Importing EU Norms

United Nations University Series on Regionalism

Volume 8

The United Nations University Series on Regionalism, launched by UNU-CRIS and Springer, offers a platform for innovative work on (supra-national) regionalism from a global and inter-disciplinary perspective. It includes the World Reports on Regional Integration, published in collaboration with other UN agencies, but it is also open for theoretical, methodological and empirical contributions from academics and policy-makers worldwide.

Book proposals will be reviewed by an International Editorial Board.

The series editors are particularly interested in book proposals dealing with:

– comparative regionalism;
– comparative work on regional organizations;
– inter-regionalism;
– the role of regions in a multi-level governance context;
– the interactions between the UN and the regions;
– the regional dimensions of the reform processes of multilateral institutions;
– the dynamics of cross-border micro-regions and their interactions with supra-national regions;
– methodological issues in regionalism studies.

Accepted book proposals can receive editorial support from UNU-CRIS for the preparation of manuscripts.

Please send book proposals to: pdelombaerde@cris.unu.edu and lvanlangenhove@cris.unu.edu.

For further volumes:
http://www.springer.com/series/7716

Annika Björkdahl • Natalia Chaban
John Leslie • Annick Masselot
Editors

Importing EU Norms

Conceptual Framework and Empirical Findings

 Springer

Editors
Annika Björkdahl
Department of Political Science
University of Lund
Lund
Sweden

Natalia Chaban
National Centre for Research on Europe
University of Canterbury
Christchurch
New Zealand

John Leslie
Victoria University of Wellington
Wellington
New Zealand

Annick Masselot
College of Business and Law
University of Canterbury
Christchurch
New Zealand

ISSN 2214-9848   ISSN 2214-9856 (electronic)
United Nations University Series on Regionalism
ISBN 978-3-319-13739-1   ISBN 978-3-319-13740-7 (eBook)
DOI 10.1007/978-3-319-13740-7

Library of Congress Control Number: 2014960059

Springer Cham Heidelberg New York Dordrecht London

Printed on acid-free paper

Springer International Publishing is part of Springer Science+Business Media (www.springer.com)

Acknowledgement

This volume is one of the outcomes of the: *Knowledge and Expertise Exchange Europe—New Zealand—International Staff Exchanges* (2011–2014) (KEEENZ-IRSES) initiative. We acknowledge and appreciate the financial support from the European Commission and the Ministry of Research Science and Technology of New Zealand and we are grateful to the KEEENZ-IRSES support which made this publication possible.

We would also like to express our gratitude to Professor Michael Bruter, Professor Martin Holland, Professor Ole Elgström, Professor Mitja Žagar, Professor David Harvey and Dr John Leslie for initiating this research collaboration. We are also grateful to our efficient project managers who assisted with our exchanges and collaborations. Our special thanks go to Sarah Christie, Yvonne Grosch and Rebecca Morgan of the National Centre for Research on Europe (NCRE), University of Canterbury, New Zealand. We thank our contributors for sharing their academic insights and knowledge in this volume.

Finally, our team of editors would like to thank our families, and especially our wonderful children.
A. Björkdahl, N. Chaban, J. Leslie and A. Masselot

Contents

Contributors

Rikard Bengtsson Department of Political Science, Lund University, Lund, Sweden

Annika Björkdahl Department of Political Science, Lund University, Lund, Sweden

Natalia Chaban National Centre for Research on Europe, University of Canterbury, Christchurch, New Zealand

Ole Elgström Department of Political Science, Lund University, Lund, Sweden

Annmarie Elijah Centre for European Studies, Australian National University, Canberra, Australia

Alison Firth University of Newcastle, Newcastle, UK

Queen Mary University of London, London, UK

University of Surrey, Guildford, UK

Maria Garcia Department of Politics, Languages & International Studies, University of Bath, Bath, UK

Toni Grace Victoria University of Wellington, Wellington, New Zealand

James Headley Department of Politics, University of Otago, Dunedin, New Zealand

Martin Holland National Centre for Research on Europe, University of Canterbury, Christchurch, New Zealand

W. John Hopkins School of Law, University of Canterbury, Christchurch, New Zealand

Serena Kelly National Centre for Research on Europe, University of Canterbury, Christchurch, New Zealand

John Leslie Political Science and International Relations Programme, Victoria University of Wellington, Wellington, New Zealand

Annick Masselot College of Business and Law, University of Canterbury, Christchurch, New Zealand

Kate McMillan School of History, Philosophy, Political Science & International Relations, Victoria University of Wellington, Wellington, New Zealand

Henrietta S. McNeill National Centre for Research on Europe, University of Canterbury, Christchurch, New Zealand

Avery Poole School of Social and Political Science, The University of Melbourne, Melbourne, Australia

Wenwen Shen School of History, Philosophy, Political Science and International Relations, Victoria University of Wellington, Wellington, New Zealand

Ivo Šlosarčík Faculty of Social Sciences, Charles University, Prague, Czech Republic

Chapter 1
Introduction: To Take or Not to Take EU Norms? Adoption, Adaptation, Resistance and Rejection

Annika Björkdahl, Natalia Chaban, John Leslie and Annick Masselot

There is no reason why, in this part of the world, we should fall short of the vision the Europeans have set themselves of a common European space. Although we have far more in common with each other than the numerous nations of Europe, we still face the same basic task of persuading ourselves that our distinct and separate national identities can continue to thrive in a supra-national framework.

Prime Minister Sir Geoffrey Palmer of New Zealand to Prime Minister Bob Hawk of Australia, April 1990.

Europe's influence as a source of norms and values shapes the world. Sometimes, as noted by the Prime Ministers of New Zealand and Australia, it offers a model of cooperation to be emulated, while in other cases Europe exercises normative power directly to set global standards for human rights and democracy as well as for intellectual property and consumers' safety. How is the normative power of the European Union (EU) perceived and received in different parts of the world?

Aiming to advance a research agenda on export and import of EU norms and values, the main focus of this volume is on the *recipients* of EU norms. We raise questions concerning when, how and why EU norms are imported. Thus, the volume

A. Björkdahl (✉)
Department of Political Science, Lund University, Lund, Sweden
e-mail: annika.bjorkdahl@svet.lu.se

N. Chaban
National Centre for Research on Europe, University of Canterbury, Christchurch, New Zealand
e-mail: natalia.chaban@canterbury.ac.nz

J. Leslie
Political Science and International Relations Programme, Victoria University of Wellington, Wellington, New Zealand
e-mail: john.leslie@vuw.ac.nz

A. Masselot
College of Business and Law, University of Canterbury, Christchurch, New Zealand
e-mail: annick.masselot@canterbury.ac.nz

© Springer International Publishing Switzerland 2015
A. Björkdahl et al. (eds.), *Importing EU Norms,* United Nations University Series on Regionalism 8, DOI 10.1007/978-3-319-13740-7_1

explores the interplay between the EU as a norm-maker and recipient countries as norm-takers. In doing so this volume explores a neglected question: How are EU norms adopted, adapted, resisted or rejected? The questions that inform the contributions of this volume include the following: How do norm-takers perceive of the EU and its norms? Is there a 'normative fit' or friction between EU norms and the local normative context? Similarly, how do EU norms impact recipients' interests and institutional arrangements?

This interdisciplinary volume brings together a variety of theoretical perspectives from the field of political science, law and EU studies to investigate norm import and to develop a conceptual framework. We emphasize translation of imported European norms into changes of institutional arrangements, policies and/or practices by recipients. We organize responses into a spectrum that stretches from unqualified *adoption* of European norms, over *adaptation* and increasing levels of *resistance* to unambiguous *rejection*. This conceptual framework provides us with tools to read a complex reality without necessarily mirroring this reality.

We analyse the norm-takers' responses to the projection of EU norms, interactions between the EU and norm recipients, and conditions within the norm-takers themselves. First, this volume maps EU norm export strategies and approaches as they affect norm-takers. Is EU influence on norm-takers *intentional, incidental, active* or *passive*? Can we make a distinction between how the EU projects norms *internally* and *externally*? The *internal* and *external* dimension of EU norm export will help to distinguish between norm-takers in various locales (inside and outside the EU as well as at various geographical and spatial distances from the EU). Second, we recognize that norm export and import takes place in a relationship between norm-maker and norm-taker that is defined by interdependence, asymmetry and power. Third, domestic circumstances within norm-takers condition the reception of norms. For example, how exported norms fit with the recipient's normative context, elites' predisposition for socialization, learning and cultural filters may shape how local actors translate (or not) norms into local institutions and practices. Constellations of material interests and institutions are also likely to affect reception of EU norms.

A rich variety of examples taken from EU Member States, European and non-European cases provides a foundation for a critical analysis of the interplay between norm-maker and norm-takers. Our empirical cases explore rejection of EU norms in Russia and Africa as well as adaptation of EU practices in Australia and New Zealand. Chapters on China, the Association of the Southeast Asian Nations (ASEAN) and the Czech Republic demonstrate resistance to EU norm export. This 'eclectic' approach includes a large number of cases in which the reception of EU norms has not yet been explored. This adds to the few cross-case analyses found in research on EU norm diffusion while making theoretical contributions to the advancement of the research agenda on norm diffusion and normative power.

1.1 Placing the Book in the Existing Debates

Opinions among scholars diverge about the role and relevance of Europe and the EU in world politics (Hyde-Price 2006). Often the EU is portrayed as a unique actor with distinct European powers essentially different from the powers of other global players. Various terms have been coined to characterize the EU and its powers: the EU as a civilian power, a post-modern power, a soft power, an ethical power and, most influentially, as a normative power (Whitman 2013). An important aspect of the normative power debate is whether the EU is normative by design or default. Thus, is normative power what the EU does or what it is? (Manners 2002, 2006a) Another dimension of the discussion about the normative power of the EU concerns the constitutive and causal effects of the EU's relations with the world–inside Europe, between regions and globally.

Shifts in power raise important questions about the relevance and role of normative power in global relations, such as who decides whether power and influence in world politics is normative or not. Assumptions about European exceptionalism are challenged, the conventional myopic focus on the EU is questioned and critical reflections on the EU 'Self' in relation to the 'Other' are provided (Manners 2006b). We 'turn the table' and critically explore how the EU normative power is perceived and received in the near and the far abroad, and how different types of societies react to the EU's global ambitions. Thus there is a need to shift focus from the EU to the world the EU engages with in order to better understand how the power of the EU is constituted, perceived and confronted and to examine critically how the norms exported by the EU are received.

'Normative Power Europe' (NPE) exerts its influence, among other ways, by projecting its norms. The existing norm diffusion literature may help us understand how such norms are perceived and received in various locales around the world. The Europeanisation research, which explores the EU's impact on domestic policies, institutions and structures within the EU, in the EU neighbourhood provides additional insights (Schimmelfennig and Sedelmeir 2004, 2005; Björkdahl 2005; Noutcheva and Duzgit 2012). However, these approaches have increasingly been critiqued for their top-down perspective (Börzel and Risse 2012). Spatial distance from the EU highlights these critiques (Jetschke and Murray 2012). Hence, conventional norm diffusion literature has paid attention to the mechanisms and channels of norm export, while neglecting strategies of norm import and the recipient. In this volume, we acknowledge the importance of norm recipients by placing them at the centre of analysis and bringing the relational character of norm diffusion to the fore. We aim to problematize and critically investigate the channels through which norms travel from place to place. We ask to what extent power relations and interdependence shape pathways of diffusion and outcomes or whether pathways of diffusion themselves shape norm import. Regardless, it is clear that the recipients of norms retain agency and the ability to exercise this agency to affect the process of norm import. Moving beyond existing research this volume accounts systematically for how norm-takers perceive EU norms.

1.2   Conceptual Framework

Bringing together insights from a variety of theoretical perspectives we investigate norm import and develop a conceptual framework to understand why norm-takers around the world adopt, adapt, resist or reject the EU's norm exports. Why are there differences in willingness to import norms exported by the EU in various parts of the world? We situate the conceptual framework within the normative power literature and we elaborate the notion of cultural filters including others' perceptions of the EU in order to understand these responses to EU norm export.

We emphasize translation of imported European norms into changes of institutional arrangements, policies and/or practices by recipients. We organize responses into a spectrum that stretches from unqualified *adoption* of European norms, over *adaptation* and increasing levels of *resistance* to unambiguous *rejection* in the following way (Table 1.1). *Adoption* reflects a conscious and unambiguous translation of exported European norms into local policies, institutions and practices. *Adaptation* requires two things. Exported European norms must be changed in some way from European practice to meet local demands. This might involve, for example, changes in institutional form and decision-making procedures. Regardless of such alterations, however, the original normative content of the export must remain unmistakeable. *Resistance*, on the other hand, demonstrates the reverse of *adaptation*. The core of recipient normative practice must remain distinct from European practice. This does not mean that engagement with European norms leaves local practice unchanged. Rather, local actors may retain previous practice or they might choose an alternative to both European norms and the *status quo*. Moreover, they may dress the *status quo* or a third alternative in the formal trappings of European institutions and policies to give an impression of *adoption* or *adaptation*. At their core, however, recipient practices are guided by norms that are distinct from European exports. Finally, *rejection* means that local norms, institutions, policies and

Table 1.1 Conceptual Framework

Encounters	Response	Outcome
Encounters between external (EU) norms and local practices	*Adoption*	Adoption at the local level of EU norms. Local practices comply with new norms
	Adaptation	Adaptation and contextualizing external (EU) norms to local characteristics and local practices comply
	Resistance	Dominance of local characteristics. Limited import of EU norms. Few local practices comply with imported norms
	Rejection	Rejection of EU norms and thus local practices do not comply with EU norms

practices diverge unambiguously and conscientiously from European norms. This conceptual framework guides the empirical analysis of the broad range of cases of recipients of EU norm exports. This volume is primarily aimed at making theoretical contributions to the advancement of the research agenda on norm diffusion and normative power while providing empirical cross-case analysis. In addition, it lays a foundation for future inquiry into the EU as a recipient of feedback and norms in a less 'EUrocentric' world.

While Table 1.1 arranges responses of norm-takers along a continuum, we do not intend to ascribe any value to these outcomes other than the degree to which they reflect norms originally projected by the EU. We recognize that movement of norms may be a frictional process. To reflect a complex, multi-layered process of norm export and import we use the metaphor of friction (Tsing 2005; Björkdahl and Höglund 2013). We ask when and how *friction* arises between the norm-maker and the norm-taker. Friction brings to the fore the give-and-take relationship that transforms both the norm recipient and the EU. By conceptualising friction in this manner we are better able to grasp the abrasive and unpredictable ways in which EU norm exports interplay with the normative context and practices of the norm-takers. For instance, attending to the frictional travel of ideas and practices from the EU means that both repressive top-down imposition of norms *and* local responses in terms of adoption, adaptation, resistance and rejection can be captured. This opens up for an understanding of the agency of norm-takers as both oppositional and accommodating. Hence, encounters may produce hybrid normative outcomes containing components of both the norm exporter and the norm importer, obscuring their boundaries. Friction is a notion that highlights vertical and asymmetrical relations between the norm-maker and the norm-taker. It reminds us, however, that, despite structural constraints such as asymmetries of economic and political power, norm-takers exercise agency.

We understand the responses developed by norm-takers as affected by external and internal circumstances. To what extent do conditions external to the norm importer affect the reception of EU norms? For example, how do power asymmetries such as EU capacity to impose conditionalities play into norm import? How do interdependencies such as trading relations influence norm import? Furthermore, to what extent do factors internal to the norm importer affect the reception of EU norms? Such factors include perceptions of the EU, normative priors, constellations of interests and domestic institutions and practices. Literature in the field of EU external perceptions explores the visions of the EU as a 'Normative Power Europe' (Chaban 2011; Holland and Chaban 2011; Chaban et al. 2013). Yet, theoreticians of EU normative identity rarely if ever consider the role of cognitive priors and EU external perceptions in their conceptualisation of the 'NPE' (cf. Larsen 2014). This is not lastly due to the fact that the 'NPE' literature has considered norm-takers only in a crude way. This oversight is puzzling as the seminal work by Manners has already attracted attention to the notion the 'cultural filters'. Those are to be 'based on the interplay between the construction of knowledge and the creation of social and political identity by the subjects of norm diffusion' (Manners 2002, p. 245). The idea of 'cultural filters' was informed by an earlier study which asserted that a cultural filter 'affects the impact of international norms and political learning in third states and organizations leading to learning, adaptation or rejection of norms' (Kinnvall 1995, pp. 61–71). This volume addresses this scholarly gap and revisits the notion of the 'cultural filters' which embraces norm-takers' perceptions and cognitive predispositions among other elements.

1.3   Outline of the Book

The volume is structured around the categories, adoption, adaptation, resistance and rejection. The introduction constructs a conceptual framework that guides the individual contributions.

In Section 1, we consider first cases exploring *adoption* of EU norms inside and outside the EU. Ivo Šlosarčík demonstrates in his contribution that even in an EU Member State, the Czech Republic, which has a legal obligation to comply with the *acquis communitaire* regulation on the Schengen and Eurozone rules, adoption may be selective and reluctant. The following chapter by Toni Grace also illustrates that norm diffusion within the EU can be contested. The chapter explores the Øresund Region as a case study of the frictions that can occur when EU 'free movement' norms are adopted and put in practice in a micro-regional border setting. Chapter 4 enquires into the role played by the EU in relation to the G20 in the process of establishing a new global economic governance regime in the wake of the financial crisis. Rikard Bengtsson demonstrates that the G20 group's willingness to adopt EU exported norms is directly related to changing perceptions of EU power before and after the Eurozone sovereign debt crisis.

Section 2 considers the more complicated cases of norm *adaptation*. Developing the concept the cultural filters, Natalia Chaban, Martin Holland and Serena Kelly focus on external perceptions towards the EU and its institutions as a 'model' of integration using data derived from a public opinion survey conducted in several Asia-Pacific 'heavyweights'. The chapter demonstrates that the process of adaptation is often based on the perception of the attractiveness of the EU as a model of integration—a perception conditioned in this case by recognition of the success or lack thereof of European Monetary Union. John Leslie and Annmarie Elijah argue that Australian and New Zealand policy makers apply selectively lessons from European economic integration in constructing a Trans-Tasman Single Economic Market (TTSEM). Chapter 7, by Kate McMillan, shows the EU's ability to export its vision of regional mobility and citizenship within a common external border has been modest in Australia and New Zealand. Instead, Australasian policy makers have constructed transnational labour markets with none of the EU's protections of migrants' social and political rights. In Chapter 8, John Hopkins and Henrietta McNeil observe how European standards and regulations find their way into New Zealand domestic law through both intentional adoption and unintentional adaptation.

Section 3 brings to the fore *resistance* to EU norm exports. Annika Björkdahl and Ole Elgström investigate how the EU is exerting normative power by exporting principles of liberalism such as trade liberalization, market economy and World Trade Organisation (WTO) compatibility through the Economic Partnership Agreements (EPA) negotiations with various African groupings. The chapter finds that recipients of norms challenge the EU normative power through resistance, foot-dragging and aversion to entering into these trade agreements. Avery Poole, in her contribution, explores the reality-expectations gap that has emerged around ASEAN's institutional developments. While ASEAN is committed to strengthening its institutions along the EU model, doing so runs afoul of existing ASEAN norms about equity and financing of operations. Chapter 11, by Alison Firth, explores implementation and interpretation of World Trade Organisation's agreement on Trade Related aspects of Intellectual Property Rights (WTO TRIPs) trademark provisions in New Zealand and compares the presence or absence of tensions with those in the UK and other EU states.

In Section 4, attention is paid to the *rejection* of EU norm exports. In Chapter 12, Maria Garcia and Annick Masselot provide a critical assessment of the tension that exists between the EU internal and international legal obligations to achieve gender equality in all its activities, and the lack of actual implementation of this value in the context of trade negotiations with the Asian region. James Headley's contribution demonstrates how Russian policymakers assert Russia's 'Europeanness', demand involvement in developing pan-European norms, while resisting EU attempts to equate EU and 'European' norms. In Chapter 14, Wenwen Shen investigates how the EU and China interact and shape each other on the issue of human rights. Central to the chapter is the assumption that the EU is a transformative power and agent of change towards China in its political, legal and cultural rhetoric and practice on human rights issues.

A concluding chapter draws together and compares the various case studies. It summarizes the relationship between EU exports, the interplay between the EU and the norm-takers, as well as the conditions in the recipient society to enhance our understanding of the EU's normative dialogue with the world. Thus, we add to the theoretical literature regarding norm diffusion and normative power by conceptualising interactions between the norm-maker and the norm-taker and by strengthening analysis of the norm-taker, while highlighting tensions between rational choice and social constructivist approaches.

1.4   Conclusion

This volume considers responses to European norms in the context of both conditions prevailing among recipients (perceptions, interests, institutions) as well as the mediating mechanisms by which norms come to recipients. It asks whether observable patterns or regularities emerge between EU propagation of norms, mechanisms through which they are mediated, the background conditions within which recipients receive them and the outcomes produced. Essentially, our emphasis on norm-takers highlights the reflexive nature of norm diffusion. Conditionality can be met with resistance and rejection, or EU examples can be adopted or adapted through emulation and learning without EU action. The reflexive nature of EU norm diffusion has implications for the EU itself as a norm exporter.

Reference list

Björkdahl, A. (2005). Norm-maker and norm-taker: Exploring the normative influence of the EU in Macedonia. *European Foreign Affairs Review, 10*(2), 257–278.

Björkdahl, A., & Höglund, K. (2013). Precarious peacebuilding: An introduction. *Peacebuilding, 1*(3), 289–299 (Special issue on Precarious Peacebuilding).

Börzel, T. A., & Risse, T. (2012). From europeanisation to diffusion: Introduction. *West European Politics, 35*(1), 1–19.

Chaban, N. (2011). Images of the EU as a social, environmental and developmental actor: Visions from Asia. *European Union External Affairs Review, 1*(1), 5–23.

Chaban, N., Elgström, O., Kelly. S., & Lai, S.-Y. (2013). Images of the EU beyond its borders: Issue-specific and regional perceptions of EU power and leadership. *Journal of Common Market Studies, 51*(3), 433–451.

Holland M., & Chaban, N. (2011). The EU as an agent for democracy: Images of the EU in the Pacific media 'Mirror'. *Journal of European Integration, 33*(3), 285–302.

Hyde-Price, A. (2006). 'Normative power Europe': A realist Critique. *Journal of European Public Policy, 13*(2), 217–234.

Jetschke, A., & Murray, P. (2012). Diffusing regional integration: The EU and Southeast Asia. *West European Politics, 35*(1), 174–91.

Kinnvall, C. (1995). *Cultural diffusion and political learning: The democratization of China.* Lund: Lund University Press.

Larsen, H. (2014). The EU as a normative power and the research on external perceptions: The missing link. *Journal of Common Market Studies, 52*(4), 896–910.

Manners, I. (2002). Normative power Europe: A contradiction in terms? *Journal of Common Market Studies, 40*(2), 235–258.

Manners, I. (2006a). The European Union as a normative power: A response to Thomas Dietz. *Millennium: Journal of International Studies, 35*(1), 167–180.

Manners, I (2006b). Normative Power Europe Reconsidered: Beyond the Crossroads. *Journal of European Public Policy, 13*(2), 182–199.

Noutcheva, G., & Duzgit, S. A. (2012). Lost in europeanization? The Western Balkans and Turkey. *West European Politics, 35*(1), 59–78.

Schimmelfennig, F., & Sedelmeier, U. (2004). Governance by conditionality: EU rule transfer to the candidate countries of Central and Eastern Europ. *Journal of European Public Policy, 11*(4), 661–79.

Schimmelfennig, F., & Sedelmeier, U. (Eds.). (2005). *The Europeanization of Central and Eastern Europe.* Ithaca: Cornell University Press.

Tsing, A. L. (2005). *Friction: An ethnography of global connections.* Princeton: Princeton University Press.

Whitman, R. (2013). The neo-normative turn in theorising the EU's international presence, *Cooperation and Conflict, 48*(2), 171–183.

Prof. Annika Björkdahl is Professor of Political Science at Lund University. She has published on ideas and norms in International Relations particularly focusing on the role of the EU as an exporter of norms as well as on conflict prevention, peacekeeping and peace-building. Among her recent publications are *War and Peace in Transition* (Nordic Academic Press 2009), *Rethinking Peacebuilding: The Quest for Just Peace in the Middle East and the Western Balkans* (Routledge 2013) (with K. Aggestam). She has also published in *European Foreign Affairs Review, Journal of European Public Policy* etc. She has also been a guest professor at National Centre for Research on Europe, Canterbury University. She is currently the editor in chief of *Cooperation and Conflict*.

Dr. Natalia Chaban is Associate Professor and Jean Monnet Chair at the National Centre for Research on Europe, University of Canterbury, New Zealand. She has significant experience in analysing EU identity outside the EU, widely publishing and advancing methodological expertise in this regard. Since 2002, she has co-led a comparative transnational project on EU external perceptions comprising a multicultural team from 20 Asia-Pacific locations, as well as a 'mirror' perceptions project "Asia in Eyes of Europe". Among her publications is *The European Union and the Asia-Pacific: Media, Public and Elite Perceptions of the EU* (2008) Routledge (N. Chaban and M. Holland, eds.) and *Communicating Europe in Times of Crisis: External Perceptions of the European Union* (2014) Palgrave (N. Chaban and M. Holland, eds.) She has also published articles in journals such as *European Foreign Affairs Review, Journal of Common Market Studies, Journal of European Integration, European Law Journal, Mobilities.*

Dr. John Leslie is a Lecturer in Political Science and International Relations at Victoria, University of Wellington (VUW). His research comparing economic integration in the European Union, between Australia and New Zealand and in the Asia Pacific has appeared recently in, among other outlets, *Journal of Common Market Studies,* Government and Opposition, Asia Europe Journal. During 2014 and 2015 John Leslie is on leave from VUW, acting as the European Union's Trade Officer in New Zealand. Research and writing for this volume were completed before he took up his position with the EU.

Annick Masselot is an Associate Professor in Law at the University of Canterbury (College of Business and Law). Her research interests focus upon European Union law, comparative law, gender equality and equal treatment, social and employment law, reconciliation between work and family life, pregnancy and maternity rights. She is the author of *Reconciling Work and Family Life in EU Law and Policy*, (2010) London: Palgrave Macmillan (with E. Caracciolo di Torella). She has published articles journals such as the *European Law Review, European Law Journal, Columbia Journal of European Law, Feminist Legal Studies.*

Part I
Adoption

Chapter 2
A Selective and Reluctant Adopter: The Czech Republic and Its (Non)Accession to Schengen and Eurozone

Ivo Šlosarčík

2.1 Introduction: General Obligation to Adopt EU Norms… and Exceptions from the Rule

Members of the European Union (EU) have a general obligation to adopt and enforce the Union's *acquis* in all its complexity unless the EU regulatory framework itself provides for an exception. Additionally, according to the principle of sincere cooperation, EU Member States are obliged not only to adopt EU rules formally, but also to enforce them in practice. This includes a duty to introduce effective and dissuasive sanctions for violations of the EU rules by private actors (Sverdrup 2008).

The same applies to EU's new-comers. New EU states have an obligation to adopt EU norms, even those created before the moment of their accession. Both the EU and candidate countries have spent considerable energy on scrutinizing potential Member States' ability to adopt the *acquis* and on negotiating temporary exceptions (transitional periods) to its application. This happened most frequently in the areas of the Common Agricultural Policy (CAP), mobility of workers and capital and environmental policy (Dougan 2004; Inglis 2004).

This chapter provides an application of the theoretical framework developed in the introductory chapter of the volume as it analyses the derogation from the EU *acquis* in the Czech Republic. It acknowledges the importance of norm-takers by placing the Czech Republic at the centre of analysis of norm diffusion within the EU. In doing so it brings the relational character of norm diffusion to the fore and critically investigates alternatives to traditional formal channels of norm transfer that are available to Member States. It focuses on two policy areas, the Eurozone and Schengen, where the Czech Republic did not adopt EU norms immediately after accession in 2004. Even if the accession treaties permitted it to postpone adopting Eurozone and Schengen rules, the (non)adoption of Schengen and Eurozone norms was the subject of controversy in a period when the Czech state was already

I. Šlosarčík (✉)
Faculty of Social Sciences, Charles University, Prague, Czech Republic
e-mail: slosarcik@fsv.cuni.cz

© Springer International Publishing Switzerland 2015
A. Björkdahl et al. (eds.), *Importing EU Norms,* United Nations University Series on Regionalism 8, DOI 10.1007/978-3-319-13740-7_2

a full member of the EU. This study explains the motivations of Czech political elites in their treatment of the Eurozone and Schengen norms and maps the alternatives to EU norm adoption that the Czech state followed.[1]

After accession in May 2004, EU norm adoption in the Czech Republic seemed to be relatively straightforward. Already in the pre-accession period, the Czech Republic, as a candidate state, was obliged to implement an extensive catalogue of EU norms. In principle, any exception from the duty to implement the Union's *acquis* in its entirety required explicit negotiation and formalisation in a transition period or transition regime written into the Accession Treaty. This was clear regarding those EU norms where formal primary or secondary law existed (e.g. consumer safety standards, environmental norms or ban on discrimination against citizens of other EU states). A much less coherent approach existed in areas where the content of the EU norms was blurred, such as the quality of civil service, rule of law or fight against corruption. This normative lacuna existed even though these areas were important for the efficient application of other EU standards in new Member States (Kochenov 2008).

With regard to Schengen and Eurozone rules, explicit transitional periods were agreed for their adoption by new EU states, including the Czech Republic. This postponement built upon existing practice in the EU before the 2004 Enlargement. Several old EU states (UK, Ireland and Denmark) had negotiated permanent opt-outs from the Eurozone or Schengen, while others (e.g. Sweden) were granted temporary exceptions (Piris 2010). The accession *acquis* for the states joining the EU in 2004 developed from the latter example: new EU members were granted a temporary exception both from Schengen and Eurozone rules.

Consequently, new Member States did not apply two significant segments of the EU *acquis* immediately after their accession. What distinguished the Eurozone and Schengen transitional regime from the other areas of temporary non-application of the *acquis* was a sophisticated procedural mechanism for its termination. This required additional cooperation between old and new EU states, including additional control mechanisms and internal EU conditionality (Marek and Baun 2011). Despite the absence of a maximum prescribed length for Schengen and Eurozone transitional regimes, the accession treaty clearly defined both exceptions as temporary. Transitional regimes were not intended as a permanent opt-out from the EU regulation comparable to those negotiated by the UK or Denmark.

Both temporary exceptions were formulated in vague terms that provided wide margins for interpretation and political bargaining. However, the respective treaty clauses supported the reading that new EU states are entitled, when they comply with the Schengen and/or Eurozone accession rules, to participate in both projects. At the same time, the Czech Republic was obliged—due to explicit rules in the accession treaties and/or its general duty under the principle of sincere cooperation—to take steps towards terminating its special treatment[2].

---

[1] This chapter covers developments in the Czech Republic until the resignation of the centre-right coalition led by Petr Nečas in June 2013.

[2] See Act Concerning the Conditions of Accession of the Czech Republic, the Republic of Estonia, the Republic of Cyprus, the Republic of Latvia, the Republic of Lithuania, the Republic of

New EU members were expected to join both the Schengen area and the Eurozone in the future, albeit without an explicit time-horizon for this being set in the accession treaties. Rather, accession to these two regimes was to take place after the EU new-comers proved their ability to comply with the specific Eurozone and Schengen rules and/or the EU's regulatory framework had adapted to the higher number of participating states. Accordingly, potential opposition to expansions of the Schengen area or Eurozone by the old EU states had to be formulated primarily in 'technical' terms, rather than as political opposition to their enlargement. The potential for such a 'technical' scenario to prevent Eurozone enlargement was demonstrated in May 2006 when Lithuanian aspirations to join the Eurozone were blocked, or significantly delayed, because its inflation rate exceeded convergence criteria marginally.[3]

The response by the Czech Republic to the EU's 'export' of norms stretches from unqualified adoption of European norms without adaptation, in the case of the Schengen rules, to increasing levels of resistance and foot-dragging as in the case of the Eurozone rules. Adoption reflects a swift and unambiguous translation of exported Schengen rules into Czech visa policy. Adaptation on the other hand requires two things. Exported European norms must be changed in some way from European practice to meet local demands. This involved changes in substance, form or procedure to fit the Czech context, while the original normative content of the export must remain untouched. The case of Eurozone can be described as resistance to EU norm export as the core of the Czech practice remained formally distinct from European norms and practices. This, however, does not mean that Czech engagement with European norms left its practice unchanged since a formal Czech *rejection* of EU exported norms was complemented by modification of the Czech domestic regulatory framework under the influence, albeit without formal transfer, of new norms applied in the Eurozone.

The analysis of Czech practical experience with adoption of Schengen and Eurozone rules provides an even more complicated (or confusing) picture than the general scenario described above. Indeed, the Czech government sought to apply Schengen rules as soon as possible, even when this meant they would not be adapted to the priorities of Czech visa policy. Thus, the Czech experience with full accession to the Schengen area can be described as 'adoption without adaptation', thus fusing two concepts formulated in the introductory chapter of this volume.

In contrast, Czech accession to the Eurozone has been postponed several times. Furthermore, Czech avoidance of the Eurozone has been combined with a refusal to participate in new forms of EU economic and fiscal governance formed during the 2010–2012 Eurozone crisis (which could be called 'Eurozone+' rules due to their connection with the rationale of the original Eurozone regulatory framework).

Hungary, the Republic of Malta, the Republic of Poland, the Republic of Slovenia and the Slovak Republic and the adjustments to the Treaties on which the European Union is founded, in particular article 3 (Schengen) and article 4 (Eurozone), the latter in connection with article 122 TEC (Nice version).

[3] Lithuania's inflation was 2.63 % instead of 2.60 % as required by the convergence criteria.

However, the Czech approach to the Eurozone and new EU economic governance has been more complex than a simple refusal to adopt the respective set of norms. While the Czech Republic has formally stayed outside the Eurozone and new EU economic initiatives, it also implemented—informally and selectively—EU rules in its—formally autonomous—domestic rules in reaction to the economic crisis. Therefore, the Czech experience with respect to Eurozone and economic governance rules can be described, using terminology of the introductory chapter, as a 'formal rejection with informal adaptation'.

This chapter develops as follows. First, the chapter provides an analysis of the diffusion of the Schengen rules to the Czech Republic and depicts how adoption can occur without adaptation as exported EU norms are integrated without alteration. The second part of the chapter presents an analysis of the diffusion of the rules pertaining to the Eurozone and demonstrates how informal adaptation can occur simultaneously with formal rejection of EU exported norms. The chapter concludes with an insightful comparison of the two cases of norm export—the Schengen and Eurozone rules—as atypical areas of European regulation and provides a discussion about the grey zone of EU norm imports.

2.2   Schengen Rules in Czech Republic: Adoption without Adaptation

The Schengen regime started as a pragmatic effort by some EU Member States to solve mobility problems within the internal borders of the European integration project. It subsequently developed into a complex package of norms that includes: standardization of control mechanisms on external EU borders, harmonization of visa and asylum procedures, increasing police and judicial cooperation within the EU and construction of the most extensive security-focused EU database available to Member States' agencies. A 'side effect' of this process was that Schengen became one of the most visible symbols of the European integration inside and outside the EU and lost (in the Amsterdam Treaty) its autonomous legal identity separate from the core of the EU (Šlosarčík 2010).

The 'Big Bang' enlargement in 2004 did not immediately include EU new-comers into all elements of the Schengen system. In particular, the 2004 Enlargement did not result in immediate abolition of border controls between old and new Member States. Instead, the Accession Treaty presumed that controls would continue until two conditions were fulfilled. First, new EU members were obliged to demonstrate their capacity to control mobility over those new EU external borders for which they were responsible (i.e. their borders with non-EU states and international ports and airports in their territory). Second, the Schengen database (Schengen Information System, SIS) had to be modernized to cope with the increased number of countries participating. However, in contrast to popular belief, new EU states were not exempted from the whole Schengen *acquis*. They were obliged to apply all Schengen rules that did not require SIS involvement. For instance, the 'immediate' Schengen rules (applied since May 2004 but usually implemented even earlier) included harmonization of the list of 'visa' and 'visa-free' third countries. An additional, albeit not explicitly formulated, element of the Schengen rules was the creation of mutual trust between the implementing authorities of the participating states, in particular with regard to the efficiency and incorruptibility of border control and visa-issuing bodies. For these reasons, the Schengen rules for new EU states were frequently formulated not in the form of a catalogue of norms to be implemented, but in the form of objectives, such as quality of border control, to be reached (Grabbe 2006).

Full accession to Schengen was among the highest priorities for Czech governments of all political colors, including the Social Democratic coalition until 2006 and the government led by Civic Democrats thereafter. Therefore, the Czech Republic was open to virtually all forms of cooperation and screening processes. Among others, these included forming joint Czech-German police teams in border areas and strengthening the general police presence in the proximity of future internal Schengen borders, with the objective of making the Schengen enlargement more acceptable by Germany and Austria. At the same time, delays in the modernization of the Schengen Information System that made some old EU states contemplate postponing the Schengen enlargement triggered a sharp and coordinated critique by new EU Member States (Marek and Baun 2011). Efforts by the new EU states resulted in the Council's decision to provide (almost)[4] all EU 2004 new-comers with full Schengen membership shortly before Christmas in 2007.

What makes Czech adoption of the Schengen rules interesting is the rigidity with which they were adopted and the absence of any significant effort to adapt them to specific Czech circumstances. In particular, the absence of any country-specific adaptation was visible in the area of visa regimes with new EU neighbours in the former-Soviet space. All non-EU, former-Soviet states were included in the EU's list of countries whose citizens are required to have a visa when travelling to the EU. This EU rule stood in contrast to the existing liberal visa policy of post-Communist Central European states toward the former-Soviet countries. In practice, the EU *acquis* required the candidate countries to make their visa policy significantly more restrictive. This was potentially costly both politically (e.g. a more restrictive visa regime might be interpreted as reflecting worsening bilateral diplomatic ties) and economically (e.g. a more restrictive visa regime might cause problems for business, labour and tourist mobility). Several new EU states, including Poland and Hungary, undertook continuous efforts to weaken the impact of the new visa regime on their relations with their Eastern neighbors, in particular with Ukraine. These efforts included: shifting the implementation of the new EU rules as close to the enlargement date as possible (the position of the old EU states and the European Commission was that new visa rules should be implemented even before the signature of the Accession Treaty); extending their consular networks in the respective third countries; and, last but not least, intensive political communication with their non-EU counterparts expressing their discomfort with the EU regime (Kazmierkiewicz 2005). No similar efforts were detectable in the Czech case. The Czech Republic

---

[4] Cyprus has remained outside the Schengen area due to a combination of practical and symbolic issues connected with the division of the island.

followed a 'technical' path in terminating visa-free travel (in form of termination of bilateral visa-free agreements) by citizens of non-EU former-Soviet states.

2.3 Eurozone Experience: Formal Rejection with Informal Adaptation

In the years directly following the enlargement, the Czech government expressed few reservations about the country's straightforward and rapid accession to the Eurozone. The strategy of the accession of the Czech Republic to the Eurozone, published by the governmental coalition lead by Social Democrats in 2003, expected the Czech currency to be replaced by the Euro in 2009 or 2010.The same target date was mentioned in the 2004 Convergence Program and in the 2007 inter-departmental National Coordination Group's plan for adoption of the Euro (Šlosarčík et al. 2011).

Enthusiasm for adoption of the Euro started to weaken after inauguration of the center-right coalition led by the Civic Democratic Party in 2006. Although the new government declared Eurozone accession a governmental priority, the focus of debate has shifted to the need for a broader adaptation of the Czech economy to Eurozone membership and a target date for accession has disappeared from official documents (Marek and Baun 2011).

The Czech National Bank's position has always been to respect the primacy of political leadership in the Eurozone accession process, but the Bank's statements have shifted gradually to a more sceptical tone (Šlosarčík et al. 2011). Central Bank scepticism toward Eurozone accession was strengthened by the gradual appointment of new members to its governing board (membership in the board is for 6 years with the possibility of re-appointment) by the sharpest and most consistent critic of the Eurozone project, the President of the Republic, Václav Klaus (in office 2003–2013).

Since the outbreak of the Eurozone crisis in 2010, Czech debate on Eurozone accession has come to a stand-still. The only innovative element was an opinion, presented by the Prime Minister Petr Nečas in October 2011, that the Czech Republic should hold a referendum before acceding to the Eurozone. The Prime Minister's key argument in favor of a referendum was that the Eurozone in the late 2010s, when the Czech Republic might join, will be substantially different from the Eurozone of 2003, when the referendum on Czech accession to the EU was held.

Czech ambivalence toward the Eurozone was reinforced by the focus and format that economic intervention took in the EU after 2010. While EU elites followed more-or-less standard EU rules on internal market and Eurozone governance before 2010, after 2010 the Eurozone crisis provoked political and institutional improvisation and a rather cavalier approach to the EU's and the Eurozone's formal rules. The immediate result of this chaotic development has been a heterogeneous package of loosely connected instruments which differ in: legal form (internal EU regulation establishing European Financial Stability Mechanism/EFSM versus external agreement establishing European Financial Stability Facility/EFSF or the Fiscal Compact), level of country specificity (single-country focused Greek Loan Facility versus EFSF/EFSM of general application), involvement of non-Eurozone states (inclusive ESFM versus exclusive EFSF versus semi-inclusive Fiscal Compact) and intensity of their preventive versus sanction elements (Louis 2010; Ruffert 2011).

Since the Czech Republic is not a full Eurozone member, its politicians were not involved in formation of several key rescue instruments, such as the Greek Loan Facility, the EFSF or the ESM, which are applicable exclusively between the Eurozone states. Therefore, Czech political leaders avoided the uneasy '*de facto* junior' position at the negotiation table. This 'outsider's' experience was not shared by the Czechs' eastern neighbor, the Slovak Republic. As a new Eurozone member since 2009, Slovakia not only shared the financial burden of the Eurozone intervention, but Slovak (non)participation in the Greek rescue package caused significant domestic political turmoil in 2010 and its delays in the 2011 EFSF reform even triggered the fall of a Slovak government.[5]

Regarding new instruments and initiatives applicable to all EU states, the Czech Republic adopted a dubious approach. Czech negotiators have not blocked adoption of those EU rules requiring participation of all EU states, such as the EFSM (adopted in form of a Council regulation). Nor have they rejected the 'six-pack' reforming and expanding the Stability and Growth Pact mechanism (adopted in the form of five regulations and one directive that are applicable, albeit with different regimes, to both Eurozone and non-Eurozone states). However, when the Czech Republic could abstain from participation without formally hampering the functioning of a new EU instrument, Czech politicians preferred to opt out. Hence, the Czech Republic was one of four EU (non-Eurozone) states outside the Euro Plus Pact (together with the UK, Sweden and Hungary). More significantly, the Czech state abstained, together with UK, from signing the Fiscal Compact.

At the same time, the Czech government expressed its support for the austerity-focused content of the EU initiatives, declaring the Czech Republic to be an integral part of the informal 'northern' group in the EU. This position broadly recognized the dependence of the Czech economy on its German counterpart. The conservative coalition's support for austerity was not only verbal. Austerity was also the core of its economic program in the years from 2010 to 2013. The government even contemplated establishing a 'debt-brake' and it presented a proposal for a corresponding constitutional amendment in 2012 (Beneš and Braun 2013).

2.4   Conclusion: Grey Zone of EU Norm Adoption

Czech experiences with Schengen and Eurozone rules provide two very different examples of adoption (or the absence of it) of complex sets of EU rules after accession. While Czech accession to Schengen was relatively straightforward, the Czech

---

[5] Slovak involvement in the Greek rescue package was condoned politically by Prime Minister Robert Fico. This act contributed to, but was not the decisive factor in, his electoral defeat in parliamentary elections. New centre-right coalition, led by Iveta Radičová, was 'trapped' by its pre-election rhetoric and refused to implement the Greek bail-out in legislation. Later, tension linked to ratification of the EFSF reform in the Slovak Parliament caused the Slovak governmental coalition to collapse in autumn 2011.

government gradually increased its resistance to Eurozone membership and this hesitation extended into Czech refusal to participate formally in new forms of European economic and fiscal governance created during the Eurozone crisis ('Eurozone + rules'). This difference is even more striking when one recognizes that both the adoption of Schengen rules and the rejection of Eurozone rules were orchestrated by the same 'moderately eurosceptic' coalitions led by Civic Democratic Party[6] and with the same politician (Václav Klaus) in the presidential office.

Both Schengen and Eurozone rules are atypical areas of European regulation. They are abnormalities with huge economic, political and symbolic importance. The institutional 'ownership' of norms is blurred in Schengen, the Eurozone and even more in 'Eurozone+'. In particular, the position of the European Commission as the 'guardian of the Treaties' is less prominent and the Commission is competing with other EU institutions, such as the European Council, the Council of the EU and the European Central Bank. Therefore, the Commission is less ready to use its formal enforcement powers (such as the action before the Court of Justice) to sanction a reluctant Member State, such as the Czech Republic, for not taking active steps towards Schengen and/or Eurozone accession. Without imminent risk of external pressure, Czech authorities had more space to choose their own approach to EU norms than was possible in other areas of integration.

The difference in Czech behavior on Schengen and the Eurozone can be explained by a combination of three factors. The first one was the Czech government's perception of its own ability to influence the development of EU rules after the Czech Republic formally adopts them. The second factor was the availability to the Czech Republic of alternative ways to gain the same objective without formally adopting the EU rules. And the third, supplementary, factor was the level of politicization of the respective agenda.

Decision-making processes in the Eurozone and the Schengen differ. The Schengen system respects the standard voting weight of the participating states (a majority of legislation is adopted by ordinary legislative procedure) and full Schengen members retain a veto over Schengen enlargement. The Czech Republic could, therefore, have relative confidence in its ability to leave an 'imprint' on Schengen rules—for instance, on EU visa policies. Czech accession to Schengen preceded the 2010 Schengen enlargement crisis, when several old EU states used a critique formulated within the Cooperation and Verification Mechanism, which is formally independent of the Schengen system, to prevent Romania's and Bulgaria's full accession to the Schengen area (Vachudova and Spendzharova 2012). Thus, the Czech elites could believe in 2007, when they acceded, that no significant gap existed between Schengen's formal and informal rules.

---

[6] Paradoxically, the Social Democratic Party, which is more sympathetic to the idea that the Czech Republic should belong to the 'hard core' of the European Union, is more likely to criticise the material essence of the EU's pro-austerity norm contained in the Fiscal Pact, as the Social Democratic Party is inclined to implement more pro-growth policies driven by investments and other forms of public spending financed from the state budget, even at the expense of increasing the public debt.

In the Eurozone, on the other hand, decision-making power reflects the relative economic strength of Member States and many competencies have been shifted to the European Central Bank, i.e. beyond direct control of Member States. The Eurozone crisis further demonstrated the importance of informal economic and fiscal power of individual Eurozone states in decision-making. This is clearly shown by the experience of Slovakia in the Eurozone—a state with particularly close historical links to the Czech Republic. Slovakia's practical inability to make autonomous decisions and the politically destabilizing consequences it had, sent warning signals to Czech political elites.

The Czech government seemed to lack confidence in its ability to pursue its interests in Eurozone decision making and, in particular, in the unpredictable and vague legal framework of the Eurozone after the crisis. In a study on the Fiscal Compact prepared by the Secretariat of the Czech Prime Minister, the possibility of the Czech Republic joining the Fiscal Compact was criticized almost exclusively from the legal perspective—it questioned the Compact's compatibility with both EU and Czech legal orders—while the economic and fiscal impact of accession received only marginal attention (Úřad vlády ČR 2012).

The second factor distinguishing Czech responses to Schengen and the Eurozone was the availability of options for the Czech Republic to reach the same objectives without formally adopting the EU rules. The core of Schengen cooperation was the removal of border controls with other EU states and this was available only via the EU channel; a similar outcome was not available through unilateral action. In contrast, the Eurozone and 'Eurozone+' rules on fiscal responsibility could be 'copied' by autonomous fiscal policy implemented by Czech authorities.

The Eurozone agenda received significant political attention in the Czech Republic. Formal rejection of the Eurozone and 'Eurozone+' rules has not, however, prevented adaptation of the Czech domestic regulatory framework to its Eurozone counterpart. The political attention given to the Schengen accession was, in contrast, exhausted by the issues directly linked with removal of border controls. There, the adaptation of the Czech rules—strengthening of police presence in border regions—emerged. In the remaining issues—such as adaptation of the Czech consular network and visa policy—the lack of political leadership led to a very 'technical' adoption of EU rules with virtually no adaptation to Czech specifics. The absence of political attention given to the external impact of the Schengen accession can be explained by the fact that the Czech Republic borders exclusively with other EU/Schengen states and the fact that there is no significant Czech minority remaining outside Schengen. In the hypothetical case of Slovakia's exclusion from the Schengen enlargement, the Czech Republic would most likely not simply have adopted the Schengen rules, but would have adapted them to politically defined priorities.

While the general framework of the EU requires adoption of EU rules by its members with limited space for adaptation (e.g. during implementation of directives), the Schengen and Eurozone segments of European integration demonstrate that—under specific circumstances—an EU member can opt for more complex forms of norm transfer, such as formal adoption without adaptation (Schengen) or formal rejection with informal adaptation (Eurozone).

References

Beneš, V., & Braun, M. (2013). Evropský rozměr české zahraniční politiky. In M. Kořán & O. Ditrych (Eds.), *Česká zahraniční politika v roce 2012* (pp. 51–72). Praha: Ústav mezinárodních vztahů.

Dougan, M. (2004). A spectre is haunting Europe… free movement of persons and the Eastern enlargement. In C. Hillion (Ed.), *EU enlargement: A legal approach* (pp. 111–141). Oxford: Hart Publishing.

Grabbe, H. (2006). *The EU's transformative power: Europeanization through conditionality in Central and Eastern Europe*. Houndmills: Palgrave.

Inglis, K. (2004). The Accession Treaty and its transitional arrangements: A twilight zone for the new members of the Union. In C. Hillion (Ed.), *EU enlargement: A legal approach* (pp. 77–109). Oxford: Hart Publishing.

Kazmierkiewicz, P. (2005). *The Visegrad states between Schengen and neighbourhood*. Warsaw: Institute of Public Affairs.

Kochenov, D. (2008). *EU enlargement and the failure of conditionality: Pre-accession conditionality in the fields of democracy and the rule of law*. Alphen aan den Rijn: Wolters Kluwer.

Louis, J.-V. (2010). The no-bailout clause and rescue packages. *Common Market Law Review, 4*(47), 971–986.

Marek, D., & Baun, M. (2011). *Česká republika a Evropská unie*. Brno: Barrister & Principal.

Piris, J.-C. (2010). *The Lisbon treaty: A legal and political analysis*. Cambridge: Cambridge University Press.

Ruffert, M. (2011). The European debt crisis and European Union law. *Common Market Law Review, 6*(48), 1777–1806.

Sverdrup, U. (2008). Implementation. In P. Graziano & M. Vink (Eds.), *Europeanization: New research agenda* (pp. 197–201). Houndsmill: Palgrave Macmillan.

Šlosarčík, I. (2010). Schengenský systém: Pragmatické řešení unijního problému se symbolickou přidanou hodnotou. In H. Scheu & M. Částek (Eds.), *Aktuální otázky migrační politiky Evropské unie* (pp. 57–65). Praha: Vysoká škola finanční a správní.

Šlosarčík, I., Kasáková, Z., Váška, J., & Weiss, T. (2011). Fragmentation and coexistence of Leitbilder in the Czech Republic. In M. Jopp & L. Rovna (Eds.), *Leitbilder for the future of the European Union* (pp. 74–119). Baden-Baden: Nomos.

Úřad vlády ČR. (2012). Smlouva o stabilitě, koordinaci a správě v hospodářské a měnové unii—Analýza. Praha.

Vachudova, M., & Spendzharova, A. (2012). *The EU's cooperation and verification mechanism: Fighting corruption in Bulgaria and Romania after EU accession*. Stockholm: SIEPS.

Dr. Ivo Šlosarčík is Jean Monnet Chair in European Law and director of European integration studies program at Faculty of Social Sciences, Charles University in Prague. He was member of governmental advisory bodies on the European Constitutional Treaty and the EU Council Presidency in 2009. Ivo Šlosarčík's area of research covers rule enforcement in the EU, the EU's cooperation in the AFSJ and the adaptation of national political, administrative and judicial structures to the European integration. In 2013, Ivo Šlosarčík published a book analyzing transformation of conditionality in the EU (Karolinum 2013) and was editor of a monograph on the EU's institutional reform after the Lisbon Treaty (Grada 2013).

Chapter 3
Mobility in Principle and Practice: Multilevel Adoption of Free Movement Norms in a European Cross-border Region

Toni Grace

3.1 Introduction

This chapter examines European Union (EU) norm adoption related to the free movement of people in European Cross-Border Regions (CBRs). Rather than focussing on the relationship between European Union (EU) norms and domestic national structures or international governance regimes, this chapter frames norm diffusion within the context of multi-level governance in Europe, particularly the micro-regional structures governing European border regions. Similarly, while much political and academic focus on European freedom of movement is placed on intergovernmental cooperation, many attempts to normalise mobility are occurring through more localised forms of regional integration (Gualini 2003). CBRs interact with both national and supranational actors in this process, creating a new arena for the study of free movement norm diffusion, adoption and resistance at multiple levels of governance.

This chapter first begins by framing 'freedom of movement' as it is related to EU norms, analysing it in economic, political and normative terms. It outlines how norms are conveyed by the EU as an integral component of regional integration and notions of European citizenship. A brief introduction of CBRs as an arena for the study of free movement norms links their development to wider European integration. The Øresund region is explored in further detail as a critical case study in this regard, with a focus on the factors that have made the region a prime site for the adoption of free movement norms.

Yet despite these ideal preconditions for the normalisation of free movement, cross-border mobility has occasionally arisen as a contested subject in the region. This chapter considers frictions over Third Country National (TCN) mobility as domestic divergence in Danish and Swedish immigration politics developed parallel to increased integration efforts over the last decade. It is posited that the politi-

T. Grace (✉)
Victoria University of Wellington, Wellington, New Zealand
e-mail: toni.lucia.grace@gmail.com

© Springer International Publishing Switzerland 2015
A. Björkdahl et al. (eds.), *Importing EU Norms,* United Nations University Series on Regionalism 8, DOI 10.1007/978-3-319-13740-7_3

cal opportunities and costs of free movement norms are not evenly spread across Member States or between different levels of governance. The chapter concludes by considering key findings from the mixed adoption and contestation of free movement norms in a bi-national border region, including the deeper implications this signals for EU free movement efforts.

3.2 Freedom of Movement in the EU

Over the past half century, freedom of movement has been one of the most fundamental principles of European integration and a central aspiration in many of the EU's founding documents (Recchi and Favell 2009). The signing of the Treaty of Rome in 1957 established the European Economic Community (EEC), putting in place the legal, institutional and political structures for deeper integration and created targeted mobility rights for the working population. The Single European Act signed in 1986 later expanded on these provisions by envisioning an area without internal borders 'in which the free movement of goods, persons, services and capital is ensured' (Single European Act, 1987; Article 13).

This earlier legislation targeted the facilitation of economic movement for labour mobility, though as integration deepened these rights were gradually extended to all citizens of European Member States. The signing of the 1985 Schengen Agreement, and the subsequent Schengen Convention in 1990, allowed participating Member States to initiate the removal of borders to movement of other categories of persons such as students, pensioners and other economically non-active persons. The Treaty of Amsterdam, signed in 1997, further incorporated the Schengen agreements into EU law and also formally took account of TCNs by introducing a number of norms related to visas, asylum and immigration policies (Baldoni 2003). With the advent of Schengen and the Amsterdam Treaty, regional mobility rights moved beyond minimal economic membership to the collective participation of Europeans in deeper political and social connectivity (Maas 2007).

3.2.1 Free Movement as a Derivative of EU Norms

The principle of free movement underlying Schengen legislation can therefore be related to norms promoted across the EU with a view to not only the need to maximise regional economic functionality, but also to uphold the liberal principles underpinning European integration and cohesion policy. In 2011 European Commission President, José Manuel Barroso reiterated these sentiments declaring 'the full recognition by the European Council of the free movement of persons as a core principle of the European Union and as a fundamental right...' (Barroso 2011, p. 3). In this sense, regional mobility emerges as both a functional and normative concept. Cross-border mobility extends beyond material flows such as socio-economic exchange and economic interdependence into the flow of norms and ideas such as shared beliefs in unity and liberal ideology. Scholars have linked freedom of movement to a number of liberal principles such as human rights and redistributive justice (Bauböck 2009), democracy and equality (Aradau and Huysmans 2009). Manners (2008) argues that these make up some of the substantive normative principles that the EU promotes as Normative Power Europe (NPE). Freedom of movement is a derivate of these as it is a means of acting out and normalising these deeper normative principles. Similarly, social constructivist scholars such as Checkel (1999) describe this as an on-going socialisation process by which actors internalise the values and norms of the European Community.

Given their centrality to the European project, EU free movement rights also comprise one of the few tangible elements of a common European citizenship (Recchi and Favell 2009). EU Directive 2004/58/EC states that 'Union citizenship is the fundamental status of nationals of the Member States when they exercise their right of free movement' (European Union 2004: preamble on line). An illustration of this internalisation of EU free movement norms is in the 2011 European Barometer survey which showed that almost half of responders mention intra-EU free movement rights as an element they associate most closely with European integration (Parkes and Schwarzer 2012).

Free movement has also been analysed as a functional political concept, with increased cross-border migration triggering the need for international cooperation, such as the establishment of regional political authorities to manage cross-border movement, serving to further legitimise European integration (Aradau et al. 2010). Through cross-border exchange, EU mobility is therefore a mechanism for promoting bottom-up regional integration and political architecture, both of which contribute to the playing down of national differences. This indicates a pattern of behaviour expected of Member States that they will progressively remove, not add, obstacles to cross-border mobility in the 'spirit' of free movement.

3.3   CBR: The 'cement' of European Integration

CBRs are particularly interesting in this regard as they are, by definition, a product of integration between two or more countries, with cross-border movement being a daily reality for many who live in the region. Local political efforts to remove cross-border obstacles are reflective of the emergence of multilevel governance, which has been a key interest of scholars in the context of European integration (Bache and Flinders 2005). The prominence of border regions has even led some observers to predict that future international competition in Europe may be more between regions and metropolitan areas rather than between nations (EURICUR 2007).

CBRs have developed across Europe as a result of initiatives that aim to transform the concept of the border from one of division to one of dynamic cross-border cooperation. Such regions emerged particularly during a boom in the 1990s as local actors, aided by EU support schemes, created transnational partnerships to build these traditionally peripheral spaces into promising locations for the creation of functional, prosperous border regions (Perkmann 2003). In line with EU integration, the logic of CBR strategies is to soften arbitrary national borders and restructure regions along functional lines for economic growth, as opposed to the traditional Westphalian notion of borders as peripheral areas that look inward towards central national activity (Mostov 2007). For this reason CBRs have been described as the 'cement of the European House', alluding to their functional role as part of the process of European integration (AEBR 2008, Online).

3.3.1 Diffusion of Free Movement Norms to CBRs

The desire to promote new and alternative forms for cross-border cooperation has followed continental European integration processes with scholars pointing out the interdependencies between micro-regional and macro-regional (EU) processes of regionalisation (Blatter 2004). The diffusion of norms related to free movement have therefore been couched in the wider diffusion of norms and practices of the new Europe, illustrated by synergistic terms such as "Euregions" or "Euroregions" (Council of Europe, Online). Additionally, cross-border efforts have been directly incentivised and sustained by EU support schemes such as the European Regional Development Fund (INTERREG), which provides funding for cross-border integration projects that further European integration goals. This can be analysed as an example of formal, vertical idea diffusion such as that described by Börzel and Risse (2009), whereby formal top-down mechanisms such as EU Treaties, policy, case law, funding regulations and institutional arrangements are used to promote supranational EU norms to Member States. In this way, EU policies and directives set the framework for regionalisation processes so that CBRs serve as both a laboratory and illustration of how EU integration can be advanced (Lyck and Boye 2009). From a political integration perspective, Hall (2008) also notes how democratic governance efforts in CBRs represent a critical case study of prospects for wider EU political integration.

   EU policies and ideas can also transform the behaviour, structures and identities of actors in qualitative terms through processes of socialisation and persuasion (Börzel and Risse 2009). This is linked to Blatter's (2004, p. 535) notion of 'consociation' where the EU influences behaviour not only by formal, vertical mechanisms but by 'symbolising ideas which shape identities and contain an encompassing 'image' of a cross-border political community.'Following this notion, EU discourses and policies of free movement can serve to idealise cross-border mobility as a 'common sense' within new special visions of European integration, including cross-border regionalism. This is related to Castells' (1996) hypothesis that the traditional notion of 'space as a place' is gradually being replaced by the concept of 'spaces of flows.' Related to CBRs, this means that the basis for political action is not territorial jurisdiction but function specific issues which require cross border cooperation (Mansfield and Solingen 2010). This demonstrates how pathways of diffusion, such as funding channels and policy frameworks, can have an influence on regional interests and institutional arrangements, shaping import norms.

3.4 The Øresund Region: The 'Human Capital of Scandinavia'

These interdependent supranational and local interests in freedom of movement are evident in the cross-border Øresund region, which sets itself out as a leader in European integration and mobility efforts (Øresund Committee 2010a). Support from multiple levels of government, financial and political, all contributed to high hopes for the Øresund region as bridge construction started in 1995. The national governments of Denmark and Sweden supported the building of the Øresund Bridge, believing that the removal of this natural geographical boundary would enhance and broaden the potential for trade and bring economic benefits for the regional economies of Scania and Zealand (Danish and Swedish Governments 1999, pp. 10–11).

Since the opening of the Øresund Bridge between Denmark and Sweden in July 2000, efforts to integrate neighbouring municipalities across the sound have intensified at both national and regional levels. Boasting the slogan 'The Human Capital of Scandinavia', this metropolitan agglomeration has a combined population of 3.7 million inhabitants; a third of which live on the Danish side of the Sound. Estimates also show that around 20,000 people commute across the Øresund Bridge on a daily basis (Øresundsbro Consortium 2010).It is hoped that the Øresund region's unique combination of a capital city (Copenhagen) with the knowledge intensive and manufacturing sectors of Scania will make the region competitive against other metropolitan regions in Europe.

The Øresund project cuts across two national jurisdiction systems, creating a space for new kinds of actors to manage cross-border interests (Löfgren 2008). The main body dedicated to managing cross-border integration is the Øresund Committee, a cross-border forum for voluntary political cooperation constituting municipal and local politicians from both countries described by the Organisation for Economic Co-operation and Development (OECD) (2003) as "governance without government." The Committee is driven by a goal that by 2020 the Region will be a model for other European CBRs 'with a common labour market—free from obstacles that complicate life for those living and working on different sides of the Sound' (Øresund Committee 2010a, p. 8). The Committee is a prominent member of the transnational Association of European Border Regions (AEBR) lobby group, having twice been awarded its annual 'Sail of Papenburg' Cross-Border Award for outstanding programmes, strategies, projects and actions within the scope of cross-border cooperation.

3.4.1 Freedom of Movement in the Øresund Region

While the removal of remaining borders to mobility is a key focus of the Øresund Committee, the region has enjoyed a long standing foundation of Scandinavian free movement provisions, though these have not always moved in tandem with European free movement developments. Since 1954, Denmark and Sweden have enjoyed formalised, passport-free travel due to their membership in the Nordic Passport Union, one of the regional precursors to the European Schengen area. The region also has a common Nordic labour market agreement and a shared social security convention (Nordic Council, online).

While the principles of Nordic and EU free movement arrangements were similar, the meeting of these Nordic and European free travel agreements initially created a dilemma due to the non-EU member status of Norway and Iceland. Schengen offered EU members Denmark, Sweden and Finland the opportunity to join a wider European community of mobility, but in doing so the survival of the Nordic Passport Union was threatened. However, in 1996, Schengen members signed a co-operation agreement with Norway and Iceland to give effect to their non-EU membership of Schengen, allowing the Nordic Passport Union to be preserved within the Schengen area (Maas 2005). In the same year the Amsterdam Treaty merged Schengen cooperation with the general legal and institutional framework of the EU and the Nordic countries signed an agreement with the EU on 18 May 1999 to join the Schengen acquis. Free movement in the Øresund region is therefore situated in a series of interwoven free movement provisions, both Nordic and European.

In addition to national economic and political investment from successive Danish and Swedish governments, the Øresund region has been supported by targeted supranational policies from both the EU and the Nordic Council, an inter-parliamentary forum for Nordic cooperation formed after World War II. The Nordic Council has been heavily involved in integration efforts, particularly those related to the promotion of free movement, adding to the dynamic multi-level governance behind the region. The Øresund region is viewed by the Council as a strong symbol of Nordic cooperation and a strategic gateway between Scandinavia and the European continent. The Nordic Council itself states that;

> the Nordic goal of an open Region harmonises well with the European ideal. The ultimate objective in both cases is to make better use of the Nordic Region's and the EU's full potential by minimising the impact of borders as obstacles.' (Nordic Council, online)

The Øresund Committee receives financial support from the intergovernmental Nordic Council of Ministers, and collaborates in several key policy areas through a partnership programme for the regional sector. In 2007 the Nordic Council of Ministers also set up a 'Freedom of Movement Forum' which has worked closely with the Øresund Committee to identify and removing cross-border obstacles within the region through constructive dialogue with national political and administrative bodies.

Aided by this, the region is already one of the most economically integrated border regions in Europe and regional politicians envision that this will deepen further over time, 'making it the most competitive, attractive and effective region in Europe.' (Øresund Committee 2005, p. 23). The region has been identified as a 'Transnational Mobility Region'within the EU special policy discourse, emphasising the region's role within a bigger picture of seamless Nordic and European economic spaces (Jensen and Richardson 2004). It is thus described by its proponents as not only one of the biggest construction projects in the history of modern Europe, but also one of Europe's biggest social experiments, alluding to the fact that the region represents a forerunner of intensive, multifaceted regional integration in Europe (Øresund Committee 2011).

Like the Nordic Council, the EU has invested strongly in the region since its inception through INTERREG—a programme of funding that aims to stimulate cooperation between regions at multiple levels in the EU. 139 cross-border projects were implemented in the Øresund under INTERREG II "Strand A" for cross-border cooperation (1994–1999) while INTERREG IIIA (2000–2006) had made over EUR 30.84 million available to the Øresund region, with the Danish and Swedish government contributing the same amount (INTERREG IIA 2005). The level of INTER-REG commitment is also exemplified by the joint technical secretariat hosted in the Øresund region for the coordination of projects and funding. INTERREG V is currently operational, covering 2014–2020, with the Øresund funded under a joint Øresund-Kattegat-Skagerrak programme involving border regions Sweden, Denmark and Norway. In addition to INTERREG funding, Jerneck (1999) suggests that the doctrine of regionalisation purported by the EU also legitimised political aspirations in the Øresund region for cross-border cooperation and self-governance.

3.4.2 Recent Efforts to Enhance Freedom of Movement

A core priority of the Øresund Committee since the early 2000s has been '…to eliminate as many as possible of the legal and regulatory obstacles that exist, so that it will become simpler to work, study, live or invest on the other side of the water' (Øresund Committee 2005, p. 23). Given the absence of formal territorial borders for movement in the region, much of the focus of the Øresund Committee has been on the removal of administrative barriers to work and welfare on both sides of the sound. Most of these issues became evident as the number of cross-border commuters increased, raising questions about contribution to, and redistribution of, national public funds and insurance schemes for mobile residents. The Nordic Freedom of Movement Forum and Øresund Committee published a joint report entitled, '33 barriers, developments and opportunities: the 2010 Øresund Model' which outlines the key obstacles to a common labour market, social rights, and free movement for all residents in the Øresund region. Gradual progress is being made, with some key achievements including agreements between Danish and Swedish Governments to prevent double taxation and allow people to be employed in both countries at the same time (Øresund Committee 2010b).

Another interesting aspect of the Øresund project is the way in which culture and economy have been intertwined in region building. Paasi (2009) notes that notions of identity and citizenship have become major buzzwords within regional integration projects, similarly identified in the EU's cohesion policy as an important element for regional development. A regional identity is promoted by Øresund actors as a means of unifying the resident population, lowering mental barriers to transnational activity and promoting the Øresund region externally as an attractive destination for skills and investment. The Øresund Consortium (2010) summing up 10 years of integration since the opening of the bridge notes:

> Across the region, many people now regard themselves as Øresund citizens. But what does it mean to be an Øresund citizen? ...Perhaps we can find it in the commitment and dynamism that many people have invested in making their daily life function just as smoothly across national borders as it did before in the two parts of the region.

O'Dell (2003; 2011) uses the term 'regionauts' to describe this routinely mobile group of regional citizens who develop skills and experience on both sides of the border, through which 'politicians and planners hoped that a new sense of regional belonging and unification would arise' (O'Dell 2011, p. 14). Visions for deeper regional integration therefore include the emergence of a common Øresund citizenship—a normative notion expressed through identity markers related to free movement norms. To be mobile across borders and to embrace freedom of movement as a norm is, in effect, to act as an Øresund citizen and to perform the necessary acts of integration.

3.4.3 Contestation of Free Movement Norms

In noting all of the above, it is clear that the adoption of free movement norms in principle and practice is essential to the Øresund project, as well as being in the interest of supranational structures that have supported the region's development. Such analyses suggest that the Øresund region encompasses the ideal conditions for EU norm adoption, which is why this chapter frames the Øresund region as a critical case study for European integration at the micro-regional level. Nevertheless, freedom of movement has not progressed smoothly nor been adopted as an uncontested norm. Since the opening of the Øresund Bridge there have been a number of surprises in this regard. Øresund promoters quickly realised that commuter numbers remained low and the appearance of unexpected obstacles to cross-border movement continued to increase (Löfgren 2008).

The notion of the Øresund as a seamless transport corridor to Europe was recently challenged when it became the site of a short-lived (though highly publicised) reinstatement of Danish customs borders in 2011. The installation of permanent checkpoints and systematic border controls was criticised by the European Commission as a possible breach of the Schengen Agreement (Malmström 2011). While swiftly overturned by the incoming Social-Democratic led government, the custom border case caused concern in the EU Commission due to the fact that a long-standing EU 15 member like Denmark would unilaterally challenge EU's Schengen arrangement, rather than working to strengthen and reinforce it (Munkøe 2012). Concerns emerged from neighbouring Sweden and regional actors, particularly over the symbolism of these border controls and mixed messages on free movement in the Øresund region. Swedish MP Hans Wallmark asserted,

> This is a very unacceptable development. While others are struggling for greater freedom of movement across our borders they are building walls in Denmark ... which goes in a

completely different direction than everything that the Nordic Council and the European Union stand for…. The idea of free movement in the Nordic countries and the EU is fundamental for co-operation. (Nordic Council 2011)

3.4.4 National Immigration Politics

The tightening of Danish immigration laws was another unforeseen development which caused tensions in the region around issues of mobility, migration and diversity. For a region where open clashes between national governments had been rare, the issue of immigration became one of the regular exceptions (Bucken-Knapp 2003). The Liberal-Conservative (L-C) Government that came into power in Denmark in 2001 made explicit promises to its voters that it would significantly change the premise of the country's immigration and migrant integration policies. At the start of 2002, the L-C coalition presented its 'New immigration politics' (*En Ny Udlændinge politik*) which included a radical shift in the country's approach to immigration and the introduction of new provisions that were some of the most restrictive in Europe (Goli and Rezaei 2007). Conversely, Rydgren (2010) describes how in Sweden, the lack of a credible anti-immigration party, and an agreed cross-party consensus not to mobilise on immigration issues, have largely limited anti-immigration policy and political discourse.

National approaches to border security, mobility, multiculturalism and transnational rights became a highly divisive issue between the two countries (Hedetoft et al. 2006). Anti-immigration political parties offered some of the most active rhetoric in this regard, mobilising voters around what Hellström and Hervik (2011) describe as core nativist messages that 'Sweden belongs to the Swedes and Denmark to the Danes'. This was expressed vividly by Danish People's Party (DPP) Leader Pia Kjærsgaard when she stated 'If the Swedish government wants to transform Sweden… into a Scandinavian Beirut with clan wars, killings and mass rapes, then let them do it. We can always put a barrier on the Øresund Bridge…' (Kjærsgaard 2002, online).

One of the prominent examples of contested immigration policy was brought about by divergent national spousal reunification policies for non-Europeans (Rubin 2005).Both Denmark and Sweden are obliged under the same EU Council Directive 2004/38/EC to allow EU/European Economic Area (EEA) Member State citizens the right to move and reside freely within Member States, along with their spouses and dependent children. However, Denmark has not signed up to EU Council Directive 2003/86/EC which asserts a right to family reunification for TCNs lawfully resident in an EU Member State. The greatest divergence between Denmark and Sweden thus related to rules regarding family reunification for TCNs, for which there is more scope for national discretion under EU law (Kofman and Meetoo 2008). From the early 2000's Denmark introduced some of the most restrictive requirements in Europe for prospective non-EU family migrants, largely influenced by the Government's support arrangement with the Danish People's Party. Of the more controversial policies enacted, the so-called '24 year rule' and 'attachment requirement' set strict requirements whereby a minimum age of 24, national affinity, level of wealth, and living arrangements are required before Danish citizens or residents may bring non-EU spouses or partners into the country (Østergaard-Nielsen 2003).

The purpose of these changes was to reduce immigration numbers and to prevent forced marriages or marriages of convenience (Hagelund 2008). In regard to the former, the policy was effective as family reunification residence permits dropped in Denmark between 2001 and 2006 by over 70 % (Danish Ministry of Refugee, Immigration and Integration Affairs 2010). One immediate effect of this divergence in family reunification laws was that mixed-marriage couples failing to get secure residence in Denmark moved instead to the more liberal neighbour state of Sweden. Danes with foreign spouses began moving to the southern Swedish city of Malmö at a rate of about 60 couples a month, continuing to work in Copenhagen by commuting across the Øresund Bridge, earning them the nickname of 'love refugees' (Rubin 2005, p. 319). This led to political debate and publicity around many Danish-TCN couples caught up in legal restrictions on spousal reunification.

The Swedish government was vocal in its misgivings about the new restrictive changes in Danish immigration policy and concerned about inadvertent migratory flows to Sweden as a result (Polakov-Suransky 2002). The Nordic Council Citizens' Committee similarly met in 2005 to discuss any contradiction between the Danish government's desire to promote freedom of movement and the tightening of the rules for family reunification (Nordic Council 2005). The sudden restrictions on spousal reunification in Denmark drew the attention of the European Commission which asserted that the rules contradicted EU Directives allowing EU citizens and their family members to move and reside freely within EU Member States (Rubin 2005). This created an interesting anomaly by which European rights to non-EU spousal reunification were essentially more generous than those afforded to Danish citizens under their own national legislation.

Even national citizens face some barriers to full cross-border rights in the Øresund region. Danes can only vote in national elections if they are normally resident in the country, so any living in Sweden and commuting to Denmark for work over the Øresund Bridge effectively lose one of their main political rights associated with citizenship. Denmark's policy of unitary citizenship also means that Øresund residents can have either Danish or Swedish citizenship—not both (Howard 2005). Different national rules about immigration, residence and citizenship policies therefore raise complications for the normalisation of seamless regional mobility and where Øresund citizens can live, work and enjoy a range of rights on both sides of the Bridge.

While there has been some success in addressing national barriers to free movement of Danish and Swedish citizens, this has proven more difficult with regard to non-European nationals, ineligible for the same cross-border labour rights and who face particular barriers to exercising free movement (Schluter 2005). Despite recommendations from the Nordic Council (Hansen et al. 2010) and the Øresund Committee (2010b), a cooperative approach to TCN cross-border rights has not yet been politically possible, and tensions are particularly evident between Denmark and Sweden on this issue. Such examples highlight on-going political tensions surrounding the movement of TCNs and the complexity of free movement principles when set in the context of wanted and unwanted forms of mobility. Just as the TCN spouses could be viewed as the unfortunate victims of tightened immigration policies, they are also members of an emerging group of mobile Øresund citizens, unintentionally embodying the kind of cross-border commuter citizenship envisaged by actors promoting cross-border integration. Examining integration in the Øresund, including adoption of free movement norms, therefore requires attention to national differences in official Danish and Swedish attitudes towards immigration policy (Bucken-Knapp 2003).

3.5   EU Free Movement Norm Adoption and Friction

When Øresund actors were building the bridge in the 1990s, it is unlikely they would have foreseen the unpredictable way in which their transnational visions would be challenged by the normative context of domestic immigration politics. Promoting freedom of movement has become an integral part of regional cohesion policy, yet the more border obstacles are overcome, the more they are reproduced along other lines (Gualini 2003). The presence of TCNs in the Øresund region challenges leaders to consider the reality of regional membership and participation, as the question of who does or does not deserve free movement in the region remains highly politicised.

This mirrors similar challenges in wider EU integration where efforts to enhance freedom of movement in Europe are challenged by those who resist the project of creating mobile European citizens, including, but not restricted to, populist national political parties. Such actors have provided a key source of resistance to free movement norms and EU integration more widely, particularly around the issue of TCN mobility (Maas 2005). More than half of the immigrants into EU Member States (approximately 1.6 million people in 2009) were TCNs (Eurostat 2011).In the absence of internal border controls in the Schengen area, any TCN admitted to one Schengen Member State has unmonitored access to travel to others, meaning that trust in each states' border and immigration controls is a necessary condition of the arrangement. TCN mobility remains a salient political issue however and Member States have struggled to form consensus on immigration policy harmonisation (Givens and Luedtke 2004). This has even led to recent EU discussion about the introduction of an Entry/Exit system as an electronic means to record whether TCNs have arrived or left the Schengen area (European Commission 2013). Conversely, other actors argue that TCNs are vital for Europe's economic future, with foreseeable labour market needs driving continued openness to immigration for economic growth (Münz et al. 2007).

One of the main areas of friction in Member States adopting EU free movement principles relates to the organisation of national citizenship, creating democratic inconsistencies between mobility and state-centred political rights. To consider issues of free movement norms in friction with national interests therefore prompts a deeper, normative reflection on the tensions between principles that underpin it.

Liberalism claims freedom of movement as an integral part of individual autonomy, while democracy also asserts national discretion over immigration control. TCNs and mobile EU citizens challenge existing concepts of democracy which entail political representation of a nationally-rooted population through domestic parliamentary elections and institutions (Isin 2008). The frictions arising from different levels of norm adoption raise an underlying paradox that European citizenship itself is marked by a tension between citizenship as derivative of the nation-state and citizenship that is activated by movement to another EU country (Bauböck 2007).

3.5.1   Key Findings

There are a number of key considerations that arise from the case study of free movement norm adoption in the Øresund region. The first is that norm export and import takes place in an interdependent relationship between norm-maker and norm-taker. The Øresund region, as a model CBR project, draws on EU norms of economic and political transnationalism (including freedom of movement) to legitimise the prioritisation of regional integration and new cross-border governance structures. Through financial, institutional and normative support, the EU has similarly demonstrated that it is investing in CBRs to deliver bottom up integration at the site of national borders. These material interests and institutions are an important condition in the diffusion of EU norms as regional political actors are predisposed to adopt and promote the positive benefits of cross-border integration and mobility. These include aims of achieving the Øresund region's 'cohesive, yet diverse labour market' (Øresund Committee 2010b, p. 6) through leading efforts to enhance freedom of movement.

Member States on the other hand are largely influenced by the tone of domestic political issues, as noted by patterns of Euro-scepticism and hostility to immigration. Scholars have long argued that the regulation of migration and cross-border movement constitutes the very 'state-ness of states', as immigration inevitably raises issues such as national security, population growth and composition, and national identity; all of which are areas that affect the role and legitimacy of the modern nation-state (Torpey 1998). Thus, it is argued that the political opportunities and costs of free movement norms are not evenly spread across different political actors, leading to differences in willingness to adopt or adapt to free movement norms at various levels of governance.

Secondly, this chapter has suggested the asymmetry of EU norm diffusion, particularly in the context of political debates on immigration. Norms are adopted for different kinds of people and purposes. Rather than stable and predictable flows of mobility, the Øresund region has shown examples of uneven and contest movements, in addition to mobility of contact and community. The ready adoption of free movement norms to promote the mobility of Øresund 'regionauts' is contrasted with other 'unwanted' forms of mobility, such as controversial movement of TCNs. Free movement norms are therefore unevenly adopted by some actors, interests and people more than others. In much rhetoric of the Øresund region, immigrants are written out of the integration narrative, despite being both a highly populous and highly mobile group (O'Dell 2011). This disjuncture speaks to a deeper conceptual struggle between European norms of individual liberalism and the democratic right of Member States to assert sovereignty over immigration and border protection. As Parkes and Schwarzer (2011) note, adopting the 'spirit' of free movement is not, it seems, as deeply anchored in many EU Member States' societies as suprar-egional actors might have hoped.

A third element emphasises that the domestic circumstances of norm-takers condition the reception of norms. Despite regional actors positioning the Øresund as the epitome of European freedom of movement and integration, it is evident that region is not free from national political resistance. However this tension is not experienced evenly across Member States, as evidenced in the case of divergent national immigration laws, policies and principles in Denmark and Sweden. National approaches to immigration and mobility still matter and have a bearing on the extent to which Øresund actors can promote free movement principles beyond those acceptable by national political circumstances. This relates to Börzel and Risse's (2009) observation that the acceptance or rejection of EU ideas depends on whether underlying assumptions are compatible with long-established domestic norms and the identities that they define. Among national political actors there remain divisions, including groups that outwardly reject Schengen and its underlying norms of free movement. In this sense, the ability to successfully adopt free movement norms in the cross-border Øresund region is reliant not only on the sum of institutional structure and economic conditions for integration, but also on whether these norms resonate with the domestic structures. In the absence of this resonance, freedom of movement norms can face political contestation and social mobilization.

All three of these points highlight the complexity of free movement norms and how they are adopted and negotiated in CBRs as frictions with national settings continue to challenge the 'European' ideal of free movement. If we consider the implication that CBRs, no matter the transnational image they promote, are entrenched to an extent in national frameworks, then certain limitations to EU norm adoption become visible. It is in bringing to the fore the tensions that lie between processes of integration and practices of mobility that we can understand the political importance of this adoption or rejection of free movement norms, and the significance that this has for prospects of regional integration, whether at the supranational or micro-regional level.

References

AEBR. (2008). Cross-border cooperation—European priority and political objective of the EU beyond 2013. http://www.aebr.EU/files/publications/CBCnach2013_M_rz_2008_EN.pdf. Accessed 5 May 2011.

Aradau, C., & Huysmans, J. (2009). Mobilising (global) democracy: A political reading of mobility between universal rights and the mob. *Millennium Journal of International Studies, 37*(3), 583–604.

Aradau, C., Huysmans, J., & Squire, V. (2010). Acts of European citizenship. *Journal of Common Market Studies, 48*(4), 945–965.

Bache, I., & Flinders, M. (2005). *Multi-level governance*. Oxford: Oxford University Press.

Baldoni, E. (2003). Free movement of persons in the European Union: A legal-historical overview. PIONEUR Working Paper No. 2, http://www.obets.ua.es/pioneur/bajaarchivo_public.php?iden=40. Accessed 8 April 2012.

Barroso, J. M. (2011). Speech by president Barroso at the EP open conference of presidents. Europa press releases. http://Europa.Eu/rapid/press-release_SPEECH-11-484_en.htm?locale=en. Accessed 8 Nov 2011.

Bauböck, R. (2007). Who are the citizens of Europe? Eurozine. http://www.Eurozine.com/articles/2006-12-23-baubock-en.html. Accessed 24 June 2012.

Bauböck, R. (2009). Global justice, freedom of movement and democratic citizenship. *European Journal of Sociology, 50*(1), 1–31.

Blatter, J. (2004). From "spaces of place" to "spaces of flows"? Territorial and functional governance in cross-border regions in Europe and North America. *International Journal of Urban and Regional Research, 28*(3), 530–548.

Börzel, T., & Risse, T. (2009). The transformative power of Europe: The European Union and the diffusion of ideas. KFG Working Paper No. 7, Freie Univ. Berlin.

Bucken-Knapp, G. (2003) Shaping possible integration in the emerging cross-border Øresund region. *European Studies: A Journal of European Culture, History and Politics, 19*(1), 55–79.

Castells, M. (1996). *Rise of the network society*. Malden: Wiley-Blackwell Publishers.

Checkel, J. T. (1999). Social construction and integration. *Journal of European Public Policy, 6*(4), 545–560.

Council of Europe. (n.d.) Local and regional democracy and good governance: What is a Euroregion? http://www.coe.int/t/dgap/localdemocracy/Areas_of_Work/Transfrontier_Cooperation/euroregions/What_is_en.asp. Accessed 14 Oct 2013.

Danish and Swedish Governments, 'Øresund—En region bliver til' (State Publications, 1999). http://www.evm.dk/resources/oem/static/publikationer/html/oresund/hele.pdf. Accessed 5 May 2011

Danish Ministry of Refugee, Immigration and Integration Affairs (2010). Annex 22: Overview of all residence permits granted in Denmark 2001–2010. In Statistical Overview—Migration and Asylum, Ministry of Refugee, Immigration and Integration Affairs, Copenhagen.

European Institute for Comparative Urban Research (EURICUR). (2007). *National policy responses to urban challenges in Europe*. Aldershot: Ashgate.

European Union. (2004). Corrigendum to Directive 2004/38/EC of the European Parliament and of the Council. http://eur-lex.europa.eu/LexUriServ/LexUriServ.do?uri=CELEX:32004L0038R(01):en:HTML. Accessed 26 June 2012.

European Commission. (2013). 2013/0057 (COD): Proposal for a regulation of the European Parliament and of the Council establishing an entry/exit system (EES) to register entry and exit data of third country nationals crossing the external borders of the Member States of the European Union. http://ec.europa.eu/dgs/home-affairs/doc_centre/borders/docs/1_en_act_part1_v12.pdf. Accessed 20 Oct 2013.

Eurostat. (2011). Migration and migrant population statistics, http://epp.eurostat.ec.europa.eu/statistics_explained/index.php/Migration_and_migrant_population_statistics. Accessed 26 June 2012.

Givens, T., & Luedtke, A. (2004). The politics of European Union immigration policy: Institutions, salience and harmonisation. *Policy Studies Journal, 32*(1), 145–165.

Goli, M., & Rezaei, S. (2007). Denmark. In A. Triandafyllidou & R. Gropas (Eds.), *European immigration: A sourcebook* (pp. 71–86). Aldershot: Ashgate. (Chapter 6).

Gualini, E. (2003). Cross-border governance: Inventing regions in a trans-national multi-level polity, disP. *The Planning Review, 39*(152), 43–52.

Hagelund, A. (2008). "For women and children!": The family and immigration politics in Scandinavia. In R. D. Grillo (Ed.), *The family in question: Immigrant and ethnic minorities in multicultural Europe* (pp. 71–88). Amsterdam: Amsterdam University Press.

Hall, P. (2008). Opportunities for democracy in Cross-border regions? Lessons from the Øresund region. *Regional Studies, 42*(3), 423–435.

Hansen, N., Seip, Å., & Eldring, L. (2010). *Rekruttering av kompetansearbeidskraft fra tredjeland til Norden– Reguleringer, strategier og realiteter*. Copenhagen: NCM Publications.

Hedetoft, U., Petersson, B., & Sturfelt, L. (2006). *Bortom stereotyperna?: Invandrare och integration i Danmark och Sverige*. Stockholm: Makadam Förlag.

Hellström, A., & Hervik, P. (2011). Feeding "the beast": Nourishing nativist appeals in Sweden and Denmark. CoMID Working Paper Series (1), CoMID, Aalborg.

Howard, M. M. (2005). Variation in dual citizenship policies in the countries of the EU. *International Migration Review, 39*(3), 697–720.

INTERREG IIA. (2005). Programme summary of the Øresund region, INTERREG IIA programme. http://event.interact-eu.net/download/application/pdf/1007227. Accessed 5 May 2011.

Isin, E. (2008). Enacting mobility: Theoretical issues. http://www.enacting-citizenship.eu/index.php/sections/blog_post/48/. Accessed 14 April 2012.

Jensen, O., & Richardson, T. (2004). Constructing a transnational mobility region—On the Øresund. In S. Dosenrode & H. Halkier (Eds.), *The Nordic regions and the European Union* (pp. 139–158). Hampshire: Ashgate.

Jerneck, M. (1999). *Integration och utveckling i Öresundsregionen: Möjligheter och utmaningar*. Lund: Lund University.

Kjærsgaard, P. (2002). Sæt En Broklap i Øresundsbroen, http://www.danskfolkeparti.dk/Pia_Kj%C3%A6rsgaard_S%C3%A6t_en_broklap_i_%C3%98resundsbroen. Accessed 17 June 2012.

Kofman, E., & Meetoo, V. (2008). Family migration. In International Organization for Migration (Ed.), *World migration 2007: Managing labour mobility in the evolving global economy* (pp. 151–172) Geneva: International Organisation for Migration.

Löfgren, O. (2008). Regionauts: The transformation of cross-border regions in Scandinavia. *European Urban and Regional Studies, 15*(3), 195–209.

Lyck, L., & Boye, P. (2009). Cross border regions as forerunners in EU Integration—an institutional perspective on structural change. Svenska Nätverket för Europaforskning i Ekonomi. http://www.snee.org/filer/papers/540.pdf. Accessed 2 Dec 2012.

Maas, W. (2005). Freedom of movement inside "Fortress Europe". In E. Zureik & M. Salter (Eds.), *Global surveillance and policing: Borders, security, identity* (pp. 233–246). Devon: Willan Publishing.

Maas, W. (2007). *Creating European citizens*. Lanham: Rowman & Littlefield.

Malmström, C. (2011). Statement by Cecilia Malmström, EU Commissioner for home affairs, on the announced permanent customs controls in Denmark. http://europa.eu/rapid/press-release_MEMO-11-296_en.htm?locale=fr. Accessed 8 Nov 2011.

Manners, I. (2008). The normative ethics of the European Union. *International Affairs, 83*(1), 65–80.

Mansfield, E. D., & Solingen, E. (2010). Regionalism. *Annual Review of Political Science, 13*(1), 145–163.

Mostov, J. (2007). Soft borders and transnational citizens. In S. Benhabib, I. Shapiro, & D. Petranović (Eds.), *Identities, affiliations and allegiances* (pp. 136–158). Cambridge: Cambridge University Press.

Munkøe, M. (2012). The 2011 debacle over Danish border control: A mismatch of domestic and European games, EU Diplomacy Paper 01/2012, Department of EU International Relations and Diplomacy Studies, College of Europe. http://aei.pitt.edu/33456/1/EDP_1_2012_Munkoe.pdf. Accessed 10 Nov 2011.

Münz, R., Straubhaar, T., Vadean, F., & Vadean, N. (2007). What are the migrants contributions to employment and Growth: A European approach. OECD. http://www.oecd.org/dataoecd/43/15/38295272.pdf. Accessed 26 June 2012.

Nordic Council. (2005). Bertel Haarder faces Nordic cross-fire, Nordic Council website. http://www.norden.org/en/news-and-events/news/bertel-haarder-faced-nordic-cross-fire/. Accessed 14 April 2011.

Nordic Council. (2011). Wallmark: Tighter border control unacceptable. Nordic Council Website. http://www.norden.org/en/news-and-events/news/wallmark-tighter-border-control-unacceptable/. Accessed 15 Nov 2011.

Nordic Council. (n.d.). 1953–1971—Nordic cooperation. http://www.norden.org/en/nordic-council/the-nordic-council/the-history-of-the-nordic-council/1953-1971. Accessed 14 April 2011.

Nordic Council Website. (n.d.). Freedom of movement. http://www.norden.org/en/about-nordic-co-operation/areas-of-co-operation/freedom-of-movement/freedom-of-movement. Accessed 14 April 2011.

O'Dell, T. (2003). Øresund and the regionauts. *European Studies, 19,* 31–53.

O'Dell, T. (2011). Mobility and the stitching together of everyday life experiences in the Øresund region. In M. Vacher, T. O'Dell, & H. L. Schollert (Eds.), *Temporal and spacial modalities of everyday integration* (pp. 14–23). Lund: Institutionen för kulturvetenskap.

OECD. (2003). OECD territorial reviews: Øresund, Denmark/Sweden, OECD, France.

Øresund Committee. (2005). 'Öresundsregionen: The human capital of Scandinavia' Øresundskomiteen, Copenhagen, 18, 23.

Øresund Committee. (2010a). ØRUS: Øresund regional strategy. Øresundskomiteen, Copenhagen.

Øresund Committee. (2010b). 33 Obstacles, challenges and opportunities: The Øresund Model 2010. Øresundskomiteen, Copenhagen.

Øresund Committee. (2011). Annual review: 2010. Øresundskomiteen, Copenhagen.

Øresundsbro Consortium Analysis Department. (2010). *10 years: The Øresund bridge and its region.* Copenhagen: Øresundsbro Konsortiet.

Østergaard-Nielsen E. (2003). Counting the costs: Denmark's changing migration policies. *International Journal of Urban and Regional Research, 27*(2), 448–454.

Paasi, A. (2009). The resurgence of the "region" and "regional identity": Theoretical perspectives and empirical observations on regional dynamics in Europe. *Review of International Studies, 35,* 121–146.

Parkes, R., & Schwarzer, D. (2012). The divisiveness of mobility: Fuelling populism in the Euro and Schengen areas. German Institute for International and Security Affairs. http://www.swp-berlin.org/fileadmin/contents/products/comments/2012C21_pks_swd.pdf. Accessed 2 Dec 2012.

Perkmann, M. (2003). Cross-border regions in Europe: Significance and drivers of regional cross-border cooperation. *European Urban and Regional Studies, 10*(2), 153–171.

Polakov-Suransky, S. (2002). Denmark: Rebuffing immigrants. *World Press Review, 49*(8), Online. http://www.worldpress.org/Europe/642.cfm. Accessed 14 April 2011

Recchi, E., & Favell, A. (2009). *Pioneers of European integration: Citizenship and mobility in the EU.* Cheltenham: Edward Elgar Publishing.

Rubin, L. (2005). Love's refugees: The effects of stringent Danish immigration policies on Danes and their non-Danish spouses. *Connecticut Journal of International Law, 20,* 319–342.

Rydgren, J. (2010). Radical right-wing populism in Denmark and Sweden: Explaining party system change and stability. *SAIS Review, 30*(1), 57–71.

Schluter, P. (2005). *The Nordic countries—One workplace, one market: A report on removal of cross-border obstacles by special envoy Poul Schluter.* Copenhagen: NCM Publications.

Torpey, J. (1998). Coming and going: On the state monopolization of the legitimate "means of movement". *Sociological Theory, 16*(3), 239–259.

Toni Grace was the recipient of a 2011 IRSES-KEEENZ Award to Lund University in Sweden which supported her Master's thesis research on regional integration, cross-border mobility and models of citizenship in the Øresund Region. She has previously lived in Denmark for 2 years and maintains an interest in Scandinavian and immigration issues. Toni holds a Master's degree (Distinction) in Political Science from Victoria University of Wellington, and is currently a Senior Advisor for the New Zealand Ministry of Business, Innovation and Employment.

Chapter 4
The EU and Global Economic Governance: Playing the Role of a Global Leader?

Rikard Bengtsson

4.1 Introduction: New Preconditions, New Challenges: Global Economic Governance in Transformation

The global political economy is in a process of fundamental transformation. Symbolized by the rise of China and the American pivot to Asia, geopolitical and geoeconomic processes are converging to form a major global shift centering on the Asia-Pacific. The implications of this for the Asia-Pacific as well as for the rest of the world, Europe included, largely remain to be seen. There are indications, however, that within the area of international organization, dramatic changes are under way in the direction away from embedded multilateralism into weaker forms of institutionalization. Perhaps the most evident example of this concerns the elevation of the Group of Twenty (G20) into the premier forum for global economic governance. Such developments are of key concern to the European Union (EU), given its values-based foreign policy and, specifically, its institutionally-oriented approach to multilateralism, at a time when consecutive crises have severely impacted its actorness. To what extent has the EU been able to promote its norms and standards in the emerging economic governance structures? Are EU norms and ideals accepted by other key actors on the global stage?

The development outlined above falls into a broader set of questions related to how existing multilateral institutions function today in view of globalization processes, new challenges and the emergence of new global and regional powers, and what needs and prospects for reform there are. The increasingly dense webs of interconnectedness and interdependence, a key reflection of growing globalization, arguably contains an enhanced community of interests among states and non-state actors and, as a result thereof, increasing calls for novel global solutions and

R. Bengtsson (✉)
Department of Political Science, Lund University, Lund, Sweden
e-mail: rikard.bengtsson@svet.lu.se

© Springer International Publishing Switzerland 2015   39
A. Björkdahl et al. (eds.), *Importing EU Norms,* United Nations University Series
on Regionalism 8, DOI 10.1007/978-3-319-13740-7_4

organizations. Simultaneously, conflict and competition seem to increase in today's world—although in a non-military fashion, a fundamental change compared to previous periods in human history.

If anything, it could be argued that the need for global governance is greater than before—processes of specialization of production and intensification of trade mean that countries and corporations are more interdependent than before in complex global value chains and that the system as such is vulnerable to disruptions of various sorts. Also, financial flows have increased dramatically in recent years, due to deregulation as well as technological developments. Foreign direct investment (FDI) trends are changing and developing economies are now receiving more FDI as a group than developed economies—a historical global shift that also reflects China's changing role in the global economy. A mismatch between the Bretton Woods institutions as they were developed in the 1940s and how the global economy has evolved is thus becoming all the more apparent. This is, in part, because new leading actors are emerging with different sets of preferences—for instance, regarding multilateralism—and, in part, because the global political economy as a system of interaction is changing in nature.

4.1.1   Conceptualizing the EU in Global Governance

This new setting begs basic questions about the future of multilateralism and how global governance instruments are to be designed. Typically, international cooperation is plagued by the dilemma of balancing efficiency and democracy. Many critics of conventional multilateralism such as the United Nations-based order refer to its lack of effectiveness as a reflection of the vast number of participants. Critics of exclusive (i.e. great-power-based) orders encompassing just a few participants, such as the Group of Eight (G8), on the other hand, point to problems of representation and transparency. Both perspectives underline the centrality of legitimacy, either as input or output legitimacy. At the heart of the notion of legitimacy is the right to govern and be supported, or at least tolerated, by those governed. The legitimacy concept is thus two-fold: 'rightful membership' and 'rightful conduct' (after Clark 2005).

The development of the G20 into the central forum for global economic governance encompasses this dilemma of striking the 'right' balance between seemingly contrasting values. As argued by Slaughter (2013) the G20 can be viewed as a policy response trying to achieve two ends at the same time—maximizing the political legitimacy for coordinated action, and maximizing the effectiveness of such a response. The G20 format thus resembles what could be called elite multilateralism (Haass 2010) or minilateralism, conceptualized as 'the smallest possible number of countries needed to have the largest possible impact on solving a particular problem' (Naím 2009, p. 135). Such a perspective underscores the necessity of creating a legitimate order in the eyes of those included *as well as* those excluded. While powerful states inside the G20 are of critical importance for leadership and implementation, and hence for legitimating the institution, it is ultimately the outsiders who determine the actual degree of legitimacy (which underlines the importance of perceptions, expectations, feelings of inclusion etc.). Thus, restricted or exclusive forms of multilateralism imply a focus on the notion of representation. In order for an arrangement to be deemed legitimate in terms of representation, non-members must feel adequately represented by those on the inside. In the G20 this is a key issue not least among developing countries. The evolution from G8 to G20 means that major developing countries, such as China, India and Brazil, are included as members, but to what extent are they representing developing countries outside of the G20? This is also a key issue for the EU, given that a few EU member states are G20 members in their own right, along with the EU in its institutional capacity, but the vast majority of EU members are not directly represented at the level of heads of state and government.

The G20 and preceding G forums were set up 'outside the normal protocols of multilateral international law and the United Nations' (Slaughter 2013, p. 43) and are largely lacking constitution, secretariat and budget. As a consequence, they have no capacity for independent policy development. Instead, member state governments are decisive, which raises the important questions about membership, representation and legitimacy introduced above. Certain measures of institutionalization have been suggested in recent years, but the overriding format of great power summitry remains. This may come as no surprise given the profile and nature of the membership—great powers often do not want to be bound by the same set of rules as ordinary countries; as is often argued, great powers rarely make great multilateralists.

Where does this leave the EU, given that the foreign policy of the EU and its member states is (to varying degrees, admittedly) built on the centrality of a rules- and an institutions-based global order? To what extent have European actors in the G20 been successful in promoting European values and standards? These questions can be addressed through the prism of leadership. Leadership may be defined as 'an asymmetrical relationship of influence in which one actor guides or directs the behaviour of others towards a certain goal over a certain period of time' (Underdal 1994, p. 178) and may come in various forms, for instance utilizing structural preconditions, entrepreneurial possibilities within institutional arrangements, and discursive resources regarding agenda-setting and framing of substantive issues. In what ways, if any, are the EU and European states playing a leadership role in developing global economic governance?

The chapter begins with a discussion on the expanding 'minilateralism' of the G20 while situating the EU in this evolving context. In so doing, the chapter reflects upon the politics of representation and legitimacy of these far from uncontroversial developments. Furthermore, the chapter assesses the performance of the EU and the distinct role of individual EU Member States in the G20 context. Returning to the question of whether or not the EU and the European actors play a leadership role in the G20, and in effect promote European norms and ideas on the global level, the concluding analysis suggests that the European influence has decreased in recent years despite substantial representation and agenda-setting potential.

4.2 From G7/8 to G20: Expanding Minilateralism?[1]

4.2.1 Aims and Rationale: First Crisis Management, Then What?

The original aim of elevating the status of the G20 to the level of heads of state and government was to restore confidence and lay the foundation for renewed growth and financial stability. Beyond immediate crisis management, a broader aim has developed that focuses on defining common development goals and establishing consensus as to how to achieve these goals. In so doing, the G20 allots for itself the role of agenda-setter and broker—laying the foundation for the operative work of and implementation through international organizations, not least the Bretton Woods institutions (the International Monetary Fund (IMF) and the World Bank group (WB)) and the World Trade Organization (WTO). This peculiarity—that agenda creation, definition of reform needs and consensus-building takes place in a small group which is then to guide the implementation in organizations with broad membership—creates a legitimacy problem. The authority and legitimacy of the G20 thus depends on the ability of the group to form consensus and deliver results in key issues of global economic governance. But differing views of what constitutes these key issues as well as how to deal with them means that the G20 is potentially vulnerable and susceptible to continued, potentially increasing, criticism.

4.2.2 Membership

As regards membership, there are no formal criteria for G20 membership, but the initiators (especially American and Canadian finance ministers) stressed that member states ought to be 'systemically important', i.e. the forum should include the largest economies in the world. Partly contradicting that economic perspective, another conventionally agreed consideration was geographic/regional balance. At the same time, effectiveness, implying a limitation of the number of participants, was a key concern. And, as in so many other contexts, membership also rests on political considerations rather than strict criteria. All-in-all, the outcome approximates the 20 largest economies in the world, but still excludes major economies such as Iran, Taiwan and Poland, and includes Argentina and South Africa instead.[2] A peculiarity of sorts is that in addition to 19 states, also the EU as an entity is a member. It has

---

[1] Factual information about the development of the G20 in this section is primarily drawn from the G20 website; for introductory analyses, see Jokela (2011a); Kirton (2012).

[2] G20 members are Argentina, Australia, Brazil, Canada, France, Germany, India, Indonesia, Italy, Japan, Korea, Mexico, Russia, Saudi Arabia, South Africa, Turkey, United Kingdom, United States and the European Union. The G20 countries account for approximately 85 % of world GDP, 80 % of world trade, 65 % of world agricultural land and 77 % of production of grain.

not been granted the right to chair the group, however; the G20 remains in that sense squarely an intergovernmental construction.

The membership profile—size and content—raises important governance questions about representation and legitimacy. As a reflection of this and deepening interdependence, a practice of inviting non-members to summits has developed in the G system. Notably, in 2005, Prime Minister Blair, as chair of the G8, invited Brazil, China, India, Mexico and South Africa, a move which became institutionalized at the 2007 summit (during Germany's presidency), in what later came to be known as the Heiligendamm Process. This practice has continued in the G20 context, and it has been expanded to international organizations.[3] In addition to this summit practice, certain countries utilize an 'outreach' strategy in their region to enable a form of 'proxy representation'. Australia is a good example of this in relation to New Zealand and other states in the region.

The G20 has stimulated interorganizational cooperation that probably would not have taken place otherwise. Because of this, there is an indirect possibility of influencing for those outside the G20. At the same time, it is obvious that if the G20 countries have established a consensus, it is in principle impossible to promote any alternative viewpoint.

In the European context, the inclusion of the EU as an institution potentially grants a degree of representation for smaller EU states. However, the institutional redesign through the Lisbon Treaty, in which the rotating presidency was abolished in external relations, diminishes this; representation depends largely on the actions of the large individual members. Jokela argues: 'Fears that the institutionalization of the European Council with a permanent President would further empower the largest member states have grown stronger under the current crisis situation' (2011b, p. 8). At the G20, the EU is represented at the leaders' level by both the Council President and Commission President. It should be added that in addition to Germany, France, the United Kingdom and Italy as permanent European members of the G20, Spain has come to be granted the status of permanent invitee.

4.2.3 Genesis: Cooperation in the Format of G20 Finance Ministers 1999–2008

The G20 was founded at a Group of Seven (G7) finance ministers' meeting in September 1999. The first meeting of G20 finance ministers and heads of central banks

---

[3] France (2011) invited the chairs of the African Union (AU), New Partnership for Africa's Development (NEPAD) and Gulf Cooperation Council (GCC), while Korea (2010) invited the chair of Association of South-East Asian Nations (ASEAN). Canada (2010) invited the Netherlands while Mexico (2012) invited Chile, Colombia and Ethiopia. Russia (2013) invited Ethiopia (chair of AU), Senegal (chair of NEPAD), Kazakhstan, and Singapore (chair of Global Governance Group (3G)) among others. The UN Secretary General is present at all leaders' summits, as are the heads of the IMF, WB, WTO, the Organization for Economic Cooperation and Development (OECD) and the Financial Stability Board (FSB). In addition, at Los Cabos (Mexican Presidency 2012), the heads of Food and Agricultural Organization (FAO) and the International Labour Organization (ILO) were in attendance.

was held in Berlin in December 1999. The rationale for global economic governance is to be found specifically in the Asian crisis, and more generally in the realization that in a deeply interdependent and interconnected world, vulnerabilities have increased and the simplistic dichotomy of North and South is no longer relevant in the same way as before. The G20 replaced the Group of 33 (G33) and the Group of 22 (G22), which had been established a few years earlier.

Annual meetings at the level of finance ministers were held for a number of years, based on a rotating chairmanship. In connection to a G7 meeting in October 2008—at the height of crisis after the fall of the Lehman Brothers—President Bush proposed that a G20 meeting should be convened in Washington in November that same year at the level of heads of state and government, for the purpose of collective crisis management of the global economy. Interestingly, from the perspective of European influence, the push for the meeting came through an initiative by President Sarkozy and Prime Minister Brown. Since 2008, G20 summits at the level of heads of state and government have taken place once or twice annually and, as we will see, the leaders have designated the G20 as the premier forum for global economic governance.

It should be noted that meetings of finance ministers have continued also after the initiation of the leaders' summits, among other things to prepare these summits. During the 2013 Russian presidency of the G20, five such meetings were taking place.

4.2.4   Upgrade 2009–2010: From London and Pittsburgh to Seoul and Toronto

Of key relevance for the continuation of the process was and still is the relationship between the G20 and the Bretton Woods institutions. The foundation of the upgrading of the G20 to its key position is to be found in the concluding declaration of the first G20 summit of heads of state and government in Washington, stating that

> we underscored that the Bretton Woods institutions must be comprehensively reformed so that they can more adequately reflect changing economic weights in the world economy and be more responsive to future challenges. Emerging and developing economies should have a greater voice and representation in these institutions. (G20 2008, p. 10)

Since then, every G20 meeting has contained discussions of multilateral governance, especially at Pittsburgh (September 2009) and Seoul and Toronto (both 2010). As a consequence, the IMF and WB have decided on reforms to increase the say of emerging and developing economies. In the IMF, the result is that the voting weights of these countries increased by 2.6–44.7%, with the corresponding decrease for developed economies. Herein lies a controversial issue: Given that these issues were settled in the G20 rather than in the respective institutions meant that most countries did not have a direct say in the negotiations. Further quota rebalancing is to be expected, and the same problem will appear again (for instance in relation to the 2015 shareholding review in the WB).

The Pittsburgh declaration is significant in terms of upgrading the status of the G20—participants 'designated the G20 to be the premier forum for our international economic cooperation' (G20 2009, p. 3).[4] The likelihood that this will materialize in formal terms (some kind of arrangement in which the Bretton Woods institutions are made formally subordinate to the G20) must be considered quite low, but a de facto development of this kind is arguably already under way and, as such, is much more problematic from the perspective of accountability and transparency.

In terms of concrete outcomes during the upgrading process, it can be noted that calls, not least from many European countries, for improved regulation resulted in the Financial Stability Board (FSB) at the G20 London meeting (April 2009).

Another sign of the upgrade is that the G20 agenda has gradually broadened after the initial crisis management summits to include development issues and climate change. In Seoul (2010), development issues (including food security and commodity price volatility) were introduced on the agenda, resulting in the so-called Seoul Development Consensus for Shared Growth. This outcome is a clear indication of the possibility that the country holding the presidency can influence the agenda. In this case, as the forum provided an opportunity for South Korea to showcase its transformation from a poor developing country to a successful and internationally important actor providing development aid for others (for further analysis, see Gnath and Schmucker 2011; Cherry and Dobson 2012).

The climate issue has been addressed in all declarations from the last few years, in the form of expressions of support for the UNFCCC process, although no substantial negotiations have taken place. While the G20 will not replace other forums in the environmental field, it could still become the political clearinghouse also in this field. Looking at the summits in Brisbane in November 2014 and in Turkey in Fall 2015 will be important in this regard.

It should be noted that there is a broad consensus in the group not to move into the area of foreign policy proper, and not to deal with issues regarding democracy and human rights—a reflection of the self-interests of the governments concerned, which comes as no surprise in a constellation that includes Saudi Arabia, China and Russia among its members.

4.2.5 Consolidation: Cannes Onwards

The process described above has been consolidated in recent years. Summits have been less frequent (annual meetings since 2011), reflecting the somewhat less acute economic situation. Little new came out of the Cannes 2011 meeting, meaning that status quo powers rather than proponents of alternative regimes won out. The major focus of the 2012 Los Cabos meeting was thus to reinvigorate the process, or as Giles put it in the *Financial Times* (2012): 'After a string of failures, the task for

---

[4] As time has passed, the word 'our' has often disappeared, and Russia has now taken this one step further by designating the G20 the 'steering group for the global economy'.

the Los Cabos G20 summit is to stop the rot and prevent the organization becoming irrelevant.' Whether that will succeed in the long-term perspective is perhaps too early to say, but significant progress was made in 2012 on designing new global rules on e.g. derivatives, credit rating agencies, gathering and keeping of financial data, and systemically important financial institutions, or so-called 'sifs'. Moreover, in February 2013, G20 finance ministers agreed to avoid precipitating currency wars through competitive devaluations and targeting of exchange rates. Rather, they resolved to let market forces determine exchange rates based on fundamentals.

On the declaratory level, the Los Cabos conclusions (18–19 June 2012) emphasized:

> Despite the challenges we all face domestically, we have agreed that multilateralism is of even greater importance in the current climate, and remains our best asset to resolve the global economy's difficulties. … we will intensify our efforts to create a more conducive environment for development. (G20 2012, p. 1)

It can be noted that that 'inclusive green growth', development issues and corruption all feature prominently in the declaration. The text can also be read as a proclamation of the self-image of the group:

> In light of the interconnectedness of the world economy, the G20 has led to a new paradigm of multilateral co-operation that is necessary in order to tackle current and future challenges. The informal and flexible character of the G20 enables it to facilitate international economic and financial cooperation, and address the challenges confronting the global economy. It is important that we continue to further improve the transparency and effectiveness of the G20, and ensure that it is able to respond to pressing needs. (G20 2012, p. 14)

Finally, another feature of the consolidation of the G20 should also be mentioned, namely its promotion of increasing contacts with civil society in the form of Business 20, Labour 20, Civil 20 and Think 20, among other constellations.

This period is largely marked by one of less proactive European profiles: the Cannes agenda, to take but one example, was overshadowed by the Eurozone sovereign debt crisis, and it was evident that the EU was weakened in its normative argumentation and agenda-setting position as a result of its internal problems (Jokela 2011b; interview Swedish government official 10 September 2013). Having said that, no one else has stepped forward as a clear leader of the G20 and the forum has not developed dramatically in a direction opposed to EU interests. Rather it seems to have taken on a different role than that of a crisis management committee. Luckhurst (2012, p. 755) argues: 'Once the initial crisis appeared to dissipate in late 2009, so did the willingness to compromise and maintain strategic cooperation within the G20. …there have not been further substantive initiatives from this group to match what was achieved in April 2009.' This also means, in effect, that the weak form of multilateralism it represents remains the organizing principle.

4.3   The Politics of Representation and Legitimacy

G20 has become a consensus mechanism among major economies and a catalyst for decisions in other international forums (IMF, WB, WTO, ILO), i.e. playing the role of global agenda-setter—it is the node of a system of international institutions and regulations. As we have seen, recent IMF reform was decided through the G20, as well as the refinancing of the IMF.

This process is not only about substantive remedies and solutions to economic crises (and potentially other issues). It also reflects the principally important issue of design of global governance regimes. States in the G20 and generally proponents of the current system argue from the standpoint of output legitimacy—there is need for effective governance of the global economy, i.e. providing global public goods, which points to the importance of leadership and encompassing the world's largest centres of population and economic activity. On the contrary, one could argue, as Slaughter, that 'effectiveness alone is not enough to sustain global forms of governance and capitalism' (2013, p. 44); rather, the arrangement must also be recognized as legitimate from an input or participatory perspective.

The development is thus not uncontroversial. The former Australian Prime and Foreign Minister Rudd is a staunch supporter: 'The G20 is the best blend of legitimacy and effectiveness the international community has had so far in dealing with the great challenges of the global economy' (cited in Slaughter 2013, p. 50). Others take a more critical standpoint. Swedish Prime Minister Reinfeldt (representing the EU at the Pittsburgh summit as Sweden was holding the EU Council Presidency) has argued that 'it should be self-evident that the countries affected by the G20's decisions should also have been allowed to have their say in making them' (Reinfeldt 2009). Norwegian Foreign Minister Gahr Støre has gone a step further in describing the G20 as

> one of the greatest set-backs since World War II… the G20 is a grouping without international legitimacy… The G20 composition is determined by the major countries and powers. It may be more representative than the G7 and the G8… but it is still arbitrary'. (Der Spiegel 2010, see also Slaughter 2013, p. 49)

Criticism can also be found in the form of institutional counter-developments, notably the formation of the so-called Global Governance Group (or 3G), consisting of 30 small and middle powers led by Singapore. The group, which defends the UN multilateral system, was formed in the spring of 2009 in New York on the initiative of Singapore. It has members from all parts of the world, sees itself as a counterweight to the G20 and promotes multilateral solutions and the interests of small states. The group contains countries such as Botswana, Chile, Malaysia, New Zealand, the Philippines, Vietnam and Switzerland—and three EU countries (Finland, Luxembourg and Slovenia), which invites interesting questions about potential tensions within the EU. The group is becoming increasingly institutionalized and has held seven ministerial meetings. The main task of 3G is described as working for 'a more effective, accountable and inclusive framework of global governance' (Global Governance Group 2013), for instance through more transparency in G20 generally and briefings in the UN before and after G20 summits. The UN is considered the backbone of a legitimate global order—the UN is "the only global body with universal participation and unquestioned legitimacy—the actions and decisions of the G20 should complement and strengthen the United Nations system" (Global Governance Group 2013). The 3G group is thus not opposed to the G20 per se, but finds the question of representation problematic as so many are affected by its decisions but are left out of the decision-making process. Additionally, it maintains that the G20 should be limited to economic and financial matters, rather than broaden its agenda: "The controversy over the G-20's role has been further fuelled as its agenda has broadened beyond core economic and financial issues" (Global Governance Group 2011). The group has asked to be systematically consulted in the G20 process. Its opinions have not gone unnoticed, and the chair of the group is now invited to the G20 summits.

What is then the EU view of the G20 in light of debates about weakening multilateralism? Reflecting changing preconditions of governance, the perspective taken is often one of output legitimacy (for overviews, see the European Commission 2013a). According to a (quite explicit) contribution by the EU Delegation to the United Nations on UN reform, the G20

> can play a catalytic and or/supportive role in specific areas, such as economic policy, development, financial sector reform, trade, energy safety and security, environment including climate change, and health… the G20 can… provide the political momentum in areas where the UN may find it more difficult to galvanise action. (EEAS 2011, p. 5)

The backdrop is primarily one of lack of efficiency at the UN level:

> In many instances, moving from broad consensus to a more operational policy-making and actual coordinated delivery of measures on the ground has been hampered by some outdated debates reflective of a North-South logic which no longer defines international relations. This severely restricts the capacity of the UN to play its full role in global economic governance. (EEAS 2011, p. 5)

Therefore, from an EU perspective, agenda development is of critical importance after the initial crisis years, as evident in the Seoul Development Consensus for Shared Growth, given that the ambition is to create a *global* system of regulating capitalism.

It may be fruitful to reiterate here that the G20 is not based on formal international treaties like other organizations but on a selective and informal agreement among participants. Rather than producing formal texts, then, it becomes largely a matter of discursive influence. But, crucially for the EU, can such an arrangement be a norm promoter in global politics? Again, the issue is decided by the recognition that non-members grant the group—minilateralism may prove legitimate, if it can deliver global public goods that the multilateral order cannot.

As an illustration, Director General Pascal Lamy spoke of WTO reform (September 2012) in terms of the 'crisis of multilateralism', arguing that 'multilateralism is struggling…. the WTO is one of the most successful examples of rule-based multilateralism at work…. but our members' difficulties to agree to update our rulebook also demonstrates that the WTO is not immune to the geo-economic and geopolitical transformations of our time' (ibid.). Again, the role of the EU, as a key trade actor, is underlined.

4.4   EU Performance at the G20

Given the great European presence in the G20—in all seven representatives, including member state representatives, EU institutional representatives and Spain as permanent invitee—favourable preconditions exist for substantial European influence in the G20 process. Resembling a 'most likely'-design, one could venture the argument that if Europe is not successful in getting its way in this context, less favourable settings will likely present problems in terms of European impact.

One overriding observation is that the EU and European states were instrumental and influential in the early phase of the G20 at leaders' level. To begin with, it was Germany and France that pushed the US to utilize the G20 for crisis management. Also, the London summit, largely perceived as a success, consolidated the forum substantially in deciding on 'unprecedented coordinated state intervention in the markets' (Jokela 2011b, p. 4). A lot of credit was given to European parties for this outcome: to the UK, and specifically Prime Minister Brown, for proactively hosting the summit, to France and Germany for driving negotiations forward, and to the European Commission for providing intellectual and conceptual leadership. It has been claimed that in the *communique* after the summit many of the Commission's suggestions were adopted word-for-word (Jokela 2011b; see also Bengtsson 2010). The EU was well coordinated and spoke with one voice ('agreed language'). The EU was also successful in its agenda-setting efforts to raise the issue of climate change at the Pittsburgh summit (2009), but did not manage to produce any decisive outcome in terms of commitments (a prelude to the Copenhagen COP 15 summit, after which the EU has had a hard time playing a leadership role in the climate sphere).

As a contrast to the impact and posture of the early years, more recent developments display that European actors have been less coordinated and that European perspectives have been less attractive to non-European participating states. The Eurozone sovereign debt crisis has dominated the agendas at Cannes and Los Cabos (although less so at St. Petersburg) and has weakened European authority. Especially the Cannes summit presented a possibility for renewed European leadership, but—due to internal European conflicts, the euro crisis, and the differing interests of other parties—it amounted to very little. No significant EU deliberations on the institutional developments in the G-20 have taken place. There has been no obvious agenda-setting role for the EU in the last years. As Jokela argues, the EU 'has failed to establish global consensus on some of the key challenges' of global economic governance (Jokela 2011b, p. 8). In summary, Europe's influence in the G20 has been declining in recent years.

Having said that, the EU's role in the expansion of the G20 agenda beyond the economic and financial sector should not be underestimated—the EU has promoted ideas of its own and added weight to those of others (development and green growth being the most obvious cases), contributing to new forms of coalitions that do not follow traditional North-South divides (for analysis see Luckhurst 2012). By and large, however, it has not managed to get the G20 to devise or adopt strong arrangements against the initial will of other major states, especially when it comes to getting others to commit to binding efforts, a pattern that is recognizable from other negotiating forums (interview Swedish government official 10 September 2013). The field of climate change is a good illustration of this problem (see further Kim and Chung 2012). Developing countries have not taken the agenda in a completely different direction than that of the developed countries, however (as shown by Luckhurst 2012). Instead they have been able to block the success of initiatives launched by the EU (and others), in effect questioning of the EU's credibility as a global discursive leader in this field (Gnath and Schmucker 2011; interview Swedish official 10 September 2013). As in other contexts, agenda exclusion proves a powerful mechanism for influence.

Things may be changing again, however. While still too early for systematic conclusions, elements of the 2013 summit process point towards an EU less paralyzed by internal crisis and more confident and potentially influential in discussions on future global governance. In the run-up to the 2013 St. Petersburg summit, Presidents Barroso and van Rompuy sent a letter to the 28 heads of state and government in an effort to reach a more proactive, concerted perspective and to have an inclusive preparatory phase (and to gain legitimacy for their own perspectives in the process—see further below on challenges of internal coordination). In doing so, they sought to pinpoint their views on issues to be prioritized at the summit: growth and employment, financial regulatory reform, tax avoidance and evasion, reform of international financial architecture, and progress in work on development, anticorruption and energy (European Commission 2013b). Conclusions from the summit were quite cheery and self-confident: 'We are pleased that the European Union's objectives for this summit have been broadly achieved', wrote Barroso and van Rompuy after the summit, highlighting the adoption of an action plan for growth and jobs and further commitment to financial regulation along European lines (European Council 2013, p. 1; see also G20 Leaders' Declaration). Moreover, they noted:

> This G20 summit cemented the global paradigm shift towards fairer taxation by endorsing the establishment of the automatic exchange of tax information. We are highly satisfied that this new standard will be implemented as from 2015 among G20 members, as the EU has pushed for. - - - The G20 finally confirmed the importance of open, free and fair trade as an important source of growth and development… stepping up efforts to roll back trade-restrictive measures as called for by the European Union. (European Council 2013, p. 2)

4.5 The Internal-External Nexus of the EU

As the preceding paragraphs underline, there is reason, as in so many other contexts, to differentiate between the EU and its member states. Quite clearly, the EU has not been a coherent actor in recent years. Commission President Barroso noted himself in the 67th UN General Assembly debate (April 2013) that the financial crisis had been a wake-up call for the EU to realize the need for a coordinated response requiring a new forum (Barroso 2013).

The issue of EU coherence and member state representation is a generic feature of EU performance in global negotiating forums. Preconditions in the G20 are potentially positive in the external dimension with its numerical dominance in relation to other actors at the G20. On the other hand, it presents a complex dynamic internally, with four (and, in effect, five) EU member states present in the G20 along with two representatives of EU institutions, resulting in difficult issues of coordination and coherence. The Lisbon Treaty has thus streamlined EU representation somewhat in doing away with the rotating presidency at the level of leaders, although not at the level of finance ministers. Still, the question of EU-internal representation looms large. To what extent do European representatives present at the G20 speak on behalf of the EU as a collective entity? The answer is 'only to a degree', if judged by existing studies and interview data. Coordination prior to G20 summits exists but does not seem to impact substantially on EU collective performance. To be sure, there are a number of channels of influence for non-G20 EU member states. All member states are represented and have the possibility of shaping discussions and coordination outcomes within the decision-making structure of the EU both in the economic and financial sector proper—in the Council for Economic and Financial Affairs (ECOFIN)—as well as in its preparatory committee, the Economic and Financial Committee (EFC). Also, G20 summits are prepared by sherpas (personal representatives) of government leaders, and in the case of the EU, the sherpa is a Commission official who interacts with all member states at the level of COREPER (the so-called committee of permanent representatives, i.e. member state ambassadors in Brussels). So, also in issues outside the economic area member states are involved in coordination. However, as the same major EU states that dominate coordination and decision-making in the EU also hold individual seats in the G20 and coordination concerns 'agreed language,' rather than legally binding provisions, the influence of non-G20 member states is often limited, albeit with some important variations (see further Debaere 2010; Nasra and Debaere 2012). Moreover, examples exist in which EU states present at the G20 have not honoured coordinated agreements (for instance concerning tax havens, see Debaere 2010).

4.6 Concluding Remarks

Are European actors, and specifically the EU, playing a leadership role in the G20? Or has the EU lost momentum due to internal crisis and splits? Answers to these questions necessitate a temporal perspective. In the early phase of the elevated G20, Europe was more important than it has been in recent years. The internal crises and weaknesses of the EU are part of the explanation for this outcome. It does not constitute the full explanation, however. Rather, it could be argued that even a stronger and more coherent EU would have had a hard time promoting a European version of multilateralism (if such a notion exists) in a loosely institutionalized great power summitry format such as the G20, in which other parties—particularly some developing countries—envisage weaker forms of multilateralism. There is a risk that difficulty will increase over time, irrespective of the internal turbulence of the EU, if others develop stronger policy preferences in directions contrary to EU interests.

In conclusion, as the G20 has changed in posture (through consolidation, agenda expansion—especially into development issues—and moving from crisis management to long-term governance), the EU's influence has decreased in recent years. This reflects circumstances—the Eurozone sovereign debt crisis and the crowding-out of proactive foreign policy—but also potentially underlying structural causes: both weakening internal cohesion and perhaps decreasing global interest in or attraction to European ideas and values. One could also argue that in areas where the G20 states have opposing views—such as how to handle trade imbalances—European perspectives have been unable to produce outcomes. Some preliminary signs indicate the return of European clout in the G20, as evident in the St. Petersburg outcomes (G20 2013; European Council 2013), but it is still too early to tell whether this is an enduring trend.

How are these developments to be understood? A fruitful frame of reflection is provided by Yves Tiberghien and others in discussions of 'Minervian actors' in global institution building. Minervian actors, argue Tiberghien (2013), seek multilateralism in three different modes of action: perceived self-interests, influence of norms and ideas (normative action), and through domestic political leadership. The EU, conceived of as a Minervian actor in global governance (ibid.; Manners 2013), displays all three characteristics in the case of the G20, albeit to different degrees in different time periods. Notably, domestic political leadership—here interpreted as the ability to project EU-internal common ideas onto the global scene –has been lacking due to multiple crises (financial, economic, and political) within the EU.

The overriding question for the future is thus twofold: Will the G20 continue to be the primary institution for global economic governance? And, will Europe (again?) be able to Europeanize the G20. Or, will we instead see a marginalization of Europe and loose and informal great power interaction (often referred to as a 'G-ization' of global politics) quite far removed from European notions of multilateralism? Jokela's conclusion from 2011 still seems to hold true:

> The key outcome of the G-20 process is nevertheless the fuller incorporation of the emerging economies into the global governance arena. So far their increased power and influence has however largely come without responsibility, i.e. without a binding commitment to common objectives in terms of traditional norms-based multilateralism. Therefore the G-20 has so far provided rather limited opportunities for the EU to forge its strategic goal of a world order based on effective multilateralism. (Jokela 2011a, p. 78)

In conclusion, European strategic action for norm export is thus trapped in a situation where it holds substantial representation, and therefore agenda-setting potential, but where it also faces difficulties over unitary/coherent action and lack of credibility. Within those parameters, however, there is room for agenda shaping, as recent developments indicate.

In closing, it may be worth pointing out that to the extent that formal preconditions matter, which seems to be the case, there are interesting times ahead in light of upcoming presidencies and varying perspectives on multilateralism—Australia takes over after Russia for 2014. Thereafter Turkey will chair in 2015. For 2016, the presidency is yet to be decided, but will come from the Asian group: reasonably not South Korea, which held the presidency in 2010, but rather China, Indonesia or Japan. A first-time China presidency would be especially significant as an illustration of the changing nature of the global political economy. This would also be a challenge to the EU in light of China's approach to multilateralism and its position on development issues/perspectives (as the world's second largest economy and, yet, still a developing country).

References

Barroso, J. M. (2013). Economic governance in the age of interdependence, speech at the United Nations General Assembly, 15 April 2013. http://europa.eu/rapid/press-release_SPEECH-13-321_en.htm. Accessed 3 Nov 2013.

Bengtsson, R. (2010). EU, krisen och den nya globala ordningen. In L. Oxelheim, L. Pehrson, & T. Persson (Eds.), *EU och den globala krisen* (pp. 143–169). Stockholm: Santérus.

Cherry, J., & Dobson, H. (2012). 'Seoul-searching': The 2010 G-20 Seoul summit. *Global Governance, 18,* 363–381.

Clark, I. (2005). *Legitimacy in international society.* Oxford: Oxford University Press.

Debaere, P. (2010). The output and input dimension of the European representation in the G20. *Studia Diplomatica, LXIII*(2), 141–154.

Der Spiegel. (2010, June 22). Norway takes aim at G-20: 'One of the Greatest Setbacks Since World War II'.http://www.spiegel.de/international/europe/norway-takes-aim-at-g-20-one-of-the-greatest-setbacks-since-world-war-ii-a-702104.html. Accessed 20 Dec 2013.

EEAS (European External Action Service). (2011). EU initial views on "the role of the UN in global economic governance and development", 18 May 2011. www.un.org/esa/ffd/economic-governance/EU.pdf. Accessed 24 Oct 2011.

European Commission. (2013a). The EU and the G20. http://ec.europa.eu/commission_2010-2014/president/g20/index_en.htm. Accessed 3 Nov 2013.

European Commission. (2013b). G20 summit: Improving global confidence and support the global recovery—Joint letter of the presidents of the European Commission and the European Council, 23 July 2013, MEMO/13/717. http://europa.eu/rapid/press-release_MEMO-13-717_en.htm. Accessed 3 Nov 2013.

European Council. (2013). Results of the G20 summit in Saint Petersburg: Joint statement by European Council President Van Rompuy and European Commission President Barroso, 12 September 2013, EUCO 182/13. http://www.european-council.europa.eu/the-president/press-releases?lang=en&page=4. Accessed 3 Nov 2013.

G20. (n.d.). Group of Twenty official website. http://www.g20.org. Accessed 22 Jan 2014.

G20. (2008). Washington summit leaders' declaration, 15 November 2008. http://www.g20.org/official_resources/library. Accessed 22 Jan 2014.

G20. (2009). Pittsburgh Summit Leaders' Declaration, 15 September 2009. http://www.g20.org/official_resources/library. Accessed 22 Jan 2014.

G20. (2012). Los Cabos summit leaders' declaration, 18–19 June 2012. http://www.g20.org/official_resources/library. Accessed 22 Jan 2014.

G20. (2013). Saint Petersburg summit leaders' declaration, 5–6 September 2013. http://www.g20.org/official_resources/library. Accessed 22 Jan 2014.

Global Governance Group. (2011). Remarks by Ambassador Vanu Gopala Menon, Permanent representative of Singapore to the United Nations in New York, at the Wilton Park conference on reforming international governance, Luxembourg, 15 June 2011 on 'To What Extent Does Global Governance Respond to The Needs of Large and Small Countries?' http://www.mfa.gov.sg/content/mfa/overseasmission/newyork/nyemb_statements/global_governance_group/2011/201102/press_201106_2.html. Accessed 22 Jan 2014.

Global Governance Group. (2013). Press statement by the Global Governance Group (3g) on its sixth 3G ministerial meeting, New York, 25 September 2013. http://www.mfa.gov.sg/content/mfa/overseasmission/newyork/nyemb_statements/global_governance_group/2013/201309/press_20130925.html. Accessed 22 Jan 2014.

Gnath, K., & Schmucker, C. (2011). *The role of the emerging countries in the G20: Agenda-setter, veto player or spectator? Bruges regional integration & global governance papers 2/2011.* Bruges: College of Europe/United Nations University.

Giles, C. (2012, June 18). Leaders aim to make a difference. *Financial Times.* http://ww.ft.com/intl/cms/s/2/ce96ba8e-b15d-11e1-9800-00144feabdc0.html. Accessed 17 April 2013.

Haass, R. (2010, January 5). The case for messy multilateralism. Financial Times. http://www.ft.com/intl/cms/s/0/18d8f8b6-fa2f-11de-beed-00144feab49a.html. Accessed 12 Sept 2013.

Interview Swedish government official 10 September 2013.

Jokela, J. (2011a). *The G20: A pathway to effective multilateralism? Chaillot papers.* Paris: EUISS.

Jokela, J. (2011b). *Europe's declining role in the G20: What role for the EU in the club of the most important powers? FIIA Briefing paper 96.* Helsinki: Finnish Institute of International Affairs.

Kim, J. A., & Chung, S. (2012). The role of the G20 in governing the climate change regime. *International Environmental Agreements, 12,* 361–374.

Kirton, J. (2012). The G20's global governance: Working for the world. http://www.g20.utoronto.ca/biblio/kirton-leuven-lecture-2012.html. Accessed 12 Sept 2013.

Luckhurst, J. (2012). The G20 and *ad hoc* embedded liberalism: Economic governance amid crisis and dissensus. *Politics & Policy, 40,* 740–782.

Manners, I. (2013). The European Union as a minervian actor in global institution building. In Y. Tiberghien (Ed.), *Leadership in global institution building: Minerva's rule* (pp. 33–48). Houndmills: Palgrave.

Naím, M. (2009). Minilateralism. *Foreign Policy, 173,* 135–136.

Nasra, S., & Debaere, P. (2012). The European Union in the G20: What role for small states? *Cambridge Review of International Studies, iFirst,* 1–22.

Reinfeldt, F. (2009, September 25). Packed agenda for G20 leaders. http://www.se2009.eu. Accessed 26 March 2013.

Slaughter, S. (2013). Debating the international legitimacy of the G20: Global policymaking and contemporary international society. *Global Policy, 4*(1), 43–52.

Tiberghien, Y. (2013). Introduction: Minervian actors and the paradox of post-1995 global institution building. In Y. Tiberghien (Ed.), *Leadership in global institution building: Minerva's rule* (pp. 1–22). Houndmills: Palgrave.

Underdahl, A. (1994). Leadership theory: Rediscovering the arts of management. In I. W. Zartman (Ed.), *International multilateral negotiation: Approaches to the management of complexity* (pp. 178–197). San Fransisco: Jossey-Bass.

World Trade Organization. (2012). Multilateralism is struggling, speech by Director-General Pascal Lamy, 24 September 2012. http://www.wto.org/english/news_e/sppl_e/sppl244_e.htm. Accessed 3 Nov 2013.

Rikard Bengtsson is Associate Professor of Political Science at Lund University, Sweden. His main research interests include global political economy, regional security and integration, and EU in international relations. His most recent research monograph is *The EU and the European Security Order: Interfacing security actors* (Routledge 2009). From 2010 to 2013 Bengtsson served as Deputy Director of the Centre for European Studies at Lund University. He has also been a guest professor at Stellenbosch University, South Africa, and Peking University, China.

Part II
Adaptation

Chapter 5
Perceptions of 'Normative Power Europe' in the Shadow of the Eurozone Debt Crisis: Public Perspectives on European Integration from the Asia Pacific

Natalia Chaban, Serena Kelly and Martin Holland

5.1 Introduction

International normative actors such as the European Union (EU) have the potential to influence norms and culture both within and beyond their borders. Mirroring constructivist theory, with its emphasis on 'social learning, socialization, and social norms' (Checkel 2001, p. 553), here diffusion is made synonymous with the 'spread', 'trickling down' or 'translation' of ideas and focus is placed on how foreign entities adopt norms (Checkel 1999, p. 85). The universal acceptance of norms acts as a stabilizer for world politics (Finnemore and Sikkink 1998, p. 894). Consequently, theories surrounding the exportation of EU norms provide a useful tool for understanding the potential impact (or actorness) of the EU and its norms outside of its enlarging borders. Specifically, this chapter is interested in the reception, in the Asia-Pacific, of what is arguably one of the EU's most successful norms—regional integration. The study argues that a key aspect of the productive dialogue between the sender and receiver of norms and values is the *cultural filter* (Manners 2002), represented in this analysis through a continuum of perceptions. By investigating images of the EU as a model of (or at least a reference for) regional integration in the Asia-Pacific, this chapter notes potential factors shaping perceptions and proposes a multi-level understanding of those factors and how they may affect the reception of normative messages sent by the EU.

Whereas most studies on norm diffusion are concerned with elites or policy-making, this study focuses on the importance of communicating with foreign publics. Our analysis explores external *public* perceptions of the EU and its institutions

N. Chaban (✉) · S. Kelly · M. Holland
National Centre for Research on Europe, University of Canterbury, Christchurch, New Zealand
e-mail: natalia.chaban@canterbury.ac.nz

S. Kelly
e-mail: serena.kelly@canterbury.ac.nz

M. Holland
e-mail: martin.holland@canterbury.ac.nz

© Springer International Publishing Switzerland 2015
A. Björkdahl et al. (eds.), *Importing EU Norms,* United Nations University Series on Regionalism 8, DOI 10.1007/978-3-319-13740-7_5

as a model of integration using data derived from a 2012 public opinion survey (10,000 respondents) conducted in ten Asia-Pacific countries (themselves members of various regional groupings and organizations): Japan, China, South Korea, Singapore, Malaysia, Thailand, India, Russia, Australia and New Zealand.[1] These data are then contrasted with findings from nine earlier public opinion surveys (covering all of the countries surveyed in 2012 except Russia), conducted either before or at the start of the Eurozone sovereign debt crisis. As such, the chapter offers unique comparative longitudinal insights into the international norm diffusion of the EU. This is achieved through tracing the dynamics of the spontaneous images of the EU as a global referent for regional integration (another promising yet rarely executed approach).

5.2 'Normative Power Europe' and the Role of a Cultural Perceptions Filter: Theoretical Insights

It has been argued that the EU's normative *global* force, or influence, beyond its borders, and the conditions necessary for diffusion to take place are poorly understood (Börzel and Risse 2009, pp. 11–12). However, in his 2002 seminal work, Manners noted that it is necessary to consider local conditions when norms and values of one international actor are positively or negatively processed and reacted to by other members of the world community. In Manners' (2002, pp. 244–245) construction of 'Normative Power Europe' (NPE), these factors included both the transmission of one- and two-way information from the sender to the receiver. In the former case, this could happen either intentionally, via strategic communication (*informational diffusion*) or unintentionally (*contagion*). In the latter case, the mutual exchange of ideas occurs—through either the institutionalisation of a relationship (*procedural diffusion*); or through substantive or financial means such as trade, aid or technical assistance (*transference*); or as a result of physical presence (*overt diffusion*). The final factor, according to Manners, is the *cultural filter*—'the interplay between the construction of knowledge and the creation of social and political identity by the subjects of norm diffusion' (Manners 2002, p. 245). While Manners lists the *cultural filter* as only one of the many factors in his paradigm, we suggest it occupies a central space in the model as it arguably underlies and shapes the other factors. Manners appears sympathetic to this argument. Referencing research by Kinnvall (1995, pp. 61–71), he states that the *cultural filter* 'affects the impact of

---

[1] The analysis draws on data from 'The EU in the Eyes of Asia-Pacific', an international comparative research project undertaken in 20 locations since 2002. This systematic investigation of EU external imagery combines how the EU has been framed by local media with perceptions of the EU held by the public and national stakeholders (Chaban and Holland 2013; Chaban and Holland 2014; Holland and Chaban 2014). For more publications see www.euperceptions.canterbury.ac.nz. The authors of this chapter would like to acknowledge support provided by the Jean Monnet Lifelong Learning Programme of the European Commission and Asia-Europe Foundation (ASEF) to this project throughout the years.

international norms and political learning in third states and organizations leading to learning, adaptation or rejection of norms' (Manners 2002, p. 245). Acharya also takes into consideration the domestic context of the importer (2004). For Checkel, '[d]iffusion is more rapid when a cultural match exists between a systemic norm and a target country, in other words, where it resonates with historically constructed domestic norms' (Checkel 1999, p. 87).

This chapter extends the notion of the *cultural filter* by utilizing the concept of 'EU external perceptions' as one way of understanding the *cultural filter*. Perception is defined here as the 'result of the subjective or psychological cognition of the observer rather than the objective reflection of the object that is being observed' (Shiming 2010, p. 269). In other words, perceptions are cognitive constructs reflecting the world which have been filtered through individual memories, experiences, attitudes or emotions. Perceptions are a concept reflecting a process of the complex interaction between reality and subjective psychological cognition. Perceptions of international actors are complex constellations of meanings shaped by a number of interacting factors, among those are the perceived relative capability of an actor, the perceived threat or opportunity represented by that actor, and the perceived culture of that actor (Herrmann et al. 1997; Herrmann 1985). In addition to these actor-centred factors, Tsuruoka (2008) argued that perceptions are shaped by both developments within an international actor (the EU in his study) and outside it (particularly, in the location in question). Research by Chaban and Magdalena (2014) extends this paradigm, arguing that in addition to *EU-* and *location*-specific factors, *global* factors are increasingly important in shaping external views of the EU.

One of the fundamental aspects of perception is the cognitive process of categorization: 'When we perceive our environment, we rapidly integrate large amounts of incoming stimulus/information into categories that help to guide our understanding of the world' (Brosch et al. 2010, p. 377). Categorizations are fundamentally part of human cognition and are a 'necessary way of organising the world in our minds, creating mental maps for working out how we view the world and negotiating our ways thought it in our everyday social relations and interactions' (Pickering 2001, p. 2). Moreover, the constantly changing world means that one must consequently make sense of these changes (Brosch et al. 2010, p. 377). In this way, new categories are being created constantly, and categories cannot be fixed and must be flexible.

Consequently, external categorizations of the EU are also expected to be constantly changing. Considering Braudel's tri-partite paradigm of geographical and historical distances (1982, considered in Didelon et al. 2008; Didelon-Loiseau and Grassland 2014), the re-categorizations could occur on the levels of (1) *micro histoire,* when major crises such as war or revolution (or, in our case, the Eurozone debt crisis) re-shape categorizations of an actor in a short timeframe; (2) *histoire conjuncture*, or permutations over 25–50 years (in our case, possibly the process of European integration itself with its many projects, from Common Agricultural Policy and Schengen Zone to Enlargement and the Common Currency); and finally (3) *histoire de longue durée*, or evolutions over centuries (in our case, Europe's discovery, exploration and exploitation of the world since the fifteenth century).

Pickering (2001) argued that categorizations should be differentiated from stereotypes. While the former are needed by human beings in order to process infinite details of the surrounding world, the latter are rigid cognitive devices. According to Pickering, 'the comfort of inflexibility which stereotypes provide reinforces the conviction that existing relations of power are necessary and fixed' (Pickering 2001, p. 3). Paradoxically, while being imprecise and inaccurate due to the homogenisation of the perceived groups, stereotypes are often used to produce an impression of knowledge. They render 'the illusion of precision in defining and evaluations of other people' (Pickering 2001, p. 4).

Stereotype resilience is common—as stereotypes are situated in the long-term memory of an individual and thus difficult, if almost impossible, to change. Stereotypes carry assessments and are marked by prejudice, judgment and/or alienation. In this way, the stereotyped is a silent and powerless 'Other' in the stereotype. Importantly, while recognising stereotypes as a concept used by one social group to justify discrimination of another group, this analysis interprets stereotyping in a broader way—as a 'process for maintaining and reproducing the norms and conventions of behavior [sic], identity and value' (Pickering 2001, p. 5).

The cognitive devices of the categorization and stereotyping derive imagery. As with perceptions, the notion of images is conceived here as a result of a complex interaction between reality and subjective psychological cognition. Since images exist in oral or written linguistic expressions, visually and intertextually, research can trace images and—through images—the cognitive processes of perceptions behind particular images. This study defines images as a

> [R]eference to some aspect of the world which contains within its own structure and in terms of its own structure a reference to the act of cognition which generated it. It must say, not that the world is like this, but that it was recognized to have been like this by the image-maker, who leaves behind this record: not of the world, but of the act. (Cohen n.d.)

It is important to stress that not all images are stereotypes, and not all perceptions lead to stereotypical images. However, the historical approach is seen as the most helpful in tracing stereotypes, and this justifies our longitudinal comparative approach.

This study explores external perceptions and images of the EU as a normative power through one specific lens—regional integration. Our analysis focuses on the categorizations and mental maps of the EU revealed through spontaneously generated verbal images. This chapter argues that any sender of a normative message (including the EU) needs to account for *cultural filters*, which include a complex set of perceptions, categorizations, stereotypes and images. Furthermore, it is paramount to incorporate this knowledge into the dialogue on norms and values between senders and receivers, as perceptions, resulting in categorizations and images (stereotypical or not), have power over the diffusion of normative ideas. Put simply, perceptions can facilitate, or obstruct, the spreading of norms and values introduced externally. In this light, the chapter traces spontaneous images of the EU as a referent for regional integration comparing them across two time periods—before and after the outbreak of the Eurozone sovereign debt crisis. Importantly, we do not equate the categorizations of the EU surfacing through spontaneous images with stereotypes. Yet, we do argue that if certain categorizations persist over time, carrying an explicit assessment/judgement of the 'Other' (the EU in our case), it means that those categorizations may become stereotypical—resistant to change and potentially prejudicial.

The explicit focus on the study of perceptions—as a precondition for various outcomes of the sender-receiver dialogue—makes this chapter stand apart in this volume. The chapter is placed in the section of 'Adaptation' because emulation of the EU's norms and values may be triggered by a particular set of EU perceptions among the receivers. Yet, perceptions can also trigger resistance and rejection (outcomes that could be initiated by many factors, including prejudice). Also of importance to note is that awareness of, and positive perceptions towards, certain norms do not automatically lead to norms and values being adapted or adopted. Nevertheless, awareness of communicated normative messages, recognition of the normative identity of the sender and positive connotations attached to that recognition by the receivers are argued here to be prerequisites in both the adaptation and/ or adoption processes.

The chapter's underlining hypothesis is that the Eurozone sovereign debt crisis has tarnished and weakened the EU's global image as an influential normative actor in the field of regional integration. Guided by this expectation, this longitudinal analysis tests whether more visible and more positive recognition of the EU as a regional integration model existed before the outbreak of the Eurozone sovereign debt crisis than after. This finding may indicate a certain fragility of EU images in the region and point to the fact that internal EU factors lead in shaping EU external perceptions. Alternatively, if our comparison between the two periods shows no change in recognition of the EU as a reference for regional integration, this would indicate that EU imagery is relatively stable when it comes to referencing the EU as a model for regional integration. In this scenario, the external audience cares (or not) about and evaluates the EU in terms of regional integration irrespective of the EU's internal crises. Arguably, this may indicate the importance of *location-specific* factors. Finally, if the comparison of typical perceptions before and after the outbreak of the crisis shows more frequent references to the EU in terms of regional integration after the outbreak, this finding may point to *global* factors in action. An increasingly multipolar world demands a heightened global visibility towards a number of 'superpowers-in-waiting'. In this light, an intensified vision of a regionally united EU, even in the times of its own crisis, suggests an external recognition of the EU as a strong competitor for this title.

5.3 Public Opinion and Foreign Policy

A novel feature of this analysis is its explicit focus on the general public's perceptions and images of the EU as a normative actor in the field of regional integration. Studies of NPE, including its most recent reiteration in the guise of diffusion theory

(Börzel and Risse 2009), have mistakenly overlooked public opinion in the dialogue between the senders and the receivers of the normative message.

A long tradition of foreign policy and international relations studies has classified the general public as the least powerful democratic actor when it comes to external affairs policy- and decision-making. Pertaining to foreign policy, Jacobs and Page (2005) argue that international business leaders and experts are more likely to have an impact. A vision of the general public as the least influential group in initiating and propagating foreign policy ideas has become a stereotype in itself. Yet, international relations in the twenty-first century take place in a rapidly changing and interconnected world. In today's globalizing environment, states are no longer the only significant global actors. State and non-state actors (including civil society and general pubic) are intertwined in a multitude of networks. Attention to domestic public opinion in the area of foreign policy-making is growing in popularity among scholars and stakeholders in both democratic and undemocratic societies.

In a democratic context, through voting, public opinion shapes political outcomes. Page and Shapiro (1983) charted public opinion and policy change and concluded that 'When Americans' policy preferences shift, it is likely that congruent changes in policy will follow' (ibid, p. 189). In undemocratic societies, 'governments are constantly polling the public to understand their aspirations and pre-empt them' (Leonard and Krastev 2007, online). As such there is nothing to prevent the scholarship on 'norm diffusion' and 'perceptions' from conceptualizing the general public as a key agent, as it may act to provide legitimacy to foreign policy and is crucial to the acceptance of institutional change at home. According to Schimmelfennig (2009, p. 9), 'The EU's conditionality and socialization can be directed at societal actors—parties, firms, interest groups, NGOs or even regional administrations—rather than central governments.' We suggest extending this list to include the general public: after all, public diplomacy—a tool to 'understand, engage, and influence publics on a wide range of other issues relating to governance, economic growth, democracy, the distribution of goods and services, and a host of cross-border threats and opportunities' (Gregory 2008, p. 276)—is a growing reality of modern-day international relations.

Despite changing global and diplomatic paradigms, for many scholars the question of democratic representation in foreign policy remains contentious (Entman 2004, p. 123). As such, Entman concludes that public opinion is typically a 'dependent variable', able to provide feedback to influence elites on external policies occasionally (Entman 2003, p. 420). The reality of globalization suggests this may be changing rapidly. Entman himself, in his 2003 publication on 'cascade activation' theory, which deals with spreading the ideas in the foreign policy process, posited that

> [P]erception of where the public stands itself becomes … an object of political power and strategy. If, say, elites are contending over an administration decision and the [government] can disseminate the notion that public opinion favors (sic) the president, that perception can help delegitimize and silence the opposition. (Entman 2003, p. 420)

The key deficit is a lack of insight into 'exactly how elites figure out what the public is thinking' (Entman 2004, p. 12). This analysis addresses this gap and contributes to research on the impact of public opinion on foreign policy via a systematic comparative empirical investigation of public opinion polls. The main focus is on the perceptions of the EU as a sender of the normative message of regional integration. The next section elaborates the phenomenon of the EU as a possible referent and self-proclaimed model of regional integration and the acceptance of this idea in the Asia-Pacific as documented in the relevant literature.

5.4 Regional Integration as a Norm Export

The EU's success at regional integration has seen it often showcased as an international role model. From the EU's perspective, its leadership abilities in this area are obvious: as the European Security Strategy (2008, p. 25) asserts, '[o]ur experiences give the EU a particular role in fostering regional integration. Where others seek to emulate us… we should support them.' Some external observers, however, are more cautious, including influential commentators such as Charles Kupchan who described the EU as 'dying—not a dramatic or sudden death, but one so slow and steady' mainly due to a 'renationalization of political life, with countries clawing back the sovereignty they once willingly sacrificed in pursuit of a collective ideal' (Kupchan 2010). Most of the recent criticism aimed at the EU is now focused on the Eurozone sovereign debt crisis, a crisis which, since 2008, has seen the EU become increasingly introspective and divided. With the crisis ongoing, what kind of external perceptions emerged of the EU's stance on the Eurozone sovereign debt crisis? Is the EU still seen globally as a significant and legitimate 'soft' power? Has the crisis undermined positive external visions of the success of the EU's regional model and even triggered the perception of a failure of this model? Is Europeanization still important for the EU's external partners? By posing these questions, the leading hypothesis of diffusion theory, developed by Börzel and Risse (2009),—that the EU's idea of regional integration is exclusively positive—is critically examined.

Scholars and practitioners have long debated the form of European regionalism. For instance, is it strictly based on gradual economic integration principles (Viner 1950), or is the European social model the most important element of the EU's regionalism? (A question central to McMillan's contribution to this volume.) According to the latter model, 'economic and social progress must go hand in hand' (Jepsen and Pascual 2005, p. 234). Another important component of European integration is its institutional set-up. According to Haas, European integration was about the establishment of supranational institutions which were suited to perform specific tasks, increase information and reduce transaction costs, resulting in a spillover into other policy areas (Haas 1968). Debate about this issue is central to the contribution of Leslie and Elijah in this volume.

The use of the Asia-Pacific region as a case-study offers the opportunity to assess the success of 'transformative power Europe' from the viewpoint of a region which is geographically distant as well as culturally, economically and historically diverse from Europe, yet has enduring links with the EU. This chapter acknowledges the diversity of regionalism in the Asia-Pacific, as well as differing degrees of EU influence. In terms of regionalism, the Asia-Pacific also has a number of regional groupings with differing definitions as well as degrees of success at regional integration.[2] As such, Asia-Pacific regionalism *may* be affected by EU norms on integration, since

> [I]nternational norms must always work their influence through the filter of domestic structures and domestic norms, which can produce important variations in compliance and interpretation of these norms. (Finnemore and Sikkink 1998, p. 893)

'Diffusion' theory articulates a paradigm of five 'diffusion' mechanisms instrumental in understanding the roles of the exporter and the importer of these ideas: coercion, manipulation, socialization, persuasion and emulation (Börzel and Risse 2009, p. 9). Although it is by no means clear how to measure each of these mechanisms, *emulation* and *lesson-learning,* are of particular interest to this study. Both rely on indirect influence and do not require the EU to actively promote its ideas. Foreign recipients of these ideas may use the EU to either draw lessons from, or mimic, the EU's processes (ibid.). Thus, the two mechanisms are argued to be paramount in the EU's dialogue with the world, since,

> [W]hile the EU can rely on legal coercion to overcome resistance in case of current and would-be members, it has to rely on indirect diffusion mechanisms in its external relations beyond Europe. (Börzel and Risse 2009, p. 18)

Importantly, the former mechanism follows from 'logic of appropriateness'— actors' behaviour follows a desire to be perceived as doing 'right' as actors seek approval from other actors (to act 'appropriately') through upholding values, cultures, *etc*. In this instance, 'Target states are persuaded to adopt EU rules if they consider these rules legitimate and [if such states] identify with the EU' (Schimmelfennig 2009, p. 7). The latter, while relying on the soft 'power of seduction' (Nye 2008, p. 96), follows from a desire to achieve some desired (material) end. In this instance, actors seek 'better' solutions for achieving concrete outcomes (often material). In this case, states are more likely to look towards the EU as a model to learn from 'if they perceive them [the EU's model] as solutions to their problems, either based on instrumental calculations or the appropriateness of the EU solutions' (Schimmelfennig 2009, p. 7).

The countries and regions identified in this case study fall under the 'logic of appropriateness' model. That is, the EU has not overtly coerced the states through conditionality and aid. Therefore, an insight into the *emulation* mechanism—admittedly 'the least researched area… with regard to the external diffusion of European ideas' (Börzel and Risse 2009, p. 13)—in the context of EU-Asia-Pacific interfaces of regionalization is intriguing. Some (e.g. von Hofmann 2007; Hänggi 1999) argue that Asia does not need to and will not 'carbon copy' the EU model; others disagree and argue that because the EU model is the most advanced, it can serve as a referent

---

[2] Consider, for example, the Association of South East Asian Nations (ASEAN), ASEAN+3, East Asian Summit (EAS), ASEAN Regional Forum (ARF), South Asian Association for Regional Cooperation (SAARC), Shanghai Cooperation Organisation (SCO), Pacific Islands Forum (PIF), Trans-Pacific Partnership (TPP), Asia-Pacific Economic Cooperation (APEC) and Closer Economic Relations (CER) between Australia and New Zealand.

at least (Hatoyama 2010; Langhamer 1999). Whatever the case, because of the EU's currently successful experiment in regional integration, it prefers to relate to third parties as regions wherever possible (Lamy 2002).[3] Areas of market and economic integration as well as the establishment of governing institutions are the priority for the EU (Bicchi 2006).

It is undeniable that EU integration is the longest and most visible example of regional integration. The countries considered in this project are signatories to various regional organizations, which have various levels of integration. Singapore, Thailand and Malaysia are part of the Association of South East Asian Nations (ASEAN), the most successful and enduring attempt at Asian regionalism. Established in 1967, it was implemented as a means of ensuring the 'survival of regimes' (Acharya 2003, p. 375). In contrast with the EU experience of a rule-based, binding institutionalization, ASEAN's integration, to date, has been based on informal consensus and operates a 'non-interference' code of conduct. Momentum for ASEAN integration increased in the 1990s (Telò 2006, p. 122), a benign, if unintentional, consequence of the 1997 Asian economic crisis (Acharya 2003, p. 382). The establishment of an ASEAN Community by 2015 poses the prospect, however, of a more rules-based level of integration. The Association is influential in wider regional cooperation through its membership of the Asia Regional Forum (ARF) and East Asia Summit (EAS). As well as members of ASEAN, ARF membership includes the EU, Australia, India, Japan, New Zealand, South Korea and Russia.

India is also a signatory to the South Asian Association for Regional Cooperation (SAARC). This was established in December 1985 and is less institutionally-focussed than ASEAN and mainly intergovernmental. China, Japan and South Korea also participate in the annual Trilateral Summit launched in December 2008, where China's, Japan's and South Korea's heads of state and Prime Ministers meet to discuss issues of common concern. Further, the Shanghai Cooperation Organisation includes Russia and China.

The Pacific component of our analysis forms a unique case-study: Australia and New Zealand are part of the Pacific Islands Forum (PIF), but are not recipients of EU aid unlike the rest of the Forum (the Pacific's reception of the NPE is also in focus in the contribution by Björkdahl and Elgström in this volume). Moreover, together they have established and promote Closer Economic Relations (CER) that rival EU economic integration in some areas, such as service and labour market integration (discussed at length in the contribution of Leslie and Elijah in this volume). Lastly, Russia is geographically close to the EU and its geopolitical location and lack of regional institutionalization (both important factors according to Börzel and Risse) as well as its close economic ties to the EU makes it a worthy and useful inclusion in our case study (Russia's reaction to the NPE is also considered in the contribution of Headley in this volume).

Importantly, all of the countries considered engage in direct, institutionalized interaction with the EU (where, presumably, socialization with the EU might occur among these elites). Along with the EU, all of the countries included in the research

---

[3] This regional interaction is evident in the EU's interregional arrangements with groupings such as ACP, ASEM, Rio Process and the Barcelona Process (Telò 2006).

presented here are members of the Asia-Europe Meeting (ASEM). Beginning in 1996, the forum now has 53 members (Russia, Australia and New Zealand joined in 2010).

5.5 Methodology

The chapter analyzes public opinion data from two periods. Data after the outbreak of the Eurozone sovereign debt crisis was collected between 1 and 23 March 2012 in ten Asia-Pacific locations. Each location sampled 1000 respondents via an online survey (margin of error ±3%), in their native language. The questionnaires were administered by TNS London. Respondents were randomly selected from an existing panel database.

The survey asked the following open-ended question: 'When you think of the term "European Union" what three images come to mind?' The responses to this question were subsequently transcribed verbatim and translated into English (translated entries went through a double-reliability check). Verified responses were scanned for the following key words: 'region', 'integration', 'integrate', 'unity/unite', 'union', 'alliance', 'community', 'association', 'model', 'reference', 'lesson', 'learn', 'blueprint', 'example', 'experience', 'alliance', 'association', 'unification/unify/unified', 'cooperation', 'coordinate/ion', 'harmony', 'together', 'argument', 'fight', 'singular/singularity', and 'group'.

The same search terms were used to analyse responses to the identical open-ended question in the 'pre-crisis' public opinion surveys in nine Asia-Pacific countries (all but Russia in our sample)—400 respondents per country (margin of error ±5%), conducted in 2004 in Australia and New Zealand (by telephone), in 2007 in China, Japan, South Korea, Thailand and Singapore, and in 2009 in India and Malaysia (all on-line).

5.6 Findings

Revealingly, the open-ended question responses featured before and after the Eurozone sovereign debt crisis displayed an overwhelming association of the EU with the idea of 'togetherness': either living together as one (in a particular place) and carrying a common identity (a concept of 'community'), or co-existing together for a joint purpose and enjoying mutual benefits based on a relationship based on an affinity of interests, nature, or qualities (concepts of 'association', 'alliance', 'single market'/'single currency'), the action or fact of joining together, or being joined together (notions of 'union' and 'unity'), the process of being united, or made into a whole ('unification'), or simply being together by being located close to each other ('group', 'together') (See Tables 5.1 and 5.2) (concepts' definitions are from Merriam-Webster Dictionary, online).

Table 5.1 Spontaneous images of the EU *before* the Eurozone sovereign debt crisis (total number of responses)

	China	India	Russia	Thailand	Japan	Malaysia	Singapore	South Korea	Australia	New Zealand	Total
Unit/ing/ed/es	11	12	N/A	4	7	10	62	58	24	5	193
Community	55			1	8		4	110	1	1	180
Union	18	13	N/A	7	6		36	37	19	12	148
Unification/unify	27	3	N/A		21		5	64	2	2	124
Group	2	9	N/A	19	6	3	21	6	16	22	104
Together	4	10	N/A		9		1	6	33	24	87
Alliance	19		N/A	3	22		1	10		1	56
Region	2	1	N/A	2	19		5		3	4	36
Cooperation	7	2	N/A	1	10		6	7	4	2	39
Integrat/e/ion	23	7	N/A				2		1		33
Harmony		2	N/A		1		4	1	4	1	13
Association	3		N/A		1		1	4			9
Singular/singularity			N/A						2		2
Coordinat/e/ion	0		N/A						1		1
Total	171	59		37	110	13	148	303	110	74	1025

Table 5.2 Spontaneous images of the EU *after* the Eurozone sovereign debt crisis (total number of responses)

	China	India	Russia	Thailand	Japan	Malaysia	Singapore	South Korea	Australia	New Zealand	Total
Union	26	129	107	16	9	28	119	13	46	52	545
Unit/ing/ed/es	78	17	78	13	4	50	61	34	64	54	453
Community	70	26	81	5	11	13	12	79	8	8	313
Group	7	28	1	31	1	27	48	2	18	43	206
Association	0	15	126	6	0	36	5	1	1	0	190
Alliance	115	0	3	0	0	1	0	8	7	6	140
Cooperation	1	6	29	20	8	16	3	16	8	3	110
Together	4	4	8	1	0	7	8	0	24	35	91
Integrat/e/ion	19	4	11	3	7	2	2	31	0	1	80
Unification/unify/unified	1	2	11	0	2	5	0	14	7	1	43
Singular/singularity (esp market and currency)	0	0	0	0	0	3	5	12	9	0	29
Harmony	0	0	0	0	2	3	3	3	1	2	14
Region	2	1	1	2	4	0	1	0	0	0	11
Coordinat/e/ion	1	0	0	0	0	0	0	0	0	0	1
Total	324	232	456	97	48	191	267	213	193	205	2226

Ideas of *disunity*, absence of unity and disturbance of unity were observed only in the survey after the outbreak of the crisis. While the word 'integrate' was notably absent in the responses, 'disintegrate' was mentioned in Australia. The term 'unity' was also transformed in Australia into 'disunity'. 'Disunity' and 'no unity' were found in New Zealand and the term 'disturbance of unity' was used in Japan. Yet, those had only a minuscule visibility in the overall pool of responses.

Significant to our investigation, images of the EU as a viable 'region' in which members are interdependent—i.e. reference to 'cooperation', 'integration', 'coordination', 'harmony' and 'region' itself—were almost invisible in both periods. Yet, images of 'region' and 'integration' were slightly more frequently referenced before the crisis: 'region' was more visible in Japan and Korea, and 'integration' in China (Table 5.1). Importantly, spontaneous associations indicating a perception of the EU's potential for emulation, or lesson learning, attitudes towards the EU—notions of a 'model', 'reference', 'lesson', 'learn', 'blueprint', 'example', and 'experience'—did not appear at all after the start of the crisis (Table 5.2). However, these images had some (also very limited) presence in the sample before the crisis.

After the outbreak of the Eurozone sovereign debt crisis, the categorizations of 'union' and 'unity' were the most popular in our sample and the most prolific in India, China, Russia, Australia, New Zealand and Singapore (Table 5.2). Before the crisis, those images were most visible in Singapore and South Korea. Concepts surrounding this term ranged from 'political and economic union' (especially economic) in all countries, to 'harmonious union' (India), and 'join the union' and 'reasonable union' (South Korea).

The results displayed in Tables 5.1 and 5.2 showed a number of consistencies and support the argument that EU external perceptions are location-specific (Chaban et al. 2013a). Certain visions (the repetition of key words and concepts) on the images and processes of regional integration in the EU were stable over time, with clear specific terms dominating each country. In both periods of observation dominant images of 'community' (in China and South Korea), 'alliance' (in China), 'unification' (in Korea) and 'group'/'together' (in Australia, New Zealand and Singapore) surfaced. It was interesting to note that the type of responses from Australia and New Zealand paralleled each other. Each has shared historical and cultural ties to the UK and an uneasy relationship with the EU since Britain joined the EEC in 1973.

Before the crisis, the highest share of responses mentioning 'integration-oriented' search terms came from South Korea (Table 5.3), followed by China and Singapore. After the outbreak of the crisis, the Russian sample profiled the highest share, followed again by China and Singapore. Over time, the share of responses relating to visions of the EU's 'togetherness' was noted to increase in India and Malaysia, while the sample in Japan and South Korea profiled a steep drop in such perceptions (Table 5.3). Singaporean perceptions remained high in both periods and the other constituencies (Australia, New Zealand and Thailand) had relatively low perceptions of the EU in this manner.

Putting this into context, Russia, China and India have been the EU's strategic partners. South Korea, who is currently an EU strategic partner, was then engaged

Table 5.3 Share of responses mentioning 'integration-oriented' search terms before and after the outbreak of the Eurozone debt crisis

	China	India	Russia	Thailand	Japan	Malay-sia	Singa-pore	South Korea	Aus-tralia	New Zea-land
Before (%)	16.6	5.7		3.6	10.7	1.3	14.4	29.5	10.7	7.2
After (%)	14.5	10.4	20.5	4.4	2.2	8.6	12	9.5	8.6	9.2

in intensive Free Trade Agreement (FTA) negotiations with the EU in the pre-crisis period (successfully completed at the time of the 2012 survey), while Singapore, India and Malaysia have been negotiating FTA negotiations with the EU. The partnership dimensions of the EU with these countries may cause a stronger focus of the EU towards communicating with these countries as well as more receptiveness of public in these countries towards understanding the EU and its (at times complicated) integration process.

Another possible factor behind these visible images is *location-specific* contexts. Although the data cannot substantiate this interpretation, a plausible explanation for these findings was that the South Korean public assigned priority to the 'integration-related' concepts in relation to the EU due to its own situation—a divided nation which aspires to peaceful reunification with its Northern neighbour. In a similar fashion, the general public in China, Russia and India—themselves multinational and multilingual states—can also easily relate to the concepts of unity and community. Singapore, on the other hand, may see itself as a hub of the South East Asian region, thus also relating to the EU's similar experiences (as the hosts of many of the region's regional institutions). On this note, Japan's presence in the 'low share' group in the second period of observation could be explained by Japan's absence as a member of any formal sub-regional grouping, making the EU's experiences irrelevant for the general public. At the same time, Japan's strategic partnership with the EU could be one explanation for the high share of examined responses before the crisis.

Of particular interest are Thailand, Australia and New Zealand. These countries are actively involved in the regional formations of ASEAN (in the Thai case) and CER and PIF (in the two other cases). Yet, they featured the lowest shares of 'integration-related' spontaneous responses both before and after the outbreak of the crisis. Thus, state-level regional experiences do not seem to trigger an appreciation of the EU's efforts at integration in the minds of the public. Arguably, public awareness of regional integration processes in the three locations is muted. This finding supports the above-cited sentiment that diffusion of norms and values is the most powerful, when it 'resonates with historically constructed domestic norms' (Checkel 1999, p. 87). On the other side, the EU is not a strategic partner for these locations and nor was it involved in securing FTA negotiations with them at a time of the surveys. This seems to support Barbe's finding that the EU's influence over third countries is dependent on interdependence with the EU (Barbé et al. 2009). In other words, high economic interaction of states with the EU coupled with resonating domestic norms and values may be the reason for a high appreciation of EU's integration efforts by the public.

These findings demonstrate that categorizations of the EU's integration processes and functions are often location-specific, relatively resistant to change, and mediated through both EU partnership arrangements and local cultural filters of experiences and histories on the ground. In the latter case, state-specific conditions echoing local intricacies, views and definitions appeared to be driving the most prominent general public perceptions of the EU in terms of 'integration-related' concepts in the Asia Pacific, with regional experiences and their awareness following.

5.7   Discussion

This study argued that understandings of European normative diffusion are incomplete without accounting for the receivers' *cultural filters*. Those filters 'sieve' the EU's normative messages and condition the success of both the EU's strategic and unintentional one-way normative communications as well as the success of its dialogic communication. The *cultural filters* considered in our analysis are external perceptions of the EU which drive categorizations and images and, therefore, serve as one of the key pre-conditions for EU influence shaping receivers' expectations and responses. The perceived success of a 'normative exporter' is an important indicator of whether or not the norm will be imported in the future. That means that in order for norms to be adopted, and adapted the norm in question first needs to be recognized and then viewed as successful (Finnemore and Sikkink 1998, p. 906; Haveman 1993, p. 598; Simmons et al. 2006, p. 789, 798). Knowledge of *how* successful the EU's regional integration is perceived to be by outsiders is largely absent. Our study addresses this deficit by tracing the content of and changes in how people perceive the EU in the Asia Pacific.

The analysis presented above is particularly useful for advancing concepts surrounding the promotion of EU norms in the Asia-Pacific as it may shed new light on why norms are adapted or adopted by some states and not others (Checkel 1999, p. 85). This chapter acknowledges that understanding different attitudes towards regionalism is a complex matter (for instance, Shu (2009) has demonstrated that in countries where there is a strong nationalist sentiment regionalism is more likely to be rejected). Nevertheless, tellingly, there was an overwhelming neutral-to-positive perception amongst the general public respondents about EU regional identity, irrespective of location. This was traced before and after the outbreak of the Eurozone sovereign debt crisis, with particular categorizations of the EU's 'togetherness' in certain locations over time. This indicates that while *EU-specific* factors (crisis in our case) were prominent influences in the second period of observation, public opinion in the Asia Pacific also revealed relatively stable location-specific categorisations of the EU as a whole. This could arguably indicate *location-specific* factors at play within a time frame of what Braudel (1982) has called *histoire conjuncture.* This finding delivers several potentially useful messages to the EU in its interaction with the Asia-Pacific. First, the general public in the Asia-Pacific is not forming negative judgmental/stereotypical images of a disjointed, challenged or weak EU 'in crisis'. On the contrary, the members of the public consistently value various aspects of the EU's regional integration process—either in terms of union, or group, or association, *etc.* Moreover, many instances of the Asia-Pacific public's positive viewing of the EU's efforts to maintain integration could translate into local public support of both the EU's integration efforts as well as support of further regional integration at home. Arguably, this would feed into a legitimizing sentiment for considering region-building experiences in the selected Asia-Pacific locations. However, this research also found a positive correlation between the Union's high profile economic involvement with the respective Asia-Pacific locations—i.e. inter-dependencies—and a high appreciation of the EU's integration efforts by the public.

Rather than being exclusively positive, there were a number of negative images of the EU in terms of 'disunity'. Although not dominant, these findings point to the fact that rather than being seen in exclusively positive terms the EU's integration process was also viewed negatively. This finding may also be reflective of the negative impact of the Eurozone sovereign debt crisis, which hampered perceptions of the EU as a significant and legitimate 'soft' power and a successful regional integration experiment. As such, *EU-specific* factors on the level of the *micro histoire* have also been involved in the formation of EU public categorisations, if only marginally. This finding carries yet another message for the EU and its (realistic) public diplomacy outreach in the Asia-Pacific. Namely, it shows a relatively slow public reaction to the *EU-specific* events—even of a large magnitude—in the locations outside of the EU's borders.

Importantly, the notions of 'region', 'integration' and 'cooperation' were only rarely mentioned. Moreover, notions of a 'model', 'reference', 'lesson', 'learn', 'blueprint', 'example' and 'experience' did not appear in the responses at all after the outbreak of the crisis. The low and period-specific visibility of these concepts was revealing. As noted, most of the countries in our sample are interested in some form of regional integration and all are members of ASEM, a forum designed to facilitate dialogue and thus greater understanding between Asia and Europe. Previous research (Chaban et al. 2013b) has noted the high prominence of EU integration themes and experiences among the Asian elites. In contrast, our study found that the EU does not represent itself instantly as a model for emulation (or lesson-drawing) for the general public. At a time of the multipolar redesign of the world, when global influences, including 'normative' ones, are highly sought after by global 'superpowers' and 'emerging powers'what are the resounding messages for the EU?

The three conclusions underline that, ultimately, systematic knowledge of the EU's external imagery is the key to the EU's successful external outreach and influence. Persistent ignorance, on the other hand, will lead to a failure to 'understand a fundamental component of the EU's international role as well as of the Europeans' self-identification process' (Lucarelli 2007, p. 4). EU foreign policy, while being to a large extent driven by internal ideas and processes, is partly shaped in response to others' expectations and reactions (Herrberg 1997). With '[o]utsiders' expectations and perceptions influenc[ing] the impact of EU foreign policy role performance' (Chaban et al. 2006, p. 248), external perceptions are a source of knowledge of EU foreign policy as they have been interpreted as 'important indicators of how well intentions have been translated into observable actions' (Rhodes 1999, p. 6). Outside approval and acceptance is important to an entity's legitimacy. Indeed, EU norm diffusion takes this consideration one step further: if the EU is not only accepted by a foreign entity but emulated as well, this could strengthen the EU's legitimacy at home. Thus, *cultural filters* of external perceptions of the EU serve as a conceptual link between theoretical models that seek to explain why and how norms are accepted or not (e.g. the diffusion theory) and models that attempt to understand the correlations between EU capabilities and external expectations of the EU (e.g. capabilities-expectations gap (Hill 1993). The focus on perceptions in this case becomes key for investigating 'not just why and how the EU behaves differently because of its different configuration…' but 'if such a distinctiveness is likely to feed back into the EU's internal and international credibility, and possibly also into the self-identification of the Europeans as a political group' (Lucarelli 2007, p. 268). Indeed, scholars agree that 'paying attention to how the EU is viewed abroad helps us to evaluate whether gaps between expectations and realities have affected the "reach" of EU influence' (Rhodes 1986, p. 6).

In scholarship on how EU norms are exported and imported, a number of deficits remain. For example, the EU norms which may be diffused are numerous (Manners 2002), and many observers dispute which of these are distinctly attached to the EU (Finnemore and Sikkink 1998, p. 89; Meyer 2001, p. 238).[4] Further, it is methodologically difficult to demonstrate whether ideas have been diffused from one entity (the EU) to another (Asia-Pacific countries and regions) (Checkel 1999, p. 86; Simmons et al. 2006). Lastly, there has been a tendency to only '…focus on successful cases of diffusion…' (Checkel 1999, p. 86). Due to the nature of our data and enquiry, this analysis was able to assess whether *the EU* is used as a reference point for regional integration. Moreover, this analysis considers both positive and negative perceptions of the EU norm in question.

In this light, the findings discussed above could be of value to the post-Lisbon EU, which seeks a more coherent and effective dialogue with the world. Importantly, the EU's political influence in Asia has traditionally been limited and official EU involvement in Asia was launched with a strategic economic goal in mind (Holland 2002, pp. 67–68). Because of the EU's success in experimenting in regional integration, it also prefers to relate to third parties as regions (Lamy 2002), a preference which is especially visible in the ACP dialogue. This preference extends to the Asia-Pacific, yet the question remains open as to whether this mode truly enables the EU to productively engage with the wider world. The process of normative adoption that engages *emulation* mechanisms—although often difficult to grasp— appears to be the most appropriate for the EU's interaction with the Asia-Pacific. In this scenario, the promoter does not impose ideas directly and is respectful of the

---

[4] They may also be universal/international or American norms.

recipients' identity, while the receiver voluntarily chooses (or not) to adopt these ideas and feels secure from direct pressure. Arguably, when it comes to the EU-Asia-Pacific interface on regional integration, the *emulation* mechanism could be the most capable in facilitating 'active responsive understanding', or 'dialogism' (Bakhtin 1986, p. 69), between the European 'Self' and the Asia-Pacific 'Other'.

Reference

Acharya, A. (2003). Democratisation and the prospects for participatory regionalism in Southeast Asia. *Third World Quarterly, 24*(2), 375–390.

Acharya, A. (2004). How ideas spread: Whose norms matter? Norm localization and institutional change in asian regionalism. *International Organization, 58*(2), 239–275.

Bakhtin, M. (1986). The problem of speech genres. In C. Emerson, M. Holquist, & M.M. Bakhtin (Eds.), *Speech genres and other late essays* (pp. 60–102). Austin: University of Texas Press.

Barbé, E., Costa, O., Herranz, A., & Natorski M. (2009). Which rules shape EU's external governance? The pattern of rule selection in foreign and security policies. *Journal of European Public Policy, 16*(6), 834–852.

Bicchi, F. (2006). Our size fits all: Normative power Europe and the Mediterranean. *Journal of European Public Policy, 13*(2), 286–303.

Börzel, T. A., & Risse, T. (2009). The transformative power of Europe: The European Union and the diffusion of ideas. KFG The transformative power of Europe, Working Paper No. 1, Freie Universität Berlin, Berlin.

Braudel, F. (1982). *On history*. Chicago: University of Chicago Press.

Brosch, T., Pourtois, G., & Sander, D. (2010). The perception and categorisation of emotional stimuli: A review. *Cognition & Emotion, 24*(3), 377–400.

Chaban, N., & Holland, M. (Eds.) (2008). *The European Union and the Asia–Pacific: Media, public and elite perceptions of the EU*. London and New York: Routledge.

Chaban, N. & Holland, M. (Eds.) (2013). Special issue. Lisbon and the changing external perceptions of the EU: Visions from the Asia-Pacific, *Baltic Journal of European Studies, 3*(3).

Chaban, N., & Holland, M. (Eds.) (2014). *Communicating Europe in times of crisis: External perceptions of the European Union*. Basingstoke: Palgrave McMillan.

Chaban, N., & Magdalena, A.-M. (2014). External perceptions of the EU during the Eurozone Sovereign Debt Crisis, *European Foreign Affairs Review, 19*(2), 195–220.

Chaban, N., Elgström, O., & Holland, M. (2006). The European Union as others see it. *European Foreign Affairs Review, 11*(2), 245–262.

Chaban, N., Holland, M., & Ryan, P. (Eds.) (2009). *The EU through the eyes of Asia: New cases, new findings*. Singapore, London: World Scientific.

Chaban, N., Elgström, O., Kelly, S., & Lai, S. -Y. (2013a). Images of the EU beyond its borders: Issue-specific and regional perceptions of European Union power and leadership. *Journal of Common Market Studies, 51*(3), 433–451.

Chaban, N., Holland, M., Kelly, S., & Lai, S. -Y. (2013b). Images of European integration in Asia. In T. Christiansen, E. Kirchner, & P. Murray (Eds.), *The Palgrave handbook of EU-Asia relations* (pp. 59–74). Basingstoke: Palgrave-McMillan.

Checkel, J. T. (1999). Norms, institutions, and national identity in contemporary Europe. *International Studies Quarterly, 43*(1), 83–114.

Checkel, J. T. (2001). Why comply? Social learning and European identity change. *International Organization, 55*(3), 553–588.

Cohen, H. (n.d.). What is an image? University of California at San Diego. aaronshome.com/aaron/publications/whatisanimage.pdf. Accessed 10 Oct 2013.

Didelon-Loiseau, C., & Grassland, C. (2014). Internal and external perceptions of Europe/EU in the world through mental maps. In N. Chaban & M. Holland (Eds.), *Communicating Europe in times of crisis: External perceptions of the European Union* (pp. 65–94). Basingstoke: Palgrave McMillan.

Didelon C., Grasland C., & Richard Y. (2008). *Atlas de l'Europe dans le Monde*. Paris: La Documentation Française.

Entman, R. (2003). Cascading activation: Contesting the White House's frame after 9/11. *Political Communication, 20*(4), 415–432.

Entman, R. (2004). *Projections of power: Framing news, public opinion, and US foreign policy.* Chicago: University of Chicago Press.

European Security Strategy. (2008). Report on the implementation: Providing security in a changing world. http://www.consilium.europa.eu/uedocs/cms_data/librairie/PDF/QC7809568ENC. pdf. Accessed 26 Oct 2013.

Finnemore, M., & Sikkink, K. (1998). International norm dynamics and political change. *International Organization, 52*(4), 887–917.

Gregory, B. (2008). Public diplomacy: Sunrise of an academic field. *The Annals of the AAPSS, 616*(1), 274–290.

Haas, E. B. (1968). *The uniting of Europe—Political, social, and economic forces 1950–1957.* Stanford: Stanford University Press.

Hänggi, H. (1999). ASEM and the construction of the new triad. *Journal of the Asia Pacific Economy, 4*(1), 56–80.

Hatoyama, Y. (2010). Public speech at the 16th International Conference on the future of Asia, Tokyo, Japan, 21 May. http://e.nikkei.com/e/fr/tnks/Nni20100520D20JFF04.htm. Accessed 21 Dec 2010.

Haveman, H. A. (1993). Follow the leader: Mimetic isomorphism and entry into new markets. *Administrative Science Quarterly, 38*(4), 593–627.

Herrberg, A. (1997). The European Union in its international environment: A systematic analysis. In A. Landau & R. Whitman (Eds.), *Rethinking the European Union: Institutions, interests and identities* (pp. 36–53). Basingstoke: Macmillan Publishers Limited.

Herrmann, R. (1985). *Perceptions and behavior in Soviet foreign policy.* Pittsburgh: University of Pittsburgh Press.

Herrmann, R., Voss, J., Schooler, T., & Ciarrochi, J. (1997). Images in international relations: An experimental test of cognitive schemata. *International Studies Quarterly, 41*(3), 403–433.

Hill, C. (1993). The capability-expectations gap or conceptualising Europe's international role. *Journal of Common Market Studies, 31*(3), 305–328.

Holland, M. (2002). *The European Union and the third world.* Houndsmills: Palgrave.

Holland, M., & Chaban, N. (Eds.) (2010). Special Issue. Reflections from Asia and Europe: How do we perceive one another?. *Asia Europe Journal, 8*(2).

Holland, M., & Chaban, N. (Eds.) (2014) *Europe and Asia: Perceptions from Afar.* Baden-Baden: Nomos/Bloomsbury.

Holland, M., Ryan, P., Nowak, A., & Chaban, N. (Eds.) (2007). *The EU through the Eyes of Asia.* Warsaw, Singapore: University of Warsaw.

Jacobs, L., & Page, B. (2005). Who influences U.S. foreign policy? *American Political Science Rreview, 99*(1), 107–123.

Jepsen, M., & Pascual, A. S. (2005). The European social model: An exercise in deconstruction. *Journal of European Social Policy, 15*(3), 231–245.

Kinnvall, C. (1995). *Cultural diffusion and political learning: The democratization of China.* Lund: Lund University Press.

Kupchan, C. (2010 August 29). As nationalism rises, will the European Union fall? *The Washington Post.* http://www.washingtonpost.com/wp-dyn/content/article/2010/08/27/AR 2010082702138.html. Accessed 26 Oct 2013.

Lamy, P. (2002). Stepping stones or stumbling blocks? The EU's approach towards the problem of multilateralism vs. regionalism in trade policy. *The World Economy, 25*(10), 1399–1413.

Langhamer, R. J. (1999). Regional integration APEC style: Lesson from regional integration EU style. *ASEAN Economic Bulletin, 16*(1), 1–17.

Leonard, M., & Krastev, I. (2007). New world order: The balance of soft power and the rise of herbivorous powers. ECFR policy brief, 24 October. http://www.ecfr.eu/content/entry/commentary_gallup_poll_results/. Accessed 26 Oct 2013.

Lucarelli, S. (2007). EU political identity, foreign policy and external image, the external image of the European Union: A global survey, GARNET Working Paper Series 17. http://www.garnet-eu.org. Accessed 12 Nov 2013.

Manners, I. (2002). Normative power Europe: A contradiction in terms? *Journal of Common Market Studies, 40*(2), 235–258.

Merriam-Webster Dictionary. http://www.merriam-webster.com/. Accessed 13 Nov 2013.

Meyer, J. (2001). The European Union and the globalization of culture. In S. Andersen (Ed.), *Institutional approaches to the European Union* (pp. 227–245). ARENA Report No 3/2001.

Nye, J. (2008). Public diplomacy and soft power. *The ANNALS of the American Academy of Political and Social Science, 616*(1), 94–109.

Page, B. I., & Shapiro, R. Y. (1983). Effects of public opinion on policy. *American Political Science Review, 77*, 175–190.

Pickering, M. (2001). *Stereotyping: The politics of representation.* New York: Palgrave.

Rhodes, C. (1986). Introduction: The identity of the European Union in international affairs. In C. Rhodes (Ed.), *The European Union in the community* (p. 6). Boulder: Lynne Rienuer.

Rhodes, C. (1999). *The European Union in the world community.* Colorado: Lynne Rienner Publishers.

Schimmelfenning, F. (2009). Europeanization beyond Europe. *Living Reviews in European Governance, 4*(3). http://www.livingreviews.org/lreg-2009-3. Accessed 15 Nov 2013.

Shiming, F. (2010). Chinese public perceptions of Japan and the United States in the post-cold war era. In G. L. Curtis, R. Kokuburn, & J. Wang (Eds.), *Getting the triangle straight: Managing China-Japan-U.S. relations* (pp. 269–291). Tokyo: Japan Center International Exchange.

Shu, M. (2009). National identity and regional integration: A comparison between Europe and East Asia. *EUSA Review, 22,* 2.

Simmons, B., Dobbin, F., & Garrett, G. (2006). Introduction: The international diffusion of liberalism. *International Organization, 60*(4), 781–810.

Teló, M. (2006). *Europe: A civilian power? European Union, global governance, world order.* London: Palgrave.

Tsuruoka, M (2008). How external perceptions of the European Union are shaped: Endogenous and exogenous sources. Presented at GARNET Conference, Brussels, 24/26 April.

Viner, J. (1950). *Customs union issue.* New York: Carnegie Endowment for International Peace.

von Hofmann, N. (2007). How do Asian's evaluate Europe's strategic involvement in East Asia? *Asia Europe Journal, 5*(2), 187–192.

Dr. Natalia Chaban is Associate Professor and Jean Monnet Chair at the National Centre for Research on Europe, University of Canterbury, New Zealand. She has significant experience in analysing EU identity outside the EU, widely publishing and advancing methodological expertise in this regard. Since 2002, she has co-led a comparative transnational project on EU external perceptions comprising a multicultural team from 20 Asia-Pacific locations, as well as a 'mirror' perceptions project "Asia in Eyes of Europe". Among her publications is *The European Union and the Asia-Pacific: Media, Public and Elite Perceptions of the EU* (2008) Routledge (N. Chaban and M. Holland, eds.) and *Communicating Europe in Times of Crisis: External Perceptions of the European Union* (2014) Palgrave (N. Chaban and M. Holland, eds.) She has also published articles in journals such as *European Foreign Affairs Review, Journal of Common Market Studies, Journal of European Integration, European Law Journal, Mobilities.*

Dr. Serena Kelly is a post-doctoral fellow at the NCRE. She has participated in several stages of the NCRE's "EU External Perceptions" project as both a researcher and trainer. Most recently she coordinated a 10 country research project involving Japan, South Korea, China, India, Singapore, Thailand, Malaysia, Australia, New Zealand and Russia. This research systematically analysed local media, elite and public opinion on local perceptions towards the European Union. For more information see www.euperceptions.canterbury.ac.nz. Her PhD was on the European External Action Service.

Prof. Martin Holland holds a Jean Monnet Chair ad personam and is Director of the National Centre for Research on Europe at the University of Canterbury, New Zealand, and of New Zealand EU Centres Network. He has published widely on EU Development Policy, Common Foreign and Security Policy as well as EU Perceptions. His most recent Palgrave title is Development Policy of the European Union (2012) (with M. Dodge).

Chapter 6
From One Single Market to Another: European Integration, Australasian Ambivalence and Construction of the Trans-Tasman Single Economic Market

John Leslie and Annmarie Elijah

6.1 Introduction

Over the past 30 years Australia and New Zealand have constructed a Trans-Tasman Single Economic Market (TTSEM) that, like the Single European Market (SEM), has substantially removed administrative barriers to the free movement of goods, services, capital and people.[1] Officially, the European Union (EU) has never recognized trans-Tasman economic integration, let alone attempted to coerce, socialize or teach Australian and New Zealand policymakers about integration. Despite this official indifference, European integration has had both direct and indirect effects on trans-Tasman developments. The United Kingdom's (UK) accession to the European Economic Community (EEC) in 1973 had a direct effect by extending the Customs Union/Common External Tariff (CET) and Common Agricultural Policy (CAP) around Australian and New Zealand agricultural producers' principal

The authors gratefully acknowledge funding from the research project 'Australia and the European Union: a study of a changing trade and business relationship' (LPO000000) supported by the Australian Research Council, as well as the European Australian Business Council, the European Commission, the Department of Foreign Affairs and Trade, the Department of Agriculture, Fisheries and Forestry and the Department of Industry and Innovation.

[1] This chapter uses the terms 'Australasian', 'Antipodean' and 'trans-Tasman' to refer to Australia and New Zealand only. Some observers have included New Guinea as part of 'Australasia'. We reject that usage explicitly. We also reject any (e.g. Eurocentric) value judgment attached to the term 'Antipodean'. Instead we use it simply to identify Australia and New Zealand together.

J. Leslie (✉)
Political Science and International Relations Programme, Victoria University of Wellington, Wellington, New Zealand
e-mail: john.leslie@vuw.ac.nz

A. Elijah
Centre for European Studies, Australian National University, Canberra, Australia
e-mail: annmarie.elijah@anu.edu.au

© Springer International Publishing Switzerland 2015
A. Björkdahl et al. (eds.), *Importing EU Norms,* United Nations University Series on Regionalism 8, DOI 10.1007/978-3-319-13740-7_6

markets. The trade diversionary effects of European integration produced a 'competitive' or 'contagious' effect that precipitated trans-Tasman economic integration. Europe has also had an indirect effect by providing an example, positive and negative, at every step of trans-Tasman integration.

Australian and New Zealand policymakers *adapted* European ideas and practices about economic integration for local use. They were particularly receptive to ideas and practices associated with the SEM. However, Australasian policymakers filtered these ideas and practices through perceptions of European integration that were coloured by their direct experience with the diversionary impact of Europe's CET and CAP. Thus, they emulated liberalizing components—like the single market—appropriated coordinating mechanisms—such as mutual recognition—and avoided elements like customs union and Europe's centralized supra-national institutions (European Commission, Court of Justice and Parliament), which they associated with illiberalism. Australasian policymakers consciously constructed trans-Tasman integration as an example of 'open regionalism' that they offered as an alternative to European experience for regional integration in the Asia-Pacific.

This chapter continues in three parts. The next section locates trans-Tasman integration in arguments about 'external' causes of economic integration. It gives particular attention to modes of diffusion from the volume's introduction that are relevant to the transfer of practices from Europe to the trans-Tasman relationship—competition, learning and emulation. A second section provides two case studies to demonstrate how Australasian policymakers adapted European ideas and practices for local use. First, it shows how Australian and New Zealand policymakers imported considerable content from the SEM but consciously transformed it into an 'open' and 'outward looking' alternative to European economic integration. A second case study demonstrates that, while the supra-national institutions Australasian policymakers constructed to govern the TTSEM served many of the same functions as the European Commission, Court of Justice and Parliament, they reflected indigenous rather than European origins. A concluding section draws lessons for future research about diffusion of integration practices.

6.2 'External' Causes of Trans-Tasman Economic Integration: Globalisation, Europeanisation and International Diffusion of Ideas

With the end of the Cold War and a multiplication of regional integration projects outside Europe, observers began to look beyond European experience and (neo-functional and liberal intergovernmental) explanations that emphasized 'internal' drivers of integration. Instead, their focus fell on the role of the international environment in integration and the impact of the changing structure of the world economy, the diffusion of political and policy ideas and the influence of European integration, in particular (Breslin and Higgott 2000; Simmons et al. 2006; Manners 2002; Jetschke and Lenz 2013). Changes in the international environment had both a direct and indirect impact on trans-Tasman economic integration. First, the changing structure of the world's economy—and European integration, in particular—had a direct influence on the material options available to economic producers and policymakers in Australia and New Zealand. Second, European economic integration offered 'lessons' to Antipodean policymakers about how to manage changes in the world's economy. Finally, the circumstances of economic changes—particularly UK accession to the EEC—shaped Australian and New Zealand policymakers' perceptions of European integration. This section considers the direct impact of the changing world economy on trans-Tasman economic integration as well as how these changes shaped Australian and New Zealand policymakers' perceptions of European integration.

The international environment and the EU, in particular, can have a direct impact on economic integration outside Europe in several ways. Powerful actors—like the EU, the United States (US) or International Monetary Fund (IMF)—may use coercion and conditionality to influence integration in other regions. They may also influence policymakers in other regions by attempting to 'teach' or 'socialize' them to particular norms, values or practices. EU policymakers, however, have never recognized trans-Tasman economic integration as such, nor have they tried to coerce, teach or socialize Australian and New Zealand policymakers about economic integration.[2] However, globalization and European integration did have a direct impact on Australasian developments in another way. Trans-Tasman economic integration reflects what some observers refer to as 'competitive', 'contagious' or 'domino' integration (Baldwin 1993; Mansfield and Milner 1999; Mattli 1999). From this perspective, the material consequences of being left out of a preferential trading scheme prompt subsequent integration efforts in which new members join existing formations or form new ones. The UK's accession (1973) to the EEC and the General Agreement on Tariff and Trade (GATT) Tokyo Round's (1973–1979) failure to liberalise European agricultural markets cut off Australian and New Zealand producers from their principal markets. These developments led directly to Australian Deputy Prime Minister Doug Anthony's overture to deepen economic ties with his New Zealand counterparts in May 1979 (Andre et al. 2003). This proposal precipitated negotiations for the 1983 Australia New Zealand Closer Economic Relations Trade Agreement (ANZCERTA). The UK's accession forced Australasian policymakers to re-evaluate the economic and political structure of the world and their place in it.

European integration also affected trans-Tasman economic integration indirectly. First, European integration provided one source of 'lessons' about economic integration. Australasian policymakers' import of European norms, ideas and practices about economic integration receives more attention below. Second, the diversionary impact of CAP and the CET on agricultural trade profoundly influenced Australasian policymakers' perceptions of European integration. As 'victims' of the CAP and the CET, many Australians and New Zealanders felt deeply ambivalent about European

---

[2] Australian and New Zealand did negotiate agreements for mutual recognition of accreditation as a single team with the EU. However, each country signed a separate agreement with the EU and the initiative for joint negotiations came from Australian and New Zealand policymakers (Mumford 2004).

integration. While they welcomed—and came to identify with—liberalization and Europe's internal market, they also abhorred its diversionary impact and defined trans-Tasman economic integration in opposition to it. Accordingly, the ANZCER-TA Preamble declares the parties' 'commitment to an outward looking approach to trade' (Australian DFAT 1995). Further, as trans-Tasman economic integration deepened, Australian and New Zealand governments refined their outward-looking approach to trade into a commitment to 'open regionalism' between themselves and in the larger Asia-Pacific. They defined 'open regionalism' as conforming to the letter and spirit of member states' GATT obligations, including Article 24. Trading arrangements must: not introduce preferences against third parties; be open to accession by new member states; permit subsequent unilateral liberalization and reform; be comprehensive (Holmes et al. 1986, p. 18; New Zealand MFAT 1993, pp. 77–78). Further, they left no doubt as to the inspiration for their commitment to 'open regionalism' by defining it in direct contradistinction to European agricultural policies (Holmes et al. 1986, p. 18; New Zealand MFAT 1993, p. 63).

External and internal developments reinforced these prejudices from the 1980s. Externally, the emerging neo-liberal orthodoxy and 'Washington Consensus' provided ideological support for 'open regionalism'. Internally, elections in 1983–1984 brought Labo(u)r governments into office, which confronted economic crises and were willing to experiment with new policy approaches. In both countries trans-Tasman economic integration became intertwined with neo-liberal, domestic reforms as part of a larger strategy to transform economies and promote competitiveness on world markets. Perhaps more than in any other set of countries, a neo-liberal policy paradigm informed Australia and New Zealand policymakers' perceptions of economic integration and European economic integration, in particular.

The international environment had three effects on trans-Tasman economic integration. UK accession to the EEC forced Australasian producers and policymakers to adjust strategically to a changing world. Second, because the EEC's CAP/CET caused this painful adjustment, it became the target of an ideologically justified antipathy. Accordingly, Australian and New Zealand policymakers defined trans-Tasman economic integration in opposition to the EEC's trade diversion, as 'open regionalism'. However, internal European liberalization meant that Australasian policymakers' attitudes were ambivalent toward European integration. The next section, therefore, considers the third effect of the international environment: how Australian and New Zealand policymakers imported and adapted European ideas and practices to trans-Tasman economic integration.

6.3 Europe as a 'Model' for Trans-Tasman Economic Integration

This section analyzes whether and how European precedent influenced trans-Tasman developments by serving as a 'model' of economic integration. In investigating this influence, it is important to recognize that European ideas and practices are only one 'cause', among several, that contributed to trans-Tasman economic integration. This observation is important in the trans-Tasman context and for investigations of policy diffusion more generally. This is because it is the 'friction', or lack of it, between imported ideas/practices and local 'causes' that determines which outcome—*adoption, adaptation, resistance* or *rejection*—comes into being.

This section has three parts. The first outlines the 'local' context and causes of trans-Tasman integration: the socio-economic, political and institutional forces that shaped trans-Tasman economic integration from the 'inside'. It demonstrates that there are strong similarities as well as considerable differences between the 'contexts' of European and trans-Tasman integration. Two case studies follow this introductory part. The first case analyzes Australasian policymakers' *adaptation* of European norms and practices in constructing a single market between the two countries. The second case demonstrates Australasian policymakers' *adaptation* of European ideas and practices in designing supra-national institutional arrangements to govern the emerging trans-Tasman single market. In both cases European precedent influenced Australasian decision making, but it was one of several causal forces.

6.3.1 Local 'Context' and Trans-Tasman Economic Integration

The 'local' context in which trans-Tasman economic integration has taken place is both similar to and different from the 'context' of European integration. The similarities help explain why policymakers imported European ideas and practices to make a single market the goal of trans-Tasman economic integration. The differences help explain why European practices were adapted in the construction of a single market and the supra-national institutions to govern it.

Both socio-economic and political similarities exist between the Australasian and the EEC Member States. Australia and New Zealand, like the original EEC Member States, were early members of the Organisation of Cooperation and Development (OECD). They satisfy the preconditions Haas (1958, pp. xv–xvi) identified as necessary for integration and 'formation of political communities': (1) developed economies deeply embedded in the international economic system, (2) a set of developed and stable organizations for interest representation, (3) a system of open and transparent competition between interests groups, and (4) a democratic and constitutional system that governs this competition.

Another critical similarity defined both Australasian and European political institutions. Like the EEC, and the European Coal and Steel Community (ECSC) before it, the tension between economic interdependence and multiple jurisdictions has played an important role in the process of trans-Tasman economic integration. In the trans-Tasman relationship, the problem of multiple jurisdictions is not limited to the sovereign boundaries that separate Australia from New Zealand. Rather, Australia's federal division into eight states and territories creates a situation in which ten, not two, governments pool their sovereignty to govern a trans-Tasman single market. The Australian Constitution and case law creates an ambiguous division of competencies between the Commonwealth and state/territory governments in matters of market regulation. As a result, in 1990 Australian Prime Minister Bob Hawke (1990) observed famously that Australia's internal market was more balkanized than Europe's internal market. Hawke's so-called 'New Federalism' speech came at critical moment that merged trans-Tasman economic integration with Australian domestic reforms. Australia's internal balkanization created opportunities for integration entrepreneurs to 'internalize externalities' and these opportunities extended across the Tasman Sea. Just as policy coordination promised to stimulate economic growth across the 'Six' in Europe, Australasian policymakers saw a similar opportunity in coordinating policies between different levels of Australian federalism as well as between New Zealand and Australia.

Significant differences, however, also distinguish the 'internal' conditions of European and trans-Tasman economic integration. First, the composition of the Australian and New Zealand economies differs from that of the original EEC members. Although some EEC Member States still had large agricultural sectors when integration began in the 1950s and 1960s, they also had significant industrial capacity and traded manufactures with each other. With time agriculture became a smaller proportion of their economies and the tertiary sector became more important for production and trade. Australia and New Zealand have both had small—but important—manufacturing sectors and their service sectors have also grown over time. In trade, however, both countries export principally primary products. Through the 1980s, agricultural products made up a large percentage of each country's exports. To the present, agriculture remains New Zealand's principal source of foreign currency earnings. In Australia, mining became a leading export sector in the late 1980s.

These differences between Australia and New Zealand and the EEC Member States have had two important consequences for the processes of trans-Tasman economic integration. First, because there is relatively little complementarity between the Australian and New Zealand economies, there is relatively little 'demand' among social interest groups for economic integration. As a result, policy coordination has been driven by policymakers' desires to restructure the Australian and New Zealand states and economies rather than, for example, business desires to access new markets (Leslie et al. 2013).[3] Second, the relative absence of complementarities meant the potential gains from both trade creation and trade diversion between the two economies were also relatively small, while both economies' vulnerabilities to third-party discrimination were all-too-apparent. These circumstances provide a material foundation for policymakers' support of 'open regionalism' in both countries. They also played a role in decisions to construct the ANZCERTA as a goods

---

[3] Australia is the largest source of imports into New Zealand and until 2013 was the largest market for New Zealand exports. Imports from and exports to Australia, however, make up no more than one-fifth of New Zealand's trade with the world (New Zealand MFAT 2012). New Zealand ranks sixth among Australia's export markets and seventh among two-way trade partners (Australian DFAT 2012).

Free Trade Agreement (FTA), rather than as customs union with a common external tariff. These issues receive more attention below.

Cultural and institutional homogeneity also distinguish Australia and New Zealand from EEC/European Community (EC)/EU Member States. The Australian and New Zealand economies both resemble *liberal market economies*, rather than the *coordinated market economies* (Hall and Soskice 2001). EU Member State economies are heterogeneous in this regard. Further, Australia's and New Zealand's welfare states both resemble the 'liberal' model of postwar welfare states (Schwarz 2000; Esping-Andersen 1990), while welfare states in the EU states have been more diverse. Australian and New Zealand economic and welfare institutions exist alongside legal systems that, while by no means identical, both evolved from UK common law. Similarly, political institutions in both countries are variants of the UK's 'Westminster System'. These similarities reflect UK colonialism as well as the dominance of the English language and British culture over alternatives in both societies. These cultural and institutional similarities reduce uncertainties and facilitate greater 'trust' between Australasian policymakers than exists among European policymakers.

Finally, an important institutional difference distinguishes the local contexts in which European and trans-Tasman economic integration took place. Europeans acknowledge the ECSC as the beginning of the European integration process because of the Schuman Plan's delegation of supra-national authority to international agencies, particularly the High Authority. Subsequent European integration has been bound up inextricably with the actions of the supra-national European Commission, Court of Justice and Parliament. The process of trans-Tasman economic integration inherited a very different—and less visible—set of institutions. Since at least the 1920s, line ministers of the Australian Commonwealth, states and territories and even the New Zealand government have been meeting in portfolio-based ministerial councils (Painter 1998). At the end of the 1980s and in the early 1990s, these ministerial councils served some of the same functions as the European Commission, Court and Parliament in facilitating 'deep' economic integration and creation of a single market. The design of these ministerial councils, and a few autonomous trans-Tasman agencies, differed importantly from Europe's arrangements. The origin, evolution and design of these institutions receive more attention below.

European ideas and practices about economic integration entered into a trans-Tasman context that was both similar to and different from the context of European integration. Perhaps most importantly, Australian and New Zealand policy makers were able to recognize enough similarities between the challenges they faced and European circumstances that they could look to Europe for policy solutions. Levels of economic development and the organization of polities in both regions were similar. Australian and New Zealand policy makers understood the tensions they faced between economic interdependence and competing jurisdictions to be analogous to those that prompted European economic integration. However, even as this fundamental similarity was apparent, Australian and New Zealand policy makers also confronted peculiarities in their own situation. The economic and, especially, trade profiles of Australia and New Zealand differed markedly from those

of the original EEC members. Institutions in Australia's and New Zealand's economies and polities were more homogeneous, and more 'liberal', than those of EEC
members. Finally, Australian and New Zealand policy makers inherited a very different set of institutions with which to coordinate trans-national policies. The next
two sections demonstrate empirically how the Australasian economic, cultural and
institutional context shaped reception of European ideas in the processes of trans-
Tasman economic integration.

6.3.2   Constructing a Trans-Tasman Single Market

European integration has had a changing influence on trans-Tasman economic integration. Construction of the SEM and the trans-Tasman single market began almost simultaneously. However, while the former grew from a blueprint set down
in the Single European Act, the latter emerged incrementally and organically over
time and subject to international influences including European integration itself.
Over time Australasian policymakers have come to associate trans-Tasman economic integration directly with the values, practices and language of SEM, while,
at the same time, taking pains to draw distinctions between the two developments.
The following demonstrates the Australasian policymakers' adaptation of European
norms and practices in construction of the TTSEM as the goal of economic integration between the two countries.

As indicated above, trans-Tasman economic integration began as a result of—
and with great ambivalence toward—the EEC's first enlargement. However, even in
this original moment of Antipodean Euroscepticism, European integration served as
a policy referent for Australian and New Zealand policymakers anticipating greater
integration of their economies. At the 1979 meeting of trade ministers, where he
proposed closer trans-Tasman economic coordination, Australian Deputy Prime
Minister Doug Anthony suggested to his counterpart, 'If the Europeans can do so,
why can't we?' (Andre et al. 2003, p. 34). While Anthony was clearly thinking of
European economic integration, he did not state what he thought the Europeans
had or had not done concretely. Nor did he offer a proposal for what he thought
Australians and New Zealanders should do to coordinate economic policies. The
task of turning aspirations for closer coordination into a negotiating agenda was left
to officials on both sides of the Tasman, who considered a menu of options. These
options were drawn directly from existing scholarship on Europe, particularly Balassa's (1961) levels of integration: FTA, customs union, common market, monetary
union, economic union (Andre et al. 2003, p. 49, pp. 41–43). Senior politicians on
both sides raised the possibility of a common market, customs and currency union
(Andre et al. 2003; Templeton 1995). At this point 'local' forces shaped outcomes.

Material interests influenced policymakers' choice to limit the initial step toward economic integration, the ANZCERTA, to creation of a comprehensive, but
conventional, free trade area for goods. Both governments observed that important
differences distinguished manufacturing industries in the two countries and that

these differences were reflected in each country's tariff profile. Tariff harmonisation within a CET/customs union would generate significant adjustment costs for manufacturers in one or both countries—a situation, they recognized, that distinguished their circumstances from, for example, the Benelux customs union (Andre et al. 2003, pp. 48–54, 159–163). As a result of the potential for a customs union to aggravate already significant resistance to liberalisation coming from New Zealand manufacturers and Australian dairy interests, policy makers determined that comprehensive free trade in goods (a 'negative list' with commitments to remove exemptions) was as far as they were willing to go. Thus, while European precedent provided Australasian policymakers a wider menu of choices for economic integration, calculations of material interests determined that a goods FTA would be their initial step.

An important cognitive transformation accompanied this initial step toward greater trans-Tasman economic integration, however. This transformation reflects Australasian ambivalence toward European integration. On the one hand, policymakers began to think of trans-Tasman integration as a process, like European economic integration, that was meant to serve grander strategic goals. On the other hand, they sought to distinguish trans-Tasman and European integration. For example the ANZCERTA's Preamble voices the broader strategic aspirations of the Agreement's architects:

> BELIEVING that a closer economic relationship will... contribute to the development of the region through closer economic and trading links with other countries, particularly those of the South Pacific and South East Asia. (Australian DFAT 1995)

The Preamble also differentiates the trans-Tasman undertaking from Europe by proclaiming the parties' 'commitment to an outward looking approach to trade' (ibid.).

Ambitions to deepen trans-Tasman economic integration beyond free trade in goods also found expression in the ANZCERTA text. Articles 11, 12, 21 and 22 extol the two governments to consider coordination of policies on taxation, company law, standards, non-tariff barriers, investment and movement of people, among others. They entail no obligations other than a 5-year review of the relationship, however. As ANZCERTA focused on eliminating tariffs and quantitative restrictions on goods, the parties undertook no commitment to construct governance arrangements, other than an annual meeting of ministers.

In the Five Year Review of ANZCERTA European norms, values and practices began to shape trans-Tasman economic integration toward construction of a 'single market'. At an August 1985 CER ministerial meeting in Canberra—two months after the European Commission released its White Paper 'Completing the Internal Market'—the Australian and New Zealand Prime Ministers, Bob Hawke and David Lange, threw their weight behind using the Five Year Review to deepen economic integration between the two countries. In defining and negotiating the agenda for the 1988 Review, Australian and New Zealand policymakers looked explicitly and repeatedly at developments surrounding the Single European Act and SEM. European practices were a model for, among other things, elimination of anti-dumping and countervailing measures, internal regulation of competition, customs cooperation and the eventual construction of a mutual recognition regime for goods standards and labour qualifications. But European influences existed next to other 'external' influences that shaped 'deepening' trans-Tasman economic integration. Policymakers expanded on a Canada-US FTA (CUSFTA) initiative by creating a 'negative list' approach for liberalisation of services markets (Thomson 1990). It is difficult to disentangle the influence of, for example, the GATT Agreement on Technical Barriers to Trade and European precedent on the trans-Tasman harmonisation of accreditation systems, product and food safety standards that also grew out of the 1988 Review process. The agreement that emerged out of the 1988 Review process pushed economic integration 'deep' behind borders, but reflected an eclectic set of European, international non-European and local influences.

It is in the framing of the overall characterisation and objectives of deepening trans-Tasman economic integration that European precedent exerted the greatest influence. After the 1985 CER ministers meeting, officials referred to potential policy areas for deepening economic integration as 'second generation' issues. In the course of the review process, 'second generation issues' were replaced by an emerging vision of the process and goal of trans-Tasman economic integration. In announcing the measures under the 1988 Review, the Australian and New Zealand Prime Ministers proclaimed

> Today we have set the final seal on a package of measures which will accelerate, deepen and widen the economic relationship between our two countries. From 1 July 1990 we will have removed virtually all the impediments to achieving a single trans-Tasman market. (New Zealand DTI 1988, p. 1)

The SEM provided Australasian policymakers with a label and ideological rationale for trans-Tasman economic integration. Yet, even as they imported European language, values and practices, Australian and New Zealand policymakers also asserted the distinctiveness of trans-Tasman integration. The same prime ministerial communique from which the passage above is taken states, 'CER is outward-looking and the impressive growth in two-way trade between our two countries has not been achieved at the expense of our other trading partners' (ibid., p. 2).

In the quarter century since the 1988 ANZCERTA Review deepening economic integration has taken place irregularly and incrementally across a broad range of issue areas, but, if anything, policymakers have come to associate these processes *more closely* with the SEM. Since the 1988 Review, policymakers have implemented hundreds, if not thousands, of *ad hoc* measures to deepen trans-Tasman integration of goods, services, capital and labour markets. The SEM has provided the referent to unify conceptually and rationalize these measures. In 2005, the two countries' governments asserted a conceptual unity around these disparate measures by making a TTSEM the official goal of efforts to integrate the two economies. In 2012, a joint report of the two countries' Productivity Commissions, *Strengthening trans-Tasman Economic Relations*, proclaimed:

> Opportunities to strengthen trans-Tasman economic ties can be classified using a framework based on what the European Union has termed the 'four freedoms'—relating to trade in goods and services, and the movement of capital and labour. (Australian and New Zealand Productivity Commissions 2012, p. 9)

Thus, Australasian policymakers define trans-Tasman economic integration explicitly in European terms, values and practices. Yet, this is *adaptation* not *adoption*. Australian and New Zealand policymakers emphasize that the TTSEM's openness and 'outward-looking' orientation distinguish it from the SEM. And, while they consider the TTSEM a 'living' or 'expanding' relationship, they regard its evolution differently than many Europeans regard the EU's evolution. While many Australian and New Zealand policymakers would like the trans-Tasman relationship to 'widen' in the Asia Pacific, they do not regard it as a station on the path toward 'ever closer union' and political integration.

6.3.3   Creating Trans-Tasman Institutions for 'Deep' Economic Integration

While the trans-Tasman single market was an adaptation of European ideas and practices to local use, the institutions Australian and New Zealand policymakers constructed to govern the single market are indigenous. Although they perform many of the same functions as the EU's more famous supra-national arrangements, they have a different institutional design that reflects local circumstances. The EU's principal supra-national institutions—the Commission, Court of Justice and Parliament—possess authority *across a broad range of issues*. Australian and New Zealand policy makers, on the other hand, have delegated supra-national authority only in *narrowly defined issues areas*. They granted supra-national legislative and dispute-resolution authority to a hand-full of issue-specific, trans-Tasman agencies and a larger number of portfolio-based ministerial councils under the Council of Australian Governments (COAG). This decentralized institutional design reflects the fact that Australian and New Zealand policymakers faced challenges similar to those European policymakers confronted in building the SEM, but they did so under political and institutional circumstances peculiar to the trans-Tasman relationship.

Constructing a single market confronted European and Antipodean policymakers with a similar set of challenges. The most basic of these challenges derives from the fact that 'deep' or 'behind borders' policy coordination—the kind central to constructing single markets—is qualitatively more difficult than cooperation to reduce tariffs and quantitative restrictions. This kind of 'deep' policy coordination distinguished the agenda of the SEM project and 1988 ANZCERTA Review process from previous European and trans-Tasman integration.

Coordination of 'behind borders' policies differ in nature from tariffs and quantitative restrictions. The latter are transparent policies that protect domestic producers from foreign competitors. The effects of—and intentions underlying—many 'behind borders' policies, on the other hand, are ambiguous. For example, policymakers may create product, sanitary and phytosanitary standards to protect consumers, animal and plant health. They may also enact these measures to protect domestic producers from external competition. Because trading partners cannot easily determine what motivates such regulations—protection or 'legitimate' public policy interests—trans-national policy coordination is qualitatively more difficult than reduction of tariffs and quotas.

Because of the ambiguity attached to 'behind borders' issues, some observers have argued that 'deep' integration requires institutional arrangements that can perform functions that sovereign parties cannot perform themselves. These functions include: interpreting obligations, monitoring compliance, resolving disputes and setting an agenda when creation of new obligations is required. The Treaties of Paris and Rome created institutions that have performed these functions for the ECSC, EEC and their successors. The 1988 Review set in motion the construction of institutional arrangements that have performed these functions in the trans-Tasman relationship.

Australia's relative size and the 'deep' integration put forward under the 1988 Review created an understandable desire for institutionalisation among New Zealand policy makers. A briefing paper for the New Zealand cabinet concluded that 'the 1988 review could result in a broader scope and coverage of bilateral trade and economic activity and therefore an expanded scope for disputes of an interpretive nature' (New Zealand MERT 1988, pp. 7–8). As the smaller partner, New Zealand officials sought to make the 1988 Review's obligations as binding as possible. New Zealand's ministers went into final negotiations for the Review seeking to bring together its various elements—liberalisation of services trade, acceleration of market access provisions, coordination of policies on TBTs—in a 'single instrument', tied to ANZCERTA, with treaty status. In addition, the New Zealanders wanted a binding dispute settlement mechanism based on the GATT model of panels of neutral experts (Hoadley 1995; New Zealand MERT 1988, pp. 7–8). Australian negotiators, however, rejected both demands, concluding that a single instrument was too cumbersome and that regular meetings of ministers had proven adequate for managing the relationship (New Zealand MERT 1988a). The Review ended as collection of 11 separate agreements without overarching institutional arrangements (Hoadley 1995). Asymmetry of power explains, at least in part, why the TTSEM and the trans-Tasman relationship, more generally, have evolved as a set of separate initiatives in different issue areas with nothing like the EU's treaty structure to bind them together.

After the 1988 Review, New Zealand's policy makers persisted in pushing integration deeper and institutionalizing the trans-Tasman relationship. The 1988 Review had set in motion integration processes in several issue areas, some of which spilled over into other issue areas and the momentum for deepening carried through well into the 1990s. After the Australian rejection of a dispute settlement mechanism in 1988, New Zealand policymakers took a different tack on institutionalisation by seeking to adapt existing institutional arrangements—the standing Commonwealth-State ministerial councils—to serve 'deep' integration. New Zealand Prime Minster Sir Geoffrey Palmer explained his vision of the evolving trans-Tasman relationship in an April 1990 letter to his Australian counterpart, Bob Hawke. Palmer began by comparing the trans-Tasman relationship with European integration directly.

There is no reason why, in this part of the world, we should fall short of the vision the Europeans have set themselves of a common European space. Although we have far more in common with each other than the numerous nations of Europe, we still face the same basic task of persuading ourselves that our distinct and separate national identities can continue to thrive in a supra-national framework. (Palmer 1990, p. 4)

Palmer extrapolated from the 1988 Review and on-going integration processes to speculate '…that as the single market develops, we must be prepared for pressure to harmonise areas of policy-making which we now regard as sacrosanct areas of national sovereignty' (ibid., p. 4). Accordingly, he suggested that the two countries prepare to discuss the broadening relationship 'including institutional relationships', although he avoided setting a concrete agenda for integration other than 'to fence off possibilities that…get too close to federation' (ibid., p. 5). He did, however, suggest that immediate progress might be made by using the standing councils within which New Zealand Ministers participate with their Commonwealth and State counterparts 'to enhance Australia/New Zealand cooperation' (ibid., p. 5). Accordingly, a joint prime ministerial statement following their July 1990 meeting announced that over the following year meetings of sectoral councils would discuss how to enhance Australia-New Zealand cooperation (Hawke and Palmer 1990, p. 7). Out of this process evolved the 'functional', or portfolio-based institutional arrangements that govern 'deep' integration of the Australian and New Zealand economies.

This outcome reflects New Zealand policymakers' persistence, but also changing Australian preferences. From the middle of 1990 Australian attitudes toward institutionalisation shifted to parallel those of New Zealand policymakers. This shift reflects the fact that the most important barriers to economic integration and growth were not necessarily those between Australia and New Zealand, but those separating the Australian states. After narrowly winning re-election in March 1990, Hawke's Labor Government sought to stimulate growth through the related processes of 'micro-economic' reform and 'New Federalism'. The former sought economic growth by integrating Australia's 'balkanized' internal market. The latter created a new layer of institutions in Australian federalism to manage conflicts arising from overlapping Commonwealth and state jurisdictions in market regulation. Like New Zealand policymakers, the Hawke Government viewed the ministerial councils as an institutional solution to the challenges of 'deep' economic integration.

Hawke's 'New Federalism' and the 'One Nation' programmes of his successor, Paul Keating, added an informal, 'cooperative' layer to Australian federalism. Commonwealth, State and Territory governments created this new institutional layer by merging the existing ministerial councils together under the oversight of heads of government and central agencies in Special Premiers' Conferences (SPCs) and, after May 1992, the Council of Australian Governments (COAG). Bringing ministerial councils under the SPCs/COAG permitted linkages between and coordination of, for example, regulatory policies and provision of government services[4] from a whole-of-government perspective (Weller 1996, pp. 103–104). The SPC/COAG

---

[4] The SPCs and COAG have had less success in coordinating policies with distributive implications and Commonwealth-State financial relations (see Weller 1996, pp. 98–99).

structures provided heads of government and central agencies with a mechanism to steer the reform agenda and oversee progress based on consultation and agreement between officials and ministers. In policy areas specifically associated with 'micro-economic' reform, this new layer pooled the authority of overlapping jurisdictions and, in some cases, introduced majority voting to replace unit veto (Painter 1998, p. 25).

This 'cooperative' layer of Australian federalism remains informal and highly segmented. It is founded on an agreement between Commonwealth, State and Territory premiers and is embedded neither in the Constitution nor in statutory law (Kildea 2010). It is functionally segmented as policy-making capacities remain concentrated within the constituent governments' line ministries, while central departments and heads of government provide political coordination. New Zealand's ministers' participation extends these arrangements across the boundaries between the two countries.

While Australasian policymakers imported many ideas and practices associated with the single market, the institutions they constructed to govern it had indigenous origins. Policymakers were aware of Europe's supra-national institutional arrangements as well as those in CUSFTA (Chaps. 11 and 19). If Europe's institutions were a model for Australasian policymakers, then they served as a model to be avoided. The European Commission, in particular, was associated with CAP/CET and, through these, the traditions of French mercantilism. Instead of European imports, the institutions of the trans-Tasman Single Economic Market were constructed from the power relationship between Australia and New Zealand, the peculiarities of Australian federalism and an existing set of sectoral ministerial councils.

6.4   Conclusions

European ideas and practices affected economic integration between Australia and New Zealand to produce an adaptation of the SEM, the TTSEM. The process of deep and deepening economic integration leading to TTSEM was a direct response to the UK's accession to the EEC and the diversionary pressures of the CAP and CET. Europe was also a source of ideas and practices about economic integration. Australasian policymakers recognized their own situation as analogous to the conditions of economic interdependence and competing jurisdictions that prompted European integration and looked to Europe for 'lessons'. However, the trauma of the UK's accession also shaped Antipodean perceptions of European ideas and practices and, therefore, how they were 'received'. They abhorred the diversionary impact of CET and CAP. Thus, while they imported European ideas and practices—particularly about the single market—they adapted them to produce a peculiar, 'outward looking' variant of the SEM.

While it is clear *that* European precedent influenced trans-Tasman economic integration, it is often more difficult to determine *how much* influence it had. The contagious effect of European integration and the growing influence of the SEM are unmistakable. However, decisions about the scope and design of institutions have origins in local conditions rather than European precedent. The decision to avoid customs union, for example, reflects the existing trade and tariff profiles of the two countries. Further, the design of trans-Tasman institutions seems to have little to do with European precedent and to be much more the product of local context, especially the asymmetrical relationship between Australia and New Zealand and the existing Commonwealth-State ministerial councils. It is difficult to untangle the relative weight of 'internal' and 'external' causes of trans-Tasman economic integration.

What does seem clear about trans-Tasman integration, however, is the importance of agency and processes of innovation. Neither Europeans nor other actors have sought to influence Trans-Tasman integration from the 'outside'. Instead, Australasian policymakers have drawn on both external examples and local resources to construct a novel and highly efficacious 'single market'. The friction produced by importing 'lessons' from Europe into 'local' conditions has prompted an interesting Australasian innovation: a deep and deepening single market that is 'outward looking' and governed by issue-specific, supra-national institutions.

References

Andre, P., Payton, S., & Mills, J. (Eds.). (2003). *The negotiation of the Australia-New Zealand Closer Economic Relations Trade Agreement 1983*. Canberra: Commonwealth of Australia.

Australian Department of Foreign Affairs and Trade. (1995). Australia-New Zealand free trade agreement. In Australian Government Publishing Service. http://www.dfat.gov.au/fta/anzcerta/downloads/anzcerta1.pdf. Accessed 15 Oct 2013.

Australian Department of Foreign Affairs and Trade. (2012). Australia's trade in goods and services 2012. http://www.dfat.gov.au/publications/tgs/index.html. Accessed 15 Oct 2013.

Australian Productivity Commission and New Zealand Productivity Commission. (2012). Strengthening economic relations between Australia and New Zealand—joint commissioned study. http://www.pc.gov.au/projects/study/australia-new-zealand. Accessed 15 Oct 2013.

Balassa, B. (1961). Towards a theory of economic integration. *Kyklos, 14*(1), 1–17.

Baldwin, R. (1993). A domino theory of regionalism. Working Paper 4465. National Bureau of Economic Research. http://www.nber.org/papers/w4465. Accessed 15 Oct.

Baldwin, R. (2009). Sequencing regionalism: Theory, European practice, and lessons for Asia, ADB Working Paper Series on Regional Economic Integration (80) Asian Development Bank, Shanghai.

Breslin, S., & Higgott, R. (2000). Studying regions: Learning from the old, constructing the new. *New Politcal Economy, 5*(3), 333–352.

Esping-Andersen, G. (1990). *The three worlds of welfare capitalism*. Princeton: Princeton University Press.

Haas, E. (1958). *The uniting of Europe*. London: Stevens and Sons.

Hall, P. & Soskice, D. (2001). An introduction to varieties of capitalism. In P. Hall & D. Soskice (Eds.), *Varieties of capitalism: The institutional foundations of comparative advantage* (pp. 1–68). Oxford: Oxford University Press.

Hawke, B., & Palmer, G. (1990). Joint prime ministerial statement. Documents of the Ministry of Economic Development, Head Office, Business & Legal central filing system. R17314864. Wellington: National Archive of New Zealand.

Hoadley, S. (1995). *New Zealand and Australia: Negotiating closer economic relations*. Wellington: New Zealand Institute of International Affairs.

Holmes, F., Harvey, M., Mason, G., & Garcia, M. (1986). *Closer economic relations with Australia: Agenda for progress.* Wellington: Victoria University Press/Institute of Policy Studies.

Jetschke, A., & Lenz, T. (2013). Does regionalism diffuse? A new research agenda for the study of regional organizations. *Journal of European Public Policy, 20*(4), 626–637.

Kildea, P. (2010). The future of COAG. NSW IPAA.

Leslie, J. & Elijah, A. (2012) Does n = 2?: Trans-Tasman economic integration as a comparator for the Single European Market. *Journal of Common Market Studies, 50*(6), 975–993.

Leslie, J., Castle, M., & LeQuesne, S. (2013). Business, policy makers and the evolution of the trans-Tasman Single Economic Market (TTSEM). Paper presented at the 2013 conference of the New Zealand Political Studies Association, University of Canterbury, Christchurch, 2–3 December.

Manners, I. (2002). Normative power Europe: A contradiction in terms? *Journal of Common Market Studies, 40*(2), 235–258.

Mansfield, E., & Milner, H. (1999). The new wave of regionalism. *International Organization, 53*(3), 589–627.

Mattli, W. (1999). *The logic of regional integration: Europe and beyond.* Cambridge: Cambridge University Press.

Moravcsik, A. (1998). *The choice for Europe.* Ithaca: Cornell University Press.

Mumford, P. (2004). A study of factors affecting regulatory cooperation between states. MA thesis, Victoria University of Wellington.

New Zealand Ministry of Foreign Affairs and Trade. (1993). *New Zealand trade policy—implementation and directions: A multi-track approach.* Wellington: New Zealand Ministry of Foreign Affairs and Trade.

New Zealand Department of Trade and Industry. (DTI 1988). *Agreed documents from the 1988 Review of ANZCERTA.* Wellington: New Zealand Department of Trade and Industry.

New Zealand Ministry of External Affairs and Trade. (MERT 1988). The Chairman, Cabinet Development and Marketing Committee, ANZCERTA 1988 Review: 20–21 June Ministerial. In: Documents of the Ministry of Foreign Affairs and Trade, Head Office, Central Filing System: Canberra High Commission. R22200915. Wellington: National Archives of New Zealand.

New Zealand Ministry of External Affairs and Trade. (MERT 1988a). 'TELEX to Wellington 01342 [Confidential] 15 June 1988 SUBJ: ANZCERTA: 1988 Review' Documents of the Ministry of Foreign Affairs and Trade, Head Office, Central Filing System: Canberra High Commission. R22200915. Wellington: National Archives of New Zealand.

New Zealand Ministry of Foreign Affairs and Trade. (2012). Global New Zealand—International trade, investment, and travel profile: Year ended December 2012. http://www.stats.govt.nz/browse_for_stats/industry_sectors/imports_and_exports/global-nz-dec-12/key-points.aspx. Accessed 15 Oct 2013.

Painter, M. (1998). *Collaborative federalism: Economic reform in Australia in the 1990s.* Cambridge: Cambridge University Press.

Palmer, G. (1990). Draft Letter to Mr. Hawke from Mr. Palmer—Message Number S 19620, 18 April, From: Wellington, To: Canberra Subject: Australia/New Zealand 1 July 1990. In: Documents of New Zealand Ministry of Economic Development. R17314864. Wellington: National Archive of New Zealand.

Sandholtz, W., & Zysman, J. (1989). 1992: Recasting the European bargain. *World Politics, 42*(1), 95–128.

Schwartz, H. (2000). Internationalization and two liberal welfare states: Australia and New Zealand. In F. Scharpf & V. Schmidt (Eds.), *Welfare and work in the open economy* (pp. 69–130). Oxford: Oxford University Press.

Simmons, B., Dobbin, F., & Garrett, G. (2006). Introduction: The international diffusion of liberalism. *International Organization, 60*(4), 781–810.

Thomson, G. (1990). A single market for goods and services in the Antipodes. *World Economy, 12*(2), 207–218.

Templeton, H. (1995) *All honourable men: Inside the Muldoon Cabinet, 1975–1984.* Auckland: Auckland University Press.

Weller, P. (1996). Commonwealth-state reform processes: A policy management review. *Australian Journal of Public Administration, 55*(1), 95–110.

John Leslie is a Lecturer in Political Science and International Relations at Victoria University of Wellington (VUW). His research comparing economic integration in the European Union, between Australia and New Zealand and in the Asia Pacific has appeared recently in, among other outlets, *Journal of Common Market Studies, Government and Opposition and Asia Europe Journal*. During 2014–2015 John Leslie is on leave from VUW, acting as the European Union's Trade Officer in New Zealand. Research for and writing of this chapter were completed before he began working for the EU.

Annmarie Elijah has worked as a policy officer in the Australian Department of Prime Minister and Cabinet, and has taught politics at the University of Melbourne, Victoria University of Wellington and ANU. Her PhD (University of Melbourne) examined the implications of British membership of the European Community for Australia. Her research interests include Australia-EU relations, European integration theory, comparative regionalism, trans-Tasman relations, Australian and New Zealand foreign policy and federalism. Annmarie is Deputy Director of the ANU Centre for European Studies.

Chapter 7
Moving Freely, but Taking a Different Route: Comparing Trans-Tasman and European Union Norms of Human Mobility

Kate McMillan

7.1 Introduction

Finnemore and Sikkink point to a 'generally agreed understanding' of a norm as 'a standard of appropriate behavior for actors with a given identity' (Finnemore and Sikkink 1998, p. 891). The norms with which this chapter is concerned are those associated with the European Union's (EU's) human mobility regime. Two broad EU norms are identifiable in respect of this regime. The first draws from economic liberalism and asserts that the removal of national barriers to the movement of people within an economically integrated region will allow for the free flow of labour, assisting with regional economic growth. The second draws from Europe's social democratic tradition, and emphasises the need to protect the social and political rights of citizenship, even as processes of regional integration proceed. Dynamic interaction of these norms has created a regime of regional mobility in which the 'right' to freedom of movement for nationals of EU Member States has been matched (if imperfectly) with legislation that allows mobile EU citizens to access at least some of the social and political rights of citizenship when resident in a Member State of which they are not a national. This chapter considers variables that affect whether the EU's model of human mobility might be successfully exported to other regions undergoing market integration. It does so by looking to the case of human mobility within the free travel area of New Zealand and Australia, here referred to as the trans-Tasman region[1] or Australasia.

---

[1] Without entering the vexed debates about what constitutes a 'region', I am here using the term 'trans-Tasman region' to refer to the combined territorial areas of Australia and New Zealand, sep-

---

The author gratefully acknowledges support for this project from the Knowledge and Expertise Exchange Europe New Zealand (KEEENZ) programme.

K. McMillan (✉)
School of History, Philosophy, Political Science & International Relations,
Victoria University of Wellington, Wellington, New Zealand
e-mail: kate.mcmillan@vuw.ac.nz

© Springer International Publishing Switzerland 2015
A. Björkdahl et al. (eds.), *Importing EU Norms,* United Nations University Series on Regionalism 8, DOI 10.1007/978-3-319-13740-7_7

97

Australasia's geographical distance and political independence from the EU makes it a valuable case study to include in a volume exploring questions of EU norm diffusion. The growing literature on the EU as an exporter of norms has tended to focus on the diffusion of norms into contexts where explicit or potential benefits accrue to the EU from such diffusion (Börzel and Risser 2009; Schimmelfennig 2012; Baracani 2009). Less attention has been paid to the EU's capacity to export norms into contexts where neither the EU nor the potential 'norm importer' stands to make gains from the other as a result of norm adoption. Such cases are, however, instructive for what they say about the persuasiveness of EU norms in contexts free of instrumental evaluations, and can help us understand the conditions under which learning or 'unilateral emulation' (Börzel and Risser 2009; Schimmelfennig 2012) might occur. They are helpful, in other words, in evaluating the extent to which the EU is a normative power (Manners 2002) capable of leading by example as well as through incentives and coercion.

The EU is not actively engaged in promoting its model of human mobility into Australasia and neither the EU nor Australia and New Zealand have much reason to expect benefits from the other as a result of an Australasian emulation of that model. Any norm adoption by Australia and New Zealand may thus be assumed to stem from either a unilateral assessment by Australasian policy makers that the EU model is likely to 'produce more efficient and effective policy outcomes than the alternatives' (Marsh and Sharman 2009) or an acceptance of the EU's 'normative', or value-based vision of human mobility, or both.

We might also expect a better 'fit' between EU norms and domestic trans-Tasman norms than in other regions, and thus, potentially, less resistance (Acharya 2004) to the transfer of norms from the EU to the TTR. Australia and New Zealand are long-standing democracies, with legal and political systems based on liberal democratic values and European traditions. Further, since the early 1980s the TTR has been engaged in a process of regional economic integration that shares much in common with economic integration in Europe (Leslie and Elijah 2012a). This process has extended deep 'behind the border' to an extent not seen outside of Europe. The TTR and the EU thus share basic values and a commitment to sustained economic integration. The TTR's adoption or rejection of the EU human mobility model can tell us more about the genuine persuasiveness of that model than is possible from cases where greater levels of friction might provide other explanations for rejection or adaptation.

The chapter finds evidence that Australasian policy-makers have, indeed, borrowed from the EU's casting of human mobility as central to the project of regional market integration. However, rather than adopting the EU model, trans-Tasman pol-

---

arated by the Tasman Sea. Trans-Tasman is used inter-changeably with 'Australasian'. The use of both terms reflects common usage but also the lack of academic consensus on the appropriate term to refer to the combined territories of Australia and New Zealand. This lack of consensus itself says something about the under-theorisation of the region. The term 'Antipodean' is not employed here because of the Euro-centric geographic relativism on which it relies.

icy makers have, since the 1980s, adapted a pre-existing trans-Tasman free travel arrangement to fit with the project of integrating the Australian and New Zealand economies, using a markedly different set of policies and institutions to those deployed in the EU. Moreover, the idea that a regime of regional free movement of people ought to protect the equality and democratic rights of those who move has been of decreasing significance in the trans-Tasman context.

We should not, perhaps, be surprised that Australasia and the EU differ so significantly in their free movement policies—in fact, in no two regions practicing a form of human mobility are the arrangements facilitating free movement identical (see IOM 2010). An examination of those differences and their causes, however, is valuable in helping us identify the conditions under which the EU's model, and its underlying norms, may prove influential—or otherwise—in other contexts.

Variations in human mobility regimes may be conceptualised along two primary axes: the extent to which barriers to individuals wishing to cross national borders are lowered; and the extent to which national welfare and labour and other policies are coordinated among Member States to ensure that regional migrants can access the social and political rights of citizenship when resident in a Member Country of which they are not a national. The first, which in the European context Scharpf has referred to as 'negative integration' (1996), is driven in most instances by the logic of liberal economics, which sees the free movement of the factors of production, including labour, as beneficial to regional economic growth. By contrast 'positive integration' attempts to coordinate national policies within an economically integrated region in order to 'shape the market conditions under which markets operate' (ibid., p. 15). Coordination of welfare policies is an example of such positive integration. In comparing human mobility regimes in the EU with those in the trans-Tasman, we find that while both regimes score highly in terms of negative integration, the EU has proceeded much more with positive integration of national welfare policies than has the trans-Tasman region.

Explanations for international variation along these two axes are many and various (IOM 2010; Strutt et al. 2008), and include institutional, historical, economic and geographical factors too diverse to cover in their entirety here. The task of this chapter is more modest: it seeks to examine the influence of four variables on trans-Tasman decisions about (a) the use of passport controls, and (b) access to social benefits for those who exercise freedom of movement across the Tasman.

The first significant factor identified below as affecting trans-Tasman mobility policies is the growing economic *asymmetry* between Australia and New Zealand. Higher levels of economic growth and significantly higher wages in Australia have led to an unbalanced flow of migrants across the Tasman since the late 1960s, with around ten times as many New Zealanders leaving for Australia as those coming in the opposite direction in recent years (Australia and New Zealand Productivity Commissions 2012). Power asymmetries also affect New Zealand's calculations about the loss of sovereignty likely to be consequent upon any political union with its much bigger partner across the Tasman.

Second, *geography* in the form of a sea border between New Zealand and Australia is found to have played an important role in trans-Tasman policy-makers' calculations about visa and passport-free travel between the two countries. The third and fourth variables discussed below are those of *timing*, argued to influence the norms underlying human mobility regimes, and the *institutionalisation* of those regimes and the norms underlying them.

In the next section the chapter examines how each of these variables helps us to understand differences between the human mobility regimes in the EU and in the trans-Tasman region, as well as to identify the influence of the EU's model of mobility on trans-Tasman decision-makers. Two case studies illustrate when and how trans-Tasman policy makers have adopted, adapted and rejected EU norms of freedom of movement.

7.2   Border Controls and the Free Movement of People in the Trans-Tasman Region and the EU Compared

At the heart of any human mobility arrangement are policies designed to reduce the barriers to the movement of people across territorial borders between Member States. In this section I examine the case of one specific type of policy designed to reduce such barriers: that of the removal of border checks for those travelling within an economically integrated region, as implemented within the EU's Schengen region. In tracing the process by which Australia and New Zealand created border control policies, I identify how trans-Tasman policy makers *adopted* the EU's language of human mobility in the late 1990s, but both *adapted* and *rejected* Schengen-style policies in favour of policies considered to better meet local needs and conditions.

Since 1995 internal border controls have been removed for all individuals travelling between France, Germany, the Netherlands, Belgium and Luxemburg under the terms of the Schengen Agreement of 1985. Although the Schengen Agreement originally existed independently of the EU, in 1997 it was incorporated into European law, and now applies to all EU members except England and Ireland (which have opted out of the rules regarding border checks) and Croatia, Cyprus, Bulgaria and Romania (as they have not yet met the criteria for implementing the Schengen *acquis*). Non-EU members Iceland, Norway, Switzerland and Liechtenstein are also members of the Schengen zone.

The removal of passport checks at national borders within the Schengen region is seen by the European Commission (EC) as removing a crucial obstacle to the EU goal of human mobility, and 'guaranteeing' to EU nationals their 'fundamental right' to free movement (European Commission 2014, online). Provisions exist for the re-introduction of national border controls in the face of an exceptional threat to public safety or internal security, but since 2013 the Commission has had competency for deciding when and where the reintroduction of border controls is appropriate

(European Commission 2013b). In the EU case, then, the removal of border controls is seen as furthering the goal of freedom of movement, and supranational governance of Member States' border controls as helpful in maintaining that freedom.

Australia and New Zealand have chosen a different set of rules to further trans-Tasman freedom of movement, even after they began to pursue an EU-style single market. Indeed, for Australia and New Zealand passport requirements were introduced in order to preserve the freedom of movement agreement, which was otherwise threatened by divergent immigrant policies. Under the terms of the 1973 the Trans-Tasman Travel Arrangement (TTTA) visa- and passport-free travel was permitted for citizens of Australia and New Zealand (and for citizens of other Commonwealth countries who had resident status in either Australia or New Zealand) when travelling to each other's country, along with the right to live and work there indefinitely. Australian concerns about New Zealand acting as a 'back door' for drug traffickers, illegal migrants and terrorists (Hoadley 2002; McPhee 1981; McMillan 1989), however, led Australia to exert pressure on New Zealand to harmonise its external entry requirements with Australia's. New Zealand twice rejected such proposals (McMillan 1989). In the absence of a harmonised immigration policy, travel arrangements between the two countries became more restrictive, with Australia introducing passport requirements for all trans-Tasman travel in 1981, and New Zealand reciprocating in 1987.

What explains New Zealand's rejection of Australia's proposal to harmonise their immigration policies, a rejection that seems to have been central to Australia's introduction of passport controls for travellers entering Australia from New Zealand in 1981? One factor, undoubtedly, was the already significant *power asymmetry* between the two countries, which lead New Zealand to assume that 'harmonisation', would, inevitably, require New Zealand to change its immigration policies in line with Australia's. McMillan (ibid.) argues that New Zealand was, at the time, particularly concerned about losing the tourism and diplomatic advantages they saw resulting from the visa-free travel it offered to a number of countries. Australia objected to these visa-free relationships on the grounds that they opened a 'back door' to Australia for migrants from countries with which Australia did not have a visa-free arrangement.

In 1981, of course, the Schengen Agreement had not been signed, and the introduction of passport requirements for free travel between New Zealand and Australia actually brought the trans-Tasman in line with the arrangements then in place in the European Community. Nor had New Zealand and Australia themselves embarked on the project of market integration that began in 1983 with the signing of Australia New Zealand Closer Economic Relations Trade Agreement (ANZCERTA), although an earlier free trade agreement, the New Zealand Australia Free Trade Agreement (NAFTA) had made some progress in reducing tariffs between the two countries.

In 2005, however, a new agenda for market integration between Australia and New Zealand was proposed, in the form of a Trans-Tasman Single Economic Market (TTSEM), strongly influenced as Leslie and Elijah outline (2012a) by the goals and vision of a Single European Market (SEM). Debate about the re-introduction of passport-free trans-Tasman travel was stimulated in 2009 with the announcement by the New Zealand Prime Minister John Key and then Australian Prime Minister Kevin Rudd of a joint plan to 'streamline' travel between the two countries. The broader political strategy to which the Prime Ministers said they were committed was to 'give new intensity and a renewed focus to delivering the practical benefits and outcomes from the Single Economic Market' (Rudd and Key 2009, p. 1).

Following the Prime Ministers' 2009 announcement the consultancy firm Capgemini was employed by Australian and New Zealand officials to identify ways in which the Prime Ministers' vision for facilitated trans-Tasman travel could be put into practice. Capgemini came up with various scenarios, including the creation of a 'common border' between Australia and New Zealand. Under this scenario all flights between the two countries would arrive and depart at domestic terminals, giving passengers a 'domestic-like' experience and negating the need for passport checks on passengers travelling on these flights. This scenario most closely approximated that within the Schengen zone. It was strongly supported by the airline industry, which had long been pressuring the two governments to free up travel between the two countries, including lobbying for passport-free travel (Korporaal 2010). In 2010 the airline Jetstar had commissioned a report that argued removing border controls between the two countries would reduce airfares by $ A76 ($ NZ94.7), increase passenger numbers by 13 % and add $ A280 million to Australia's GDP (NZPA 2010).

In what might be seen as a rhetorical *adoption* of the EU norm of a common border, the trans-Tasman response to the Capgemini Report was to identify a common border as an 'aspirational goal for both countries' (Australian Customs and Border Security 2011, p. 10). In practical terms, however, Australia and New Zealand agreed in 2010 to *reject* a Schengen-style removal of border controls. Instead, they opted to retain the practice of trans-Tasman flights departing and arriving at international terminals and advocated greater reliance on pre-clearance procedures in order to speed up the processing of travellers.

Here we see *geography*, and specifically the presence of sea borders, as playing a significant role in trans-Tasman policy-makers' rejection of EU practice. Their view was that abandoning passport checks for intra-regional movement did not offer the same advantages to trans-Tasman travellers, businesses or governments that it offered their equivalents in the continental European context. Virtually all travel between the two island nations occurs by aeroplane (the shortest travel time by air between them is over 3 hours); quite different to the experience of travelling across the European continent by road or rail. Contemporary airline travel, whether domestic or international, commonly requires passenger and luggage check-in, as well as security scans, particularly in the post-9/11 security environment. Even without passport controls it is, therefore, impossible in the trans-Tasman context to replicate the seamless border crossings possible in the European continent. Trans-Tasman border agencies questioned whether any reduction in passenger transit time achieved by removing passport controls would compensate for the loss of information regarding who is moving across the national borders (Davison 2012).

Sea borders were also a central consideration in relation to bio-security checks, identified as crucial to protecting both the natural environment and the primary industries of New Zealand and Australia. Sea borders and geographical isolation have allowed for the evolution of unique indigenous flora and fauna in both countries, which, like their agricultural industries, are highly vulnerable to imported bio-pests. Given this, officials argued that risk profiling strategies designed to speed up the movement of goods and the people who carry them across the trans-Tasman borders were preferable to the removal of customs and immigration checks.

The claim that sea borders played a significant role in the 2010 decision to retain passport controls for trans-Tasman travel is given some support by the example of the United Kingdom and Ireland, which like New Zealand and Australia, are separated by a sea border from other member states. Their decision to remain outside of Schengen undoubtedly gave heft to trans-Tasman policymakers' suspicion that the removal of borders within the Schengen region was, at least in part, formalising *de facto* practice for continental countries already struggling to maintain land borders.

Trans-Tasman border agencies (Customs, Immigration and the Ministry of Agriculture and Fisheries) did, however, aspire to simulate some of the 'borderless experience' enjoyed by those moving within the Schengen region whilst retaining sovereign control of the borders. In December 2009, New Zealand introduced electronic self-processing kiosks at major New Zealand airports for trans-Tasman travel. 'Smartgate', as the system was called, used electronic information from biometric e-passports, and digital facial recognition technology to allow New Zealand and Australian e-passport holders to process themselves through immigration kiosks at the airport, bypassing the need for a customs officer to perform identity checks. By 2013 Smartgate kiosks were available in all major airports in Australia for eligible passenger arrivals, and in all major New Zealand airports for eligible passengers at departures and arrivals (New Zealand Customs Service 2013).[2] In this way they *adapted* the EU norm of 'borderless' travel to suit local circumstances.

A comparison of the role border controls play in EU and trans-Tasman mobility regimes needs, however, to also consider what has been presented by the EC as the *quid pro quo* of passport-free travel in the EU: the creation of a common external EU border. According to the EC,

> The removal of internal borders means that the Schengen countries need to cooperate with each other to maintain a high level of security within the Schengen area. It also means that they need to share responsibility for and cooperate in managing their common external borders. (Europa 2013b)

A range of policies now exist to coordinate management of this border, including the application of a common set of rules for EU Member States carrying out external border checks; a common visa policy for third country nationals entering the Schengen area for a stay of up to three months; the EU Schengen Information

---

[2] Significantly, however, procurement decisions relating to Smartgate were taken at a national level, not inter-governmental level, albeit with high-level official discussion. In late 2013 it was not clear whether Australia would adopt the Smartgate system for its departures. The system, in other words, fell short of a coordinated trans-Tasman approach to passenger processing.

System II, which allows Member States to share information about things such as missing persons, and stolen cars and firearms; and the Visa Information System, which allows them to share information on applicants for a Schengen Visa. Member States share the costs of controlling the external borders through the External Borders Fund, while the European Agency for the Management of Operational Cooperation at the External Borders of the Member States of the EU (Frontex) facilitates common management of that border (Europa 2013a). Europol (the European Police Office) exists to assist Member States fight intra-regional crime.

Schengen has also given Member States a vested interest in each other's immigration and asylum policies. While Member States retain responsibility for setting their immigration entry criteria and determining the number of migrants they will accept, the EU has created a common legal framework for migration policies across Europe. For certain categories of migrants—students, highly qualified workers and researchers—common entry requirements have been established, and their rights 'homogenised' across the Union (Europa 2013b). Highly skilled and qualified migrants can apply for an EU Blue Card, eligibility criteria for which have also been standardised across the Union.

Progress has been slower in relation to the development of a Common European Asylum System (CEAS) to which the EU is committed (Europa (2013b); European Council on Refugees and Exiles 2013; European Commission 2013a; Article 78 Treaty on the Functioning of the EU). Large asylum flows at the end of the Cold War pushed the issue up the EU agenda in the early 1990s, amid concerns that the financial, administrative and social burdens associated with hearing asylum claims were unevenly distributed throughout the Union. Concerns were also expressed by Member States that the conditions experienced by asylum seekers varied considerably around the Union, as did an asylum seeker's chance of having her/his claim recognised. The Common European Asylum System aims to standardise the reception and treatment of asylum seekers, the procedures for granting or denying asylum, and the processes for determining which country is responsible for hearing the claims of any particular asylum seeker (Article 78 (1–2) of the Consolidated Treaty on the Functioning of the EU 2013).

Each of the 'common EU border' policies discussed above works to articulate a vision of the EU as a region in which freedom, experienced in part through regional mobility, is only made 'secure' through the imposition of controls on what is now conceptualised as a common external border. Australasia has not adopted this vision as appropriate for its own region, but Australia's 1981 request for a harmonisation of Australian and New Zealand immigration policies demonstrated a similar logic. In 2014, the absence of that common border continues to make the prospect of the re-introduction of passport-free travel remote. And, as was the case in 1981, *power asymmetries* between New Zealand and Australia make that an unattractive option for the smaller party. In 2014 New Zealand will, undoubtedly, still regard proposals for a common border as an exertion by Australia of the demand that New Zealand alter those aspects of its immigration policy that irritate Australia. These aspects include New Zealand's visa-free relationship with 58 countries, which Australia continues to view as providing a 'back door' into Australia; policies that provide annual quotas for Pacific migration each year; and skilled and business stream migration policies that, while broadly similar to Australia's, are more lenient in some respects.

Australia and New Zealand also have very different experiences with asylum-seekers. Geographical proximity to Asia has seen Australia become a destination for asylum-seekers able and willing to make the frequently perilous journey by sea from the Indonesian coastline. New Zealand, by contrast, is yet to receive a boat carrying asylum seekers, although there have been repeated media reports that such an arrival is imminent (Fairfax 2013; Ansley 2013). Nonetheless, in 2013 the National Government in New Zealand introduced changes to the New Zealand Immigration Act that allowed for the detention of asylum seekers who form part of a 'mass arrival' by sea, bringing New Zealand's immigration laws closer to those of Australia's. In January 2013, the New Zealand Prime Minister John Key also agreed to take 150 refugees from Australia per year, saying the asylum issue was 'an Australasian and a regional' one that required 'strong cooperation' between the two countries, and a 'regional solution' (Watkins 2013b; Nicholson 2013). While this suggests that in respect of asylum policy, at least, Australia and New Zealand are moving closer towards conceptualising a common approach to dealing with external migrants, it does not yet look like an EU-style common border.

This section has illustrated that Australia and New Zealand have, variously, *adopted*, *adapted* and *rejected* EU free movement policies with respect to the removal of border controls for trans-Tasman travellers. Geography, and asymmetrical power relations and migration patterns were identified as important variables in determining when and how Australia and New Zealand imported EU norms associated with removing border controls.

The next section turns to a study of the EU's practice of social security coordination, and examines the variables that have affected Australasian policy-makers growing *rejection* of the EU norm of social democracy in relation to intra-regionally mobile citizens.

7.3 Social Security Coordination in the Trans-Tasman and the EU Compared

This section compares the portability of social benefits for intra-regional mobile citizens in the EU and the trans-Tasman region. One of the main findings is that although historically Australia and New Zealand extended welfare benefits to each other's citizens on an equal basis with their own nationals, this non-discriminatory treatment has been eroded since the 1980s. Moreover, the processes of market integration, which have led to pressure for the coordination of social security policies in the EU context, have in the trans-Tasman case led to pressure for their divergence. *Timing, institutions* and *asymmetry* are identified as significant variables affecting different outcomes in the two contexts.

Under the EU's Social Security Coordination system EU citizens who are resident in an EU Member State of which they are not a national have the same legal rights and obligations with respect to social security benefits as nationals of that state (European Commission 2013a). This includes their health, maternity, unemployment, pension and parental benefits. Nationals of one EU state, who are entitled to a benefit from that state, may for a period of time receive that benefit when living in another EU state (ibid.). Member States are still responsible for determining their own social security rules, but under the modernised Regulations of 2010 (883/2004 and 907/2009) those rules apply equally to EU nationals resident in that state (ibid.).

Justifications for the provision of social security to mobile EU citizens can be traced back to the Treaty of Paris in 1951. Article 69.4 of that Treaty identified the non-portability of social security arrangements as a potential barrier to the free movement of workers, and something that ought, therefore, be avoided (Treaty of Paris 1951). Over time, and particularly as a result of rulings by the European Court of Justice (ECJ), arguments that draw from a social democratic perspective have provided an alternative set of justifications for the provision of behind-the-border policies (Baldoni 2003; Cornelissen 2009; Hansen and Hager 2012; McMillan 2014). *Timing* and *institutions* have been significant in this: the EU continues to be influenced by the post-war social democratic consensus in ascendancy at the time its foundational documents were drafted. Those documents, such as the 1951 Treaty of Paris and the 1957 Treaty of Rome, inextricably bound the project of human mobility with that of European economic integration, and thus with the supranational institutions and rules governing European integration. Social democratic values embedded in such foundational documents continue to exert influence.

Historically, Australia and New Zealand also treated each other's citizens as equals with respect to the provision of social security rights—rights that were generous by international standards. *Asymmetrical* migration patterns, however, combined with a lack of *institutional* protection of mobile citizens' rights, have seen Australia progressively withdraw New Zealanders' access to a range of welfare benefits in Australia since 1986 (Australia and New Zealand Productivity Commissions 2012). As New Zealand has not imposed similar restrictions on Australians resident in New Zealand, a stratification of access to social benefits has emerged among those who move within the trans-Tasman region.

Australian citizens and permanent residents living in New Zealand have access to all the income support benefits available to nationals after a two-year waiting period. Those intending to live in New Zealand for two or more years are also able to access public health care and education and disability support immediately on arrival and are eligible for the Working for Families tax credit system after one year's residence. Under the cost-sharing Social Security Agreement of 2001 they are eligible for New Zealand superannuation, Veteran Pension and Invalid Pension. New Zealand nationals resident in Australia are similarly able to access public health and education services, and child-related tax benefits there. After a two-year period seniors are eligible for a Commonwealth Seniors Card and Health Care Card. And, under the cost-sharing agreement, New Zealanders are also eligible for the Australian Old Age Pension, Disability Support and Carers payment (Productivity Commissions 2012).

In 2001, however, Australia removed access for Australian-resident New Zealanders arriving under the TTTA to a number of federally-administered social security benefits. New Zealanders arriving after 26 February 2001 were no longer eligible for the unemployment benefit (although they could apply for a one-off six month payment after ten years' continuous residency), sickness benefit, youth allowance, sole parent benefit, National Disability Insurance payments (although they were required to pay the levy) or student loans. In some cases, Australian State governments matched the Federal Government's restrictions with their own in relation to State-provided services. These changes to social security assistance were effected via changes to Australian domestic legislation. Of particular significance were changes to the *Social Security Act 1991*, amended to exclude New Zealanders who arrived under the auspices of the TTTA after 26 February 2001 from the definition of Australian Permanent Resident, and thus from eligibility for a range of social security benefits available to permanent residents.

Australia's decision to implement these changes arose from a long-standing irritation in the relationship over trans-Tasman migration (Goff 2001), at the heart of which were claims that asymmetrical immigration flows across the Tasman imposed an unsustainable and inequitable cost on the Australian welfare system. New Zealand disputed the Australian costings, and pointed out, moreover, that their figures did not take account of the tax revenue provided by New Zealand workers in Australia. Nor did the figures take into account the fact that the workers had been trained in New Zealand, at the expense of the New Zealand taxpayer. Other sources of concern from the Australian side included the increasing number of non-New Zealand-born New Zealand citizens who were moving to Australia (28 % of all New Zealanders moving in 2000 were non-NZ-born), and the skill and age profile of New Zealand migrants compared with non-New Zealand migrants (Australian Department of Family and Community Services and the New Zealand Ministry of Social Policy 2000).

Determined to find a solution to these long-standing irritations, Australia and New Zealand began to draft a new Social Security Agreement that would provide some benefits on a cost-sharing basis, whilst other benefits would be provided at the discretion of each government. Australia indicated that they intended to amend their domestic legislation to impose new restrictions on Australian-resident New Zealanders' access to a range of welfare benefits. Officials from the New Zealand Ministry of Social Policy highlighted for their Minister the potential disadvantage Australian-resident New Zealanders would face if Australia implemented this policy, saying:

> There will be a very sharp rise in the number of economically distressed New Zealanders living in Australia. Some of those who manage to struggle through and remain in Australia will tend to drift down into an underclass status. This problem will be exacerbated by the fact that they will not be entitled to some other forms of social assistance for which permanent residency or beneficiary status are entry gates. (Ministry of Social Policy 2000)

Trans-Tasman policy makers were also made aware that the new Social Security Agreement, and Australia's associated changes to their domestic legislation, went against the European trend of opening up welfare availability for mobile EU nationals. Officials advised that:

The Australian measures restricting social security access represent a move in the opposite direction from the pattern seen in other developed countries that have formed common labour markets. For example, in the European Community the trend has been to open up labour market benefit rights to workers from other Community countries. The 3rd and 4th regulations made by the original EEC were on social security for migrant workers, a demonstration of the fact that the Community founders considered adequate social protection a prerequisite to the development of a common labour market. Social Security protection for legal migrant workers in the EC is now largely automatic, since most such benefits are funded by social insurance contributions linked to employment. The New Zealand and Australian pattern of tax-funded benefits gives no such protection to employees, and, in the absence of specific social security agreements, leaves workers vulnerable to changes in the social security policies of the host government. (ibid.)

New Zealand Ministry of Foreign Affairs officials, however, were concerned that failure to address Australian concerns would threaten both the TTTA and the wider trans-Tasman project of economic integration, broadly labelled Closer Economic Relations (CER):

In our view, NZ should take great care to avoid any direct or indirect diminution of this historic cornerstone of the bilateral relationship. Another potential consequence of failure to resolve the Social Security issue is the sapping of Australia's political commitment to further development of CER. (Heenan 2000).

The resulting Social Security Agreement represented a *rejection* of the EU practice of social security coordination, and undermined the social democratic norms that had previously guided both EU and trans-Tasman domestic welfare policies. It illustrated the difficulty Australia and New Zealand had in protecting the social rights across the TTSEM in the context of asymmetry in migration patterns and power relations.

Timing and *institutions* also help explain why the trans-Tasman mobility regime proved so susceptible to the pressures of asymmetry. Free movement across the Tasman Sea emerged during nineteenth century under British colonial rule, and was characterised by a laissez-faire liberalism (except, from the late nineteenth century, in relation to 'race aliens') resulting from an absence of strongly delineated national identities during that early colonial period. Even when the historical practice of free movement was formalised with the TTTA in 1973, the arrangement did not take the form of a binding bilateral treaty. Rather, it was and remains, simply, a 'series of immigration procedures applied by each country and underpinned by joint political support' (New Zealand Ministry of Foreign Affairs and Trade 2013). Not only is the TTTA entirely subject to inter-governmental decision-making, it remains institutionally quite independent both from the various social security agreements developed to support those who exercise mobility under its auspices, and from the ANZCERTA of 1983. This institutional independence from the social security measures that buttress it, and the highly neo-liberal nature of the TTSEM process with which it became associated, provided little protection for social democratic norms in its application.

By 2013 media attention in New Zealand and Australia began to focus on the parlous situation of New Zealanders who had fallen on hard times in Australia as a result of their inability to access full welfare assistance (e.g. Heather 2012a, b;

Kilgalen 2013) While there was some popular sentiment that people struggling in Australia should just go home (Dominion Post 2013), others began to query whether Australia's social security rules in relation to New Zealanders were appropriate. Aspirations for a trans-Tasman single economic market, and the operation of a highly integrated trans-Tasman labour market were identified as reasons why New Zealanders ought to receive less discriminatory treatment (OzKiwi 2013; Australia and New Zealand Productivity Commissions 2012; McMillan 2014).

In their joint report on how to strengthen trans-Tasman relations, commissioned by both governments, the Productivity Commissions of New Zealand and Australia addressed social security issues between the two countries in the context of the TTSEM goal (Australian and New Zealand Productivity Commissions 2012, pp. 45–46). Drawing directly on the principles underlying the EU system of social security coordination the Productivity Commissions suggested that 'consideration could usefully be given to developing similar principles under the CER agreement', among them 'equal treatment (subject to relevant waiting periods or other initial conditions, individuals should have the same rights and obligations as citizens or permanent residents); and portability' (Australian and New Zealand Productivity Commissions 2012, p. 45).

Implementation of an equal treatment principle in the trans-Tasman region would represent a very significant step towards a more coordinated trans-Tasman system of social security. Obstacles to its implementation remain, however, high. Pre-eminent among those obstacles is, again, the need for a common external border. In the Productivity Commissions' view:

> In theory, the principle of equal treatment could only be implemented if there were effectively full alignment of the two countries' migration and citizenship programs with respect to nationals from third countries. (Australia and New Zealand Productivity Commissions 2012, p. 47)

As of October 2013 the governments of New Zealand and Australia had yet to respond to the Productivity Commissions' Report, but in early October 2013, newly-elected Australian Prime Minister Tony Abbott ruled out any changes to Australia's treatment of New Zealanders in Australia (Watkins 2013), saying that New Zealanders 'had better access to the country [Australia] than any other citizens, and that's as it should be' (ibid.). His was an endorsement of the emerging trans-Tasman model of human mobility—one that significantly lowered barriers to cross-national human mobility, but which saw limited scope for national governments to coordinate their policies to ensure the social rights of intra-regionally mobile citizens.

7.4 Conclusion

This chapter has asked when and how Australia and New Zealand have adopted, adapted, resisted or rejected EU norms as expressed in human mobility regime. Two policy case studies have been presented: the removal of border controls within the Schengen region and the creation of a system of social security coordination for mobile EU citizens. It has found that, in the broadest and perhaps most important sense, the two countries have *adopted* the EU's conception of free movement of people across national borders as beneficial and indeed central to the process of market integration. The long-standing practice of Australasian free movement has been rebranded in line with this liberal, market-making norm, with 'people movement' now explicitly identified as one of the 'four freedoms' of a trans-Tasman Single Economic Market (Australian and New Zealand Productivity Commissions 2012).

Even with the inscription of this liberal norm onto pre-existing practices of trans-Tasman mobility, however, Australia and New Zealand have largely *rejected* the policies through which the EU has achieved its model of human mobility. In respect of border controls, Australasian policy-makers have assessed the benefits of passport controls as outweighing the possible benefits of a Schengen-style removal of those controls. Nonetheless, the removal of barriers to the free movement of people has been described by both countries as desirable, indicating, at minimum, an evaluation by policy makers that border-free travel is normatively appropriate for regions with integrated markets. Local conditions, however, have been deemed to be sufficiently different to those in the EU to render the removal of border controls inappropriate in the trans-Tasman context.

In respect of developing an EU-style system of portable social rights across a trans-Tasman SEM, Australasian policy makers have similarly *rejected* an EU model of social security coordination. Historical practices of mutual assistance and equal treatment were undermined by the growth of highly asymmetrical immigration flows from New Zealand to Australia. Under these conditions, and in the absence of supranational law or institutions mandated to protect the equal rights of regionally mobile citizens, Australia's interests, as the most powerful player in the relationship, have come to dominate decision-making in this policy area. Australia's progressive removal of New Zealanders' access to a range of social benefits in Australia has created a regime of mobility in the trans-Tasman increasingly characterised by inequality among and disadvantage for those who exercise trans-Tasman mobility.

These findings have implications for the claim that the EU is a normative power, whose model of human mobility is both appropriate for and exportable to other regions undergoing market integration. They suggest that the exportability of the EU's model of human mobility to other integrating regions is affected by variables such as the *symmetry or asymmetry* of migration flows among or between the member states, with asymmetrical flows making EU-style positive integration more difficult and less likely. *Geography*, particularly the presence of sea borders, may also play an important role in member states' decisions about whether to adopt Schengen-style border policies. *Timing* is also found to be an important variable, as the social and political values of the period during which foundational policies and norms are developed within any specific region will influence whether they are compatible with EU norms of regional mobility. How and when those policies are *institutionalised* will similarly affect compatibility with EU norms, and thus the persuasiveness of those norms.

References

Acharya, A. (2004). How ideas spread: Whose norms matter? Norm localization and institutional change in Asian regionalism. *International Organization, 58*(2), 239–275.

Ansley, G. (7 May 2013). Refugees were heading for New Zealand. *New Zealand Herald.* http://www.nzherald.co.nz/nz/news/article.cfm?c_id=1&objectid=10881949. Accessed 21 Oct 2013.

Australian and New Zealand Productivity Commissions. (December 2012). Trans-Tasman joint study final report Supplementary paper D: People movement. http://transtasman-review.productivity.govt.nz/sites/default/files/13-trans-tasman-supplementaryd.pdf. Accessed 14 Oct 2013.

Australian Customs and Border Security. (2011). Capgemini paper. Streamlining trans-Tasman passenger travel terms of reference for scoping study (Draft).

Australian Department of Family and Community Services and the New Zealand Ministry of Social Policy. (July 2000). Report of the joint review of SS arrangements between Australia and New Zealand New Zealand archives. Reference Number: ABGX W5190 16127 Box 310.

Baldoni, E. (2003). The free movement of people in Europe: A legal historical overview. Pioneur working paper no. 2. http://www.aip.pt/irj/go/km/docs/aip/documentos/estudos%20publicacoes/centro%20documentacao/Capital%20Humano/I.Livre_Circulacao_Trabalhadores/A3.Projecto_Pioneur/Free_Movement.pdf. Accessed 26 April 2013.

Baracani, E. (2009). The European neighbourhood policy and political conditionality: Double standard in EU democracy promotion? The external dimension of EU justice and home affairs: Governance, neighbours, security. In T. Balzaq (Ed.), *Palgrave studies in European Union politics* (pp. 133–153). Basingstoke: Palgrave Macmillan.

Börzel, T., & Risser, T. A. (2009). The transformative power of Europe. The European Union and the diffusion of ideas. KFG working paper. 1. http://userpage.fu-berlin.de/kfgeu/kfgwp/wpseries/WorkingPaperKFG_1.pdf. Accessed 2 June 2013.

Cornelissen, R. (2009). 50 years of European social security coordination. *European Journal of Social Security, 11*(1–2), 9–45.

Davison, I. (25 April 2012). Passport-free 'Anzac expressway' ditched by NZ. *New Zealand Herald.* http://www.nzherald.co.nz/nz/news/article.cfm?c_id=1&objectid=10801244. Accessed 12 Sept 2013.

Dominion Post. (4 October 2013). Editorial: Unlived Kiwis should come back. http://www.stuff.co.nz/dominion-post/comment/editorials/9241297/Editorial-Unloved-Kiwis-should-come-back. Accessed 20 Oct 2013.

Europa. (2013a). Free movement of persons, asylum and immigration. http://europa.eu/legislation_summaries/justice_freedom_security/free_movement_of_persons_asylum_immigration/. Accessed 1 July 2013.

Europa. (2013b). The European Union explained. Building an open and safe Europe: Migration and asylum. European Commission, Luxembourg. http://europa.eu/pol/justice/flipbook/migration/en/files/migration-and-asylum_en.pdf. Accessed 12 Oct 2013.

European Commission. (2013a). Home affairs: Common European asylum system. http://ec.europa.eu/dgs/home-affairs/what-we-do/policies/asylum/index_en.htm. Accessed 2 Oct 2013.

European Commission. (2013b). Press release. http://europa.eu/rapid/press-release_MEMO-13–536_en.htm. Accessed 10 Jan 2014.

European Commission. (2014). Home affairs. Schengen. http://ec.europa.eu/dgs/home-affairs/what-we-do/policies/borders-and-visas/schengen/. Accessed 11 Jan 2014.

European Council on Refugees and Exiles. (2013). History of CEAS. http://www.ecre.org/component/content/article/36-introduction/194-history-of-ceas.html. Accessed 25 Oct 2013.

European Union Directorate-General Justice Freedom and Security European Commission. (2013). Right of Union citizens and their family members to move and reside freely within the Union. How to get the best out of Directive 2004/38/EC. http://ec.europa.eu/justice/citizen/files/guide_2004_38_ec_en.pdf. Accessed 23 Sept 2013.

Fairfax. (4 April 2013). Asylum seekers headed for New Zealand. Stuff. http://www.stuff.co.nz/world/australia/8529602/Asylum-seekers-headed-for-New-Zealand. Accessed 20 Oct 2013.

Finnemore, M., & Sikkink, K. (1998). International norm dynamics and political change. *International Organization, 52*(4), 887–917.

Goff, P. (2001). The trans-Tasman relationship: A New Zealand perspective. *The Drawing Board: An Australian Review of Public Affairs, 2*(1), 1–9.

Hansen, P., & Hager, S. B. (Ed.). (2012). The politics of European citizens deepening contradictions in social rights & migration policy. New York: Berghan Books.

Heather, B. (6 October 2012a). Australia not so lucky for some Kiwis. *Dominion Post*, p. A 6.

Heather, B. (16 November 2012b). Anti-Kiwi law slated by Aussie Commission. Stuff. http://www.stuff.co.nz/national/politics/7957561/Anti-Kiwi-law-slated-by-Aussie-commission. Accessed 2 Nov 2013.

Heenan, P. (17 August 2000). Official advice to the Minister of Foreign Affairs and Trade. NZ Archives: File 2 (International Treaty- A NZ SSA, Advice. Reports File 2 ABGX W5190 16127 Box 310 Record number FD 8/4/3 Part 2).

Hoadley, S. (2002). Trans-Tasman migration: Issues and politics. In B. Catley (Ed.), *New Zealand-Australian relations: Moving together or drifting apart? Papers from the 36th Otago Foreign Policy School*. Wellington: Dark Horse Publishing.

International Organisation for Migration. (2010). *International dialogue on migration No. 13. The free movement of persons in regional integration processes*. Geneva: IOM.

Kilgalen, S. (2013). No benefits for Kiwis battling in Australia. Stuff. http://www.stuff.co.nz/national/8633665/No-benefits-for-battling-Kiwis-in-Australia. Accessed 3 Oct 2013.

Korporaal, G. (15 July 2010). Jetstar chief calls to drop passports for NZ. *The Australian*. http://www.theaustralian.com.au/business/jetstar-chief-calls-to-drop-passports-for-nz/story-e6frg-8zx-1225891816856. Accessed March 2011.

Leslie, J., & Elijah, A. (2012a). Does n=2?: Trans-Tasman economic integration as a comparator for the Single European Market. *Journal of Common Market Studies, 50*(6), 975–993.

Leslie, J., & Elijah, A. (2012b). Deep economic integration and political ambivalence: Popular constraints on elite driven integration between Australia and New Zealand. UACES Conference, Passau.

Manners, I. (2002). Normative power Europe. *Journal of Common Market Studies, 40*(2), 235–258.

Marsh, D., & Sharman, J. C. (2009). Policy diffusion and policy transfer. *Policy Studies, 30*(3), 269–288.

McMillan, N. (1989). Pressures for change to the trans-Tasman travel arrangement. Unpublished MA Thesis, University of Canterbury.

McMillan, K. (2014). Political and social rights for second country nationals: Freedom of movement and citizenship in Australasia. *Citizenship Studies, 18*(3-4), 349–364.

McPhee, I. (24 April 1981). News release by the Minister of Immigration. https://www.dfat.gov.au/geo/new_zealand/02ttta.pdf. Accessed 30 June 2011.

Ministry of Social Policy. (17 November 2000). Report to the Minister of social services and employment. New Zealand National Archives Reference Number: ABGX W5190 16127 Box 310. Record Number FD 8/4/3, Part 1.

New Zealand Customs Service. (2013). Smartgate. http://www.customs.govt.nz/features/smartgate/pages/default.aspx. Accessed 25 Oct 2013.

New Zealand Ministry of Foreign Affairs and Trade. (2013). Australia: The trans-Tasman travel arrangement. http://www.mfat.govt.nz/Foreign-Relations/Australia/0-trans-tasman-travel-arrangement.php. Accessed 6 Sept 2013.

Nicholson, B. (2013). New Zealand to take 150 asylum-seekers from Australia. *The Australian*. http://www.theaustralian.com.au/national-affairs/new-zealand-to-take-asylum-seekers-from-australia/story-fn59niix-1226574373242. Accessed 3 Nov 2013.

NZPA. (3 August 2010). Call for reduced Tasman immigration checks. http://tvnz.co.nz/travel-news/call-reduced-tasman-immigration-checks-3682326. Accessed 10 Oct 2010.

OzKiwi. (2013). Campaigning for fair treatment of New Zealanders in Australia. http://ozki-wi2001.org/. Accessed 6 Nov 2013.

Rudd, K., & Key, J. (20 August 2009). Joint statement of intent: Single economic market outcomes framework. http://www.med.govt.nz/upload/76796/soi.pdf. Accessed July 2010.

Scharpf, F. (1996). Negative and positive integration in the political economy of European welfare states. In G. Marks, F. Scharpf, P. Schmitter, & W. Streek, (Eds.), *Governance in the European Union* (pp. 15–39). Houndsmills: Macmillan.

Schimmelfennig, F. (2012). Europeanisation beyond Europe. *Living Reviews of European Governance, 7*(1), 1–24.

Strutt, A., Poot, J., & Dubbeldam, J. (2008). International trade negotiations and the trans-border movement of people: A review of the literature, report prepared for the NZ Department of Labour.

Watkins, T. (13 October 2013a). Aus PM rules out change to Kiwi citizenship status. Stuff. http://www.stuff.co.nz/national/politics/9235949/Aus-PM-rules-out-change-to-Kiwi-citizenship-status. Accessed 14 Oct 2013.

Watkins, T. (9 February 2013b). NZ-Australian asylum-seeker deal. Stuff. http://www.stuff.co.nz/national/politics/8282972/NZ-Aust-asylum-seekers-deal. Accessed 13 Oct 2013.

Kate McMillan is a Senior Lecturer in Politics at Victoria University of Wellington, New Zealand. Since 2010 she has been Co-Editor of *Political Science* (SAGE). In 2012 she was a visiting researcher at Lund University, Sweden, as part of the Knowledge and Expertise Exchange Europe New Zealand (KEEENZ) programme to compare freedom of movement arrangements in the European Union with those existing between New Zealand and Australia. She publishes in the fields of immigration and citizenship politics, and media politics.

Chapter 8
Exporting Hard Law Through Soft Norms: New Zealand's Reception of European Standards

W. John Hopkins and Henrietta S. McNeill

8.1 Introduction: Adoption, Adaptation and Legal Transplants

The adoption of legal norms from one legal system into another (or reception as it is called in Comparative Law) is not a new phenomenon, neither is the globalisation of legal systems nor its recognition in academic literature (Twinning 2000). However, the mass of such work has focussed on the creation of global legal norms through the traditional medium of international law. As a result, international treaties and, more recently, customary international law are seen as the major drivers of this global phenomenon (Shelton 2011). This work challenges this presumption.

Legal globalisation consists of more than the formal adoption of international legal norms into domestic legal orders. Although such a process is clearly part of the story, and an important one at that, it would misunderstand the nature of legal globalisation to focus only on this element. It is the premise of this work that such a narrow focus on formal legal mechanisms risks failing to truly understand the mechanisms that create global legal norms. This chapter examines one particular example of the wider 'softer' elements of the global law making process and more specifically the role that the European Union (EU) has played in influencing it.

Dr. Hopkins wishes to thank members of the International and Comparative Law Group at the University of Canterbury for their support in developing the theoretical framework for the chapter. The empirical element of this chapter is based upon work undertaken by Henrietta McNeill as part of a 2013 University of Canterbury Summer Scholar Project.

W. J. Hopkins (✉)
School of Law, University of Canterbury, Christchurch, New Zealand
e-mail: w.j.hopkins@canterbury.ac.nz

H. S. McNeill
National Centre for Research on Europe, University of Canterbury, Christchurch, New Zealand
e-mail: henrietta.mcneill@canterbury.ac.nz

© Springer International Publishing Switzerland 2015
A. Björkdahl et al. (eds.), *Importing EU Norms,* United Nations University Series on Regionalism 8, DOI 10.1007/978-3-319-13740-7_8

This chapter focuses on the adoption of non-compulsory standards as a method of exporting norms between, and across, jurisdictions. As recognised by global administrative law, the development of global standards has created a conduit for the development of global law, outside the formality of the international legal system (Davis et al. 2012). It is the view of the authors that the technical nature of many of these standards belies a deeper economic and political reality.

The importance of 'behind-the-border' standards and regulation has long been recognised as a barrier to cross-border trade. Standards provide a way to alleviate such issues but in doing so they raise questions about whose standards are being adopted. Such standards are rarely value neutral. They reflect the values of the systems in which they are created, whether intentionally or not. As a result they provide a mechanism for the extension of the values of that legal system as well as providing the potential for economic advantage. Where the legal system is perceived as 'compatible' with the receiving state's system or enjoys a high reputation, reception will be easier. These 'cultural filters' mean that not all third-party standards are received equally (See Manners 2002: 245 as well as Chaban et al. and Headley in this volume).

As the following examples show, such subtle mechanisms exist alongside, but are no less important than the traditional economic and political pressure that larger markets and influential jurisdictions may bring to bear upon smaller third party states. In the field of standard reception, 'culture' matters.

8.2   Standards, Soft Law and Hard Realities

Standards today apply to a wide range of products, processes and activities as diverse as food, health, business practices and technology. Defining what we mean by a legal standard can be difficult. The traditional starting point is that of the World Trade Organisation (WTO) Agreement on Technical Barriers to Trade which defines standards thus:

> [a] ... document approved by a recognised body, that provides, for common and repeated use, rule, guidelines or characteristics for products or related processes and production methods, with which compliance is not mandatory. It may also include or deal exclusively with terminology, symbols, packaging, marking or labelling requirements as they apply to a product, process or production method. (WTO 1994)

In this chapter we draw the net a little wider and adopt a more functional approach to the topic (Michaels 2006). In practice, international standards can arise from a variety of sources including the hard-law of individual states or trans-national jurisdictions. The important point for us is that such standards, whatever their specific origin, have no formal jurisdiction in third-party states outside the norm creator. It is this lack of formal authority that defines them as an informal 'standard' rather than hard-law norm of international or trans-national law.

The fact that a standard has 'soft law' status at the international level equally does not preclude their use as hard-law in third-party domestic jurisdictions. Standards may be adopted by third countries, through a variety of means, including formal legislative processes. They may equally be functionally implemented through more informal methods through adoption by state agencies or professional bodies through codes of practice or other 'soft law' methods. If such methods have the impact of creating rules within the legal system, they should be regarded as 'legal' according to the legal functionalist tradition (Llewelyn 1940). A regulatory standard is thus one that provides 'the ability of a jurisdiction to define and implement a set of market rules and to monitor firms' compliance with them' (Bach and Newman 2010). In this chapter we examine the impact of standards, whatever their specific status, which emanate from beyond the jurisdiction of the state but have functional legal status within it.

The specific case study itself looks at this phenomenon in the context of New Zealand's relationship with the EU's legal system. New Zealand has a long history of being a good 'international citizen' in this regard and the judiciary's openness towards international legal norms is at the higher end of the scale (Hopkins 2011a). The process by which New Zealand has adopted non-national norms has usually been seen as an extension of international law. However, as already mentioned, the reality is far more subtle and is as much about adoption and adaptation of overseas domestic or trans-national standards as it is about reception of truly international norms.

International standards are incorporated into the New Zealand legal system by a number of methods (see also Firth in this volume). The formal adoption of true Standards occurs under the Standards Act 1988. Through this framework, the New Zealand Standards Council can adopt or adapt standards from overseas, where it deems this appropriate. In addition, specific agencies and legislation can create standards in particular fields, either through explicit adoption or *de-facto* adaptation.

The primary standards examined in this survey (pharmaceuticals, cosmetics, toys and food standards) were chosen specifically as initial research had identified them as major areas in which international influences were prevalent. The aim was not to assess the overall impact of international standards on the New Zealand regulatory system but to recognise their importance within specific fields and examine how such extra-jurisdictional soft law (particularly that emanating from the EU) enters into a domestic regulatory framework.

This survey concentrates primarily upon the explicit incorporation of EU standards directly into the New Zealand legal system although some examples of informal and indirect influences (particularly through national influences upon international standards) are also examined. In the view of the authors, there are likely to be many more of these indirect examples, but the complexity of tracing their etymology has precluded further examination in this particular project. The primary focus of this work is on the broader question of how 'soft' law is transformed into functional 'hard' law in the New Zealand example.

Adoption and adaptation is not universal, and the severe sectoral variation in New Zealand raises questions about how and why adaptation and adoption occurs.

As the following examples make clear, while EU standards are at the core of some New Zealand regulatory schemes (such as toys), in other cases they are rejected or ignored almost entirely (as in the case of food standards). At the broadest level of abstraction, it appears from our work that the existence of gaps in the domestic legal regulatory 'market'; acceptance in New Zealand of the quality of EU decision making; and EU reputation or perceived reputation (Chaban et al. in this volume) in a field all play an important role in the acceptance of EU standards. These operate in addition to the more recognised drivers of market access and conditionality but, at least in some regulatory fields, these 'softer' drivers may play the dominant role.

To examine how EU standards enter the New Zealand regulatory model, the chapter examines the interplay between EU standard setting (in a variety of forms) and the recipient of that standard. In doing so it analyses how such reception or rejection occurs and the drivers that underpin it. To do this, emphasis is placed upon the relationship between the standard-setting actor and the recipient of that standard through a focus on reputation, asymmetric expertise and competition between standards regimes. The work also recognises the importance of domestic circumstances within New Zealand when 'decisions' are taken to adopt EU standards. In practice, the adoption, resistance or adaptation of EU standards in New Zealand occurs as a consequence of all these factors, in addition to the traditional pressures of market access and political influence.

The overall argument presented in this chapter is that distance is not always an obstacle to the EU's normative power and extra-jurisdictional influence. In fact, the factors briefly mentioned above and explored in more detail below are of more direct relevance to the likelihood of adoption of EU standards outside the EU's jurisdiction. By looking at New Zealand, the physically most distant developed economy from the EU, one might expect that EU regulatory influence would be minimal in accordance with Schimmelfennig and Sedelmeier's theory (2004). Yet, the adoption and adaptation of EU standards in New Zealand is extensive, if variable across sectors.

This conclusion appears to challenge the physical proximity model and it should perhaps cause us to pause for thought when considering the extra-jurisdictional influence of EU norms when the issue concerns legal regulation. Such a conclusion perhaps suggests the increasing importance of networks in modern governance as regulators, judges and lawyers operate increasingly in an international space (Rhodes 1997; Peters 2000). Such law making through socialisation further emphasises the argument in favour of cultural filters advanced elsewhere in this volume. These variables, rather than distance, may be the key to understanding the fate of EU legal norms in developing global legal system.

These interactions between the standard provider and the recipient must also be seen in the context of competitive international standard setting as the two competing global legal orders of the United States (US) and the EU vie for the right to regulate global standards. The EU has long recognised the importance of such 'soft law' mechanisms to the development of global trade. The influence of the EU in creating global standards is thus not accidental.

Such an active approach to standard export continues to be a feature of EU policy and the creation and export of standards remain a priority for the EU (EXPRESS Panel 2010). According to some commentators, the reasons behind the push for extra-jurisdictional standards have changed as 'the form of governance has shifted from occasional international spill-over of domestic rules to first deliberate extra-territorial imposition of domestic laws and subsequently to trans-governmental co-operation aimed at policy harmonization' (Bach and Newman 2010). The choices inherent in such 'technical' harmonization further emphasise the political nature of standard export and reception. There is therefore little likelihood that the EU will reduce its efforts in this field. The question is whether norm recipients will remain receptive to these approaches.

8.3 Adoption of EU Standards in New Zealand—Soft Conditionality

Perhaps the clearest examples of EU regulatory norms being exported to third parties are driven by the conditionality imposed by the EU on its partners, particularly in its geographic back yard (Schimmelfenig and Sedelmeir 2004; see also Šlosarčík in this volume). However, even in New Zealand, there is evidence of a 'soft' form of conditionality at work in a number of regulatory sectors. This has been particularly true in relation to product standards and environmental protection (Fini 2011). In both cases, the key driver has been the need for New Zealand products to meet EU standards to avoid exclusion from the European market. Such examples of standard adoption are thus not part of a competitive process but become a condition of entry to the market. In several areas, the EU standards are higher than those found in the US leading New Zealand agencies and, to a lesser extent, legislation to adopt EU rules.

One of the clearest examples of this relates to the influence of the *Conformité Européenne* (CE) mark in New Zealand. Like Canada, the USA, Australia and Switzerland, New Zealand has agreed a Mutual Recognition Agreement (MRA) on Conformity Assessment with the EU. This allows New Zealand products to be endorsed by the CE mark through International Accreditation New Zealand (an autonomous New Zealand Crown Entity). This means that standards bodies in the exporter country can assess if a product conforms to the destinations' standards before it leaves the export country. Meeting the requirements for the European market is essential for a large number of producers. The importance of exports to many domestic producers leads most to adopt these CE standards despite the fact that they are not a legal requirement. In New Zealand, lacking a New Zealand mark of product safety, the 'CE' has become a *de-facto* sign of quality in a New Zealand market dominated by Asian imports.

The clearest example of this occurs in the toy sector. The EU has taken a leading role in toy safety standards through the CE mark scheme. Where New Zealand manufacturers produce toys for the European market, they must establish an CE

Declaration of Conformity, which is a market-influenced 'soft law' requirement (Standards New Zealand 2012b). However, in practice, New Zealand standards follow most of the EU examples. The speed by which New Zealand responds to changes in the EU standards can be seen by the response to the new EU toy safety directive launched in 2011. This Directive forced major brands and retailers to assess their safety regulations, just to be able to continue marketing toys to the EU (SGT-CSTC Standards Technical 2012). New Zealand (and Australia) immediately sought to 'align AS/NZS [Australian Standards/New Zealand Standards] Standards with International and European Standards' (Standards New Zealand 2012a). As a result, EU toy standards are the default in New Zealand.

In the pharmaceutical field, Medsafe (the New Zealand pharmaceutical regulation agency) also seeks compliance with the standards of key trading partners, particularly the EU, when updating the Code of Good Manufacturing Practise for Manufacture and Distribution of Therapeutic Goods (Medsafe 2009). This applies to both exported and imported goods and would appear to be an example of EU standards being applied domestically while being driven by export priorities. Incorporating market standards (that are thoroughly enforced) is a priority for retaining essential market access by third countries. Given the size of the EU market for New Zealand, EU standards again seem to be the default non-Australian model in these key export areas.

The export of such EU standards to New Zealand through soft conditionality appears very market specific. For example, despite a lack of EU influence on food standards as a whole (see below), some aspects of the food standard field exhibit major EU influences due largely to market access requirements and specification concerns. In the dairy industry, for example, concerns over ensuring that products meet the highest available specifications lead to exporters applying EU standards even though no specific legislation or requirement exists to implement them in New Zealand (Dairy NZ 2009).

Perhaps the best example of this market specific EU standard setting occurs in the wine sector. The EU remains the largest wine market in the world (taking around 70% of global production). For New Zealand, the EU is the largest export market, taking around one third of the exported product (NZTE 2010). For this reason, New Zealand wine regulation has largely adopted the EU model, if not always through legislation, but certainly in practice. The advice given to wine exporters is to apply EU wine regulations even if they go beyond the New Zealand rules to ensure that they meet import standards across several jurisdictions. For example, wine producers are likely to comply with EU standards restricting them to using 100 % of the stated grape variety, rather than New Zealand law which only requires 85 % of the stated grape variety. New Zealand wine growers also comply with the EU standard on wine labeling, requiring New Zealand wines to include mandatory information on wine labels in one field of vision (European Commission 2009).

Although the Wine Act 2003 and the Wine Regulations 2006 both adopt lower standards than the European Wine Regulation 479/2008, the Ministry of Primary Industries advises that the Overseas Market Export Requirements comply with the later Regulation (MPI 2013). In practice, wine exporters do not make a distinction between market compliance requirements and instead meet the EU Export Requirements as a matter of course (Fini 2011).

Further evidence of EU influence is clear from the requirement that all export wine undergo laboratory testing. The EU is the only market to require this action (NZFSA 2006). The result of this voluntary conditionality is to push New Zealand wine regulation towards the EU standard. While compliance with EU regulation and standards in this area seems complete, it is not immediate. When EU Regulation 203/2012 was introduced involving the production of organic wine, New Zealand's Mutual Recognition Agreement with the EU did not cover labeling wine 'organic'. New Zealand's organic certification agency expects these regulations to be upgraded for the 2014 export year (Biogro 2012).

Direct important of EU standards in these instances, among others, are still clearly driven by a desire to easily enter the European market. The conditionality may not be formal but the impact is the same as if it were so. The narrow nature of these individual examples is clear evidence of *de-facto* 'soft' conditionality as, outside these specific market led examples, the importation of EU standards in the area of food is weak, as is explored below.

8.4 Adaptation and Adoption of European Standards in New Zealand—Regulation through Reputation

The importance of the market to the import of EU norms through standards is only part of the story. In fact, in the bulk of the examples found, it would appear that the market was not the key driver. The adoption or adaptation of EU standards, in New Zealand seems largely driven not by economics but by the perceived quality of processes provided by the EU in its development and setting of standards, as well as the quality of the standards themselves. Ready-made justifications can make 'instant' standards acceptable to third countries, allowing officials to easily justify their implementation to opponents, the wider public and even overseas trade partners.

The fact that the European Commission or a relevant EU agency will have already justified its arguments in front of 28 Member States and countless lobbyists certainly aids the use of such standards in New Zealand as the same justifications can be used to defend its application in New Zealand. However, what makes EU Standards different is that they have already undergone a process to ensure that they can be applied in multiple and varied jurisdictions across 28 Member States. As a result, in many cases, they can be virtually 'copied and pasted' into national standards or legislation. In 2012, for example, the New Zealand Building Code was changed to include the European standard EN14604, which allows certain types of fire safety devices to be used in New Zealand buildings. The EU standard was copied almost exactly (DBH 2012). Such off-the-shelf trans-national standards are particularly attractive for a small jurisdiction such as New Zealand.

This reputational strength and ease of application leads New Zealand standards agencies to often justify their own approach with reference to EU examples. In the case of food colourings, for example, Food Standards Australia New Zealand requires them to undertake a safety assessment before being used in food products. This is justified with evidence from the European Food Safety Authority (FSANZ), which has published six opinions based on scientific studies undertaken in the EU. FSANZ specifically notes that the EU requires some colours to have warnings on them, as food colouring has been thought to cause hyperactivity in children (FSANZ 2012). The point here is that the New Zealand public and the relevant stakeholders will accept such evidence. The EU's standards and justification pass the cultural filter test and are thus acceptable to the New Zealand audience.

The wholesale adoption of EU standards in New Zealand appears particularly common in areas such as medical devices and cosmetics where the EU has a level of expertise and sophistication of regulation that is beyond the capacity of most states. In these areas, smaller jurisdictions such as New Zealand do not have either the domestic expertise or the resources to develop independent standards. In effect, the existence of a high status standard allows for New Zealand to piggy-back upon it and reduces the need for additional investigation of the issue. Large jurisdictions, such as the EU, have the ability to research, develop and create individual product standards across a wide range of technical areas. They also have the ability to influence their international counterparts.

Although it is beyond the specific scope of this chapter, it is nevertherless worth noting at this point that the adoption by the International Standards Organisation (ISO) of many EU standards both provides additional evidence of the EU's reputation as norm creator and provides another source by which EU standards enter the New Zealand jurisdiction. Some examples, incorporated into New Zealand, include EN1050 (risk assessment for machinery) which became ISO14120 in 1999, and EN292 (machinery safety) became ISO1200-1 and ISO1200-1 in 2003 (Manuele 2005). Such EU influence on ISO health and safety standards provides additional legitimacy to the EU standards themselves. A study of how European standards are implemented through ISO standards would provide a clearer picture of the EU's global influence on this area of soft law.

A key area of growing EU influence through reputation is in the field of pharmaceuticals. New Zealand appears to be increasingly following European practice in relation to the adoption of pharmaceutical standards and their implementation. In 2010, for example, New Zealand withdrew medicines containing dextropropoxyphene after the products were withdrawn from the EU market (Medsafe 2010a). A similar response occurred after the EMA reviewed the side effects of bufexamac-based medicines (for dermatitis) leading to an EU ban on the product. As a direct result, a similar review was undertaken in New Zealand, using the same studies (with some additional New Zealand data). This led to Medsafe revoking the consent to sell bufexamac-based products in New Zealand in 2010 (Medsafe 2010b).

Further examples of this regulation through reputation can be found in the cosmetic industry where similar imperatives exist to that of pharmaceuticals. Recent changes to New Zealand cosmetic standards for example explicitly recognised and substantially reproduced the EU Cosmetic Regulation (1223/2009) which came into force in July of 2013. This was justified under the presumption that, 'New Zealand considers changes in regulatory requirements of other major markets for adoption in their own jurisdictions', despite the lack of global agreement on these standards (NZEPA 2012). However, the choice of the EU as the source of the adoption is interesting. In this field, New Zealand appears pre-disposed to adopt EU cosmetics standards both because of the perceived quality of the standard and the fact that the New Zealand scheme already complies with EU standards. The similarity of approach provides a cultural filter, which favours the EU model. Both the EU and New Zealand define sunscreen as a cosmetic, for example, whereas the US and Canada define sunscreen as a medicine. Australia defines sunscreen as both a medicine and a cosmetic depending upon circumstances (NZEPA 2012). The planned creation of a new trans-Tasman Australia New Zealand Therapeutic Products Agency (ANZ-TPA) has the potential to change this dynamic.

The pharmaceutical field is therefore one where high reputation overseas standards and testing are regarded as appropriate and valuable. Where the standard producer is of sufficient status it will thus passe through the cultural filter. The 'status' may also be related to the Euro-centric nature of the New Zealand legal model. Whatever the exact reason, the European Medicines Agency falls into this category. It does not do so accidentally and it actively promotes itself as a global norm producer in the field. This reliance on third parties to create and assess the standards of medicines in New Zealand shows an extreme level of confidence. The heavy reliance upon EU standards in this field is clear evidence of the global influence that EU 'soft law' can have on third countries through reputational authority.

In recognising and implementing external standards, third countries are making a conscious cost-benefit analysis to allocate their limited time and expertise elsewhere. Adoption may simply be more cost-effective than any attempt to create domestic standards. This is a particularly effective strategy for developing nations and smaller jurisdictions such as New Zealand. However, national regulatory bodies have a choice in selecting which standards to implement. In choosing the EU in areas where the market influence is limited, New Zealand is influenced by the EU's reputation as a provider of high quality and precise technical norms. In these cases, reputation, however gained, passes through the cultural filter when other standard options do not.

Such an adoption approach is not without controversy, however. Adoption is, in effect transplantation of legal norms from one jurisdiction to another and can be seen as legislation by proxy. As such, adoption comes with the same risks associated with legal transplants generally (Legrand 1997). In our case study, the New Zealand practice of adopting overseas (and particularly EU standards) in technical areas has seen a number of EU standard failures being transplanted along with the standard itself.

A recent example of this occurred in 2012 when an investigation into hip replacement regulations in the EU exposed flaws within the system to approve medical devices (Radio New Zealand 2012). As mentioned above, New Zealand relies heavily upon overseas regulators (particularly the EU) to determine whether a device is able to be used in New Zealand. In this particular case, the reliance upon the EU standard and its subsequent use led to a European failure being directly transplanted into the New Zealand jurisdiction, with serious consequences for domestic consumers.

Despite the controversy that surrounds the import of some standards, adoption of EU standards has become commonplace in the New Zealand jurisdiction. This has occurred where the expertise and reputation of the EU allows New Zealand to accept its norms as worthy of adoption. However, although there are many areas in which New Zealand's regulatory model has clearly been influenced by EU norms, there are others where such influence has been minimal or non-existent. This would suggest that at times other drivers can override both the EU's exporter as a trusted producer of technical norms as well as the market imperative already examined. The cultural filter may allow European standards to enter the New Zealand regulatory system, but it does not guarantee that other factors will not trump their acceptance.

8.5   Resistance to European Standards—Rejection or Regime Choice?

Decisions to accept technical norms are driven by more than just perceived quality or market access. At times there is a specific regime choice to be made, as the above sections have hinted at. In this section we address this issue directly and examine whether rejection of EU standards, in some areas, in fact represents the adoption of alternative regimes. The global regulatory field is dominated by two players (the EU and the US). When the two 'heavyweights' agree on a standard it becomes the *de-facto* global approach in all but a small minority of cases. Smaller markets have little real choice but to abide by the rules of the dominant standard-setting powers unless a domestic imperative is so strong that isolation from the global market is deemed an acceptable price. If the two major players disagree, there is a risk of rival regulatory standards and a bifurcated system. In such cases, smaller jurisdictions are faced with a clear regime choice. The key to the EU's influence in these cases appears to at least partially be the size of the market. Where a standard exists across all 28 Member States, the EU's influence is great. Where variation exists (as in food safety), the EU's influence is significantly reduced. As a result, smaller countries are likely to adopt the EU's standards, as part of the proposed 'Kissinger Effect', where one standard is available for all of the EU (Bach and Newman 2010). Coherence and unity is essential to the EU's influence.

The weakness of EU influence in food standards (with exceptions in areas such as wine where the EU is actively pursuing international standards) can be contrasted with the situation in pharmaceuticals. In the latter, the EU presents a single regulatory face, while in the former, until recently, variations occurred across the Union. The rise of EU influence in the field of pharmaceutical regulation has come at the expense of traditional US dominance in the field. This appears to reflect a growing conflict between the two jurisdictions for control of the global regulatory space. The US has had a long tradition of strong federal regulation in this area through the Food and Drug Administration (FDA). In the past, international pharmaceutical producers have often taken the view that FDA standards provide the means to satisfy global standard requirements. In effect, if the FDA standards can be satisfied, other states will accept this as proxy for acceptance of national standards in their own state (Hairston 1997).

However, the increasing adoption of ISO standards in the field of pharmaceuticals has changed the context of this particular regulatory environment. Observers note that the ISO standards bear a significant EU imprint as the FDA has in the main operated outside them. Their growing influence is seeing a European influence on developing global standards that is difficult to gauge but no less real for this subtlety (Hairston 1997).

In 1997, the EU and the US signed a Mutual Recognition Agreement, sharing pharmaceutical certifications and findings, to eliminate overseas inspections. The US failed to certify findings to be shared with the EU, meaning that the EU was regulating both their own companies and US companies producing pharmaceuticals, giving the EU larger influence than previously over global pharmaceutical standards: EU domestic audits are said to be more thorough and harder to pass than US audits (Bach and Newman 2010). For all these reasons, the EU's influence on pharmaceutical standards (primarily through the EMA) is in the ascendency.

We can contrast this EU 'primacy' in pharmaceuticals with its failure to exert influence in the field of food standards. Globally, EU food product standards do not appear to have influenced non-EU jurisdictions. This is primarily due to significant variation in food standards amongst EU Member States and thus the lack of a single voice in the field. Member States continue to dispute the need for standardisation (instead utilising mutual recognition mechanisms) for food products and food safety. As a result, EU influence has been more muted in this area (Milmo 2001). Although, EU competences have recently expanded in these areas, the EU model has not, as yet, proved exportable. Global popularity for EU food product and safety regulations continues to be limited.

New Zealand has followed this global trend and has followed EU pharmaceutical standards but not EU food product standards. In addition, the fact that in this area New Zealand and Australia have developed a regional standards authority of their own (Food Standards Australia New Zealand) also gives them greater capacity and thus less need to adopt external standards. This agency has developed harmonized standards for the Trans-Tasman market and there is little current evidence of adoption of EU standards as part of this process.

Despite the prevalence of overt rejection in this field, some informal adaptation is also evident. EU standards, in particular, can prove an obstacle to common Trans-Tasman regulation. As an economy more reliant on trade than its Australian partner—and with the EU being New Zealand's third largest trading partner—EU standards are perhaps more central to the New Zealand market. Where these conflict with Trans-Tasman efforts to harmonise, New Zealand has been known to oppose such attempts at standards convergence and to favour the continuance of variation (and the practical continued use of EU standards) when the specific case warrants such an exception.

One such illustrative example of this was the failed 2011 Draft Australian/New Zealand Standard for Olive Oil. It was rejected by New Zealand (and adopted in Australia), as New Zealand feared that the new standard would turn away

Mediterranean imports, which make up 95% of New Zealand olive oil sales. The increased labeling requirements (specific only to New Zealand and Australia) could prove disincentives for EU producers to export to New Zealand (Cord 2011). In practice, this could mean increased reliance on more expensive Australian products (New Zealand's limited Olive Oil production is largely a high end boutique product). In addition, such unnecessary (in New Zealand terms) barriers to trade have the potential to cause retaliation or at least weaken arguments for mutual recognition and open access, so crucial to New Zealand exports (Cord 2011). For these reasons, the EU's labeling standard continues to be held acceptable in New Zealand and trumps aims to create a single standard across the Trans-Tasman area.

8.6 Conclusion: Why the EU is the External Regulator of Choice?

Schimmelfennig and Sedelmeier (2004) suggest three models to explain the institutionalization or adoption of EU legal norms in non-Member States in the Union's geographic area. The first is a rationalist bargaining power, where the EU requires that third states follow clear EU rules and conditions as a condition of receiving EU 'rewards'. This conditionality is not passive, however, as third countries undertake cost-benefit analyses to determine whether the benefits/rewards are great enough to justify the cost of implementing the EU rules or standards (Schimmelfennig and Sedelmeier 2004, p. 671). This model of conditionality is most often associated with states in geographic proximity to the EU where partnership agreements or even membership can be held out as incentives to such conditions.

Our research suggests that conditionality does play a role in the New Zealand example, although the mechanism is more subtle and may be related to the perceived quality of the standards in question. In the case of several sectors, New Zealand decisions to implement EU standards appear directly related to market access being granted on condition of their being followed. The CE mark and standards relating to wine are just two examples. The important point to note here is that the need to accord with EU standards to access the EU market has been translated into a *de-facto* standard for these products generally. Such processes create their own dynamic as the implementation of EU standards domestically in itself legitimates those standards in the eye of the domestic legal order and encourages further adoption, whatever the original driver.

The second model identified by Schimmelfennig and Sedelmeier (Ibid.) recognizes a role for the EU in providing legitimacy to norms in what is described as a 'social learning model'. This is where states' behavior is incentivised by EU values and norms. The EU justifies its existence with a collective identity of common values and norms, which creates rules that gain legitimacy as more states and groups are party to those rules. Third countries are likely to become party to these rules if they resonate with their existing standards and norms and the system is receptive to the ideas being promulgated. In such cases, the cultural filter will privilege them.

The third model sees third party states drawing on EU norms in a more pragmatic sense. With no explicit incentive this model sees third states acquiring regulatory standards, usually when they express dissatisfaction with the incumbent domestic regulatory standards: 'a state adopts [an] EU rule if it expects these rules to solve domestic policy problems effectively' (Schimmelfennig and Sedelmeier 2004, p. 676).

It is argued that the dynamic in the area of norm adoption/adaptation of EU 'soft law' standards, at least in New Zealand, is driven by a combination of these latter models with a significant element of 'soft' conditionality. New Zealand may not be seeking to become part of the EU community through conditionality or identity and thus the lesson drawing model may appear on the surface the only mechanism likely to apply. However, the concept of community needs to be expanded to truly understand the mechanisms at work here. Legal systems have a long history of non-geographical reception, and the creation of non-geographic legal communities, are both a product and the cause of such relationships. New Zealand may have no desire to become part of the EU, but it does have an affinity with European norms and values and as such it is receptive to EU-based standards. Such norms will pass through the Eurocentric New Zealand cultural filter and thus domestic regulators will consider accepting standards based upon them. This may be explained by the long legal relationship with the United Kingdom but may also be influenced by the fact that the only alternative legal 'market' is the US. The EU is both a larger economic partner for New Zealand than the US and a greater norm provider, at least in the areas examined in this chapter. When this is allied with the fact that New Zealand's major Asian economic partners (particularly China) seem also more willing to accept EU regulations rather than US models—compounded by the fact that the US has failed to engage with ISO standards in key areas—the alignment toward the EU model, where such a regime choice exists, appears the rational choice.

If New Zealand tilts towards the US, as it would be expected to do should the proposed Trans-Pacific Partnership (TPP) be enacted, the dynamic would undoubtedly change. Although the cultural filter may favour the EU's standards, the regulatory restrictions that the TPP could impose (particularly through the rumoured investor-state tribunal system) may preclude their adoption without the risk of high-cost litigation. In such a scenario, the influence of EU standards upon New Zealand domestic regulation would be expected to decline. In the Trans-Tasman case, as explored above, examples exist of New Zealand failing to agree to Australian standards when the result would strategically damage New Zealand. It is less than clear that the TPP would offer such an opportunity. New Zealand may therefore find it increasingly difficult to keep a foot in both regulatory camps.

It would be arrogant to provide a conclusive statement on the reasons why geographically distant states such as New Zealand adopt EU standards in such a limited study such as this. However, by examining a small jurisdiction such as New Zealand it should be clear that over a diverse range of fields, including pharmaceuticals, toy safety and cosmetics, EU 'soft' law has a significant influence far beyond its borders. This perhaps tells us something about the EU's extra territorial influences generally and may require us to revisit the traditional norm export theories that currently predominate. In particular, geographic distance seems to play little or no role in the export/import of these technical and legal norms, at least in New Zealand. Given the history of global legal exports and reception, this should perhaps not surprise us.

While no overarching theory exists for why EU standards create influence in some areas but not in others, the broader context may be an era of bipolar global regulatory competition between the US and the EU. Asian players are clearly influential in the development of global regulation, but although they are now key players in arguments around standard adoption and application, in the context of both global and bi-lateral free trade agreements they, as yet, remain largely adopters and adapters in terms of the technical standards themselves. In this particular element of globalisation, the choice seems to be purely one of domestic, international or EU/US standards. In many cases, ISO and EU standards appear to amount to the same thing.

For New Zealand, the end result appears to be that as the influence of standards grows and global regulation increases on the back of standardisation, external influences will be a growing feature of the New Zealand regulatory model. Through the use of standards the regulatory landscape of New Zealand can be expected to remain heavily influenced by EU institutions, unless and until, pragmatics override the cultural filter. Despite its 'soft' nature, such globalisation will continue to have hard consequences for the future of the New Zealand legal order.

References

Bach, D., & Newman, A.L. (2010). Governing lipitor and lipstick: Capacity, sequencing, and power in international pharmaceutical and cosmetics cegulation. *Review of International Political Economy, 17*(4), 665.

Biogro. (2012). Guide for wine labelling, ingredients and market access. (Lenau L, White J). http://www.biogro.co.nz/mm_uploads/Wine_notification_No1_21_11_12_ver4.pdf. Accessed 30 Oct 2013.

Cord, C. (2011, July 24). New Zealand says 'No Thanks' to new olive oil standards. *Olive oil times.* http://www.oliveoiltimes.com/olive-oil-business/australia-and-new-zealand/new-zealand-no-new-olive-oil-standards/18547. Accessed 30 Oct 2013.

Dairy NZ. (2009). Strategy for New Zealand dairy farming 2009/2010. Hamilton NZ.

Davis, K., Fisher, A., Kingsbury, B., Merry, S. E. (Eds.). (2012). Governance by indicators: Global power through classification and rankings. Oxford: Oxford University Press.

DBH. (2012). New Zealand building code: Warning systems. department of building and housing, New Zealand. http://www.dbh.govt.nz/UserFiles/File/Publications/Building/Compliance-documents/F7-warning-systems-4th-edition.pdf. Accessed 30 Oct 2013.

European Commission. (2009). EC Regulation 607/2009, Article 50.

EXPRESS Panel. (2010). Report of the expert panel for the review of the European standardization system. http://ec.europa.eu/enterprise/policies/european-standards/files/express/exp_384_express_report_final_distrib_en.pdf. Accessed 30 Oct 2013.

Fini, M. (2011). The EU as force to 'o Good': The EU's wider influence on environmental matters. *Australian and New Zealand Journal of European Studies, 3*(1), 26.

FSANZ. (2012). Compliance Document for Food Standards Australia New Zealand Food Colours (n.d.). http://www.foodstandards.gov.au/scienceandeducation/factsheets/factsheets/foodcolours.cfm. Accessed 30 Oct 2012.

Hairston, D. (1997). Hunting for harmony in pharmaceutical standards. *Chemical Engineering,* *104*(20), 51.

Hopkins, W.J. (2011a). New Zealand. In D. Shelton (Ed.), *International law and domestic legal systems* (pp. 429–447). Oxford: Oxford University Press.

Legrand, P. (1997). The impossibility of legal transplants. *Maastricht Journal of European and Comparative Law*, *4*, 111.

Llewelyn, K. (1940). The normative, the legal and the law jobs. *Yale Law Journal,* 49(8), 1355.

Manuele, F.A. (2005). Global harmonization of safety standards. *Professional Safety, 50*(11), 41.

Medsafe. (2009). Proposed update to the New Zealand code of good manufacturing practice. http://www.medsafe.govt.nz/hot/consultation/gmp review.asp. Accessed 30 October 2013.

Medsafe. (2010a). Paradex and capadex will be withdrawn from New Zealand market on 1 August 2010. http://www.medsafe.govt.nz/hot/media/2010/paradexandcapadexmarch2010.asp. Accessed 30 Oct 2013.

Medsafe. (2010b). Summary of data on the benefits and risks for bufexamac-Containing medicines indicated for the relief of dermatitis, rash and hives. http://www.medsafe.govt.nz/profs/adverse/Minutes145Bufexamacattachment.pdf. Accessed 30 Oct 2013.

Michaels, R. (2006). 'The functional method of comparative law.' In M. Reimann & R. Zimmermann (Eds.), *The Oxford handbook of comparative law* (pp. 339–382). Oxford: Oxford University Press.

Milmo, S. (2001). European food safety faces regulatory reform. *Chemical Market Reporter,* 259(26), FR12.

MPI. (2013). 'Overseas market export requirements (Omars) for wine.' Ministry for Primary Industries, New Zealand Government. http://www.foodsafety.govt.nz/industry/sectors/wine/exporting/grape/market-access.htm. Accessed 30 Oct 2013.

NZEPA. (2012). Cosmetic products group standard. New Zealand environmental protection authority. http://www.epa.govt.nz/hazardous-substances/approvals/group-standards/Pages/cosmetic.aspx. Accessed 30 Oct 2012.

NZFSA. (2006). *New Zealand grape wine export code. New Zealand food safety authority.* New Zealand: Wellington.

New Zealand Trade and Enterprise. (2010). Wine market in continental Europe. http://www.nzte.govt.nz/explore-export-markets/market-research-by-industry/food-and-beverage/pages/wine-market-in-continental-europe.aspx. Accessed 30 Oct 2013.

Peters, G. (2000). Governance and comparative politics. In J. Pierre (Ed.), *Debating governance* (pp. 36–53). Oxford: Oxford University Press.

Radio New Zealand. (2012). Hip implant probes sparks call for better NZ standards. http://www.radionz.co.nz/news/national/119160/hip-implant-probe-sparks-call-for-better-nz-system. Accessed 30 Oct 2013.

Rhodes, R.A.W. (1997). *Understanding governance: Policy networks, governance, reflexivity and accountability.* UK: Open University Press.

Schimmelfennig, F., & Sedelmeier, U. (2004). Governance by conditionality: EU rule transfer to the candidate countries of Central and Eastern Europe. *Journal of European Public Policy, 11*(4), 661–79.

SGS-CSTC Standards Technical. (2012). China takes toy safety standards seriously—Interview with SGS's toy business director in China. http://www.sgs.com/en/Our-Company/News-and-Media-Center/News-and-Press-Releases/2012/09/China-Takes-Toy-Safety-Seriously.aspx. Accessed 10 Jan 2014.

Shelton, D. (Ed.). (2011). *International law and domestic legal systems.* Oxford: Oxford University Press.

Standards New Zealand. (2012a). Draft standards on toy safety available now for public comment. http://www.standards.co.nz/news/Media+archive/July+-+Sept+07/Toys+and+safety.htm. Accessed 30 Oct 2013.

Standards New Zealand. (2012b). European toy safety directive changes for first time in 20 years and a new BS toy standard published. http://www.standards.co.nz/touchstone/Issue+30/Consumer+Safety/European+toy+safety+directive+changes+for+first+time+in+20+years+and+a+new+BS+toy+Standard+published.htm. Accessed 30 Oct 2013.

Twining, W. (2000). *Globalisation and Legal Theory.* UK: Butterworths.
World Trade Organisation. (1994). Agreement on technical barriers to trade. 1868 UNTS 120, Annex 1 (Terms and their Definitions for the Purpose of this Agreement).

Dr. W. John Hopkins is an Associate Professor and Associate Dean of Law at the University of Canterbury Law School, Christchurch, New Zealand. He has published widely in the fields of comparative public law and international law. His work has examined the development of federal and multi-level governance at both domestic and international levels, with particular reference to the European Union. His recent research examines the connection between domestic and international public law and the application of federal ideas to international organisations and governance. In 2012 he was the New Zealand Fulbright Scholar to Georgetown University, Washington DC. He was the 2014 MUNDUS-MAPP Visiting Fellow at the Central European University, Budapest

Henrietta McNeill was a recipient of a 2012-13 University of Canterbury Summer Research Scholarship which supported her research into the influence of European Union standards on New Zealand law. She has presented this research at national and international conferences in the Asia-Pacific region, and has recently returned from an internship at the European Parliament. Henrietta holds an MA from the National Centre for Research on Europe at the University of Canterbury, Christchurch, New Zealand.

Part III
Resistance

Chapter 9
The EPA-Negotiations: A Channel for Norm Export and Import?

Annika Björkdahl and Ole Elgström

9.1 Introduction

In 2002, the Economic Partnership Agreement (EPA) negotiations were initiated between the European Union (EU) and the 77 Africa, Caribbean and Pacific (ACP) countries organized in regional groupings. 12 years after the start, 43 ACP countries have concluded some type of agreement. Paradoxically, the EPAs were intended to strengthen the economic relationship between the EU and the ACP countries, but the EPA-negotiations seem to have had the opposite effect as ACP countries have resisted the EU press for domestic reforms and ambitious commitments while a number of contentious issues are obstacles to moving the negotiations forward. The ACP countries' resistance, foot-dragging and aversion to entering into these trade agreements have challenged the EU as an attractive partner for development and as a normative power. This chapter offers an understanding of the asymmetrical relations inherent in the EPA negotiations between the EU, represented by the European Commission, as a norm exporter and the ACP countries as norm importers. It uses EU negotiations with African regional groupings as empirical illustrations. The analysis is informed by the norm diffusion literature, insights from negotiation theory, and it draws on the body of literature on the EU as a normative power. In the case of the EU exerting normative power, the emphasis is on the role and influence of the EU as a 'norm-maker' and exporter of principles of liberalism such as trade liberalization, market economy and World Trade Organization (WTO) compatibility.

The authors gratefully acknowledge support for this project from the Knowledge and Expertise Exchange Europe New Zealand (KEEENZ) programme.

A. Björkdahl (✉) · O. Elgström
Department of Political Science, Lund University, Lund, Sweden
e-mail: annika.bjorkdahl@svet.lu.se

O. Elgström
e-mail: ole.elgstrom@svet.lu.se

© Springer International Publishing Switzerland 2015
A. Björkdahl et al. (eds.), *Importing EU Norms,* United Nations University Series
on Regionalism 8, DOI 10.1007/978-3-319-13740-7_9

Conventional literature on this topic ignores or downplays the recipients of norms and the agency of the 'norm-takers'. In contrast, this chapter aims to upgrade the norm importers and shed light on the critical agency and the negotiation strategies expressed by African countries resisting EU norms and standards, and refusing or being reluctant to move towards interim EPAs, comprehensive EPAs or a full EPA.

This chapter is theoretical in scope as it conceptually explores complex relationships between the norm-maker and the norm-taker, and, consequently, between the processes of norm export and norm import. The chapter stems from dissatisfaction with the dichotomy that privileges the norm exporter at the expense of the norm importer (cf. Chakrabarty 2007). It is critical of the bias in the norm diffusion literature that focuses on the diffusion of 'good' norms. This is expressed for example in the 'Normative Power Europe' literature, which is often at risk of assuming a European exceptionalism, while denying others the capability to define, launch and consolidate normative frameworks on their own (Björkdahl 2012; Nicolaïdis and Whitman 2013). Following Thomas Diez's critical intervention (Diez 2005), the bulk of theories on norm export and normative power lacks a reflection of 'the self', and, more problematically, 'the other', and the link between norm export and norm import often remains vague. Thus, this chapter questions the tendency to think of the norm diffusion processes as a smooth, uncontested almost automatic process. It concerns itself with questions such as *how can we better understand the relationship between norm-makers and norm-takers? Through what mechanisms and processes are norms diffused? How does norm diffusion affect the norms and practices of the norm-taker?*

To empirically illustrate the theoretical reasoning, the chapter draws on insights from the EPA negotiations between the EU and the ACP countries. In the case of the EPA, the EU seeks to establish a new trade regime in order primarily to foster democracy and stability (Stevens 2006; Bilal and Stevens 2009; Börtzel and Langbein 2013). The chapter depicts the power asymmetries in the relationship between the EU as a norm-maker and its counterparts, the ACP countries, as norm-takers in the EPA negotiations. It focuses on the negotiation processes as a venue for norm-maker–norm-taker interaction and consequently highlights the negotiation process as a channel of norm diffusion.

The chapter unfolds in three main parts. First, it provides an overview of a constructivist view on norm diffusion and presents a theoretical framework that critiques the mainstream constructivist interpretations of the interplay between norm-maker and norm-taker in negotiations. Second, this is followed by a critical theoretical examination of negotiation processes as a channel of norm diffusion. Third, after providing a background to the EPA-negotiations, the chapter analyses processes of norm-making and norm-taking in these negotiations with the help of our theoretical framework and with an emphasis on strategies of norm resistance.

9.2   Towards a Reflexive Study of Norm Diffusion

A reflective study of norm transfer builds on critical constructivist insights and takes into account the critique of the norm diffusion literature. First, there is a need to overcome the social constructivist tendency to privilege structures over agency. We need to move beyond the conventional understanding of norms as a 'result of common practices among states' (Gurowitz 1999, p. 417; Björkdahl 2002b). Norms and actors are here perceived as mutually constitutive as also norms express values that create rights and responsibilities of actors (Klotz 1995; Keck and Sikkink 1998; Finnemore and Sikkink 1998; March and Olsen 1998). The norm of sovereignty for example, defines what a state is, enables the state to take certain actions in the international society as well as regulates the interaction of states in international affairs (cf. Risse 1999, p. 5). This leads us to understand the mutual constitution of norms and actors in the following way: Norms are intersubjective understandings that constitute actors' interests and identities, and create expectations as well as pre-scribe what appropriate behaviour ought to be by expressing rights and obligations (see also Björkdahl 2002a, 2005).

Second, the norm diffusion literature tends to assume that norms exported are also imported—that the process would be self-perpetuating and that the inherent persuasiveness of the diffused norms will ensure norm adoption and socialization. However, the process of norm diffusion is not automatic—it requires agency. Thus, there is a need to develop an understanding of the norm-makers promoting, per-suading, convincing and negotiating with the norm-takers. In addition, norm import often requires active re-interpretation and re-representation of the external norms by the norm-taker in order to adopt the new norm and develop congruence with the norms and practices of the norm-taker (Acharya 2004). Of course, norms may be adopted due to imitation and voluntary borrowing from a successful model of norm-guided action (cf. Olsen 2002; Nicolaïdis and Howse 2002). In such case the norm-maker may be passive. It is furthermore important to pay attention to existing 'cultural filters', which may affect 'the impact of international norms and political learning in third states and organizations leading to learning, adaptation or rejection of norms' (Kinnvall 1995, p. 61–71). According to Manners (2002, p. 245), cultural filters are 'based upon the interplay between the construction of knowledge and the creation of social and political identity by the subjects of norm diffusion'. The impact of culture is potentially important not least in relations between entities as culturally diverse as the EU and African ACPs.

Third, we need to expose the asymmetrical relationship between the norm-maker and norm-taker and to move beyond the traditional bias that favours norm-makers by highlighting the agency of the norm-taker (cf. Björkdahl 2012; Diez 2013). The norm-maker is frequently perceived as a superior actor with a strong commitment to a particular norm or set of norms and a will to advocate these norms to bring about normative change, while the norm-taker is perceived to be a passive recipient of norms. A norm-maker possesses a normative power, i.e. a capacity to change nor-mative convictions of others. Over the years, the EU has demonstrated that a norm community can successfully take on the role as a norm-maker. The EU's 'power in trade' is well recognized by trade experts (Meunier and Nicolaïdis 2006).[1] Yet, the norm-taker is not to be perceived as passive in the process of norm diffusion, but influential and responsible for selecting the norms and constructing a normative fit between the transferred norms and the local normative context and this is regarded as the first phase of norm import (cf. Risse-Kappen 1996; Finnemore and Sikkink 1998). Norm adoption can be viewed as the result of adaptation and adjustment of the external norm by the norm-taker.[2] Norms that have not been internalized and institutionalized into the normative structure in a way that redefines the norm-taker's identity, preferences and interests cannot be considered successful norm import (Payne 2001, p. 41). Authentic, or genuine, norm adoption is thus seen to involve changing normative convictions in the absence of overtly material or psychological coercion. However, it may be difficult to disentangle authentic and non-authentic approaches of norm adoption, as part and parcel of the norm export is the carrot and the stick affecting the norm adoption process by providing material or immaterial incentives (Lenz 2013, p. 216–218). Traditionally, the constructivist literature has been reluctant to attach material carrots or sticks to the efforts of norm transfer, claiming that authentic norm adoption is a matter of a normative change that cannot be forced by carrots or sticks. Socialization is the second phase of norm import and refers to the processes in which the adopted norm becomes widely accepted and allowed to affect the practices of the norm-taker (Risse and Sikkink 1999; Lenz 2013, p. 216–217). Often both the norm-maker and the norm-taker are involved in a dynamic process, which can be viewed as 'matchmaking' (Acharya 2004, p. 243). Clearly, all norms are not adopted. Some may be resisted and rejected, certain norm-takers may be resistant to change, and particular normative contexts may be more or less receptive to new norms. A norm that has been imported may still meet resistance, challenging its translation into practice. There may for example still be pockets of resistance where old normative convictions persist and where a normative fit could not easily be constructed.

Fourth, there is an inherent normative bias towards liberal international norms such a free trade and an assumption that the adoption of these norms represents positive progress in terms of economic growth and development. The perception of these norms as 'universal' means that the appeal of 'norms that are rooted in other types of social entities regional, national and sub-national groups' is often ignored (Legro 1997). It should also be pointed out that so called 'universal norms' are always subject of communicative and interpretive processes, yet this interactive dimension is seldom addressed. For instance, the norms pertaining to 'trade liberalization' are often regarded as universal with a convincing track record of transforming societies in a globalized world. However, while portrayed as transcending borders on a global scale, their impact on the ground in various localities is rarely

---

[1] The concept of norm community used here is similar to the concept norm cascade used by Finnemore and Sikkink (1998).

[2] For analytical reasons these processes are presented as sequential, but in reality these processes are more likely to be parallel (Björkdahl 2002a, p. 58).

identical (Lenz 2013, p. 217). On the contrary, depending on where the norms are adopted, they are being changed through the process of norm translation.

Thus, we can conclude that norms are no typical export good that transfer from one context to another without changes in quality. Norm translation is communicative and interpretive processes, during which the norm is changed in content and meaning. Terms such as norm transfer, norm diffusion or norm export suggest a quasi-automatically expansion of a certain normative paradigm. Instead, both the norm translation, and the meaning of the norm itself undergo complex processes of re-interpretation, re-negotiation and even norm erosion as the process of norm negotiations indicates.

9.3   Norm Negotiations in Asymmetrical Relationships

The processes by which norms are diffused are often referred to by constructivists as processes of emulation or mimetic—actors see others behaving in a certain way and copy these behaviours (Katsumata 2011; Lenz 2012). Alternatively, it is depicted as a relatively simple teaching and learning process (Finnemore 1996). While learning is a process internal to an actor, teaching occurs when there are external agents who actively engage in teaching activities. This role is often performed by the norm-maker. Still, however, the process is largely seen as problem-free and non-conflictual. This chapter 'marries' a constructivist approach to norm transfer with a negotiation perspective to better grasp the contestation inherent in processes of norm diffusion and to highlight the often-ignored aspect of the venue for norm diffusion i.e. the institutional setting where the norm-maker and the norm-taker interact. Both norm-makers and norm-takers may choose between different venues for their interaction (Coleman 2013). We single out negotiation processes as such institutional settings where norms are transferred in a give-and-take process. This translation process highlights compromises and shared, as well as competing, objectives: it is a negotiation process (Elgström 2000). Elgström (2000, p. 462) argues that 'norm negotiations are special in the sense that norms are claimed to be essential elements in an actor's cognitive world' and that the norm-taker is likely to defend the essential values they hold. Such negotiations are thus likely to be conflictual to the extent that the new norm is regarded as challenging existing ones. On the other hand, if the new norm fits into the existing normative context, negotiations will most likely be more co-operative.

When norms are not adopted by imitation, with the EU acting as a role model, they are thus normally transferred by means of negotiation, in 'bilateral partner dialogues' or in regional multilateral talks (Sheahan et al. 2010; Lenz 2013). The adoption of some norms, such as democracy and good governance, are required elements in most EU agreements with weaker third parties; without the acceptance of these norms, no agreement will be concluded. Such was the case also in the Cotonou Agreement (Holland 2002). In other negotiations, however, the negotiation process itself is the means through which the EU seeks to promote its norms. This is usually the case in trade negotiations, including the EPA negotiations where the Union tried to spread norms such as free trade, internal liberalization and regional integration.

As argued above, negotiation is about interaction and give-and-take between all parties. This holds true also of asymmetrical negotiations, even if the weaker party's room of manoeuvre is more limited in such talks. There are ways (strategies and tactics) also for less powerful actors to enhance their interests and to resist unwanted norm export (Zartman and Rubin 2000; Habeeb 1988). Some of these are described below. Furthermore, the nature of negotiations matters: preconditions for norm export differ between deliberative or problem-solving modes of negotiation and a negotiation characterized by hard bargaining (cf. Kotsopoulus 2012). In a situation where communication is open, where all actors listen and explain and where negotiators meet frequently, and may develop shared understandings and trust, the chance for norm transfer is relatively high—but may go in both directions. In asymmetrical negotiations, the norm-maker may be tempted to use coercive means to push the norm diffusion process forward, ensure adoption of the new norms and compliance with the new norms. In tough bargaining, where threats, manipulation and unilaterally imposed decisions dominate, the chance for declaratory norm acceptance by the weaker actor may perhaps increase, but the prospect of norm internalization becomes unlikely. Obviously, most empirical situations lie in between these two opposites.

The interpretation and understanding of norms often differ between parties, especially in negotiations between actors with differing cultures and historical circumstances. This may create tension and ambiguities in negotiation processes as parties put different meanings into agenda items and understand the meanings and consequences of negotiation outcomes in their own way. Furthermore, actors may entertain conflicting views on causes and effects, for example concerning the links between trade liberalization, regional integration and development. In the end, a weaker norm-taking state party may use its sovereign prerogative to interpret a negotiated agreement in a way that secures its normative preferences.

A first opportunity for the weaker power to influence outcomes occurs already in the pre-negotiation stage, when the agenda is to be decided. If it succeeds in avoiding agenda items with negative normative implications, for example items that are expected to curtail its sovereignty or its policy space, much has been gained. In general, a weak party may use various tactics to further its interests in actual negotiations. In the words of Zartman and Rubin (2000), it can 'borrow power' from different sources. It may appeal to existing or previous relationships or to common interests with the stronger party. It may try to create rhetorical entrapment (Schimmelfennig 2003) by referring to the stronger party's official proclamations and promises—grandiose principled statements that were often made without considering their potential normative implications for concrete negotiations. It may also borrow power from third parties, for example in terms of public opinions in EU Member States or globally. Finally, power may be borrowed from other contexts, notably from previous or on-going negotiations that may have created precedence or rules with relevance for the negotiation at hand. Many tactics thus involve argumentation that refers to appropriate behaviour or outcomes. The weaker party may also try to mitigate the unwanted consequences of norm export by either suggesting text formulations that are so vague as to make them difficult to interpret or evaluate, or by trying to insert exceptions and long implementation periods into the final agreement (Elgström 2000). In the first instance, it can ensure that its own interpretation of imported norms is the one to be spread and implemented. In the second case, it can at least postpone difficult decisions that may raise domestic criticism. Regimes that are satisfied with the normative *status quo* and are fearful of potential consequences of norm import, may ultimately settle for a *strategy of procrastination*, including deliberate attempts to hinder the ratification or implementation of negotiated agreements.

9.4   Background to the EPA Negotiations

The EU has had preferential trade and aid agreements with the ACP states since 1975. They have been trading, first, under the four Lomé Conventions, where poverty reduction, non-reciprocal trade and aid combined with the notion of partnership and regionalism were key elements (Stevens 2006). Additional conditionalities were added in the 1990s representing the emphasis the EU started to place on norms such as human rights, good governance, rule of law and democracy (Forwood 2002). The trade provisions of the Lomé Convention were the subject of adverse rulings during the 1990s within the General Agreement on Tariffs and Trade (GATT) and then within the WTO because the Convention discriminated in favour of some developing countries (the ACP) and against others in a way that clashed with WTO norms and regulations (Bilal and Stevens 2009). After negotiations the WTO granted the EU a waiver to continue trading under those provisions until 2007. Thereafter the EU would have to make its trade regime with the ACP countries WTO-compatible. The Cotonou Agreement, which adopted all the norms included in the Lomé Convention and solidified the norms, clarified the EU's ambition to export them to its trading partners. The Cotonou Agreement continued to provide the ACP with a very favourable trade regime, a substantial aid budget and a set of joint institutions. Whilst the Cotonou Agreement lasts until 2020, its trade component was due to be replaced by 2007 by a set of EPAs (Stevens 2006).

The negotiations of EPAs between the EU and the ACP states were to alter the trade provisions of the Cotonou Partnership Agreement and replace the previous norm of non-reciprocal trading relations with the growing norm of trade liberalization to gradually incorporate the developing countries in the global economy (Sheahan et al. 2010, p. 350). The EPA negotiations began in 2002 and aimed to recast the relationship between the EU and the ACPs in such a way as to justify them under the WTO provisions. However, the EPAs also included liberalization of trade in services and investment, aspects of government procurement and rules on competition policies and have, in doing so, been controversial and resulted in a slow and turbulent negotiation process. According to Bilal and Stevens (2009, p. 1), 'the EPA process has not been an easy or friendly one; words and deeds have often been at odds, and tension has flared up'. From the outset, the EPA negotiations have been challenging both in terms of process and in substance. According to Stevens (2006) Sub-Saharan African (SSA) negotiated the new trade regime with the EU under the threat of increased barriers against its exports if agreement was not reached before 2008. Most SSA states were, at best, acquiescent or, more often, reluctant parties to the process. A few months ahead of the 31 December 2007 deadline only limited progress had been made and the negotiators had not been able to reach a common understanding on the underpinning norms of the new trade arrangement. The European Commission (EC) then decided to split the negotiations into two stages (1) the conclusion of an interim EPA to be concluded by the end of 2007 to prevent the ACP states' loss of market access after 2007 and (2) further negotiations towards comprehensive EPAs to be concluded at the regional level. By now, three out of five regional groupings, have agreed on Regional Economic Partnership Agreements.

After a decade of slow negotiations, the EPA saga took a new, but not entirely unpredicatable turn. In September 2011, the European Commission proposed to re-move trade preferences for seventeen ACP countries that have been exporting duty-free and quota-free to the EU under MAR 1528/2007 on the grounds that they had not gone on to sign, ratify or implement the EPA. The countries involved were: nine LDCs: Comoros, Mozambique, Rwanda, Lesotho, Zambia, Haiti, Uganda, Burundi, Tanzania; and eight African non-LDCs: Côte d'Ivoire, Cameroon, Ghana, Kenya, Namibia, Botswana, Swaziland, Zimbabwe (Zimbabwe ratified the EPA in 2012). Following negotiations between the different EU institutions, it was decided that removal of trade preferences would take place by 1 October 2014. The eight non-LDCs that by 2012 had not signed the EPAs, came under pressure to sign or ratify an EPA before this deadline in order to ensure continued preferential access to the EU market that they enjoyed under MAR 1528/2007.

Table 9.1 gives a regional picture where three regional configurations, the East African Community (EAC), South African Development Community (SADC) and Economic Community of West Africa (ECOWAS) have signed EPAs. In the other regions, at least one member has signed, but not the region as such.

9.5   Norm-Making and Norm-Taking in the EPA Negotiations

It seems safe to conclude that the European Union saw the EPA negotiations as a channel for norm export to African countries. In former Trade Commissioner Man-delson's words, 'the EPAs are not typical, hard-nosed free trade agreements. I see them as tools for development and the promotion of regional economic integration' (Mandelson 2005a). In contrast to ordinary trade negotiations, the EPA negotia-tions were not, according to the Commission, about promoting EU self-interests; 'Our EPA agenda is emphatically not about opening markets to our own exports' (Mandelson 2005b). At the same time, Commission officials were careful to empha-size the development aspect of EPAs. These were aimed to be 'pro-development,

Table 9.1 The EPAs between the EU and the African States. (Source: Adapted from Bilal and Stevens 2009; overview of EPA negotiations Oct. 2014; ecdpm EPA updates Sept. 2014.)

Negotiating Regional Configuration	Members	Signatory states (*LDCs)	Countries falling into EBA/*Standard* generalized system of preferences (*GPS*)	EPA was initialed
ESA Eastern and Sothern Africa	Comoros Djibouti Eritrea Ethiopia Madagascar Malawi Mauritius Seychelles Sudan Zambia Zimbabwe	Comoros* Madagascar* Mauritius Seychelles Zambia* Zimbabwe	Djibouti Eritrea Ethiopia Malawi Sudan	
EAC East African community	Burundi Kenya Rwanda Tanzania Uganda	all member states of EAC		October 2014
SADC (South African development community)	Angola Botswana Lesotho Mozambique Namibia South Africa Swaziland	all member states of SADC		July 2014

Table 9.1 (continued)

Negotiating Regional Configuration	Members	Signatory states (*LDCs)	Countries falling into EBA/*Standard* generalized system of preferences (*GPS*)	EPA was initialed
CEMAC (Communauté economique et Monétaire de l'Afrique centrale)	Cameroon Chad Cent. African Republic Congo DR Congo Eq. Guinea Gabon St.Tomé/Principe	Cameroon	Chad Cent. African republic *Congo* DR Congo Eq. Guinea *Gabon* St.Tomé/Principe	
ECOWAS (Economic community of West African states)	Benin Burkina Faso Cape Verde Côte d'Ivoire Gambia Ghana Guinea Bissau Liberia Mali Mauritania Niger Nigeria Senegal Sierra Leone Togo	all member states of ECOWAS		July 2014

pro-reform instruments' (Mandelson 2005b). Mandelson explained that his 'driving mission as Commissioner is to put trade at the service of development and to ensure [that] the needs of the poorest are at all times at the forefront of our European policy' (Mandelson 2005a). In general, the EU portrayed itself as a promoter of norms and values: the stated goals of the EU in the EPA process were to encourage a process of 'economic reform, regional integration and progressive trade opening' (Mandelson 2005a). As the EU sees development being driven by increased trade and regionalism, the EU perceived itself as a promoter of global free trade and development, and as a model for and a promoter of regional integration.

9.5.1   Tough Bargaining

Preconditions for genuine norm transfer were, however, far from ideal. In the first place, negotiations were characterized by tough bargaining rather than soft tactics and deliberation. In December 2007, just after the agreements had been initialled, the ACP Council of Ministers collectively 'deplore [d] the enormous pressure that has been brought to bear on the ACP States by the European Commission … contrary to the spirit of the ACP-EU partnership' (ACP 2007). Similar statements, echoing disquiet and frustration over EU 'undue pressure' and a 'rushed process', are frequent in the material (interviews 3–6; ECOWAS official in Daily Graphic 2008; Tankeu 2008; cf. Stevens et al. 2008, pp. 70–85). Malawi's President Mutharika accused the EU of 'imperialism', saying it was punishing countries that resisted the EPAs by threatening to withhold aid from the European Development Fund (EDF), reportedly adding 'if the agreement is so good, why do they have to force people to sign?' (AllAfrica 2008, online). The Commission negotiators' behaviour and attitudes have been described by interviewees as 'patronizing', 'paternalistic', 'condescending and very rude', 'intimidating' and as 'showing disrespect' (interviews 4, 6, 7).

Many ACP representatives insisted that EPAs were signed 'under huge duress and with little enthusiasm' (South Africa's deputy trade minister in Ipsnews 2008). The reason interim EPAs were initialled was, in this view, that the alternative—GSP status for non-LDCs—was far worse (interviews 2–6); many ACP countries had no alternative but to initial. The EU repeatedly referred to the looming deadline (interview 4) and thereby put enormous pressure on ACPs that at the same time faced intense lobbying from domestic producers that foresaw disaster if the preferential exports to the EU were stopped. The economies of many ACPs were so reliant on the EU that EPAs were considered necessary, especially as no alternative was acceptable to Union negotiators. Under 'the shadow of GSP', they felt that they were presented with a 'take it or leave it'-proposal (interviews 3, 4): 'Under pressure and the threat of disruption of their trade with the EU and of losing their preferential access to the EU market if they reject the proposal … 18 African countries have had to initial [EPA] agreements' (Tankeu 2008, online). What the Commission regarded as an explanation of objective consequences, if EPAs were not signed (that is, as a warning), was interpreted as a threat by many ACP representatives.

Secondly, there was a fundamental divergence in how the EU and its African partners understood, or framed, the negotiations. While these were for EU Commission negotiators interpreted as trade negotiations, albeit not 'typical trade negotiations', their ACP counterparts defined them as having a development focus (Elgström 2009). And while 'it is a shared overall objective that EPAs should promote development, it is clear that parties have different perceptions of the development merits of some of the specific EPA provisions' (Bilal and Ramdoo 2010a, online). Furthermore, the two parties had different views on the relationship between trade and development, on the effects of liberalization and on the consequences of regional integration (Elgström 2009). This ambiguity created tensions in the negotiation process but also opened up the possibility that actors could interpret negotiation outcomes in different ways.

The EU's intentions and official goals were repeatedly questioned. In the eyes of ACP officials, the EU was clearly driven by commercial concerns and its main goal was to safeguard against (notably Chinese) competition and open up ACP markets (interviews 2, 5, 6). DG Trade is claimed to have carried out EPA negotiations with a narrow trade approach, treating EPAs as 'any other free trade agreement', while, in the process, giving scant attention to the ACP's development agenda (interviews 1, 2). The EU was thus seen as a self-interested actor that utilizes its superior power to further its own 'mercantilist interests' (ACP 2007, online). The EU was furthermore considered insensitive to African needs and demands and as unwilling to seriously integrate the main interests of the ACP into the agreements. An African Union representative complained about 'the failure of the EC to address issues of major interest and concern to Africa' (Tankeu 2008, online). For the African states, development was all the time the main interest. In their thinking, large amounts of additional assistance were necessary to enable them to take advantage of any increased access to EU markets. Therefore, their focus in the negotiations was often on the inclusion of an explicit 'development dimension' and, more concretely, on promises of 'more money' (interview 5). Directorate General (DG) Trade, seeing EPAs as trade agreements, for a long time rejected the demand to include a development chapter in EPAs, arguing that the aid dimension was taken care of in the Cotonou agreement and was to be handled in other forums (and by DG Development) (Southcentre 2008). In the end, development chapters were actually part of the interim EPAs, but did not include any concrete details regarding sources and volumes of funds. There is widespread agreement among the interviewees—despite frequent EU assertions to the contrary—that, in reality, no additional funding has been provided to cover the huge expenditures needed to overcome the ACP countries' trade capacity problems and to meet their adjustment costs (interviews 2, 5, 6, 7; cf. AU 2008, para 8).

Finally, the EU was accused of a 'divide-and-rule' strategy because of its willingness to sign interim EPAs with individual countries—and not exclusively with entire regions—and because it allowed different provisions and rules in different agreements (interviews 1, 6). Being extremely sensitive about its internal cohesion and regional harmonization (AU 2008; Tankeu 2008; Birru 2008), many ACP spokespersons rejected every move by the EU that could be interpreted as creating divisions within the group. Furthermore, the Commission was accused of withholding information on developments in parallel negotiations, of claiming progress in a contentious area in one region to convince others to agree to the same, and of not honouring commitments (interviews 1, 3; Stevens et al. 2008, p. 81). Thus, there existed a fundamental disagreement regarding the effects on regional integration of the EPA agreements: while EU actors claimed that their insistence on negotiating with regional groupings has had positive consequences for African regional integration efforts, their counterparts emphasized the deleterious, divisive effects of such region-based negotiations.

9.5.2 Resisting EU Norm Export

The incompatible interpretations of the nature of the negotiations and of key causal relationships between trade, development and regional integration created, in our view, major obstacles to genuine norm export. If parties do not agree on fundamental conceptual issues, there is a high risk of confusion and tension when they are to transform an agreement into concrete action. Successful norm transfer requires, we argue, that the key norms at stake hold at least approximately the same meaning for norm-maker and norm-taker. It is not enough for a norm-maker to get the intended norm recipient to generally embrace 'regional integration' as a basic value: the norm-taker also has to interpret this goal in the same way as the norm-maker.

The nature of the negotiation process also has an influence on norm export. Tough bargaining and issuing ultimatums may lead to an agreement, but is not conducive to the genuine transfer of norms. One interviewee claimed that the good relationship between the EU and ACP countries that had been built up over the years was now hurt because of the 'ill-will and bad political feelings' generated by EU behaviour during the EPA process (interview 6). Likewise, Stevens et al. (2008, p. 84) conclude that 'too much pressure in an asymmetric relationship like that between the EU and the ACP, can lead to a lot of suspicion and a lack of ownership of the final result ... not conducive to a harmonious relationship'.

Though it is difficult to trace actual norm transfer from the EU to the African ACP countries as a result of the EPA-process, existing scattered evidence seems to indicate that African governments have not been convinced by the Commission's argument that the liberal trade order envisaged by the EU is desirable for them. They still, for example, resist importing rules on investments, government procurement and competition (the 'Singapore issues'), and doubt the automatic benefits of market opening. While there has certainly been a superficial norm export, in terms of rhetorical allegiance to overarching goals, there are few indications of genuine norm transfer.

In actual negotiations, the African states made use of most of the bargaining tactics suggested in the literature on asymmetrical negotiations. Most notably, they succeeded in keeping the Singapore issues out of the 2007 interim agreements. Arguably, this can be explained as an instance of borrowed power, where the ACPs could refer to and utilize the previous exclusion of these issues from the negotiations in the WTO Doha Development Round. The *vagueness* of several articles in the agreement, or in the relevant WTO provisions, inspired different interpretations and is still the root of some of the most contentious controversies. For example, the WTO provision that 'substantially all trade' has to be included in a free trade agreement was a bone of contention, with the EU taking a strict approach, while being accused by African representatives as going 'beyond the requirements of the WTO' (Chambas 2010, online). The possible *length of transition periods* was another contentious issue, with the ACP interpreting WTO rules in a way that the EU deems far too generous. Throughout the negotiations, African state representatives stressed the need for 'sufficient' transition periods (20–25 years) and that implementation should be related to development indicators rather than 'arbitrary time frames' (Agbadom 2007, online) In the end, the EU's interpretation of both these issues won out. The African ACP countries, however, gained at least a partial victory, as they were granted 15 years of transition, rather than the 10 years that the WTO considers normal.

9.5.3 A Strategy of Procrastination

After the interim agreements were concluded in 2007, the African states that initialled an agreement have resorted to the *strategy of procrastination*. All countries that concluded an interim EPA have benefited from a duty-free and quota-free market access to the EU. Though the EU Market Access Regulation requires that the countries sign, ratify and implement their interim EPAs 'within a reasonable period of time', no negative effects have occurred for those who have not done so. This situation is rather convenient for many African countries, which can enjoy the positive aspects of EPAs without implementing its details. In the words of two well-informed observers, 'many ACP countries have also implicitly revelled in the delayed EPA negotiation process … many ACP have "settled" into the status quo' (Bilal and Ramdoo 2010b, online). The former president of Tanzania, Benjamin Mkapa, for example, has stressed that signing the full EPA between the EAC and the EU would derail the EAC's development and weaken its economy as a result of the entry of EU goods into the East African market and tariff revenue losses for affected countries (Wambi 2011). This is certainly a major explanation for the frustrating deadlock in the EPA negotiations and for the rather ritualistic nature of negotiations in recent years, where both parties repeat the same arguments over and over again.

Arguably, the African states have also been able to use the EU's own partnership and development discourse to prolong negotiations. In the words of Hurt et al. (2013, p. 75), they have constructed a '"mimetic challenge" within the negotiations in order to resist the pressures to sign full EPAs'. EU negotiators may have been rhetorically entrapped (Schimmelfennig 2003) by its own declarations, while ACP negotiators have been able to 'pursue a strategy highlighting the disjuncture between the EU's rhetoric and the highly coercive negotiating tactics that have been adopted during the negotiation process' (Hurt et al. 2013, p. 75). In this way, the prevailing discourse, emphasizing the developmental character of the EPA negotiations, has become a weapon in the arsenal of the weaker states.

9.5.4 Losing Patience—Using Coercion

In 2013, the EC issued a statement that states that have concluded an EPA but not taken the necessary steps to ratify and implement it would no longer benefit from the EPA market access to Europe as from October 2014:

> The EC Market Access Regulation (MAR) 1528 of 1st January 2008 provides duty free quota free market access for African Caribbean and Pacific countries that have concluded an EPA. The Regulation requires countries to sign, ratify and implement the Agreement within a 'reasonable period of time'. At it currently stands, the MAR is a temporary, unilateral instrument of the EU to ensure that, pending the implementation of the agreement by ACP countries, there would be no trade disruption.

The message from the EC was clear: states that want to continue to benefit from EPA market access will have to sign and start implementing their existing EPA or conclude a new regional EPA. For others, they will trade with the EU under one of the schemes of the new GSP (i.e. EBA, Standard GSP or GSP Plus). The explicit deadline and credibility of the threat indicated that the EU was decidedly serious and that procrastination was no longer an alternative (Bilal 2012).

In terms of negotiation theory, this strong signal from the EU may be seen as an *ultimatum*, a threat with a definite deadline. A credible ultimatum—which this probably is, as it can be implemented by a unilateral EU decision—would clearly indicate that a strategy of procrastination is no longer a viable alternative. As in 2007, some states might have been pressured to adopt the norms exported by the EU by agreeing to an EPA, although it might not fulfil their ambitions and interests in terms of content, timing and geographical configuration due to fear of market disruption, and fear of losing their preferential access to the EU-market.[3] Under these circumstances, the risk is high that no genuine norm import will take place. The fact that there are still two African regions that have not concluded EPAs with the EU indicates, that norm resistance is still there. In these cases, no normative match between the liberal free trade norm package and the existing normative context of the norm-takers has been found. Furthermore, it remains to be seen how the regional EPA agreements that have been agreed upon will be implemented in each specific case.

---

[3] The unilateral new deadline seems to have had its intended effects: in July 2014, regional EPAs were initialled by the ECOWAS and the SADC countries and in October the EAC followed suit, after the temporary loss of Kenya's preferences to the EU market (GREAT insights 2014).

9.6 Conclusion

27 September 2014, marked the twelfth anniversary of the beginning of negotiations for EPAs between the EU and the ACP-group. But, international trade experts, stakeholders as well as civil society organizations throughout Europe and in the ACP countries claim it is not a time for celebration. Perhaps with few exceptions, the EPA agenda has not generated the enthusiasm for effective development partnership and normative change it was meant to stimulate. Many uncertainties, and the disappointing experience of protracted negotiations definitely challenged the processes of norm export and import. The EPAs have been presented as holding a normative package pertaining to trade and development that will have impact on the societies once adopted. As such the EPA-negotiations need broad support and 'buy-in' from various stakeholders in order to adjust and anchor the norm package on trade liberalization exported through the EPAs. Yet, there seems to be limited possibilities for civil society, business community and other stakeholders to influence the elite-based EPA-negotiations and assist in the process of norm translation. The EPA negotiations and the process of norm import could well be seeing a backlash as the numbers of critical voices are swelling and it is most likely that some African and/or Pacific countries will not want to conclude an EPA with the EU as no normative match can be found.

This chapter demonstrates that norm transfer through the channel of the EPA-negotiations is a give-and-take process. The EPA-negotiations clearly depict the asymmetrical relationship between the EC as a norm-maker and the ACP-countries as norm-takers. Although the negotiations are clearly characterized as asymmetrical, the norm-taker is not passive. The various African regional groupings have utilized a variety of tactics to delay the negotiations such as averseness, foot dragging, and strategies of procrastination to resist the adoption of the EU exported norms. Potential reasons for this are that the African countries found the timeframes for the negotiations too short and that the regional foundation for negotiations rushed the regional integration processes in Africa. In addition, the EPAs are not seen as benefiting African economic development, and as time has passed the EPAs are not in tune with global economic changes and the increased weight of the emerging economies that challenge the EU as a major norm exporter and trading partner in Africa.

Interviews

1. Ambassador, African initialling country, 12 June 2007.
2. Ambassador and First Secretary, African non-initialling country, 23 June 2008.
3. Minister, African non-initialling country, 24 June 2008.
4. Minister Plenipotentiary, African initialling country, 24 June 2008.
5. Ambassador, African initialling country, 25 June 2008.
6. Ambassador, African non-initialling country, 25 June 2008.
7. Official at ACP Secretariat in Brussels, 6 March 2007.

References

Acharya, A. (2004). How ideas spread: Whose norms matter? Norm localization and institutional change in Asian regionalism. *International Organization, 58*(2), 239–275.

ACP (2007). Declaration of the ACP Council of Ministers at its 86th Session, ACP/25/013/07, 13 December. http://www.acp.int/en/com/86/ACP2501307_declaration_e.pdf. Accessed 14 Oct 2013.

Agbadome. (2007). Interview with A.S. Agbadome, Conseiller Régional en Négociations Commerciales ã la CEDEAO. In acp-eu-trade newletter No.8. Conseiller en négociations Agbadome interview published in acp-eu-trade.org newsletter 2007. http://www.ecdpm.org/Web_ECDPM/Web/Content/Navigation.nsf/index2?readform&http://www.ecdpm.org/Web_ECDPM/Web/Content/Content.nsf/0/F70BE31FF15EDB84C12572B2003F1849?Opendocument. Accessed 15 Oct 2013.

AllAfrica. (2008). If EPAs are so good, why force us to sign, by P. Semu-Banda, 23 April. http://www.ipsnews.net/2008/04/trade-malawi-if-epas-are-so-good-why-force-us-to-sign/. Accessed 14 Oct 2013.

AU (African Union). (2008). Addis Ababa Declaration on EPA Negotiations. African Union Conference of Ministers of Trade and Finance, 1–3 April, AU/EXP/CAMTF/Decl. (1).

Bacrot, C. (2012). Authors' interview: Celine Bacrot, Consultant on Regional Integration and Transport at UNCTAD, Arusha July 2012.

Bilal, S. (2012). EPAs 10th Anniversary: The never ending story, ecdpm, talking points. http://www.ecdpm-talkingpoints.org/epa-anniversary-the-never-ending-story/. Accessed 14 Oct 2013.

Bilal, S., & Ramdoo, I. (2010a). Riding out the storm: Will the EPAs sink? *Trade Negotiations Insights 9*(9), http://ictsd.org/i/news/tni/94199. Accessed 14 Jan 2014.

Bilal, S., & Ramdoo, I. (2010b). Losing old friends: The risk of an EPA backlash. *Trade Negotiations Insights 9*(8), http://ictsd.org/i/news/tni/87811. Accessed 14 Jan 2014.

Bilal, S., & Stevens, C. (Eds.) (2009). The interim economic partnership agreements between the EU and African states. Policy Management Report no. 17. Ecdpm.

Birru. (2008). Statement by His Excellency Ato Girma Birru, Minister of Trade and Industry, the Federal Democratic Republic of Ethiopia, at the African Trade and Finance Ministers Meeting, Addis Ababa, 1–3 April.

Björkdahl, A. (2002a). *From idea to norm—Promoting conflict prevention.* Lund: Lund University Press.

Björkdahl, A. (2002b). Norms in international relations: Some conceptual and methodological reflections. *Cambridge Review of International Affairs, 15*(1), 9–23.

Björkdahl, A. (2005). Norm-maker and norm-taker: Exploring the normative influence of the EU in Macedonia. *European Foreign Affairs Review, 10*(2), 257–278.

Björkdahl, A. (2012). Towards a reflexive study of norms, norm diffusion and identity (re)construction: The transformative power of the EU in the Western Balkans. *Canterbury Law Review, 18*(2), 33–51.

Börzel, T., & Langbein, J. (2013). Convergence without accession? Explaining policy change in the EU's eastern neighbourhood. *Special Issue of Europe-Asia Studies, 65*(4), 571–580.

Chakrabarty, D. (2007). *Provincializing Europe: Post-colonial thought and historical difference.* Princeton: Princeton University Press.

Chambas, M. (2010). An interview with H.E Dr. Mohammed Chambas, Secretary General of the ACP Group of States, *Trade Negotiation Insights 9*(10). http://ictsd.org/i/news/tni/97960/. Accessed 14 Jan 2014.

Coleman, K. (2013). Locating norm diplomacy: Venue change in international norm negotiations. *European Journal of International Relations, 19*(1), 163–181.

Daily Graphic. (2008). EU support not enough—Ecowas Commission, 10 June. http://www.modernghana.com/news2/169190/1/eu-support-not-enough-ecowas-commission.html. Accessed 14 Oct 2013.

Diez, T. (2005). Constructing the self and changing others: Reconsidering normativepower Europe. *Millennium—Journal of International Studies, 33*(3), 613–636.

Diez, T. (2013). Normative power as hegemony. *Cooperation and Conflict, 48*(2), 194–210.

Elgström, O. (2000). Norm negotiations. The construction of new norms regarding gender and development in EU foreign aid policy. *Journal of European Public Policy, 7*(3), 457–476.

Elgström, O. (2009). From Cotonou to EPA Light: A troubled negotiating process. In G. Faber & J. Orbie (Eds.), *Beyond market access for economic development* (pp. 21–37). London: Routledge.

Finnemore, M. (1996). *National interests in international society*. Ithaca: Cornell University Press.

Finnemore, M., & Sikkink, K. (1998). International norm dynamics and political change. *International Organization, 52*(4), 887–917.

Forwood, G. (2002). The road to Cotonou: Negotiating a successor to Lomé. *Journal of Common Market Studies, 39*(3), 423–442.

GREAT insights. (2014). Special issue, Economic partnership agreements and beyond vol. 3. October/November. http://ecdpm.org/great-insights/financing-development/epa-update-september-2014/. Accessed 25 Oct 2014.

Gurowitz, A. (1999). Mobilizing international norms: Domestic actors, immigrants, and the Japanese state. *World Politics, 51*(3), 413–445.

Habeeb, W. M. (1988). *Power and tactics in international negotiations. How weak nations bargain with strong nations*. Baltimore: Johns Hopkins University Press.

Holland, M. (2002). *The European union and the third world*. Houndmills: Palgrave.

Hurt, S., Lee, D., & Lorenz-Karl, U. (2013). The argumentative dimension to the EU-Africa EPAs. *International Negotiation, 18,* 67–87.

Ipsnews. (2008). TRADE: Barroso's EPA intervention to be 'more than symbolic', by D. Cronin, 31 January. http://www.ipsnews.net/news.asp?idnews41015. Accessed 14 Oct 2013.

Katsumata, H. (2011). Mimetic adoption and norm diffusion: 'Western' security cooperation in Southeast Asia. *Review of International Studies, 27*(2), 557–576.

Keck, M. E., & Sikkink, K. (1998). *Activist beyond borders: Advocacy networks in international politics*. Ithaca: Cornell University Press.

Kinnvall, C. (1995). *Cultural diffusion and political learning: The democratization of China*. Lund: Lund University Press.

Klotz, A. (1995). *Norms in international relations: The struggle against Apartheid*. Ithaca: Cornell University Press.

Kotsopoulus, J. (2012). *Do perceptions matter? Negotiating EU-Africa relations*. Brussels: University of Kent, diss.

Legro, J. (1997). Which norms matter? Revisiting the 'failure' of institutionalism. *International Organization, 51*(1), 31–63.

Lenz, T. (2012). Spurred emulation: The EU and regional integration in Mercosur and SADC. *West European Politics, 35*(1), 155–173.

Lenz, T. (2013). EU normative power and regionalism: Ideational diffusion and its limits. *Cooperation and Conflict, 48*(2), 211–228.

Mackie, J., Görtz, S., de Roquefeuil Q. (2011). Questioning old certainties. Challenges for Africa-EU relations in 2012. *Policy and Management Insights No. 3*, December 2011. ECDPM. http://www.ecdpm.org/Web_ECDPM/Web/Content/Download.nsf/0/453BBE89B6BF6CF0C12579 6800398DD9/$FILE/11-PMI03-challenges%20final.pdf. Accessed 14 Jan 2014.

Mandelson, P. (2005a). Statement to the development committee of the European Parliament, 17 March, Speech/05/182. http://ec.europa.eu/commission_barroso/mandelson/speeches_articles/. Accessed 15 Oct 2013.

Mandelson, P. (2005b). Remarks to the trade committee of the European Parliament, 23 May, Speech/05/295. http://europa.eu.int/rapid/pressReleasesAction.do?reference=SPEECH/05/29 5&format=HTML & aged=0&language=EN & guiLanguage=en. Accessed 15 Oct 2013.

Manners, I. (2002). Normative power Europe: A contradiction in terms? *Journal of Common Market Studies, 40*(2), 235–258.

March, J. G., & Olsen, J. P. (1998). Institutional dynamics of international political order. *International Organization, 52*(4), 943–969.

Meunier, S., & Nicolaïdis, K. (2006). The European union as a conflicted trade power. *Journal of European Public Policy, 13,* 906–925.

Nicolaïdis, K., & Howse, R. (2002). 'This is my Eutopia…': Narrative as power. *Journal of Common Market Studies, 40*(4), 767–792.
Nicolaïdis, K., & Whitman, R. G. (2013). Preface. *Cooperation and conflict, 48*(2), 167–170.
Olsen, J. P. (2002). The many faces of Europeanization. *Journal of Common Market Studies, 40*(5), 921–952.
Overview of EPA negotiations. (Oct. 2014). http://trade.ec.europa.eu/doclib/docs/2009/september/tradoc_144912.pdf. Accessed 25 Oct 2014.
Payne, R. (2001). Persuasion, frames and norm construction. *European Journal of International Relations, 7*(1), 37–61.
Risse, T. (1999). International norms and domestic change: Arguing and communicative behavior in the human rights area. *Politics and Society, 27*(4), 529–560.
Risse, T., & Sikkink, K. (1999). The socialization of international human rights norms into domestic practices: Introduction. In T. Risse et al. (Eds.) *The power of human rights: International norms and domestic change* (pp. 1–38). Cambridge: Cambridge University Press.
Risse, T., Ropp, S. C., & Sikkink K. (Eds.). (1999). *The power of human rights: International norms and domestic change*. Cambridge: Cambridge University Press.
Risse-Kappen, T. (1996). Collective identity in a democratic community: The case of NATO. In P. Katzenstein (Ed.), *The culture of national security. Norms and identity in world politics* (pp. 357–399). New York: Columbia University Press.
Schimmelfennig, F. (2003). *The EU, NATO and the integration of Europe. Rules and rhetoric*. Cambridge: Cambridge University Press.
Sheahan, L., Chaban N., & Elgström O. (2010). Benign partner or benign master? Economic partnership agreement negotiations between the European Union and the Pacific Islands. *European Foreign Affairs Review, 15*(2), 347–366.
Southcentre. (2008). EPA negotiations: State of play and strategic considerations for the way forward, analytical note SC/AN/TDP/EPA/13. http://www.southcentre.org. Accessed 14 Oct 2013.
Stevens, C. (2006). The EU, Africa and economic partnership agreements: Unintended consequences of policy leverage. *The Journal of Modern African Studies, 44*(3), 441–458.
Stevens, C., Meyn M., Kennan J. (2008). The new EPAs: Comparative analysis of their content and the challenges for 2008. ODI and ECDPM, London and Maastricht. http://spiderman.ecdpm.org/Web_ECDPM/Web/Content/Download.nsf/0/E8036BBF7CB4214BC12574210 02B30D2/$FILE/ODI-ECDPM%20EPA%20Analysis%20-%20Final%20Report%2031-03-08%20Amended%2003-04-08.pdf. Accessed 14 Jan 2014.
Tankeu, E. (2008). Statement by Mrs. Elisabeth Tankeu, AU Commissioner for Trade and Industry at the Conference of AU Ministers of Trade and Finance, Addis Ababa, 1–3 April. http://www.acp-eu-trade.org/library/files/Tankeu_EN_030408_AU_statement-trade-and-finance-ministerial.pdf. Accessed 14 Oct 2013.
Wambi, M. (2011). East Africa wants to trade beyond the EU. http://www.globalissues.org/news/2011/09/12/11141. Accessed 14 Oct 2013.
Zartman, I. W., & Rubin, J. (2000). Symmetry and asymmetry in negotiation. In I.W. Zartman & J. Rubin (Eds.) *Power and asymmetry in international negotiations* (pp. 271–293). Ann Arbor: The University of Michigan Press.

Annika Björkdahl is Professor of Political Science at Lund University. She has published on ideas and norms in International Relations particularly focusing on the role of the EU as an exporter of norms as well as on conflict prevention, peacekeeping and peace-building. Among her recent publications are *War and Peace in Transition* (Nordic Academic Press 2009), *Rethinking Peacebuilding: The Quest for Just Peace in the Middle East and the Western Balkans* (Routledge 2013) (with K. Aggestam). She has also published in *European Foreign Affairs Review, Journal of European Public Policy* etc. She has also been a guest professor at National Centre for Research on Europe, Canterbury University. She is currently the editor in chief of *Cooperation and Conflict*.

Ole Elgström is Professor of Political Science at Lund University, Sweden. He has published on internal and international negotiations involving the EU, and notably on external perceptions of the EU, in a number of journals such as *Foreign Policy Analysis,* the *Journal of Common Market Studies, Journal of European Public Policy* and *European Foreign Affairs Review*. He is the co-editor (with Christer Jönsson) of European Union Negotiations (Routledge 2005) and (with Michael Smith) of *The European Union's Roles in International Politics* (Routledge 2006).

Chapter 10
Ambitions Versus Capacity: The Role of Institutions in ASEAN

Avery Poole

10.1 Introduction

This chapter considers whether the European Union (EU) acts as a regional 'model' for the Association of Southeast Asian Nations (ASEAN). It does this by exploring a particular empirical puzzle. In recent years, ASEAN has set out plans to become more institutionalised.[1] The 2007 ASEAN Charter purportedly establishes a 'legal and institutional framework' for ASEAN. It contains several apparent institutional innovations, including the strengthening of the ASEAN Secretariat, more frequent Summits and a new ASEAN Coordinating Council. Why are these ambitions not matched by institutional capacity?

Some observers see the ASEAN Charter as a signal that the Association is moving towards 'EU-style regionalism'. There is certainly some evidence that ASEAN officials have considered the relevance of the EU as a model. However, ASEAN's brand of regional integration continues to reflect the importance of local norms. There is incremental change in ASEAN institutions over time, but this is contingent upon traditional interpretations of ASEAN norms—particularly sovereignty, non-interference and the 'ASEAN Way' of consensus decision-making.

This chapter reviews the institutional innovations made by the ASEAN Charter—in particular, the supposed 'strengthening' of the Secretariat (based in Jakarta). It argues that the pursuit of ambitious goals is constrained by limitations given ASEAN's 'traditional' norms. There are tensions among ASEAN norms, as some member state representatives attempt to introduce new institutions which challenge ASEAN's traditional normative understandings. The political diversity of member states underpins their disparate interpretations and visions of ASEAN's role and

---

[1] This chapter employs Keohane's (1988) oft-cited definition of institutions as 'persistent and connected sets of rules that prescribe behavioural roles, constrain activity, and shape expectations' (386). Thus, 'institutionalisation' refers to the degree to which institutional rules regulate (or attempt to regulate) the behaviour of actors.

A. Poole (✉)
School of Social and Political Science, The University of Melbourne, Melbourne, Australia
e-mail: adpoole@unimelb.edu.au

© Springer International Publishing Switzerland 2015
A. Björkdahl et al. (eds.), *Importing EU Norms,* United Nations University Series on Regionalism 8, DOI 10.1007/978-3-319-13740-7_10

mandate. In general, however, they continue to regard ASEAN as distinct, and thus to resist EU norm exports.

10.2 Comparative Regional Analysis: The EU as a 'model'?

Is it appropriate to judge ASEAN in comparison to other regions? The question of whether ASEAN is 'unique' is not a new one (for example, see Sharpe 2003). It is only relatively recently, however, that scholars have begun to consider this question by undertaking comparative regional analysis.[2] For example, Acharya's and Johnston's (2007) volume undertakes a systematic comparative regional analysis, with a focus on institutional design and its relationship to regional cooperation.[3] More recently, a volume by Börzel et al. (2012) explores different 'roads to regionalism';[4] the authors compare the regional cases of ASEAN, the Economic Community of West African States (ECOWAS), the League of Arab States, *Mercado Común del Sur* (MERCOSUR) and the North American Free Trade Agreement (NAFTA). These are certainly important and fruitful areas of research, particularly because it is only through comparative analysis that claims of uniqueness can be 'disaggregated': *in which respects* can ASEAN or any other regional organisation be regarded as unique? As Goltermann et al. (2012, p. 9) point out, regional organisations 'may all be unique in some way—but that does not preclude a comparative perspective'.[5]

One approach to comparative regional analysis is to explore the notion of 'models' of regional integration. For example, several scholars (e.g. Beeson 2005; Börzel and Risse 2009; Murray 2010) engage in comparative analyses of Europe and Asia, and investigate claims that the EU—the most highly institutionalised regional organisation—is a 'model' of regional integration. Börzel and Risse (2009, p. 11) claim that 'ASEAN's recent efforts to jump start its regional integration has [sic] been inspired by the European Union'. In particular, they argue, 'the Secretary-General of ASEAN as the Chief Administrative Officer, his/her four Deputies and the ASEAN Secretariat (Art. 11) may look like a nascent European Commission' (ibid.,

---

[2] Johnston noted in 2005 the 'almost nonexistent' comparative work on regional institutions (Johnston 2005, p. 1036).

[3] The volume compares and contrasts the features of various regional institutional institutions, including membership; scope; formal rules; norms and ideology; and mandate. The contributors' case studies are the EU, ASEAN, the League of Arab States, the Organization of American States and the African Union. The volume thus provides a useful typology of regional institutional design.

[4] These 'roads' are: the genesis and growth of regional organisations, institutional design, member states' behaviour in regional organisations and the effects of regional organisations on their member states.

[5] Some scholars (e.g. De Lombaerde et al. 2010; Söderbaum and Sbragia 2010) explore the conceptual and methodological aspects of comparative regional analysis, particularly with a view to interrogating the (lack of) dialogue between scholars of EU studies and regionalism elsewhere in the world. This too is an important line of inquiry.

p .11). Further, they argue, the ASEAN Summit and its Chairmanship resembles the European Council and its Presidency, and the Committee of Permanent Representatives was modelled on that of the EU. Jetschke and Murray (2012, p. 177) agree that 'there are similarities with an EU-style regional organisation, at least in terms of some features of its formal institutional set-up'.

These institutional similarities are explained, these scholars argue, by ASEAN drawing on lessons from the EU, and engaging in 'normative emulation'. Börzel (2012, p. 261) argues that emulation 'might be driving the recent deepening and broadening of ASEAN, whose new charter bears some striking resemblances to EU institutions'. Jetschke and Rüland (2009, p. 181) argue that 'members of ASE-AN continuously engage in cooperation rhetoric and devise cooperation projects because they emulate the European integration project'. Another term they use to describe this situation is 'institutional isomorphism', which is assumed to increase legitimacy of the organisation (Ibid., p. 183). Similarly, Katsumata (2009, p. 619) refers to 'mimetic adoption' by ASEAN of external norms (in the issue-areas of security and human rights) in the interests of 'securing ASEAN's identity as a legitimate institution'.

However, similarities in institutional design are not sufficient evidence of emulation. It is difficult to establish such a causal relationship. ASEAN officials do seek, from time to time, to learn from the EU. For example, the Eminent Persons Group (EPG), which produced a set of recommendations for the ASEAN Charter, travelled to Brussels in July 2006 to 'study the integration experience and problems in the European Union (EU)' (ASEAN 2006). The EU has promoted itself as a model of regionalism, for example through the ASEAN-EU Programme of Regional Integration Support (APRIS, established in 2003). As part of APRIS, the EU provides some financial support to ASEAN, 'aiming particularly at strengthening the institutional capacity of the ASEAN Secretariat and generally fostering regional cooperation' (Jetschke and Murray 2012, p. 178). However, while inter-regional dialogue can surely be productive and useful for both regional organisations,[6] there are certain risks in scholars outside the region making the assumption that ASEAN is progressing on a 'path' towards the EU model.

Such initiatives tend to rest on the assumption among EU officials that the EU has worthwhile lessons to impart to ASEAN and other regional organisations. Murray (2010, p. 308) identifies what she refers to as 'integration snobbery' in the 'positioning of the EU on a rather unsteady pedestal'. This, she argues, may overlook the 'profound historical differences' between the regions, and their different experiences of society, civil society and the role of the state. There is a danger in treating the EU as an 'ideal-type' of regional integration towards which ASEAN should progress.

---

[6] Former ASEAN Secretary-General Surin Pitsuwan has said that 'the APRIS support from the EU has been successful and helpful to ASEAN...The EU's experiences in integrating their economies are certainly good pointers for ASEAN and will help us realise these gains faster' (ASEAN 2011). Such comments do not, however, 'prove' emulation.

There are other implications of assuming that ASEAN 'emulates' the EU. Such arguments imply that ASEAN is something of a normative vacuum. It neglects the existence of what Acharya (2004, pp. 247–248) calls 'prior local norms'—in other words, existing normative standards. ASEAN is a site of 'competing normative terrains', which cannot be simply identified as a repository of various 'global' norms. Neither are they a neat collection of global and local norms. Rather, ASEAN norms have been advanced, negotiated, and evolved over time—in some cases, 'localized' as Acharya (2004) puts it—and reflect competing interests, ideas and values from a variety of sources. The Secretariat may gain greater capacity in the future, but we should not necessarily assess its 'progress' as relative to the EU. It is important to remain cognisant of the EU 'lens' through which observers and analysts often perceive ASEAN.

10.3   ASEAN: Origins and Norms

ASEAN was established in 1967 by five states: Singapore, Malaysia, Indonesia, the Philippines and Thailand. It has since expanded to include Brunei Darassalam (admitted in 1984), Vietnam (1995), Myanmar (1997), Laos (1997) and Cambodia (1999). The 1967 *Bangkok Declaration* states that ASEAN 'open for participation to all States in the South-East Asian Region', and 'represents the collective will of the nations of South-East Asia to bind themselves together in friendship and cooperation' (ASEAN 1967, online). The founding member states wanted to pursue regional stability following several bilateral disagreements. They were also concerned about internal stability, and were keen to protect sovereignty and support mutual state-building efforts. Member states also recognised the potential for economic growth through intra-regional trade.

ASEAN's foundational norms were articulated in the 1976 *Treaty of Amity and Cooperation* (TAC). The 'principles' governing relations between member states, which may be referred to as ASEAN's core *constitutive norms*, include: mutual respect for independence, sovereignty, equality, territorial integrity and national identity of all nations; the right of every State to lead its national existence free from external interference, subversion or coercion; non-interference in the internal affairs of one another; the settlement of differences or disputes by peaceful means; the renunciation of the threat or use of force; and effective cooperation (ASEAN 1976, Article 2). These norms are clearly influenced by the Westphalian principles articulated by the UN Charter, and are reiterated in various core ASEAN documents (including the Charter).

The norms of respect for *sovereignty* and *territorial integrity* reflect the founding states' agreement to respect each other's borders and treat each other as sovereign states, with exclusive rule over a delimited territory. ASEAN member states are self-governing political communities, and believe (or at least agree) that they should treat each other as such. The norm of *equality* reflects the notion that 'all states, as sovereign entities, are formally equal within the society of states' (Lake

2008, p. 54). In ASEAN, the norm of equality implies that all member states have equal status; former ASEAN Secretary-General Rodolfo Severino (2006, p. 32) refers to the 'scrupulous observance of the sovereign equality of the member-states'. The norm of *non-interference* in internal affairs entails that domestic governance is excluded as a criterion of membership of ASEAN, and as a topic for (official) dialogue. It also means that member states traditionally have refrained from publicly criticising one another (Haacke 2005, p. 189; Katsumata 2004, p. 243).[7]

These constitutive norms are complemented by the *procedural norms* of the so-called 'ASEAN Way'. The core procedural norms are decision-making by consensus; informality and non-binding commitments; pragmatism; and moving at 'a pace comfortable to all'. Member states have traditionally rejected the 'legalistic', formal style of Western institutional structures, and instead favour a private and informal political culture embodied by small elite networks. They are spared the embarrassment of dissent, through closed-door dialogue that precedes formal meetings (Acharya 2001, p. 68); thus, final decisions are officially made by 'consensus'.

Member states prefer to move at 'a pace comfortable to all', which, as Severino explains, 'is a favourite phrase in ASEAN documents, [and] means advancing as fast, or as slowly, as the most reluctant or least confident member allows' (Severino 2006, p. 18). Member states prefer caution and gradualism; this explains the 'relative rarity of legally binding agreements in ASEAN' (Severino 2006, p. 18). Thus, the ASEAN Way 'stresses patience, evolution, informality, pragmatism, and consensus' (Capie and Evans 2007, p. 9). It provides a code of conduct for member state relations; in their interactions, ASEAN members focus on accommodation and consultation. They prefer 'non-binding commitments rather than legalistic formulae and codified rules' (Capie and Evans 2007, p. 11).

The Association is thus characterised by relatively low levels of institutionalisation and legalisation. While the founding states hoped that ASEAN would facilitate 'regional peace and stability' (ASEAN 1967), the entity began as a grouping or association rather than a *formal* international organisation. This is not to suggest that ASEAN was without purpose; rather, ASEAN members have traditionally preferred an informal arrangement with less institutionalisation. Alagappa (1987, p. 183) has described this as a 'loose framework [which] provides opportunities for 'face saving' which is considered vital for Asean solidarity and cohesion'. The member states' preference for consensus decision-making reflected their cautious approach to regional cooperation.

ASEAN's approach to regional order is thus based on a combination of the procedural norms of the ASEAN Way, and the constitutive norms discussed above, rather than formal, explicit 'rules' (Acharya 2001; Busse 1999; Collins 2003). It has sought to admit all Southeast Asian states as members, and to avoid confrontation through gradual institutional change using consensus decision-making. In this context, since the Association's establishment, member states have managed to prevent intra-regional disputes from escalating into full-scale conflict; this led

---

[7] Other constitutive norms—the peaceful settlement of disputes, the non-use of force, effective cooperation, and the norm of inclusion—are not discussed here given space constraints.

observers by the early 1990s to regard ASEAN as 'one of the most successful experiments in regional cooperation in the developing world' (Acharya 2001, p. 5).
However, one could argue that this is in part because the norm of consensus means
that ASEAN is beholden to the 'lowest common denominator' in decision-making.
Thus, institutional developments are tempered by the interests of the most reluctant
member. ASEAN norms effectively provide a pragmatic way for very diverse states
to interact within the same regional organisation, but also raise questions about the
Association's credibility and effectiveness.

10.4   The ASEAN Charter: Institutional Innovations?

ASEAN adopted its first Charter on November 20, 2007 (ASEAN 2007). ASEAN
leaders hailed it as a 'milestone' for regional cooperation. Particularly after the
Asian financial crisis of 1997–1998, several leaders and ASEAN officials (particularly from Malaysia, Indonesia, the Philippines and Singapore) appeared keen to
'reinvigorate' ASEAN and make it more relevant and cohesive. For example, Tun
Musa Hitam, a former Malaysian deputy prime minister and Malaysia's representative to the EPG, argues that the ASEAN leaders' desire for a Charter 'demonstrated
that they wanted to be much more cohesive against the earlier arrangement of a
loose kind of club' (quoted in Hong 2007). Singapore's then Deputy Prime Minister, Shunmugam Jayakumar (more widely known as S. Jayakumar), also expressed
concern that unless it reinvents itself, 'ASEAN—as an organisation—will atrophy
and become marginalized' (quoted in Zee News 2007).

The ASEAN Charter was intended to strengthen the Association and to elevate
both its international (extra-regional) standing and its significance to its own members. It was designed to provide the 'legal and institutional framework' for ASEAN
and to 'codify all ASEAN *norms, rules and values*' (ASEAN 2005; emphasis added). This suggests, *prima facie*, that ASEAN intended to become a more institutionalised and legalised organisation.

The EPG submitted its report in December 2006. Among other recommendations, the EPG referred to the importance of 'strengthening organisational effectiveness' by 'empowering' the Secretary-General. This reflects the growing recognition that the Secretariat has long been underfunded and understaffed (for example,
Narine 2004, p. 438).[8] The EPG also argued that ASEAN should be 'conferred legal
personality and be able to engage in legal proceeding [sic]'. While the EPG report
did not specifically define 'legal personality', it suggested that it included 'granting
ASEAN the capacity to own property, enter into contracts, and for ASEAN to sue

---

[8] The ASEAN Secretariat was established in 1976, at the first ASEAN Summit in Bali, Indonesia.
The member states signed the *Agreement on the Establishment of the ASEAN Secretariat*, which
states that the basic mandate for the Secretariat is 'to provide greater efficiency in the coordination of ASEAN organs and for more effective implementation of ASEAN projects and activities'
(ASEAN 1976).

and be sued' (ASEAN 2006, p. 44). This implies an enhanced role for the Secretariat as representative of the Association in such transactions.

However, the Charter adopts only some of these recommendations. It grants ASEAN 'legal personality' but does not further specify what this entails in practice—for example, it does not grant the Secretary-General the ability to sign any agreements on behalf of ASEAN. As such, it is unclear how granting ASEAN 'legal personality' differs from the traditional arrangement of ASEAN declarations and agreements being signed by its member states.[9] In regard to Secretariat officials, the Charter states (in keeping with previous protocol) that the Secretary-General is to be 'appointed by the ASEAN Summit for a non-renewable term of office of 5 years, selected from among nationals of the ASEAN Member States based on alphabetical rotation' (ASEAN 2007, Article 11). The Secretary-General shall be assisted by four Deputy Secretaries-General (rather than only two) 'with the rank and status of Deputy Ministers' (ibid.).

However, the Charter makes other changes to ASEAN's structure which enhance the role of the *member states*. For example, it states that the ASEAN Summit—the primary meeting of Heads of State or Government of the member states—will be held twice a year instead of annually (ASEAN 2007, Article 7). It also asserts that each member state shall appoint a Permanent Representative to ASEAN, making up a Committee of Permanent Representatives (CPR) based in Jakarta (Article 12). The CPR facilitates a greater presence of each member state in Jakarta, and thus, potentially greater oversight of the Secretariat (ASEAN 2013d). The Charter also establishes an ASEAN Coordinating Council comprised of member states' foreign ministers (Article 8), which will meet 'at least twice a year' (ASEAN 2013a).[10] ASEAN also now has three 'Community Councils' for each of its three 'Communities'—Political-Security, Economic and Socio-Cultural—comprising the relevant ministers from each member state (ASEAN 2013b).

These changes—more Summits, new Permanent Representatives in Jakarta, more frequent and formal meetings of ministers—increase the frequency and scope of interaction of member state representatives. Thus, there are tensions among particular provisions of the Charter which nominally strengthen the position of the Secretariat—raising the possibility of greater centralisation of ASEAN—while also reaffirming the significance of member states and augmenting their interaction in ASEAN forums.

Moreover, the increase in the number of meetings also increases the administrative workload for the Secretariat. In apparent recognition of this, the Charter goes on to state that the Secretariat 'shall be provided with the *necessary financial resources* to perform its functions effectively' (Article 30, emphasis added). However, there were no changes made to the formula for member state contributions. As Chin

---

[9] Interviews conducted by the author with various Southeast Asian commentators and Secretariat staff in 2008–2009 did not clarify how ASEAN would 'enter into contracts' of its own accord; the interview subjects could not (or would not) provide an answer.

[10] The foreign ministers have traditionally wielded significant influence in ASEAN decision-making, and have long met regularly in ASEAN Ministerial Meetings.

(2009, p. 32) points out, 'the strengthening of ASEAN institutions as promised by the Charter is not matched by a commensurate increase in the annual budget for the ASEAN Secretariat, or any substantive adjustments in financial contributions from ASEAN members to the organisation'. Indeed, the Charter reiterates that 'the operational budget of the ASEAN Secretariat shall be met by member states through equal annual contributions which shall be remitted in a timely manner' (Article 30).

The Secretariat has long been funded by equal contributions by member states, which are kept low enough for the less developed states to manage. ASEAN does not routinely release publicly its financial statements, but around the time of the Charter, total contributions were usually around US\$ 8–9 million per year, and had not changed for some time. Termsak Chalermpalanupap, the ASEAN Director for Research and Special Assistant to the Secretary-General, reports that in 2007–2008, each member state contributed \$ 905,000, providing an operating budget to the Secretariat of \$ 9.05 million. As he notes, 'a Secretariat budget barely larger than US\$ 9 million is miniscule when viewed against the combined nominal GDP of the member states—more than US\$ 1 trillion in 2007' (Termsak Chalermpalanupap 2008, p. 122). In May 2011, Noel Morada reported that contributions had increased to \$ 1.4 million per member state; thus, the total budget has increased to \$ 14 million (Morada 2011, p. 24). Nevertheless, the Secretariat's resources remain limited.

This is explained in part by ASEAN's adherence to the norm of equality as it has expanded to include less developed states as members. Upon admission of the so-called 'CLMV' states (Cambodia, Laos, Myanmar and Vietnam), the need for low contributions has been compounded so that they can afford member contributions.[11] At the same time, ASEAN has established a huge number of regular meetings, formal and informal summits, dialogues and standing committees, and the Secretariat 'manages this complex arrangement' (Jones and Smith 2007, p. 156). ASEAN provides only limited information about its Secretariat (e.g. ASEAN 2013d), but Bower (2010, online) reports that in August 2010, the Secretariat had about 300 staff, 'including 65 managers and experts, 180 local staff, and 55 staff from donor organizations'.

Thus, there appears to be an incongruity in increasing the number of Secretariat officials (Deputy Secretaries-General) and the range of administrative activities, while failing to ensure sufficient funding for the Secretariat. As Bower (2010, online) asks, 'How, then, will ASEAN meet its international expectations and realize the vision of its leaders with a Secretariat that is understaffed and underfunded?' Member states ostensibly aim to strengthen ASEAN and provide it with greater institutional and legal capacity, yet fail to increase its resources. Maintaining an underfunded Secretariat clearly imposes limits on the administrative and planning functions of ASEAN.[12]

---

[11] At the time of writing, these states each have a significantly lower Gross Domestic Product (GDP) per capita than most other member states.

[12] It also constrains important functions such as ASEAN's ability to respond collectively to regional crises remains constrained. For example, in the aftermath of Cyclone Nargis in May 2008, 'ASEAN was not able to shell out monetary resources on its own'; rather, the crisis fund was

Of course, member states contribute to ASEAN in other ways. They each have a National Secretariat, housed in their respective foreign ministries, which propose and administer policies (once they have been accepted at ASEAN Summits). Further, each year a member state acts as chair of ASEAN, by alphabetical rotation, and the chair hosts many ASEAN meetings. However, if ASEAN wishes to achieve its goals, it needs a Secretariat and Secretary-General with more resources and autonomy. As Jusuf Wanandi, a prominent Indonesian analyst, argues, 'The system now, whereby every member pays the same amount, is no longer realistic. A new formula that is more tenable and could increase the budget adequately should be contemplated' (Wanandi 2006, online). Some members, such as Singapore and Indonesia, could certainly manage higher contributions; the current contribution of $ 1.4 million each is a tiny fraction of their GDPs.[13]

The gap between (purported) ambitions and capacity may be explained by the notion that, by maintaining the arrangement of equal contributions, member states are complying with, and reaffirming, the norm of equality. Equal contributions would, *prima facie*, represent equal influence. However, I argue that the explanation is somewhat more nuanced. After all, norms are dynamic, and are subject to reinterpretation and thus evolution over time. The norm of equality does not actually mean that member states have equal influence in ASEAN dialogue and decisions.[14] The tension between capacity and the norm of equality reflects a more fundamental dynamic in the relationship between member states and the Secretariat. Clearly, views differ as to the role of the Secretariat and the degree of autonomy it should have.

However, it is difficult to accurately gauge the nature of these different views, and who holds them. There is limited available evidence about the discussions of the High Level Task Force (HLTF) which drafted the Charter. Tan Sri Ahmad Fuzi bin Abdul Razak, Malaysia's Ambassador-At-Large and representative to the HLTF, refers to the absence of a provision in the Charter for the 'mobilisation of resources'; he notes that 'many within the HLTF itself were unhappy with its inability to achieve a consensus on this. Various proposals put forth on the table were not even considered' (Fuzi 2008, p. 22). He does not identify which members supported and which rejected the revision of contributions, or the basis of contention. It is likely that the norm of equality (at least ostensibly) shaped the ultimate decision to retain the system of equal contributions. However, we should note that emphasis-

---

provided by private organisations (Amador 2009, p. 11). The Secretariat lacks fiscal, human and other resources, and thus it 'could not have responded to the situation on its own initiative had the member states not contributed' (11). Instead, Surin had to appeal for aid from the member states in order that some relief efforts could be undertaken.

[13] According to the World Bank (2013), Singapore's GDP was US$ 275 billion in 2012 and Indonesia's GDP was US$ 878 billion (in current US dollars).

[14] In other words, the norm of equality is not reflected in the practical reality of ASEAN dialogue. As Emmerson (2007) notes, 'acknowledging the formal equality and autonomy of member states need not deter big states from informally "persuading" small ones' (438). Naturally, all member states do not have equal *influence* in ASEAN. Some member states—particularly the founding member states of Indonesia, Singapore, Thailand, Malaysia and the Philippines—undoubtedly have more influence than others in regional dialogue and decision-making. The so-called 'CLMV' states, which are newer members (having been admitted to ASEAN between 1985 and 1999), and are less developed and less economically significant, tend to have less clout.

ing the norm of equality suits member states who do not *want* an Association with increased capacity. It may be that the lack of resources historically devoted to the ASEAN Secretariat is a deliberate (if implicit) strategy to limit its autonomy.

This perspective emphasises the continued importance of 'traditional' ASEAN norms. One could argue that 'cognitive priors' shape the introduction of institutional innovations in ASEAN. Acharya (2009, p. 21) defines cognitive priors as 'an existing set of ideas, belief systems, and norms, which determine and condition an individual or social group's receptivity to new norms'. Thus, for Acharya, 'normative change and institution-building in Asia are better viewed as evolutionary processes contingent upon prior regional norms and processes' (ibid., p. 7). Keeping the locus of decision-making with the member states is congruent with ASEAN's 'cognitive priors'; the founding member states never intended to create a supranational organisation like the EU. This provides the context for ASEAN's role as a 'resister' of the EU's norm exports. Several ASEAN officials have stated in interviews with the author that ASEAN 'is not the EU'.

10.5   How Should we Analyse ASEAN?

The difficulties of interpreting member states' visions of ASEAN are reflected in scholarly debates about the significance of the Association as a regional organisation, and about the role of institutions in ASEAN. After the Charter came into force, the members of the HLTF which drafted it each contributed a chapter to a volume entitled *The Making of the ASEAN Charter*. The editors[15] write in the preface:

> It is said that a camel is a horse designed by a committee. The ASEAN Charter is the diplomatic equivalent of a camel. It may not have the good looks of a thoroughbred, but the camel is a perfectly good and reliable animal. When the terrain is tough and dry, a camel will survive trials that would kill the toughest horse. (Koh et al. 2009, p. xxi).

This is an interesting analogy. ASEAN sceptics might be expected to argue the opposite: that the Charter—and perhaps, ASEAN generally—has the 'good looks' but not the toughness or reliability of a camel. To the extent that ambitions outweigh institutional capacity, and/or member states lack the political will to make changes to improve that capacity, ASEAN is more of a thoroughbred.

Thus, despite the creation of the Charter, perceptions persist that 'ASEAN has long been seen as operating mainly in the realm of symbolic politics rather than of concrete obligations and policies' (Hurd 2011, p. 255). Certainly, it seems that at least some members do not *want* an Association with increased capacity. As Amador (2009, p. 14) argues, 'The Secretariat is indeed ready to take on responsibility. The member states, which are the political principals of ASEAN, may not be ready'.

---

[15] The editors were Tommy Koh, Rosario G. Manalo, and Walter Woon. Tommy Koh is an Ambassador-At-Large in Singapore's Ministry of Foreign Affairs and was Singapore's representative to the HLTF. Rosario G. Manalo is a career diplomat from the Philippines and acted as its Special Envoy for the Drafting of the ASEAN Charter (ie. its representative to the HLTF). Koh and Manalo shared the role of Chair of the HLTF. Walter Woon is a Singaporean lawyer, academic, diplomat and former Attorney-General; he was part of Singapore's delegation to the HLTF.

The latter reaffirm the intergovernmental nature of ASEAN, and the cognitive priors or norms of sovereignty and non-interference. From this perspective, the locus of decision-making in ASEAN will remain with the member states, and ASEAN initiatives will continue conceived within the national secretariats based in each member state's foreign ministry.

Indeed, Jetschke and Rüland (2009, p. 198) themselves argue that 'the ASEAN Charter is... testimony to the persisting aversion that the majority of ASEAN members nurture against deep institutionalization of regional cooperation'. Their argument about emulation of the EU is qualified by the acknowledgment that 'Southeast Asian leaders and scholars persistently stress that ASEAN is no Southeast Asian version of the European Union' (ibid., p. 181). Thus, ASEAN quite consciously lacks the mechanisms necessary for international cooperation, such as a 'legacy of legalism' or 'mechanisms of monitoring' (ibid., p. 181). In a sense, then, ASEAN member states set out *ambitions* for deeper and broader regionalism through increased institutionalisation, but create a 'reality-expectations' gap. The implication is that the member states hope to gain benefits, in the form of legitimacy, from creating these expectations.

Thus, certain institutional innovations—particularly in the ASEAN Charter—appear to signify (*prima facie*) an intention to change. However, traditional ASEAN norms remain important and the Association remains intergovernmental. Member states are faced with the dilemma of wanting to be regarded as part of a credible and relevant regional organisation, while also resisting the ceding of institutional and financial autonomy to the Secretariat. They regard ASEAN as distinct vis-à-vis other regional organisations, particularly the EU. As such—while the incremental pace of change within ASEAN has led to criticism[16]—member states continue to resist EU norm exports.

10.6   Conclusions and Future Research

This chapter argues that the purported ambitions to strengthen the capacity of the ASEAN Secretariat have been stymied by the reluctance to revise the formula for member contributions. This reflects the significant tensions among ASEAN norms. Plans to make the organisation more institutionalised are hindered by traditional interpretations of ASEAN norms of sovereignty and the equality of member states.

---

[16] For example, Hurd (2011) calls ASEAN 'a framework of possible future cooperation but not much more than that'. It is characterised by a 'substantive emptiness...that is remarkable' (256). Other scholars, such as Jones and Smith (2002), have referred to ASEAN as an 'imitation community' and 'rhetorical shell' that gives 'form but no substance to domestic and international arrangements' (93). Khoo (2004) and Sharpe (2003), among others, have referred to ASEAN as merely a 'talk shop'. This criticism has been motivated in part by ASEAN's perceived failures in responding to regional problems (particularly since the Asian financial crisis of 1997–1998, and Burma's admission as a member in 1998). This, for critics, reflects the limits of ASEAN's regional 'experiment'.

This raises a question for future research: does ASEAN (or any other regional organisation) *need* a large, well-funded Secretariat to be effective, credible, and/or relevant? How can we assess the role and influence of regional bureaucracies?

It is only relatively recently that a body of literature has emerged examining international bureaucracies—how they work, whether and how they assert influence, and under what circumstances they may become dysfunctional. For example, Barnett and Finnemore (2004) explore these issues in regard to the International Monetary Fund (IMF), the United Nations High Commissioner for Refugees (UNHCR) and the United Nations (UN) Secretariat.[17] Contributors to Biermann's and Siebenhüner's (2009) volume examine international environmental bureaucracies (e.g. the UN Environment Programme Secretariat and the OECD Environment Directorate), and map out the mechanisms (such as persuasion and socialisation) through which they exercise influence. However, there is a lack of comparative analysis of *regional* bureaucracies, and (relatedly) of theorising about regional bureaucracies. Börzel (2012, p. 260) argues that 'theories of regionalism provide a whole range of explanatory factors for the genesis and growth of regional organizations. They are less equipped to account for the differential outcomes and (changes in) institutional designs we find across different regions'.

We can make some observations that suggest that further comparative work would be useful. Bower (2010, p. 2) points out that the ASEAN Secretariat budget is about 0.137% of the EU's administrative cost, and its staff is about 7.86% the size of the EU's staff. In comparison, the ASEAN Secretariat certainly appears to have low capacity. While 'ASEAN remains an intergovernmental organisation' (Börzel and Risse 2009, p. 12) without supranational ambitions, it seems intuitive that ASEAN needs a larger, more well-funded Secretariat to be effective, credible and relevant, particularly given the difficulties experienced in addressing regional crises in a coordinated manner. However, we need more research to understand exactly how or why this might be the case. Moreover, if ASEAN member states wish to resist the greater centralisation of the organisation, the needs of the Secretariat may not be met. ASEAN is thus an interesting case study for comparative analyses of regional bureaucracies. Other regional organisations, including the EU, Organisation of American States and the African Union, should also be studied with a view to understanding the impact of variations in Secretariat capacity.

This chapter raises a number of questions: Should we only assess regional organisations in relation to their own goals? Must regional organisations have a certain degree of institutionalisation, legalisation and supranationalism to be considered credible and/or effective? Or—considering the case examined in this chapter—can a 'looser and less regulated' (Murray 2010, p. 312) style of interstate regional cooperation be 'successful'? These questions highlight the need for further comparative regional analysis, particularly in regard to regional bureaucracies and their relationships with member states. While the case of ASEAN suggests that a regional organisation may 'resist' the export of norms from another region, a comparative

---

[17] Note, however, that Barnett and Finnemore (2004) conceptualise international organisations *as themselves* bureaucracies—rather than focusing only on the secretariats of those organisations.

analysis of regional bureaucracies would help us to understand why, and under what conditions, this might be the case.

References

Acharya, A. (2001). *Constructing a security community in Southeast Asia: ASEAN and the problem of regional order*. London: Routledge.

Acharya, A. (2004). How ideas spread: Whose norms matter? Norm localization and international change in Asian regionalism. *International Organization, 58*, 239–275. doi:10.1017/s0020818304582024.

Acharya, A. (2009). *Whose ideas matter? Agency and power in Asian regionalism*. Ithaca: Cornell University Press.

Acharya, A., & Johnston, A. I. (Eds.). (2007). *Crafting cooperation: Regional international institutions in comparative perspective*. Cambridge: Cambridge University Press.

Alagappa, M. (1987). Asean institutional framework and modus operandi: Recommendations for change. In N. Sopiee, L. S. Chew, & S. J. Lim (Eds.), *ASEAN at the crossroads: Obstacles, options and opportunities in economic cooperation* (pp. 183–230). Kuala Lumpur: Institute of Strategic and International Studies.

Alatas, A. (2001). ASEAN in a globalizing world. *Asia-Pacific Review, 8*(2), 1–9. doi:10.1080/09544120120098645.

Amador, J. S. (2009). Community building at the time of Nargis: The ASEAN response. *Journal of Current Southeast Asian Affairs, 28*(4), 3–22.

ASEAN. (1967). The ASEAN declaration (Bangkok Declaration). http://www.asean.org/news/item/the-asean-declaration-bangkok-declaration. Accessed 28 Oct 2013.

ASEAN. (1976). Treaty of amity and cooperation in Southeast Asia. http://www.asean.org/news/item/treaty-of-amity-and-cooperation-in-southeast-asia-indonesia-24-february-1976-3. Accessed 28 Oct 2013.

ASEAN. (2005). Kuala Lumpur declaration on the establishment of the ASEAN charter. http://www.asean.org/news/item/kuala-lumpur-declaration-on-the-establishment-of-the-asean-charter-kuala-lumpur-12-december-2005. Accessed 28 Oct 2013.

ASEAN. (2006). Report of the eminent persons group on the ASEAN charter. http://www.asean.org/archive/19247.pdf. Accessed 28 Oct 2013.

ASEAN. (2007). Charter of the Association of Southeast Asian Nations. http://www.asean.org/archive/publications/ASEAN-Charter.pdf. Accessed 28 Oct 2013.

ASEAN. (2011). ASEAN and EU: Family matters. http://www.asean.org/news/asean-secretariat-news/item/asean-and-eu-family-matters. Accessed 28 Oct 2013.

ASEAN. (2013a). ASEAN coordinating council. http://www.asean.org/asean/asean-structure/asean-coordinating-council. Accessed 28 Oct 2013.

ASEAN. (2013b). ASEAN community councils. http://www.asean.org/asean/asean-structure/asean-community-councils. Accessed 28 Oct 2013.

ASEAN. (2013c). Committee of permanent representatives. http://www.asean.org/asean/asean-structure/committee-of-permanent-representatives. Accessed 28 Oct 2013

ASEAN. (2013d). The ASEAN secretariat: Basic mandate, functions and composition. http://www.asean.org/news/item/asean-secretariat-basic-documents-asean-secretariat-basic-mandate-2. Accessed 28 Oct 2013.

Barnett, M., & Finnemore, M. (2004). *Rules for the world: International organizations in global politics*. Ithaca: Cornell University Press.

Beeson, M. (2005). Rethinking regionalism: Europe and East Asia in comparative perspective. *Journal of European Public Policy, 12*(5), 969–985. doi:10.1080/13501760500270620.

Bellamy, A. J. (2004). *Security communities and their neighbours: Regional fortresses or global integrators?* New York: Palgrave Macmillan.

Biermann, F., & Siebenhüner, B. (Eds.). (2009). *Managers of global change: The influence of international environmental bureaucracies*. Cambridge: The MIT Press.

Börzel, T. A. (2012). Do all roads lead to regionalism? In T. A. Börzel, L. Goltermann, M. Lohaus, & K. Striebinger (Eds.), *Roads to regionalism: Genesis, design, and effects of regional organizations* (pp. 255–268). Surrey: Ashgate.

Börzel, T. A., & Risse, T. (2009). The rise of (inter-) regionalism: The EU as a model for regional integration. Paper presented at the Annual Convention of the American Political Science Association, Toronto, Canada, 2–6 September 2009.

Börzel, T. A., Goltermann, L., Lohaus, M., & Striebinger, K. (Eds.). (2012). *Roads to regionalism: Genesis, design, and effects of regional organizations*. Surrey: Ashgate.

Bower, E. Z. (2010). Balance & good health come from a strong core: Is the ASEAN secretariat properly resourced? Center for Strategic and International Studies, Washington, DC. http://csis.org/publication/balance-good-health-come-strong-core. Accessed 28 Oct 2013.

Busse, N. (1999). Constructivism and Southeast Asian security. *The Pacific Review, 12*(1), 39–60. doi:10.1080/09512749908719277.

Capie, D., & Evans, P. (2007). *The Asia-Pacific security lexicon*. Singapore: Institute of Southeast Asian Studies.

Central Intelligence Agency. (2012). The world factbook. https://www.cia.gov/library/publications/the-world-factbook/index.html. Accessed 28 Oct 2013.

Chalermpalanupap, T. (2008). Institutional reform: One charter, three communities, many challenges. In D. K. Emmerson (Ed.), *Hard choices: Security, democracy and regionalism in Southeast Asia* (pp. 91–131). Stanford: Walter H. Shorenstein Asia-Pacific Research Center.

Chin, K. W. (2009). Emerging East Asian regional architecture: ASEAN perspectives. In W. T. Tow & K. W. Chin (Eds.), *ASEAN-India-Australia: Towards closer engagement in a New Asia* (pp. 22–39). Singapore: Institute of Southeast Asian Studies.

Collins, A. (2003). *Security and Southeast Asia: Domestic, regional, and global issues*. Singapore: Institute of Southeast Asian Studies.

De Lombaerde, P., Söderbaum, F., Van Langenhove, L., & Baert, F. (2010). The problem of comparison in comparative regionalism. *Review of International Studies, 35,* 731–753. doi:10.1017/S0260210510000707.

Emmerson, D. K. (2007). Challenging ASEAN: A "topological" view. *Contemporary Southeast Asia, 29*(3), 424–446. doi:10.1355/cs29-3c.

Finnemore, M., & Sikkink, K. (1998). International norm dynamics and political change. *International Organization, 52*(4), 887–917. doi:10.1162/002081898550789.

Fuzi, A. (2008). Facing unfair criticisms. In D. K. Emmerson (Ed.), *Hard choices: Security, democracy and regionalism in Southeast Asia* (pp. 17–26). Stanford: Walter H. Shorenstein Asia-Pacific Research Center.

Goltermann, L., Lohaus, M., Spielau, A., & Striebinger, K. (2012). Roads to regionalism: Concepts, issues, and cases. In T. A. Börzel, L. Goltermann, M. Lohaus, & K. Striebinger (Eds.), *Roads to regionalism: Genesis, design, and effects of regional organizations* (pp. 3–21). Surrey: Ashgate.

Haacke, J. (2005). "Enhanced interaction" with Myanmar and the project of a security community: Is ASEAN refining or breaking with its diplomatic and security culture? *Contemporary Southeast Asia, 27*(2), 188–216.

Hong, C. (2007, February 3). Consensus builder for ASEAN Charter. *The Straits Times,* 23.

Hurd, I. (2011). *International organizations: Politics, law, practice*. Cambridge: Cambridge University Press.

Jetschke, A., & Murray, P. (2012). Diffusing regional integration: The EU and Southeast Asia. *West European Politics, 35*(1), 174–191. doi:10.1080/01402382.2012.631320.

Jetschke, A., & Rüland, J. (2009). Decoupling rhetoric and practice: The cultural limits of ASEAN cooperation. *The Pacific Review, 22*(2), 179–203. doi:10.1080/09512740902815326.

Johnston, A. I. (2005). Conclusions and extensions: Toward mid-range theorizing and beyond Europe. *International Organization, 59*(4), 1013–1044. doi:10.1017.S0020818305050344.
Jones, D. M., & Smith, M. L. R. (2002). ASEAN's imitation community. *ORBIS, 46,* 93–109. doi:10.1016/S0030-4387(01)00108-9.
Katsumata, H. (2004). Why is ASEAN diplomacy changing? From "non-interference" to "open and frank discussions". *Asian Survey, 44*(2), 237–254. doi:10.1525/as.2004.44.2.237.
Katsumata, H. (2009). ASEAN and human rights: Resisting Western pressure or emulating the West? *The Pacific Review, 22*(5), 619–637. doi:10.1080/09512740903329731.
Katsumata, H. (2011). Mimetic adoption and norm diffusion: 'Western' security cooperation in Southeast Asia? *Review of International Studies, 37*(2), 557–576. doi:10.1017/S0260210510000872.
Katzenstein, P. (1996). *The culture of national security: Norms and identity in world politics.* New York: Columbia University Press.
Keohane, R. (1988). International institutions—two Approaches. *International Studies Quarterly, 32*(4), 379–396.
Khalik, A. (2007, April 19). FM: ASEAN charter to have dispute settlement mechanisms. *The Jakarta Post.*
Khoo, N. (2004). Rhetoric vs. reality: ASEAN's clouded future. *Georgetown Journal of International Affairs, 5*(2), 49–56.
Koh, T., Manalo, R. G., & Woon, W. (Eds.). (2009). *The making of the ASEAN charter.* Singapore: World Scientific.
Lake, D. A. (2008). The state and international relations. In C. Reus-Smit, & D. Snidal (Eds.), *The Oxford handbook of international relations* (pp. 41–61). Oxford: Oxford University Press.
Morada, N. (2011). The role of regional and subregional arrangements in strengthening the responsibility to protect: ASEAN and the ARF. In The Stanley Foundation (Ed.), *The role of regional and subregional arrangements in strengthening the responsibility to protect* (pp. 19–29). New York: The Stanley Foundation.
Murray, P. (2010). Comparative regional integration in the EU and East Asia: Moving beyond integration snobbery. *International Politics, 47*(3/4), 308–323. doi:10.1057/ip.2010.13.
Narine, S. (2004). State sovereignty, political legitimacy and regional institutionalism in the Asia-Pacific. *The Pacific Review, 17*(3), 423–450. doi:10.1080/0551274042000261524.
Severino, R. C. (2006). *Southeast Asia in search of a community: Insights from the former secretary-general.* Singapore: Institute of Southeast Asian Studies.
Sharpe, S. (2003). An ASEAN way to security cooperation in Southeast Asia? *The Pacific Review, 16*(2), 231–250. doi:10.1080/0951274032000069624.
Söderbaum, F., & Sbragia, A. (2010). EU Studies and the 'New Regionalism': What can be gained from dialogue?' *European Integration, 32*(6), 563–582. doi:10.1080/07036337.2010.518716.
Wanandi, J. (2006). ASEAN future challenges and the importance of an ASEAN charter. *ASIEN, 100,* 85–87.
World Bank. (2013). Data: Countries and economies. http://data.worldbank.org/country. Accessed 28 Oct 2013.
Zee News. (2007, January 1). ASEAN risks irrelevance unless it transforms: Singapore.

Dr. Avery Poole is a Lecturer in International Relations at the University of Melbourne. She is also Deputy Director of the Master of International Relations program in the Melbourne School of Government. Her research interests include regional architecture in the Asia-Pacific region, with a particular focus on ASEAN; the nexus between Indonesian foreign policy and domestic politics; and human rights institutions in Southeast Asia. She obtained her PhD from The University of British Columbia.

Chapter 11
Reception of EU Trade Mark Law in New Zealand

Alison Firth

11.1 Introduction

This chapter investigates the indirect transmission of the European Union (EU) trade mark norms to New Zealand and their reception. Adaptation took place *en route*, as the norms found their way to New Zealand through the text of the World Trade Organisation's (WTO) agreement on Trade Related Aspects on Intellectual Property Rights (TRIPs) and the legislative models used by New Zealand to implement TRIPs. One may observe the adoption of beneficial norms and the rejection of problematic ones. New Zealand seems to have taken this 'legal transplant'[1] well and avoided importing ills which have befallen trade mark law in Europe. First we shall consider briefly what trade marks are and what trade mark laws do. Then we shall consider how New Zealand has responded to some 'negative' EU trade mark norms.

Trade mark laws protect distinctive signs, or 'marks', used in the course of trade to distinguish between the goods or services of different enterprises (WIPO 2014; Sumpter 2011; Pires de Carvalho 2012).[2] Trade marks are the principal components

---

[1] The phrase and the underlying model of diffusion of legal norms are Watson's: Alan Watson *Legal Transplants: An Approach to Comparative Law* (Edinburgh 1974). A 'Bibliography on Legal Transplants and the Diffusion of Law' may be found at http://www.alanwatson.org/readings.html, including work critical of the theory. See also Garcia and Masselot in this volume.

[2] Nuno Pires de Carvalho (2012) argues that all intellectual property serves a differentiating function.

A. Firth (✉)
University of Newcastle, Newcastle, UK
e-mail: alison.firth@ncl.ac.uk

Queen Mary University of London, London, UK

University of Surrey, Guildford, UK

© Springer International Publishing Switzerland 2015
A. Björkdahl et al. (eds.), *Importing EU Norms,* United Nations University Series on Regionalism 8, DOI 10.1007/978-3-319-13740-7_11

of 'brands' (Davis 2011).[3] Trade mark laws indirectly protect the interests of consumers[4], support international trade in goods and services[5] and foster the competitive process[6] as well as directly protecting the interests of proprietors/users (Finch 2012)[7] of the marks. Proprietors can register their marks for an identified range of goods and services and then sue unauthorized users for infringement. There is benefit to trade mark owners and competitors alike in international harmonization of trade mark norms.

In the field of registered trade marks, New Zealand and the United Kingdom (UK) laws share a common origin. Unlike earlier statutes, however, which embodied the development of a shared *common law* heritage, these countries' current trade mark statutes derive much of their 'legislative DNA'[8] from EU law (Wiener 2001).

The chapter will explore how this migration of EU trade mark norms came about, discuss some problems of interpretation and practice that have developed in UK/EU law and consider whether New Zealand law has succumbed to them or not. Put shortly, four problems will be considered here: The first is 'cluttering' of trade mark registers, with marks which are not used, or which are registered for an over-broad range of goods and services. The second problem relates to the assessment of 'double identity' infringement (where claimants' and defendants' marks and products are identical). The third problem concerns the practice of 'comparative advertising', where a competitor promotes its own products by reference to another's products and distinguishing marks. The fourth issue is that of 'parallel imports'—the importation of otherwise legitimate products without the rights owner's permission for circulation in the territory of import (called 'grey goods' in US parlance). Another current challenge, that of assessing whether sale and use of trade marks as internet search terms infringe registered rights, has already been the subject of erudite commentary in New Zealand (Greene 2007).[9]

---

[3] Examples of 'brands' and their global rankings may be found at http://www.interbrand.com/en/best-global-brands/2013/top-100-list-view.aspx. Leading brands and sectors include 'APPLE'/technology; 'COCA-COLA'/soft drinks; 'VISA'/credit cards; 'MERCEDES-BENZ'/motor cars.

[4] WIPO remarks that a trade mark protection system 'helps consumers identify and purchase a product or service because its nature and quality, indicated by its unique trademark, meets their needs': http://www.wipo.int/trademarks/en/trademarks.html.

[5] http://www.wipo.int/trademarks/en/about_trademarks.html#function.

[6] Chronopolous (2011) analyses the operation and proper scope of trade mark law by placing it within a wider set of norms regulating the competitive process.

[7] Ian Finch (2012, p. 3), referring to legal recognition of trade mark licensing.

[8] Jonathan B Wiener (2001, p. 1371) describes the transplanting of national regulatory text into international law as '...selecting a bit of regulatory DNA from national law, inserting it into an international law embryo, and hoping that this new legal hybrid will grow to be a hardy offspring...'.

[9] Subsequent development of European case-law in this area, in the shape of Case C-323/09 *Interflora v Marks & Spencer* [2012] FSR 3, is considered briefly below.

11.2 How Did EU Trade Mark Norms Arrive in New Zealand?

The UK has inevitably embraced EU trade mark norms by virtue of her membership of the EU, implementing harmonizing legislation[10] into national law and influenced by a parallel, unitary, Community Trade Mark system[11] UK adoption of EU norms was therefore conscious, internal, and direct. But why should New Zealand also have taken up EU trade mark norms? Answers lie in New Zealand's membership of the WTO and in the source of the trade mark text in the WTO agreement on Trade Related Aspects of Intellectual Property rights ('TRIPS').[12] In 2006 the General Agreement on Tariffs and Trade ('GATT') Uruguay Round documents relating to the negotiation of TRIPS were derestricted, enabling scholars to trace versions of the TRIPS text (Wadlow 2007).[13]

As Wadlow notes, it was originally proposed to introduce an anti-counterfeiting code into the GATT Uruguay Round; however, negotiations on this eventually spawned the TRIPs agreement, which has much wider scope (Wadlow 2007, p. 351). Much early negotiating time (1986 to April 1989) was taken up with discussion as to whether the negotiating group had a mandate covering intellectual property generally, or one limited to trade in counterfeit goods, as argued by developing country representatives (Taubman et al. 2012, p. 6). At mid-term review of the Uruguay round, the negotiating group was expressly given full mandate (Taubman et al. 2012, p. 6).

There were many position papers and much discussion (Wadlow 2007, p. 375), but in 1990 the TRIPS text began to take its final shape from drafts tabled by the European Community (EC) and the United States (US). The first of these, document MTN.GNG/NG11/W/68, of March 29, 1990, was from the then European Community.[14] This was a draft agreement dated 27 March 1990 and proffered by the EC delegation to the GATT Secretariat 'with the request that it be circulated to members of the Negotiating Group'. By this time the EC's Trade Marks Harmonization Directive 89/104/EEC had been promulgated and the process of implementa-

---

[10] Council Directive 89/104/EEC to approximate the laws of the Member States relating to trade marks, 21 December 1988, [2009] OJ L40/1, later replaced by codified version 2008/95/EC, 22 October 2008, [2008] OJ L299/25, implemented by way of the UK Trade Marks Act 1994.

[11] Council Regulation (EC) No 40/94 of 20 December 1993 on the Community trade mark, [1994] OJ L11/1, replaced by codified Reg (EC) 207/2009 of 26 February 2009 [2009] OJ L78/1.

[12] The TRIPs agreement is Annex 1C to the Final Act of the Marrakesh Agreement Establishing the World Trade Organisation (Marrakesh, 15 April 1994). http://www.wto.org/english/tratop_e/trips_e/trips_e.htm.

[13] Accessible via links at http://www.wto.org/english/tratop_e/trips_e/trips_e.htm. Christopher Wadlow (2007) identifies a conveniently searchable database of these *travaux preparatoires* in the shape of Stanford University's GATT Digital Library at http://gatt.stanford.edu/page/home.

[14] GNG stands for 'Group of Negotiations of Goods' and NG11 for 'Negotiating Group on Trade-Related Aspects of Intellectual Property Rights, including Trade in Counterfeit Goods'. The drafts may also be searched and sourced at http://gatt.stanford.edu/page/home; http://sul-derivatives.stanford.edu/derivative?CSNID=92100042&mediaType=application/pdf.

tion into the laws of Member States had begun. Community Trade Mark Regulation 40/94 was under preparation;[15] its main substantive provisions are identical with those of the Directive. It was not surprising, therefore, that much of the trade mark section of the TRIPs draft offered by the EC negotiators closely resembled contemporaneous EC legislation.

The next significant draft, MTN.GNG/NG11/W/71, was tabled by the US. It was discussed (with other proposals) at a negotiators' meeting on May 14–16, 1990.[16] At this point the texts and negotiations begin to take a complex hue. Two dynamic chairmen of the group progressed matters further by producing reports with hybrid drafts. Chairman Anell's report and draft of 23 July 1990[17] shows a piecing together of the EC draft with elements from the US proposal, although trade mark provisions remained close to the EC version. A further draft final act, MTN.TNC/W/35/Rev.1 of December 3, 1990, was dubbed the 'Brussels' draft as it was forwarded to a Brussels meeting of the Trade Negotiations Committee at Ministerial level.[18] Finally, Chairman Dunkel drew up and tabled the so-called 'Dunkel draft' embodying the results of negotiations to date.[19]

In 1994, the TRIPS agreement was signed at Marrakesh[20] by New Zealand and other founder members of the WTO, in substantially the form of the Dunkel draft (Taubman et al. 2012). The close alignment with EC law meant that the UK was already TRIPS-compliant in trade mark terms, having enacted the Trade Marks Act 1994 to comply with Directive 89/104/EEC.

In implementing TRIPs, New Zealand enacted a new Trade Marks Act in 2002. She followed other Commonwealth jurisdictions,[21] especially Singapore, in adopting text from the UK Trade Marks Act 1994 to ensure TRIPs compliance.[22] New

---

[15] See, now, the trade mark pages of the Office for Harmonization in the Internal Market ('OHIM', the Community Trade Mark and Design registration Office) at http://oami.europa.eu/ows/rw/pages/index.en.do.

[16] MTN.GNG/NG11/21 of June 22, 1990.

[17] MTN.GNG/NG11/W/76; trade marks provisions are at p 18–23. http://sul-derivatives.stanford.edu/derivative?CSNID=92110034&mediaType=application/pdf.

[18] http://sul-derivatives.stanford.edu/derivative?CSNID=92120144&mediaType=application/pdf.

[19] Document MTN.TNC/W/FA of 20 December 1991 TRIPS is at pp Y57–90. http://gatt.stanford.edu/bin/detail?fileID=430670083X.

[20] Alongside the Marrakesh agreement creating the WTO on 15 April 1994. As the WTO puts it 'The 'Final Act' signed in Marrakesh in 1994 is like a cover note. Everything else is attached to this. Foremost is the Agreement Establishing the WTO (or the WTO Agreement), which serves as an umbrella agreement. Annexed are the agreements on goods, services and intellectual property [which is Annex 1C], dispute settlement, trade policy review mechanism and the plurilateral agreements. The schedules of commitments also form part of the Uruguay Round agreements.' http://www.wto.org/english/docs_e/legal_e/legal_e.htm#TRIPs.

[21] Hong Kong's Trade Marks Ordinance 2003, (Cap. 559); the Hong Kong database of trademark cases contains many decisions referring to UK, EU and Commonwealth case law: http://www.ipd.gov.hk/eng/intellectual_property/trademarks/trademarks_decisions/cap559.htm.

[22] Sumpter (2010) puts it thus 'The New Zealand Trade Marks Act 2002, again largely cut and pasted from the United Kingdom (and therefore European) law' and notes that European law comes 'complete with the, largely incomprehensible, European Court of Justice decisions'. The

Zealand's statute is closely modeled on Singapore's Trade Marks Act 1998 (Finch 2012, p. 409).[23]

11.3 The Trade Mark Provisions—Comparison

The evolution of important sections of treaty text was tracked and compared with EU and New Zealand legislative texts. The results of this process are exemplified below, using different fonts to highlight functionally equivalent words or phrases. (Table 11.1)

Again, there is significant correlation between the EU and New Zealand legislation. However, the next provision under study shows clear divergence. As can be seen from the table below, this occurred in the documents *preparatory* to TRIPs. It gave New Zealand considerable freedom to draft exceptions to infringement. Some she adopted voluntarily from EU law, others represent adaptive divergence, as permitted by TRIPs, (Table 11.3)

11.4 A Conundrum

The phrase 'fair use of descriptive terms' which appears in the March 1990 European Commission's proposal (on behalf of the EC) has a distinctly US flavour.[24] Why did the EC's draft diverge from its own legislative text at this point? 'Fair use' language was already present in Guidelines and Objectives proposed by the EC in 1988,[25] as Pires de Carvalho (2006) has pointed out,[26] but that still does not explain the discrepancy. Attempting to trace further back, one finds that the 1988 proposal refers to Guidelines proposed by the European Commission in November 1987,[27] but these do not contain detailed texts. However, they do announce that their proposed goals, including protection against misuse of rights, should apply to all intellectual property rights, including trade marks.

---

latter sentiment is echoed by Jacob LJ in *O2 Holdings Ltd v Hutchison 3G Ltd* [2006] EWCA Civ 1656 at [35].

[23] The text of the Singaporean statute, Cap332, may be consulted at http://statutes.agc.gov.sg/aol/home.w3p.

[24] For a history of the fair use defence in the US, now encoded as § 33(b)(4) of the Federal 'Lanham' trade mark Act, see, eg, Fuller (2006). For argument that there is growing convergence between EU and US legislation and judicial doctrines in relation to defenses, see Ramsey and Schovsbo(2013).

[25] MTN.GNG/NG11/W/26. Thanks to Prof Duncan Matthews, Queen Mary, University of London.

[26] Document MTN.GNG/NG11/W/26 of 8 July 1988, (Pires de Carvalho 2006).

[27] MTN.GNG/NG11/W/16.

Table 11.1 Definitions of 'trade mark'

Version	Text
Directive 89/104/EEC, codified as 2008/95/EC, Art. 2(1)	*A trade mark may consist of any signs capable of being represented graphically*, particularly words, including personal names, designs, letters, numerals, the shape of goods or of their packaging, *provided that such signs are capable of distinguishing the goods or services of one undertaking from those of other undertakings*
EC proposal, March 1990, Art. 10(1)	Trademark protection shall be granted. *Trademarks may consist of any signs* capable … [thereafter identical with directive text above]
Anell draft, July 1990 Sect. 2, Art. 1	Protectable Subject Matter 1A.1 *A trademark is a sign capable of distinguishing goods or services of one undertaking from those of other undertakings.* It may in particular consist of words and personal names, letters, numerals, the shape of goods and of their packaging, combinations of colours, *other graphical representations*, or any combination of such signs
Dunkel draft	As TRIPs, below, except that 'Members' appeared as 'Parties' in the Dunkel draft
TRIPs Art. 15(1)	*Any sign, or any combination of signs, capable of distinguishing the goods or services of one undertaking from those of other undertakings, shall be capable of constituting a trademark.* Such signs, in particular words including personal names, letters, numerals, figurative elements and combinations of colours as well as any combination of such signs, shall be eligible for registration as trademarks…
Singapore Trade Marks Act 1998, s 2(1)	*'trade mark' means any sign capable of being represented graphically* and *which is capable of distinguishing goods or services dealt with or provided in the course of trade by a person from goods or services so dealt with or provided by any other person;* 'sign' includes any letter, word, name, signature, numeral, device, brand, heading, label, ticket, shape, colour, aspect of packaging or any combination thereof

11.5   Exhaustion

Another area of divergence is the doctrine of 'exhaustion' of trade mark rights. In service of market integration, EU trade mark law contains provisions whereby first sale on the internal market, by the trade mark owner or with its consent, 'exhausts' trade marks rights. This means that they cannot be used to prevent further circulation of products within the internal market, across the borders between Member

Table 11.2 Scope of protection for identical or similar signs/products (A similar exercise was carried out, tracing text through the documents leading from EU to New Zealand legislations; for brevity the intervening stages are omitted here)

Version	Text
Directive 89/104/EEC, codified as 2008/95/EC Article 5(1) 'Rights conferred by a trade mark'	The registered trade mark shall confer on the proprietor exclusive rights therein. *The proprietor shall be entitled to prevent all third parties not having his consent from using in the course of trade:*
	(a) any sign which is identical with the trade mark in relation to goods or services which are identical with those for which the trade mark is registered;
	(b) any sign where, because of its identity with, or similarity to, the trade mark and the identity or similarity of the goods or services covered by the trade mark and the sign, there exists a likelihood of confusion on the part of the public; the likelihood of confusion includes the likelihood of association between the sign and the trade mark
New Zealand TMA 2002, s89(1)	(1) *A person infringes a registered trade mark if the person does not have the right to use the registered trade mark and uses in the course of trade* a sign—
	(a) identical with the registered trade mark in relation to any goods or services in respect of which the trade mark is registered; or
	(b) identical with the registered trade mark in relation to any goods or services that are similar to any goods or services in respect of which the trade mark is registered, if that use would be likely to deceive or confuse; or
	(c) similar to the registered trade mark in relation to any goods or services that are identical with or similar to any goods or services in respect of which the trade mark is registered, if that use would be likely to deceive or confuse;...

States, unless there exists some legitimate reason to oppose circulation, such as deterioration of goods.[28] However, products first marketed outside the EU, in 'third countries', are not subject to exhaustion and require the consent of the trade mark owner to import and circulate within the EU.[29]

---

[28] Directive, Art 7; Regulation Art. 13

[29] Case C-355/96 *Silhouette International Schmied GmbH & Co KG v Hartlauer Handelsgesellschaft mbH* [1998] ECR I-4799 and subsequent cases, including case C-173/98 *Sebago Inc v GB Unic SA* [1999] ECR I-4013; case C-414/99 *Zino Davidoff SA v A&G Imports Ltd* [2001] ECR I-8691; case C-16/03 *Peak Holding AB v Axolin-Elinor AB* [2005] ETMR 28.

Table 11.3 Defences/exceptions

Version	Text
Directive 89/104/EEC, codified as 2008/95/EC, Article 6 'Limitation of the effects of a trade mark'	*1. The trade mark shall not entitle the proprietor to prohibit a third party from using, in the course of trade:*
	(a) his own name or address;
	(b) indications concerning the kind, quality, quantity, intended purpose, value, geographical origin, the time of production of goods or of rendering of the service, or other characteristics of goods or services;
	(c) the trade mark where it is necessary to indicate the intended purpose of a product or service, in particular as accessories or spare parts; provided he uses them in accordance with honest practices in industrial or commercial matters.
	2. The trade mark shall not entitle the proprietor to prohibit a third party from using, in the course of trade, an earlier right which only applies in a particular locality if that right is recognised by the laws of the Member State in question and within the limits of the territory in which it is recognised
EC proposal, March 1990, Art. 13	*Limited exceptions to the exclusive rights conferred by a trademark*, such as fair use of descriptive terms, *may be made*, provided that they take account of the legitimate interests of the proprietor of the trademark and of third parties
Anell draft, July 1990 Sect. 2, Art. 4	4A *Limited exceptions to the exclusive rights conferred by a trademark*, such as fair use of descriptive terms, *may be made*, provided that they take account of the legitimate interests of the proprietor of the trademark and of third parties
Dunkel draft, Art. 17	As TRIPs, below, except that 'Members' appeared as 'Parties' in the Dunkel draft
TRIPs Art. 17,	*Members may provide limited exceptions to the rights conferred by a trademark*, such as fair use of descriptive terms, provided that such exceptions take account of the legitimate interests of the owner of the trademark and of third parties
New Zealand TMA 2002, s 94 'No infringement for comparative advertising of registered trade mark'	*A registered trade mark is not infringed by the use of the registered trade mark for the purposes of comparative advertising*, but any such use otherwise than in accordance with honest practices in industrial or commercial matters must be treated as infringing the registered trade mark if the use, without due cause, takes unfair advantage of, or is detrimental to, the distinctive character or the repute of the trade mark

Table 11.3 (continued)

Version	Text
New Zealand TMA 2002, s95 'No infringement for honest practices'(as amended by the Trade Marks Amendment Act 2011, w.e.f. 16 September 2011)	*A person does not infringe a registered trade mark if*, in accordance with honest practices in industrial or commercial matters, the person uses—
	(a) the person's name or the name of the person's place of business; or
	(b) the name of the person's predecessor in business or the name of the person's predecessor's place of business; or
	(c) a sign to indicate—
	(i) the kind, quality, quantity, intended purpose, value, geographical origin, or other characteristic of goods or services; or
	(ii) the time of production of goods or of the rendering of services

The Anell draft contained a WTO-wide exhaustion provision but TRIPS as finally drafted is neutral on exhaustion of IP rights.[30] Pires de Carvalho (2006, p. 627, citing MTN.GNG/NG11/14) regards the characterization of exhaustion as an exception to protection as having been a conceptual mistake, the provision was eventually deleted from TRIPs drafts. It is included in a synoptic table of existing international texts and proposals dated 29 September 1989;[31] this shows considerable divergence of views on exhaustion. New Zealand has chosen to implement worldwide exhaustion of trade mark rights,[32] thus rejecting the regional version developed under EU law.

Defences apart, these examples serve to demonstrate that many aspects of EU trade mark law became embedded in TRIPS and thus a matter of international obligation for New Zealand. Greene has opined 'While New Zealand and Australia may derive much of its trade mark jurisprudence from English common law tradition, the passage of [the] 1994 Act and implementation of the Trade Mark Directive will likely result, I would suggest, as a point of divergence between the two systems' (Greene 2007, p. 31) It is submitted that current trade mark laws in the UK and New Zealand are both firmly rooted in EU law—in the UK directly by virtue of her membership of the EU; in New Zealand indirectly through her membership of the WTO and the TRIPS agreement. Divergences will not be a result of the break with common law tradition, but rather of adaptation, resistance or rejection of EU norms in New Zealand.

---

[30] Art 6 TRIPs states 'For the purposes of dispute settlement under this Agreement, subject to the provisions of Articles 3 and 4 nothing in this Agreement shall be used to address the issue of the exhaustion of intellectual property rights.'

[31] MTN.GNG/NG11/W/32/Rev. 1.

[32] Trade Marks Act 2002, s 95.

11.6   TRIPs Compliance and Flexibilities

As can be seen, the definitions of 'trade mark' and the cited provisions on scope of rights in New Zealand closely follow those in TRIPS. As regards defences, TRIPs gives only general guidance as to the permitted exceptions and is neutral on international exhaustion. New Zealand law may be regarded as compliant with the specific provisions. Furthermore, TRIPS Article 7 provides some additional flexibilities: 'The protection and enforcement of intellectual property rights should contribute to the promotion of technological innovation and to the transfer and dissemination of technology, to the mutual advantage of producers and users of technological knowledge and *in a manner conducive to social and economic welfare, and to a balance of rights and obligations.*' As Yu points out 'the latter two [objectives] have a much broader focus and cover virtually all forms of intellectual property rights' (2009, p. 46). In relation to exhaustion of trade mark rights, for example, it could be argued that the amended New Zealand provisions[33] provide an appropriate balance for a country in her geographical location. Nonetheless, Frankel has criticized the introduction of international exhaustion as possibly 'a mistake as far as local industries are concerned' (Frankel 2001, p. 52).

It follows that, although New Zealand legislation follows EU law closely on registrable marks and the cited provisions on infringement, transmission of norms through the medium of TRIPs has allowed New Zealand to diverge from EU law in terms of legislative defences to infringement.[34] Furthermore, a sense of judicial[35] and administrative[36] continuity may have supported resistance to importing problems of EU trade mark law. We consider next some areas where the UK courts and others[37] have expressed dissatisfaction with EU law and then whether New Zealand's legislative and interpretative approaches have allowed her to escape unsatisfactory outcomes.

---

[33] Sect. 97A, as substituted by s16 of the Trade Marks Amendment Act 2011.

[34] Interestingly, one finds examples of reference to EU jurisprudence even here—for example on the concept of 'consent': *Leisureworld Ltd v Elite Fitness Equipment Ltd* HC AK CIV 2006-404-3499 [2006] NZHC 849 (21 July 2006), following Joined Cases C-414 to 416/99 *Zino Davidoff v A&C Imports* [2001] ECR I-869, noted by Finch 2012 at p. 604.

[35] Eg *Intellectual Reserve Inc v Sintes* [2009] NZCA 305 at [22].

[36] Despite recognition at Sect. 00, para 3.2.2 of IPONZ's trademark Guidelines that the classic case on distinctiveness, *W&G du Cros Ltd's Application* (1913) 30 RPC 660 might no longer be the most appropriate, given the change in wording of the Act, perusal of cases noted as significant in NZJIP for 2011 and 2012 shows frequent citation of *W&G du Cros*.

[37] Notably respondents to surveys for the Max-Planck 2011'Study on the Overall Functioning of the European Trade Mark System', coordinated by Annette Kur, Reto Hilty and Roland Knaak, available at http://ec.europa.eu/internal_market/indprop/docs/tm/20110308_allensbach-study_en.pdf.

11.7   Dissatisfaction with EU Trade Mark Law

Three areas are selected for discussion, to illustrate how New Zealand has managed to reject or resist problems which might have accompanied adoption of EU law via TRIPs:

1. whether the rules on registration of marks are leading to 'cluttering' of registers, in the sense of their becoming clogged with overbroad or unused registrations, and the related issue of registration of marks of low distinctiveness;
2. EU law on 'double identity' infringement, where the defendant uses a sign identical with the registered mark in relation to goods or services for which the mark is registered;
3. the defence available to competitors who use marks for 'comparative advertising'.

11.8   Cluttering of Registers

According to von Graevenitz et al. (2012, p. 5) 'cluttering arises where firms hold trade marks that are overly broad or unused raising search costs for later applicants'. It was identified as a problem for the Community Trade Mark Register by respondents to the 'Allensbach' survey (Institut für Demoskopie Allensbach 2011), which formed the basis of the Max Planck Institute's 'Study on the Overall Functioning of the European Trade Mark System'.[38] Cluttering is a problem because the rights of a trade mark proprietor to block others' registrations and to sue for infringement extend beyond the exact mark and specification of goods or services recorded on the register. It can only be exacerbated by enlargement of the EU. The main evidence for and causes of the problem, if it exists, appear to stem from five factors:

a. The main, culprit[39] appears to be OHIM's fee structure for the registration of marks—their '3 for 1' policy, of allowing applicants to designate up to 3 'Nice' classes of good or services for the same price as a single class application.[40]
b. Another administrative policy—to allow applicants to specify goods and services for which marks are to be registered by reference to class headings of the Nice Classification. This was recently challenged in IP TRANSLATOR,[41] where

---

[38] See pp. 39–40.

[39] Cited by the Max Planck Study, which recommends at p270 that OHIM charge per class, and von Gravenitz et al. 2012, p. 32.

[40] Goods and services are divided into 34 classes for goods and 11 for services in the international classification founded and updated under the Nice Agreement of 1957. The classification is widely used by trade mark offices around that world to structure their registers, reducing searching costs and the complexity of international registration of marks.

[41] The application identified services by reference to the heading of class 41, 'Education; providing of training; entertainment; sporting and cultural activities'.

the Court of Justice of the European Union produced a rather unsatisfactory ruling—that some class headings might be appropriate for use as specifications of
goods and services, and others not.[42] OHIM and national offices of EU Member
States have been working together to clarify and harmonise practice.[43]

c. Thirdly, pressure of numbers on the register for trade marks for ethical (prescrip-
tion) drugs may be caused by the requirement for these names to be approved
by medical regulators.[44] Pharma companies insure against regulatory refusal by
devising and submitting three or four names per drug, registering them all as
trade marks (Von Graevenitz August 2012, p. 1, citing de Benedetti et al. 2006).

d. A possible fourth cause is OHIM's failure to examine on relative grounds, ie for
conflict with earlier marks and rights. Von Gravenitz et al. (2012) have used data
triggered by the UK's abandonment of relative examination in 2007 to test this.
Their analysis suggests that the availability of third party opposition takes care
of this.

e. The 5 year period allowed by the legislation before a trade mark may be challenged on the grounds of non-use may exacerbate the problem of clutter.[45]

Cause c. is out of the hands of both legislator and registry. In the other four cases,
the problem of cluttering has been associated with specific practices in administration of the trade mark registration process. The New Zealand trade mark system
does not appear to have fallen prey to similar errors, for the following reasons:-

a. IPONZ trade mark fees are calculated on a per-class basis, without any reduction, unlike OHIM's '3 for 1'.[46]

b. In relation to specification of goods or services, Sect. 32(2) of the Trade Marks
Act 2002[47] and Sect. 3, para 4.1 of IPONZ Trade Mark Practice Guidelines[48]
recognize and guard against clutter and the danger of broad specifications.

As for the use of class headings, IPONZ Guidelines are very specific:

> When a class heading is used as a specification, it loses its capacity to function as a class
> heading and becomes part of an application or registration as a statement of goods or ser-
> vices. Therefore, a claim for a class heading does not equate to a claim for all the goods
> or services that may be in that class. An application which specifies a class heading only

---

[42] Case C-307/10 *Chartered Institute of Patent Attorneys v Registrar of Trade Marks* 19 June
2012. [2013] RPC 11; ECJ (Grand Chamber).

[43] Resulting in 'Common Communication on the Implementation of `IP Translator' v1.1, 20 No-
vember 2013.

[44] Eg the (Invented) Name Review Group of the European Medicines Agency. See von Graevenitz
August 2012.

[45] Von Graeventiz (August 2012, 13); Directive 2008/95/EC, Art 10; Regulation (EC) No
207/2009, Art 15.

[46] http://www.iponz.govt.nz/cms/trade-marks/fees.

[47] 'The Commissioner must not register a trade mark in respect of all of the goods and services
included in a class, or a large variety of goods or services, unless the specification is justified by
the use or intended use of the sign.'

[48] http://www.iponz.govt.nz/cms/trade-marks/practice-guidelines-index.

claims protection in respect of the goods or services actually stated in the heading, or that may be clearly encompassed by the heading. (IPONZ, Sect. 3, para 4.2)

c. IPONZ has maintained examination on relative grounds under Sects. 22–30 of the Trade Marks Act 2002.[49]
d. The period after which a trade mark can be challenged on the grounds of non-use was reduced by Sect.66(1)(a) of the Trade Marks Act 2002 to 3 years, the minimum required by TRIPS Art. 19.

These instances show that while New Zealand has unambiguously adopted substantive EU law on registrability of marks, rejection (or at least non-following) of administrative practices has allowed more robust local approaches to prevail. It is submitted that overall, this section can be regarded as adaptation.

11.9 Non-Distinctive Marks and Cluttering

New Zealand's trade mark administration appears to have avoided or rejected many causes of the cluttering problem. However, another type of cluttering problem, alluded to though not investigated by von Graevenitz et al. (2012, p. 10–11, citing Landes and Posner 1987, p. 274), results from admission to the register of marks of marginal distinctiveness. Unlike highly distinctive invented words or symbols, quasi-descriptive and laudatory marks are likely to be limited in supply.

Marketing people are fond of quasi-descriptive marks because less effort is required to educate the consumer; the appeal of laudatory marks is obvious. The low-water mark for distinctiveness in the EU was a decision of the European Court of Justice (ECJ) that BABY-DRY for babies' disposable nappies (diapers) was a 'lexical invention' and registrable as a Community trade mark.[50] The decision received a mixed reception (Griffiths 2003, p. 2; Davis 2004). However, the Court of Justice subsequently seems to have retreated from this position in DOUBLEMINT, holding that 'A sign must therefore be refused registration …if at least one of its possible meanings designates a characteristic of the goods or services concerned'.[51] Curiously, this case seems to be cited considerably less often in New Zealand registry decisions than *BABYDRY*,[52] suggesting that an opportunity is being missed to adopt *DOUBLEMINT* as a helpful precedent. Here we find the apparent rejection, or at

---

[49] See IPONZ trade mark Guidelines, Sect. 02A, para 2.2.
[50] Case C-383/99 P *Procter & Gamble v OHIM (BABY DRY Trade Mark)* [2001] CEC 325. See the caution expressed on the significance of lexical invention by IPONZ in its trade mark Guidelines at Sect. 05, para 4.2.6, citing *McCain Foods (Aust) Pty Ltd v Conagra Inc* (6 June 2002) unreported, Court of Appeal CA176/01(HEALTHY CHOICE).
[51] Case C-191/01P *OHIM v Wm Wrigley Company* [2003] ECR I-12447 at [32] (Judgment of the court: Presiding, Skouris P; Jann, Timmermans, Gulmann, Cunha Rodrigues and Rosas PP.C.; Edward, La Pergola, Puissochet (Rapporteur), Schintgen, Macken, Colneric and von Bahr, Rosas JJ.).
[52] As indicated by a search on NZLII.

least a failure fully to adopt, a helpful EU norm in the form of a ruling of the Court of Justice.

In relation to laudatory marks, BRAVO for writing instruments was considered by the European Court of Justice in *Merz & Krell*[53] Article 3(1)(d) of the Directive,[54] prohibits the registration of

(d) trade marks which consist exclusively of signs or indications which have become customary in the current language or in the bona fide and established practices of the trade.

On a reference from the German Federal Patents Court, the Court of Justice held

2… It is immaterial, when [Art. 3(1)(d)] is applied, whether the signs or indications in question describe the properties or characteristics of those goods or services.[55]

Thus, if a mark is a stock laudatory term (when considered in relation to the relevant goods and services—a question of fact), it should be refused. The New Zealand trade mark register shows several registrations of the word BRAVO for different goods and services, the most recent from 1989. Finch (2012, pp. 458–490) note some laudatory marks that have been refused or allowed registration in New Zealand, such as a three dimensional heart shape for retail services and toys[56] (refused; other traders were likely to wish to use such a shape), HONEST for smoothies, etc. (refused),[57] ULTRA for lighting apparatus etc. (accepted, on the basis that the word was not usually used on itself but as qualifying an adjective),[58] WORLD FAMOUS IN NEW ZEALAND for mineral water, etc. (allowed on the basis that it was an invented, fanciful and oxymoronic slogan).[59] It is submitted that too much weight is given in these latter cases to their lexical inventiveness, but nonetheless EU and NZ trade mark laws have both arrived at a reasonably robust approach to laudatory marks. We may regard this as parallel development of the adopted norms.

11.10 Double-Identity Infringement

Turning from registration to scope of trade mark rights, recital 11 to Directive 2008/95/EC states

---

[53] Case C-517/99 *Merz & Krell GmbH & Co* [2001] ETMR 105.

[54] The New Zealand equivalent is found in s18(1) 'The Commissioner must not register- … (d) a trade mark that consists only of signs or indications that have become customary in the current language or in the bona fide practices of trade'.

[55] Case C-517/99 *Merz & Krell GmbH & Co* [2001] ETMR 105 at Order, para 2, second sentence.

[56] *Build-a-Bear Workshop Inc's Appl* IPO T01/2007, upheld on appeal HC Wellington CIV-2007-485-196.

[57] *Charlies' Trading Ltd v Frucor Beverages* IPO T25/2007.

[58] *Marexim Import-Export Ltd's* Appl IPO T10/2007.

[59] IPO T02/2010, upheld on appeal, *Coombe v Coca-Cola Amaril (NZ) Ltd* (2011) 9 NZBLC 103. The mark is actually used on a lemon and piroa flavour.

> The protection afforded by the registered trade mark, the function of which is in particular to guarantee the trade mark as an indication of origin, should be absolute in the case of identity between the mark and the sign and the goods or services.

This is reflected in the provisions of Art. 5(1), set out in Table 11.2 above, which does not require proof of confusion, or any kind of detriment. However, the Court of Justice of the EU, through a series of decisions, has reached the position where harm to the functions of the trade mark may need to be shown in double-identity cases. It has been argued that this state of affairs was caused by a combination of relaxation of eligibility and scope of protection with an inadequate system of defences (eg Ramsey and Schovsbo 2013, p. 677; citing Senftleben 2011, p. 73; 2013). However, in the first such case before the Court of Justice, defences were available but disregarded. That case involved the phrases, 'SPIRIT SUN' and 'CONTEXT CUT' for gem-stones.[60] They were registered as trade marks, and used descriptively in discussions between another jeweller and customer to denote particular cuts of stone. The Court of Justice opined that this was not infringement. Rather than reach this conclusion by employing a defence of descriptive use from Art. 6(1)(b) of the Directive, or even to detect an implied requirement of the legislation that infringing use be use as a trade mark,[61] the Court held (in accordance with the question posed by the German court) that Art. 5(1) did not confer exclusive rights where there was 'no question of the trade mark used being perceived as a sign indicative of the undertaking of origin'.

This turn of events was compounded by the ruling of the Court of Justice in *Arsenal Football Club v Reed*,[62] where it held that damage to one of the functions of the trade mark need be shown for there to be infringement in double-identity cases. In a series of cases involving internet keywords, the significance of potential confusion has been highlighted; Morcom has argued that these cases erroneously imported a requirement of confusion into Art. 5(1)(a).[63]

Whether the requirement of damage to trade mark functions equates to a requirement of 'trade mark use' in infringement is debated. For example, the English Court of Appeal in *Arsenal v Reed* has said that 'the ECJ's judgment had made it clear that the material consideration was whether the use complained of was liable to jeopardise the guarantee of origin, not whether the use was trade mark use',[64] suggesting that the two considerations are different. Conversely, Kulk (2011, p. 609) has asserted by reference to the case of *Google France v Louis Vuitton*[65] that in the

---

[60] Case C-2/00 *Hölterhoff v Friesleben* [2002] ECR. I-4187.

[61] *Hölterhoff* at [17] In *O2 Holdings Ltd v Hutchison 3G Ltd* [2006] EWCA Civ 1656 at [36] Jacob LJ noted that invalidity could also have been pleaded.

[62] Case C-206/01 [2003] ETMR 19.

[63] Morcom 2012, 43, referring specifically to case C-278/08 *Die BergSpechte Outdoor Reisen und Alpinschule Edi Koblmuller GmbH v Guni* [2010] ETMR 33 (ECJ).

[64] [2003] EWCA Civ 696; [2003] E.T.M.R. 73 at [48]. See, also, case C-323/09 *Interflora Inc. and Interflora British Unit v. Marks & Spencer plc et Flowers Direct Online Ltd* [2012] FSR 3.

[65] Case C-236/08 *Google France Sarl v Louis Vuitton Malletier SA* [2011] All E.R. (EC) 411 (ECJ (Grand Chamber)).

EU 'trade mark use as a requirement for trade mark infringement is vibrantly alive'. As discussed by Greene (2007, pp. 8–12), trade mark use as a concept has its proponents and its detractors. However, it is submitted that, by using it to create a statutory defence in s 89(2) of the Trade Marks Act 2002,[66] New Zealand has sidestepped a costly controversy of EU law—a wise adaptive strategy

11.11 Comparative Advertising

European law has a code for misleading advertising, including provisions on comparative advertising. This was not incorporated into TRIPs, indeed it postdated the trade marks harmonization directive. New Zealand's Trade Marks Act 2002, Sect. 94, permits one trader to use another's trade mark for the purposes of comparative advertising on certain conditions, including that the use must be 'in accordance with honest practices in industrial or commercial matters'. 'Comparative advertising' is not defined in the Act[67] but New Zealand's Advertising Standards Authority has recently issued a new Code[68] which equates it to—'advertising that identifies a competing product or service (directly or by implication)'.[69]

Section 94 is a cousin of Sect. 10(6) of the UK Trade Marks Act 1994, which has been described judicially as a 'home-grown provision'.[70] Its text reflected proposals at the time to amend the directive on misleading advertising[71] and Art. 10*bis* of the Paris Convention for the protection of industrial property.[72] The UK judiciary traditionally has been robust to allow use of trade marks in comparative advertising which is not misleading when viewed as a whole. For example in *British Airways*

---

[66] 'Subsection (1) [infringement] only applies if the sign is used in such a manner as to render the use of the sign as likely to be taken as being use as a trade mark.'

[67] Sumpter (2011, p. 184) suggests that it includes implicit comparison.

[68] 'Code for Comparative Advertising', January 2013, available at http://www.asa.co.nz/revised-codes.php.

[69] EU law contains a similar definition 'Any advertising, that explicitly or by implication, identifies a competitor or goods or services offered by a competitor': Art. 2a of Directive 84/450/EEC on misleading advertising, as amended by Directive 97/55/EC to include comparative advertising; consolidated text available at http://ec.europa.eu/consumers/cons_int/safe_shop/mis_adv/index_en.htm; 'The test for determining whether an advertisement is comparative in nature is thus whether it identifies, explicitly or by implication, a competitor of the advertiser or goods or services which the competitor offers.' Case C-533/06 *O2 Holdings Ltd v Hutchinson 3G UK Ltd* [2008] 3 CMLR 14. And see case C-657/11 *Belgian Electronic Sorting Technology NV v Peelaers* [2013] ETMR 45: 'advertising' includes use of a domain name, but not its registration, and use of metatags.

[70] Pumfrey J. in *Pag Ltd v Hawke-Woods Ltd* [2002] ETMR 70; [2002] FSR 46 Ch D at [24].

[71] 'Misleading Advertising Directive' 84/450/EEC, in due course amended by Directive 97/55/EC to include comparative advertising and again by Directive 2005/29/EC concerning unfair business-to-consumer commercial practices.

[72] *Barclays Bank v RBS Advanta* [1996] RPC 307; http://www.wipo.int/treaties/en/ip/paris/.

Plc v Ryanair Ltd it was held that Ryanair's advertisements with fare comparisons and the slogan 'EXPENSIVE BA----DS' did not infringe British Airways' registered mark 'BA'.[73] Likewise in *Benchmark Building Supplies Ltd v Mitre 10 New Zealand Ltd*, Sect. 94 of the New Zealand Trade Marks Act was applied to hold that there would be no infringement of the plaintiff's trade marks by the defendants, who stickered copies of the plaintiff's brochures (which showed the plaintiff's trade marks) with prices for the same or equivalent products at their Bunnings stores.[74]

Conversely if the comparative advertisement misleads consumers, for example if they are confused as to who is supplying which products, it will infringe. This position seemed to be confirmed by the ECJ in the *O2* case.[75] Indeed, as Claire Howell (2008, p. 155) has put it, 'if confusion does occur the medium [comparative advertising] has failed to produce the desired result'

By 2010, we find one of the most robust English judges, Jacob LJ, bewailing:

> The problem, stated at its most general, is simple. Does trade mark law prevent the defendants from telling the truth? Even though their perfumes are lawful and do smell like the corresponding famous brands, does trade mark law nonetheless muzzle the defendants so that they cannot say so?
> I have come to the conclusion that the ECJ's ruling is that the defendants are indeed muzzled. My duty as a national judge is to follow EU law as interpreted by the ECJ. I think, with regret, that the answers we have received from the ECJ require us so to hold. Before I consider why in detail [citations omitted] I wish to say why I regret those answers.[76]

The *L'Oreal* case involved sellers of smell-alike perfumes. They used 'comparison sheets' linking their perfumes to the names of the claimant's perfumes, which were registered as trade marks. The ECJ had ruled that, although there was no confusion, the use was not permitted by the Misleading Advertising Directive[77] and infringed the trade marks. This was because the defendants presented 'goods or services as imitations or replicas'[78] and took unfair advantage of the reputation of the marks.[79] As Jacob LJ pointed out, the EC had asked in another case for its ruling in *L'Oreal* to be reconsidered[80] and the ruling has attracted criticism from commentators (Bjorkenfeldt 2010; Horton 2011).

Is the ruling in *L'Oreal* likely to be influential in New Zealand in the interpretation of s94? Although the *L'Oreal* ruling hinged upon application of the

---

[73] [2001] FSR 32. Although the advertisement was withdrawn after the UK Advertising Standard Authority had upheld a claim of offensiveness.

[74] [2003] NZCA 213; [2004] 1 NZLR 26. Although s94 was not in force when the cause of action arose, it was considered relevant to the continuation of an injunction.

[75] Although the Court of Justice went beyond its remit by ruling that there was no confusion, contrary to the findings of fact by the English High Court.

[76] *L'Oreal v Bellure* [2010] EWCA Civ 535 at [6]–[7].

[77] N. 70 above.

[78] Contrary to Art. 3a(1)(h) of the Misleading Advertising Directive.

[79] Contrary to Art. 3a(1)(g) of the directive.

[80] *Interflora Inc v Marks & Spencer plc (No 2)* [2010] EWHC 925 (Ch) per Arnold J at [17]; for subsequent developments, including CJEU rulings, see [2013] EWHC 1291 (Ch); [2013] FSR 33.

Misleading Advertising Directive, the authors of Finch (2012) consider that the same result would obtain in New Zealand, because the Advertising Standards Agency's (ASA's) code of conduct contains prohibitions on upgrading by association and taking advantage of goodwill. The new code on Comparative Advertising contains provisions similar to those in the earlier code. Sumpter (2011) takes the view that *L'Oreal* considerations are irrelevant, because of a provision in s89(3) that s94 overrides the infringement provisions. But this does not take into account the ASA's code, which may not be binding on the Court but evidence of perception of the fairness of practices. Here we may see a combination of formal and informal adoption of norms.

11.12   Conclusion

Important EU trade mark norms have found their way into New Zealand law by way of the WTO TRIPs agreement and the international obligations it imposes. To comply with TRIPs, New Zealand has adopted many features of EU law as reflected in the UK's Trade Marks Act 1994. However, flexibility given under TRIPS for defences, and wise and adaptive legislative and administrative choices made by New Zealand, mean that her trade mark law shows high resistance to some of the ills from which EU trade mark law is currently suffering. However, resistance to other problems may be low; here careful scrutiny of developments under EU law and discriminating use of judicial decisions may enable New Zealand to reject these problems as well. This chapter's findings may be summarised as follows: (Table 11.4).

Table 11.4 Summary of conclusions

'Ailment' of EU trade mark law	NZ response
Cluttering of trade mark registers due to administrative practices	Combination of adoption of legislative norms and resistance to administrative practices; may be regarded overall as an adaptive response
Cluttering of trade mark registers with marks of low distinctiveness	Low level of resistance; danger of adopting this problematic norm
The characterization of double-identity infringement as requiring damage to trade mark functions	Defence of non-trade mark use demonstrates resistance
L'Oreal v Bellure: trade mark rights as a high barrier to comparative advertising	NZ Practitioners disagree. Similar problems may be observed; if ASA codes given weight by the courts. May be an example of informal adoption of norms
International exhaustion of trade mark rights (for so-called 'parallel imports')	International exhaustion implemented in New Zealand legislation; EU's regional-only approach rejected

References

Bjorkenfeldt, M. (2010). The genie is out of the bottle: The ECJ's decision in L'Oreal v Bellure. *Journal of Intellectual Property Law & Practice, 5*(2), 105.

Chronopoulos, A. (2011). Determining the scope of trademark rights by recourse to value judgements related to the effectiveness of competition. *International Review of Intellectual Property and Competition Law, 42*(5), 535–570.

Davis, J. (2004). A European constitution for intellectual property rights. *Common Market Law Review, 41*(4), 1005.

Davis, J. (2011). Between a sign and a brand: Mapping the boundaries of a registered trade mark in European Union trade mark law. In L. Bently, J. Davis, & J. C. Ginsburg (Eds.), *Trade marks and brands—an interdisciplinary critique* (pp. 65–71). Cambridge: Cambridge University Press.

de Benedetti, F., Clayton, M., Shire, H., & Stone, D. (2006). Meeting the pharma challenge. *World Trademark Review*, November/December 2006, 52.

Finch, I. (Ed.). (2012). *James and Wells intellectual property law in New Zealand* (2nd ed.). Auckland: Brookers.

Frankel, S. (2001). *Towards A Sound New Zealand Intellectual Property Law 32 VUWLR*, pp. 47–74.

Fuller, M. (2006). 'Fair use' trumps likelihood of confusion in trademark law: The Supreme Court rules in KP permanent v. lasting impression. *BC Intellectual Property and Technology Forum, 11*(1), 1.

Greene, P. J. (2007). Keyword advertising, and other invisible uses of third-party trade marks in online advertising. Victoria University of Wellington Law Review Working Paper Series 2.

Griffiths, A. (2003). Modernising trade mark law and promoting efficiency: Evaluating the babydry judgment and its aftermath. *Intellectual Property Quarterly, 1*, 1–37.

Horton, A. (2011). The implications of L'Oreal v Bellure—a retrospective and a looking forward: The essential functions of a trade mark and when is an advantage unfair? *European Intellectual Property Review, 33*(9), 550.

Howell, C. (2008). *O2 v Hutchison 3G* comparative advertising: European trade mark law beyond compare? *Communications Law, 13*(5), 155.

Institut für Demoskopie Allensbach. (2011). Study on the overall functioning of the European trade mark system; metnhodology and results published as part of Max Planck Institute for Intellectual Property and Competition Law Munich (2011) Study on the overall functioning of the European Trade Mark System. http://ec.europa.eu/internal_market/indprop/docs/tm/20110308_allensbach-study_en.pdf. Accessed 18 Dec 2013.

Kulk, S. (2011). Search engines—searching for trouble? *European Intellectual Property Review, 33*(1), 607.

Landes, W., & Posner, R. (1987). Trade mark law: An economic perspective. *Journal of Law & Economics, 30*(2), 265–309.

Legrand, P. (1997). The impossibility of 'Legal Transplants'. *Maastricht Journal of European and Comparative Law, 4*(4), 111.

Morcom, C. (2012). Trade marks and the internet. *European Intellectual Property Review, 34*(1), 40.

Pires de Carvalho, N. (2006). *The TRIPS regime of trademarks and designs* (pp. 298–299). Alphen an de Rijn: Kluwer Law International.

Pires de Carvalho, N. (2012). Towards a unified theory of intellectual property: The differentiating capacity (and function) as the thread that unites all its components. *The Journal of World Intellectual Property, 15*(4), 251–279.

Ramsey, L., & Schovsbo, J. (2013). Mechanisms for limiting trade mark rights to further competition and free speech. *International Review of Intellectual Property and Competition Law, 44*(6), 671.

Senftleben, M. (2011). Keyword advertising in Europe—how the internet challenges recent expansions of EU trademark protection. *Connecticut Journal of International Law, 27*(1), 39.

Senftleben, M. (2013). Adapting EU trademark law to new technologies: Back to basics? In C. Geiger (Ed.), *Constructing European intellectual property–achievements and new perspectives* (pp. 145–146). Cheltenham: Edward Elgar.

Sumpter, P. (2010). We're a weird mob. *New Zealand Intellectual Property Journal, 6*(1), 667–669.

Sumpter, P. (2011). *Trade marks in practice* (2nd ed.). Auckland: LexisNexis.

Taubman, A., Wager, H., & Watal, J. (Eds.). (2012). *A handbook on the WTO TRIPS agreement.* Cambridge: Cambridge University Press.

von Graevenitz, G. (22 August 2012). Trade mark cluttering—Evidence from EU enlargement. http://dx.doi.org/10.2139/ssrn.2145588, or http://www.wipo.int/edocs/mdocs/mdocs/en/wipo_ip_econ_ge_1_13/wipo_ip_econ_ge_1_13_ref_graevenitz.pdf. Accessed 17 Jan 2014.

von Graevenitz, G., Greenhalgh, C., Helmers, C., & Schautschick, P. (2012). Trade mark cluttering: An exploratory report (UK Intellectual Property Office), 3.

Wadlow, C. (2007). 'Including trade in counterfeit goods': The origin of TRIPS as a GATT anti-counterfeiting code. *Intellectual Property Quarterly, 3,* 350–402.

Watson, A. (1974). *Legal transplants: An approach to comparative law.* Edinburgh: Scottish Academic Press.

Wiener, J. B. (2001). Something borrowed for something blue: Legal transplants and the evolution of global environmental law. *Ecology Law Quarterly, 27,* 1295–1371.

World Intellectual Property Organisation. (WIPO). (2014). 'Trademarks' http://www.wipo.int/trademarks/en/. Accessed 24 Dec 2014.

Yu, P. (2009). The objectives and principles of the TRIPS agreement. *Houston Law Review, 46*(5), 46.

Alison Firth read physics at Oxford University and taught physics and mathematics in London and Lima before qualifying as a barrister and practising in England and Wales. She was a full time legal academic in the UK from 1985 to 2012 and a professor in law at Newcastle and Surrey Universities, as well as being a visiting Professor in Law at Queen Mary, University of London. Her research centres on intellectual property and related areas of the law, such as competition (anti-trust) law, unfair competition and contract. She has published on design law, trademarks, copyright, confidential information, patents, competition law, licensing and procedural law relating to intellectual property.

Part IV
Rejection

Chapter 12
The Value of Gender Equality in EU-Asian Trade Policy: An Assessment of the EU's Ability to Implement Its Own Legal Obligations

Maria Garcia and Annick Masselot

> *'For money, you would sell your soul.' Sophocles,*
> Antigone

12.1   Introduction

This chapter aims to assess the tensions and contradictions that exist between the European Union's (EU) internal and international legal obligations to achieve gender equality in all of its activities, and its engagement in the competitive global economy. The context of the economic relations negotiations between the EU and the Asian region provides a useful vantage point to highlight the significant difficulties in diffusing gender norms through the medium of trade policies and the potential consequences of not doing so.

The EU portrays itself as a normative leader promoting values such as democracy, gender equality or environment and it has ambitions to lead the global debate on sustainable development (see inter alia Manners 2002, 2008; Aggestam 2008; Lightfoot and Burchell 2005; Vogler and Stephen 2007; Allwood et al. 2013; Bain and Masselot 2013). Using discourse and legal analysis, this chapter demonstrates that in all these areas and 'as a policy entrepreneur in the field of gender' (David and Guerrina 2013, p. 53), the EU raises the expectation of diffusing these values that are declared 'universal' in the preamble of the Lisbon Treaty. However, despite the existence of legal obligations and much political rhetoric, it is argued that the EU succumbs to internal and external resistance to the promotion of these fundamental

M. Garcia (✉)
Department of Politics, Languages & International Studies, University of Bath, Bath, UK
e-mail: m.garcia@bath.ac.uk

A. Masselot
College of Business and Law, University of Canterbury, Christchurch, New Zealand
e-mail: annick.masselot@canterbury.ac.nz

© Springer International Publishing Switzerland 2015   191
A. Björkdahl et al. (eds.), *Importing EU Norms,* United Nations University Series
on Regionalism 8, DOI 10.1007/978-3-319-13740-7_12

values. Values such as gender equality appear to clash with the EU's desire and interest to foster good economic relations with key rising economic markets. For instance, EU economic relations with Asia have focused almost exclusively on the promotion and facilitation of trade and investment through the negotiation of far-reaching trade agreements with the aim of enhancing economic growth. As such, there is virtually no space left for including a gender dimension to these negotiations. Ultimately, this current situation benefits EU-Asian trade at the expense of the promotion of core EU values such as gender equality. This chapter argues that the lack of reflexivity has implications for the EU's external actions and its own internal order.

This chapter relies on diffusion theory, as laid out in the introduction to this volume, (Björkdahl et al. in this volume) to explain the interplay between the EU as a norm-maker and the recipient states in Asia as potential norm-takers (Börzel and Risse 2012). The mechanisms of trade policies and negotiations by which norms such as gender equality are exported from the EU to third countries often include compulsion and conditionality, which is especially visible in the relationships between the EU and its neighbours and between the EU and the Africa Caribbean Pacific (ACP) countries. However, these specific mechanisms are often not applicable in the EU-Asia relationship because of the distance, and more importantly, the political as well as economic power imbalance (Schimmelfennig and Sedelmeier 2004). Socialisation, persuasion and emulation appear to be more relevant in the EU-Asian context. In the interaction resulting from norm maker and norm takers, diffusion theory considers a continuum of reactions from recipients states from adoption, to adaptation, to resistance, to unambiguous rejection of the norms. Even with such soft mechanisms, this chapter shows that in the context of the EU-Asia trade negotiation, the recipient states (the Asian states) firmly reject the transfer of gender equality norms.

By way of disclaimer, it is appropriate to note here that this chapter is not intended to serve as 'testing grounds for the universalization of western social sciences' (Mitchell 2003, p. 98). While acknowledging the heterogeneity of women across the Asian region, the chapter nevertheless recognises that gender, as an analytical category, has universal relevance. Women as a group are more vulnerable to poverty because of the unequal distribution of income and assets, access to credit, business services, control over the income and structural gender market bias (UN ESCAP 2013). It is also recognised that 'gender' should not be understood as 'women' but that women are part of 'gender' (Derichs 2013, p. 126). Gender is a relational term, which includes men and women. In this chapter 'gender' points to a set of learned qualities and behaviours influenced by factors such as education or economics and social expectations of men and women.

The chapter begins by providing a critical assessment of the legal background to the EU's obligations in the field of gender equality. It then focuses on EU official trade policy, which reveals internal barriers and a systemic failure to implement gender equality norms. Against this backdrop, the chapter then investigates the impact of the lack of gender perspective on trade negotiations in the Asian region. The final section of this chapter addresses the external resistance to EU attempts at linking its trade policy with broader values including social and gender rights. It critically assesses these external barriers specifically related to the Asian region and the possible consequences for the EU's relationship with that region of the world as well as for the EU internal policy.

12.2   The EU's Obligations and Commitments to Gender Equality in External Relations

The EU has entrenched the principle of 'gender equality as one of the central missions and activities of the Union' (Bell 2011, p. 629) and it is one of its fundamental values (Koukoulis-Spiliotopoulos 2008). Indeed, Article 2 of the Treaty on European Union (TEU) proclaims that equality is one of the *values* on which the Union is founded. As such, the EU has an obligation to take into account the principle of gender equality when planning and enacting all types of legislation. This so-called obligation of 'gender mainstreaming' (Pollack and Hafner-Burton 2000) is now contained in Article 8 of the Treaty on the Functioning of the European Union (TFEU) and provides that '[i]n all its activities, the Union shall aim to eliminate inequalities, and to promote equality, between men and women.' Thus, a gender dimension should be incorporated in every single area of the EU's activity (including external trade).

The obligation to achieve gender equality has further been confirmed as a constitutional fundamental right legally guaranteed by Article 23 of the EU Charter of Fundamental Rights (the Charter), which provides that

> Equality between women and men must be ensured in all areas, including employment, work and pay. The principle of equality shall not prevent the maintenance or adoption of measures providing for specific advantages in favour of the under-represented sex.

The constitutionalisation of gender equality law has also triggered its externalisation. The expansion of the scope of EU gender equality under the EU Treaty has had international ramifications. Indeed, since 1999 the Treaty grants the EU competences relating to freedom, security and justice to which equality between women and men apply when negotiating with external partners. Article 21(1) of the TEU clearly states that the EU's Common Foreign Policy and Security Policy

> shall be guided by the principles which have inspired its own creation, development and enlargement, and which it seeks to advance in the wider world: democracy, the rule of law, the universality and indivisibility of human rights and fundamental freedoms, respect for human dignity, the *principles of equality* and solidarity, and respect for the principles of the United Nations Charter and international law (emphasis added).

In addition, the European Commission's Roadmap for Equality between Women and Men (2006–2010) and the Strategy for Equality between Women and Men (2010–2015) cover both internal and external EU policies with a view to improving the coherence between these two pillars. The Strategy provides in particular that 'equality is one of five values on which the Union is founded. The Union is bound to strive for equality between women and men in all its activities' (European Commission 2010). In relation to gender equality in external actions, the Strategy for Equality states that

> EU policy on the promotion of gender equality within the EU is closely linked to the work undertaken by the Union in third countries. Through all relevant policies under its external action, the EU can exercise significant influence in fostering gender equality and women's empowerment worldwide.

It further adds that the 'EU will continue to use its development policies to promote gender equality and women's empowerment' (ibid.). As a result, any international action undertaken by the EU must be guided by the principle of EU gender equality and should be included in the EU's relationship with third countries. The highest law of the EU has therefore clearly established a strong commitment to a reflective[1] process involving the consideration of the promotion of gender norms both within and outside the EU's boundaries in all policy areas.

At the international level, the EU's most powerful tools for normative influence have been in the fields of development cooperation and trade. Both these areas are perhaps potentially areas where the EU's powerful normative action could be best used to their fullest capacities in relation to the acceptance and implementation of EU values, and engagement with multilateral bodies (see Björkdahl and Elgström; Bengtsson in this volume). As the world's largest trading entity, the EU has long used the attraction of its market and leveraged it in its trade policy in exchange for other foreign policy aims, thus using trade as a genuine foreign policy tool (Smith 2006). Indeed this has even been described as a 'market' rather than a normative power (Damro 2012), yet there is no evidence of the EU using its trade policy to encourage the external promotion of gender equality. However, the EU has been relatively successful in incorporating the promotion of gender equality norms into some of its development policies as, for instance, in the context of the United Nations' Millennium Development Goals and the co-operation and development in the African, Caribbean and Pacific regions, where the EU is concerned with aid and humanitarian development (Allwood 2013; Arts 2006). By contrast, EU-Asia co-operation and development policy was, from the outset, directly linked to the growing economic and political power of the Asian region (European Commission 1994, 2001), leaving little space for EU normative influence in the fields of gender equality and gender mainstreaming (Masselot 2013).

Unfortunately, the tension between the EU's gender equality agenda and economic interests is even more evident in the EU's trade policy towards the Asian region. As Asian consumers have gained purchasing power, Europe has become concerned with negotiating access to these emerging markets. Negotiations for comprehensive free trade agreements (FTA) between the EU and Asian states commenced in 2007 and are correspondingly accompanied by the negotiation of overarching Framework Agreements (FA) or Political Cooperation Agreements (PCA) that establish the legal basis of the relationship with the EU. FAs encapsulate the EU's core values of democracy and respect for human rights and make the entire relationship (including

---

[1] Reflexivity here means that there is a state of consistency between the internal and the external EU actions (David and Guerrina 2013).

the FTA) conditional on these values, with a suspension clause that gives the EU a possibility to cancel trade preferences if these core values are breached. FAs also incorporate many of the EU's more recent normative concerns, including sustainability, nuclear non-proliferation, counter-terrorism cooperation, support for multilateral organisations, yet these are included in non-binding terms (Horn et al. 2010). For example, the EU-Korea FTA only commits the parties to 'cooperate' and 'exchange information' in various sectors including labour conditions and social issues (including gender equality), and disputes are merely referred to an expert panel (European Union 2010a). More importantly, as subsequent sections reveal, gender is conspicuous for its absence in the EU's trade policy, despite gender equality being an EU value, and despite Directorate General (DG) Trade's acknowledgement that 'as we pursue social justice and cohesion at home,[2] we should also seek to promote our values, including social and environmental standards and cultural diversity, around the world' (European Commission 2006, p. 5).

The tension between market needs and equal rights is not new and therefore it is not surprising to find the same struggle in EU-Asian trade relations. Commitment to equality in the EU has always been entangled with economic and market-based considerations (Hoskyns 1996; True 2009a), yet gender equality (as other kind of fundamental rights) often conflict with the free market. In reality, the neo-liberal project and economic considerations have often taken precedence over fundamental rights (MacRea 2013) despite legal statement to the contrary.[3] However, what we witness in the context of trade negotiations with the Asian region is the complete abdication of the EU in engaging with (gender) equality in order to complete the economic project of market liberalisation, open competition and free market. Arguably this is not merely an issue of competing policies areas but it can be construed that the EU is not acting within its legal constrains and boundaries.

12.3   Genderless Trade Policy

As the EU's oldest external policy, trade policy has always served economic and broader foreign policy objectives (Baldwin 2006). On the one hand, EU trade policy has always had a mandate to open markets for European business:[4]

---

[2] Acknowledging the unequal effects of trade liberalisation, 'Global Europe' establishes the European Globalisation Fund to help stem some of the negative effects, and 'Trade, Growth and World Affairs' aims to extend and simplify the fund.

[3] Indeed in C-270/97 *Deutsche Post v Sievers & Schrage* [2000] ECR I-929, the Court of Justice held unambiguously that the economic aims are now only secondary to the social aims, therefore providing a clear ideological motivation for the application of European Union law. See also Case 149/77 *Defrennes* (no. 3) [1978] ECR 1365, paragraphs 26 and 27; Joined Cases 75/82 and 117/82 *Razzouk and Beydoun* v *Commission*, [1984] ECR 1509, paragraph 16, and Case C-13/94 *P.* v *S. and Cornwall County Council* [1996] ECR I-2143, paragraph 19; (Arnull 1990; Docksey 1991).

[4] Studies of the EU's trade policy have highlighted its inherent bias towards free trade and liberalisation. Proponents of the collusive delegation thesis argue this derives from the institutional

> By establishing a customs union [...] the Member States intend to contribute, in conformity with the common interest, to the harmonious development of world trade, the progressive abolition of restrictions on international exchanges and the lowering of customs barriers. (Article 110 of the Treaty founding the European Economic Community 1957)

The emphasis on trade liberalisation represents a material interest-driven policy, and an institutional ideational belief in the developmental power of trade (see Garcia 2013). Particularly under the stewardship of Trade Commissioner Pascal Lamy (1999–2004), the EU's trade policy was discursively linked to its development policy goals, and attempts were made to articulate Lamy's 'managed globalisation', which subordinated trade policy to multilateralism, sustainability and social justice (Meunier 2007) at the World Trade Organisation (WTO) (see Abdewal and Meunier 2010). On the other hand, being the EU's earliest and most 'communitarised' external policy, trade policy has also been used to pursue other EU foreign policy aims (Smith 2006; Baldwin 2006), *inter alia* democratisation, regional integration or stability, albeit with mixed results (Youngs 2004). Where economic interests were important due to market growth or competition from other actors, and where partners' situations involved resistance to EU proposals, the EU has been willing to forgo some of its foreign policy aims in favour of trade and economic relations. Bilateral FTAs with Peru and Colombia, and with individual ASEAN states as opposed to the region-to-region EU-Andean Community and EU-ASEAN FTAs originally projected are examples of this (Garcia 2012; Björkdahl and Elgström in this volume).

Commitments to external norm promotion are reflected in DG Trade's policy, even in the liberal and competitiveness-driven post-'Global Europe' policies, which acknowledge

> we are paying systematic attention to coherence with development policies, such as poverty eradication and insisting on the promotion in trade negotiations of sustainable development (i.e. decent work, labour standards and environmental protection). (European Commission 2010, p. 4).[5]

---

arrangement whereby Member States transferred EU trade policy to the European Commission, creating a principal-agent relationship (Elsig 2007), which isolated the Commission from the protectionist impulses of domestic economic sectors (Meunier and Nicolaidis 1999; Meunier 2000). Others argue the policies result from competition amongst interest groups and effective lobbying of the European Commission and Member States (De Bieve and Dür 2005; Dür 2008). Focusing on effective lobbying, the Corporate Europe Observatory think-tank based in Brussels, (see Eberhardt and Kumar 2010) maintains that the business lobby's access to the European Commission and other institutional actors is reflected in a liberal trade policy focused on opening markets abroad for services and investment, which downplays the possible negative effects of trade liberalisation. The complex interactions between principals, agents, interest groups and the folding of foreign policy aims into trade policy have led Meunier and Nicolaidis (2006) to describe the EU as a 'conflicted trade power'.

[5] In 2006 Commissioner Peter Mandelson published the 'Global Europe' trade policy which focuses on market opening, especially in emerging markets, pursuing comprehensive 'deep' trade agreements including public procurement, services, competition policy and intellectual property rights, and is driven overall by a concern with 'competitiveness' (Woolcock 2007) Commissioner De Gucht's 2006 'Trade, Growth and World Affairs' trade strategy follows the same lines.

Normative promotion in the EU's trade policy revolves around the incorporation of a democracy clause in FAs, which makes the FTA contingent on the respect of human rights and the rule of law. Recent FTAs also seek to externalise the concept of sustainability through the incorporation of social and environmental sustainability clauses. Social sustainability in terms of EU trade policy is defined in narrow terms as referring to 'decent work' and to upholding the core conventions of the International Labour Organisation (ILO). Other social issues such as poverty reduction, health and education matters or discrimination are beyond the scope of DG Trade,[6] even though some of its actions in the field of trade could impact upon these matters (e.g. liberalisation of health services in FTAs). DG Trade's social focus, thus, lies in the field of basic workers' rights and basic labour standards.[7] Perhaps not surprisingly, of the EU's values and normative objectives, breach of these abroad could result in trade advantages for partners as they can realise lower labour costs, and in a worst case scenario social dumping, potentially leading to downward pressures on EU internal employment and social policies. The EU faces the import of cheap products produced from third states with low or inexistent legislation protecting workers. These cheap products compete directly with EU products which bear the cost of higher labour protection. In order to gain or regain international competitiveness EU states might consider weakening their own internal social protection so as to reduce labour costs, the so-called 'social dumping'.

Not surprisingly, the DG most closely engaged with the neo-liberal economic project are the least likely to implement a gender mainstreaming strategy or to recognise that their policy and activities are in any way gendered (MacRae 2013). DG Trade's limited interpretation of social sustainability translates into policies that fail to explicitly incorporate some of the EU's mandated values. Unlike the EU's development policy, EU trade documents lack explicit mention of gender mainstreaming or equality. In one of her studies, Holskyns notes that DG Trade has no time and little expertise to do work on gender and that despite the existence of mainstreaming programmes, officials did not believe that they have the responsibility of addressing gender (2004, p. 15). Debusscher and True (2008) have highlighted the absence of systematic gender mainstreaming in DG Trade, and the lack of a dedicated gender officer, which other externally-focused DGs have. In particular, DG Development appears to have made the greatest head-way in gender mainstreaming, in part the result of the lobbying of action networks (e.g. Women in Development Europe WIDE) (Debusscher and True 2008). Through its collaboration with UN Women, the EU has developed training materials for gender considerations, but these apply only to development planning and aid delivery mechanisms and not to trade (Gender Matters 2013). Although concerns about women's issues in poverty al-

---

[6] DG Trade leads the FTA negotiations with third parties, but aspects of the FAs are negotiated by officials in other Commission DGs and in the External Action Service, as the competences for those areas (e.g. development cooperation or education) lie with them. Although DG Trade takes the lead, it coordinates policies with the EU Member States and with increasingly with the European Parliament, to ensure the agreements will not be voted down once finalised.

[7] The EU is using ILO core conventions as a reference point for this.

leviation are present in the EU's development policy, these are not translated into Trade policy, despite seeking coherence with development policies. To some extent DG Trade's concern with sustainability, especially regarding labour standards, and environmental consequences includes women (and men), however, no specific references to equality are made, making it easy for specific gender issues to fall off the negotiation agenda.

12.4 EU's FTA Negotiations with Asian States: The Impact of Gender Absence

Despite the absence of a specific gender mainstreaming culture in DG Trade, as the European Commission has associated gender equality with issues of development, there is some generic incorporation of these matters in EU FTA negotiations with developing and emerging states in Asia. All of the Sustainability Impact Assessments (SIAs)[8] for the region take into account gender matters by looking at women's education and employment rates through United Nation (UN) Human Development Indicators, but this focus on development indicators serves to further the development-gender link. The SIA for the EU-South Korea FTA, claims that 'no significant adverse effects on gender can be forseen' (IBM Belgium 2008, p. 15), despite acknowledging that age discrimination at work affects women more than men in Korea (IBM Belgium 2008, p. 65). More significantly, the final Framework Agreement (FA) with South Korea, for instance, only mentions in Article 22 that the parties 'agree to cooperate in the field of employment and social affairs' and that 'cooperation may include gender equality' among other issues mentioned. The EU-Korea FA did commit Korea to join the ILO and to apply the core conventions. This is expected to have an impact on 'decent work' and impact all workers, be they men or women (IBM Belgium 2008, p. 65). The SIA for negotiations with ASEAN, looking at similar indicators as well as the UN Human Development Indicators highlighted that, with the exception of Singapore, women suffer more poverty in ASEAN, have lower literacy rates and work mainly in the service sectors and agriculture and that the FTA could result in a worsening of the gender balance in employment because a higher proportion of women are employed in these sectors

---

[8] Since the early 2000s DG Trade commission's independent studies to consider the potential effects of FTAs on the EU and partner states so as to incorporate that knowledge into the negotiations. The Civil Society Dialogue and though the Sustainability Impact Assessments stakeholders', including social actors', interests in the negotiations are fed-into trade policy. Critics argue civil society positions are heard but rarely make it into the actual negotiations with partners (Maes 2009). Moreover, SIAs tend to have a pro-liberalisation bias in-built as they tend to model for positive growth in trade and investment once barriers are removed, and their quantitative methodology overlooks sectors where little data is available (i.e. informal sector, and which may disproportionately affect women) (Sprecht 2009).

compared to others (ECORYS 2009a, p. 117, 123).[9] In the case of EU-India FTA negotiations, the SIA claims that, as the textile sector concentrates a high proportion of women workers in India, and the FTA is likely to result in increased exports to Europe, the effect will be more jobs for women (ECORYS 2009b, p. 164). However, the SIA recognises that the overall impact on existing gender inequalities in high-skilled jobs will be negligible (ECORYS 2009b, p. 294). It merely suggests technical assistance to support Indian productivity and support for India's own programmes in favour of education, training and employment for low-skilled women in particular (ECORYS 2009b, p. 396). As negotiations with various ASEAN states (such as Malaysia, Vietnam, Thailand) are on-going and the text agreed with Singapore are awaiting signature and not available, it is impossible to determine at the time of writing whether more gender elements will be incorporated in these agreements. What the FTA with Korea has highlighted, however, is the EU's insistence on extending international 'decent work' standards of the ILO rather than the use of specific gender clauses or even the reliance on the Convention on the Elimination of All Forms of Discrimination Against Women (CEDAW) (True 2009a, 2009b). Thus, in a case of competing cross-cutting issues, it is clear that the EU has prioritised 'decent work' over gender equality for its trade negotiations.

Extending compliance with international agreements on labour (ILO) and environmental standards has been a particular normative goal supported by the European Parliament (EP) in an attempt to achieve coherence between internal and external policy making. It also represents a way to articulate the neo-liberal project with the human and social rights framework (ibid.). The ILO standards are particularly relevant to the gender norms agenda setting because they include the principles of non-discrimination on the grounds of sex (ILO Convention 111) and equal pay for men and women (ILO Convention 100) as well as being relevant to women who more often than men hold insecure and precarious employment. Since the entry into force of the Lisbon Treaty, the EP, who is generally favourable to fundamental rights, has become more involved in oversight of the European Commission whilst it undertakes negotiations with third parties, thus enhancing its leverage in impacting the negotiations. In a Resolution dated 11 May 2011 on negotiations with India, the EP argued in favour of the inclusion not only of 'legally binding clauses on human rights', which FAs typically contain, but also of 'social and environmental standards and their enforcement, with measures in the event of infringement' (EP 2011). This view was reiterated by the European Economic and Social Committee (2011). However, as negotiations are on-going it is difficult to ascertain whether legally-binding social and environmental standards will appear in the final FTA and FA.

Commitments to social and environmental clauses notwithstanding, the EU has been criticised for insisting on 'deep' trade[10] negotiations with developing states,

---

[9] In 2007 the EU launched FTA negotiations with ASEAN, but these were abandoned in 2010 and replaced with individual negotiations with the most advanced economies in ASEAN.

[10] 'Deep' trade refers to the incorporation of issues in trade relations that go well-beyond traditional matters of tariffs and quotas as restrictions to trade, and include the harmonisation of

and in particular for the inclusion of services liberalisation in negotiations. From a gender perspective the incorporation of these matters in FTAs with Asia has been considered particularly worrying. Ranja Sengupta and Narendra Jena (2009) argue that liberalisation of health services could lead to pricing-out vulnerable sectors, especially low-income women, and could result into a loss of qualified health care personnel in India, if the liberalisation in labour movement for service provision that India is pushing for is included in the FTA. Women in Development Europe (WIDE) warns of constrained policy space resulting from the inclusion of services and public procurement in the negotiations, potentially hindering India's government's possibilities of using policies which empower vulnerable social groups[11] (Paulus 2009, p. 8; Wichterich and Menon-Sen 2009). WIDE's overarching criticism is that in separating negotiations of social (including gender) and environmental chapters, these concerns are segregated from the rest of the negotiations and are therefore not mainstreamed into the various trade sectors (Wichterich and Menon-Sen 2009, p. 37). Significantly, negotiations in other trade sectors may result in damaging outcomes that contradict the very values the EU is trying to protect and promote in the social and environmental chapters.[12]

The underlying irony is that whilst the EU supports normative exports and has mandated itself to actively pursue this in the Lisbon Treaty under Article 21 TEU, DG Trade's commitment to 'deep' trade (see Young and Peterson 2006)[13] may be hampering the incorporation of its normative agenda as its comprehensive approach is rejected by others. Perhaps various sets of negotiations on different issues, as opposed to 'the all or nothing' approach might garner more support from partners.

'Global Europe' and 'Trade, Growth and World Affairs' trade policies, designed in the shadow of a blocked WTO Doha Development Round,[14] both focus on pursuing the EU's material interests, and externalising liberalisation as mandated by

---

partners' phytosanitary measures and various standards, intellectual property rights, competition policy, liberalising the rules for service provision (including movement of people), and opening access to public procurement markets.

[11] This might happen for instance when public procurement contracts are reserved for local companies and contracts are made contingent on the thresholds for the employment of various groups.

[12] This is particularly relevant as the different chapter will be negotiated in detail by different officials, possibly form different Ministries. Prior to the creation of the European External Action Service in the Lisbon Treaty, the FAs were negotiated by officials from the Commission's DG Relex, while the FTA part was negotiated by DG Trade. Although the parties' chief negotiators have a global vision of the agreement it is unreasonable to expect them to have every single detail and possible interference of one article with issues elsewhere in the treaty.

[13] This was unequivocally expressed by Trade Commissioner Karel De Gucht (2010) himself when he announced the launch of FTA negotiations with Singapore: 'we are not available to do shallow FTAs.'

[14] During Pascal Lamy's term as EU Trade Commissioner (1999–2004) he promoted a moratorium on new FTA negotiations to devote all efforts to supporting the WTO Doha Round. As the round faltered and it became clear by the 2005 Hong Kong Ministerial meeting that the EU's 'deep trade' agenda of liberalisation would be impossible at the WTO, DG Trade, now under the stewardship of Peter Mandelson, re-directed trade policy to foster bilateral FTAs in which the EU could push for the liberalisation of sectors excluded from the WTO (see Young and Peterson 2006).

Article 206 TFEU. The policies prioritise negotiating FTAs with partners with large market potential and higher barriers to EU trade (European Commission 2006a, p. 11) and the liberalisation of services, public procurement markets and regulatory regimes (ibid., p. 6).[15] Various studies argue that without further access to emerging markets in these controversial areas, the EU stands to gain little in economic terms from enhanced relations and FTAs with these markets (ECORYS 2009a, 2009b; Decreux and Mitaritonna 2007). Yet, DG Trade's insistence on these matters could undermine the norm-driven aspects of the EU's Trade and FTA policy.

12.5   The External Rejection of the EU Normative Promotion of Gender Equality

Reflexivity and norm diffusion are both influential over the way the EU as an external actor (and a self-proclaimed normative leader) is able to shape global gender equality values. As we have seen, in spite of the legality, there is great disparity between the EU's internal rules and its external EU relations with regards to the application of gender equality norms. This lack of reflexivity is compounded by the fact that the EU's actions cannot only be judged on its endeavour to diffuse its fundamental values but also on the level of which these values are adopted (Browning and Christou 2010). Arguably the process is twofold: without the actual import, there is no export of EU values.

Beyond internal inconsistencies, a core difficulty lies in persuading partners to accept the EU's intentional linkage of trade with other norms. Europe's partners in developing and emerging countries have protested the inclusion of sustainability and environmental clauses in negotiations. India has objected to their inclusion in the FTA, as it sees these as a form of European protectionism (Paulus 2009, p. 7), which is consistent with the widely held perspective in India that the EU is a 'protectionist club' (Lisbonne de Vergeron 2006, p. 25). For example, Indian small and medium producers may struggle to comply with EU environmental certification requirements and sanitary and phytosanitary standards for imports, and critics argue that EU requirements tend to benefit larger firms and agricultural producers (Wichterich 2009, p. 17).

In terms of social clauses, trade unions from around the world affiliated to the International Trade Union Confederation are strong supporters of the inclusion of EU core values in FTAs, however, other civil society groups question their usefulness. Naila Kaber (2004) fears that the enforcement of labour standards through trade sanctions could increase labour market inequalities through a shift of jobs towards the informal sector where those labour-standards would not be applied and lead to

---

[15] Emerging and developing partners have criticised the EU's and USA's insistence on these 'deep' trade matters at the WTO and in FTAs. NGOs and civil society groups have also critiqued the fact that these issues would restrict future policy space, a concern that has also been raised by gender-sensitive critiques of this neoliberal trade model (Sen 2005; Shivpuri 2010).

fewer women in employment. Likewise, Kevin Kolben's (2006) analysis in India found wide-spread opposition to the inclusion of labour standards in FTAs (with the exception of trade unions), as they were feared that they would protect Western markets from cheap goods, thereby adversely impacting trade and employment in India.

Objections to this comprehensive approach by the EU have been raised in particular by all its Asian partners, a region that has held non-interference in domestic matters as a centre-piece of 'Asian values'.[16] Thus, even a developed and highly competitive state like Singapore has lengthened FTA negotiations with the EU due to systematic objection to the inclusion of sustainability and environmental clauses in the agreement (Europe World 2010), potentially interfering with domestic policies on these matters. South Korea, too, had important internal debates about the Framework Agreement, the EP and the EU's general FTA/FA approach.[17] Significantly, when the conclusion of negotiations with Singapore was announced in December 2012 no announcement was made on the conclusion of the Partnership and Cooperation Agreement (PCA) that was being negotiated alongside the FTA, which was only finalised in June 2013. Prior to this, FTAs and FAs had either been completed simultaneously, or FA/PCAs had preceded FTAs, as the EU used its most powerful foreign policy tool, the 'carrot' of trade, to gain acquiescence for broader regulatory and normative aims in the FA/PCAs, by making market access conditional on acceptance of a broad FA/PCA. Negotiations with Malaysia and Vietnam which were launched in 2010, only entered the real negotiation stage in late 2012 (DG Trade 2013), again due to differences over the EU's mandated comprehensive approach to FTAs, covering WTO-plus liberalisation,[18] as well as different understandings of sustainability and environmental matters (Yean 2012, p. 10).

The case of negotiations with India represents this fundamental objection even more clearly. As a democratic state, India shares many of the EU's values, meaning that facilitation of agreement in these matters should be easier than with other countries in Asia. However, as Sen and Nair (2011, p. 434) argue when referring to the incorporation of human rights (including social and labour rights) in FTAs, India 'is of the opinion that such an issue does not belong in a market opening agreement'. In the first round of EU-India negotiations in 2007, the issue of human rights was not raised (Business Standard India 2007), but the EU subsequently incorporated the issue as part of its global approach to FTAs, as well as the result of domestic pressure by civil society citing labour abuses in India (EU 2010b). Fears have been expressed in India that the European Parliament's greater trade supervisory powers since the Treaty of Lisbon, will result in human rights being used as a 'trade

---

[16] 'Asian values' refer to Asian doctrines of developmentalism based on Confucian communitarian values, rejection of Western liberal democracy and foreign interference in domestic affairs. For a summary of the debates around the concept see Thompson 2001.

[17] From authors' phone discussions with Korean trade official (17 March 2012).

[18] WTO-plus liberalisation refers to the inclusion in bilateral or plurilateral agreements of issues that are not being negotiated in the WTO Doha Round, in particular competition policy, intellectual property rights, government procurement and services. Attempts by the EU and USA to include these in the WTO negotiations were blocked by emerging states, and were withdrawn from the agenda after the collapse of negotiations at the 2003 WTO Cancún Ministerial Meeting.

weapon' by the EU (Business Standard India 2010).[19] However, the EU's soft law approach towards these issues, as in the enforcement mechanism of the EU-Korea FTA which is through cooperation and expert panel advice, is unlikely to result in the aggressive trade protectionism feared by Indian and other Asian partners (Sen and Nair 2011, p. 435), and reflects the EU's 'soft law' to these matters which weakens the implementation and export of its core values. This notwithstanding, Asian partners perceive the EU's comprehensive approach as domineering and intrusive,[20] and the EU as a mighty trade competitor whose normative projection could hamper punctual economic interests of partners.

Ultimately, whilst the gender-development nexus has been established within the EU, the gender-trade nexus is largely absent. Instead, it has collapsed into the labour aspects of the concept of sustainability in trade relations. More importantly, with weak enforcement mechanisms in FA/PCAs for the non-trade matters negotiated alongside trade liberalisation in FTAs, EU normative extension through FA/PCAs and FTAs will remain limited, especially as long as partner states systematically oppose the linking of trade and normative issues. Organisation for Economic Co-operation and Development (OECD) partners such as Canada, Australia and New Zealand are likewise reluctant to sign FAs that may affect trade agreements with the EU.[21] As the EU embarks on negotiations with the USA a similar situation is likely to arise. If the EU were forced to alter its approach to FTAs for its OECD partners this would limit its future ability to link the trade incentive in exchange for the exportation of normative values in other parts of the world, as it would create a precedent of trade-only FTAs.[22]

12.6   Conclusion

The narrative reveals that the EU has developed strong gender equality legal obligations framed in constitutional and fundamental terms. Moreover, the EU is unambiguously politically and legally committed to achieving gender equality in its internal order and its external actions via the process of gender mainstreaming. This is clearly visible in both the EU's legal obligations and the rhetoric displayed in co-operation and development policy documents. However, when considering

---

[19] EU-India negotiations have been mired by different economic interests of the parties (see Khorana and Perdikis 2010; Khandekar 2012; Modwel and Singh 2012; Khorana and Garcia 2013).

[20] From interviews with Asian diplomats (Brussels, 30 October 2013, 27 October 2013), see also Sen and Nair 2011.

[21] From authors' discussions during research interviews with trade officials conducted in Wellington 10 December 2012; Canberra 8 October 2012; Brussels 31 October 2013. FAs represent the overarching legal framework of the relationship, and could be invoked to revoke trade preferences if the core democratic values of the FA were breached by the third party. This is unlikely to ever happen with OECD partners, which nevertheless object to the EU's 'everything goes into the agreement' approach to FTAs.

[22] Furthermore, as McGuire and Lindeque (2010) argue, the greater economic relevance of emerging markets is also lessening the EU's potential for exploiting the attraction of its market.

the EU's trade policy, explicit references to equality are conspicuous for their absence. Arguably, the prospect of access to key rising markets weakens EU efforts at achieving gender equality by creating a compromise between economic gain and a fundamental value. This is compounded by the absence of gender mainstreaming in trade negotiations, which is otherwise used as the main method in the exportation of the EU's value placed on gender equality (e.g. in development policy).

The rejection of EU gender equality values (as well as other human and social rights) from the Asian region contributes to the further weakening of the EU's ability to implement gender equality through its broader social sustainability principles. A fundamental problem lies in the fact that other actors in Asia regard this normative insistence as a protectionist reflex on the EU's part. Even states with similar social standards to the EU reject its legalistic approach in linking of these matters to trade agreements. It is, not always a case of rejection of the values *per se*, but of the EU's mechanism for their extension via conditionality clauses in its Framework and Partnership and Cooperation Agreements with applicability to the FTAs.

The nature of the EU as a normative power relies on the soft advocacy of human rights and democratisation. These values are at the core of the EU historical and fundamental's *raison d'être*. The consequences of compromising these values for economic gain are serious on many levels. Indeed, the EU's economic power is supposed to serve as a springboard for diffusing fundamental and democratic values to third countries (Manners 2002; McCormick 2007). David and Guerrina (2013, p. 56) therefore ponder rightfully the logic of the EU: 'If norms are the cart, economic power is the horse. The question is, has the EU put the cart before the horse?' The EU genderless external trade relations send a negative message about EU priorities. Moreover, the concession on fundamental norm-setting and the lack of coherence between the internal and the external EU actions also impacts on the EU's identity building (Bain and Masselot 2013), arguably creating a 'double identity' (Stratigaki 2004, p. 5).

The EU's inability or unwillingness to implement the general principle of gender equality through international actions creates a lack of reflexivity, which in turn compromises the EU as a gender actor, as an international normative power. The inconsistencies between the EU internal and external value norms create an overall watering down of the internal (universal) value and precipitate the retrenchment of well-established fundamental values. This in turns provides space for increasing internal challenges (David and Guerrina 2013). It also opens up further pockets of resistance or rejection in other area of EU external actions, for instance in co-operation and development. Already, we note a seriously weak standard for gender equality norms in co-operation and development in the Asian region (Masselot 2013) which parallels the absence of core EU value in external trade policies in the same region. It further encourages countries which normally would be more willing to accept EU values to reject them. Ultimately, these challenges and resistance pose the question of the credibility and the global reputation of the EU (Schimmelfennig 2001), casting serious doubts about the EU's international 'actorness' and, more seriously perhaps, failing to serve women in Asia.

Acknowledgements Maria Garcia wishes to acknowledge the support of the European Union, under the outgoing Marie Curie Fellowship grant PIOF-GA-2009-254239.

References

Abdewal, R., & Meunier, S. (2010). Managed globalisation: Doctrine, practice and promise. *Journal of European Public Policy, 17*(3), 350–367.

Aggestam, L. (2008). Introduction: Ethical power Europe? *International Affairs, 84*(1), 1–11.

Allwood, G. (2013). Gender mainstreaming and policy coherence for development: Unintended gender consequences and EU policy. *Women's Studies International Forum, 39,* 42–52.

Allwood, G., Guerrina, R., & MacRae, H. (2013). Unintended consequences of EU policies: Reintegrating gender in European studies. *Women's Studies International Forum, 39,* 1–2.

Arnull, A. (1990). *General principles of EC law and the individuals.* Leicester: Leicester University Press.

Arts, K. (2006). Gender in ACP-EU relations: The Cotonou agreement. In M. Lister & M. Carbone (Eds.), *New pathways in International development* (pp. 31–43). Aldershot: Ashgate.

Bain, J., & Masselot, A. (2013). Gender equality law and identity building for Europe. *Canterbury Law Review, 18,* 99–120.

Baldwin, M. (2006). EU trade politics—heaven or hell? *Journal of European Public Policy, 13*(6), 926–942.

Bell, M. (2011). The principle of equal treatment: Widening and deepening. In P. Craig & G. De Búrca (Eds.), *The evolution of EU law* (2nd ed., pp. 611–639). Oxford: Oxford University Press.

Börzel, T., & Risse, T. (2012). From Europeanisation to diffusion: Introduction. *West European Politics, 35*(1), 1–19.

Browning, C., & Christou, G. (2010). The constitutive power of outsiders: The European neighbourhood policy and the Eastern dimension. *Political Geography, 29*(2), 109–118.

Business Standard India. (2007). EU may not put human rights condition for FTA. http://bilaterals. org/spip.php?article8925. Accessed 16 Jan 2014.

Business Standard India. (2010). Hope floats for EU-India free trade pact talks. http://www. business-standard.com/india/news/hope-floats-for-india-eu-free-trade-pact-talks/391740/. Accessed 16 Jan 2014.

Damro, C. (2012). Market power Europe. *Journal of European Public Policy, 19*(5), 682–699.

David, M., & Guerrina, R. (2013). Gender and European external relations: Dominant discourse and unintended consequences of gender mainstreaming. *Women's Studies International Forum, 39,* 53–62.

De Bieve, D., & Dür, A. (2005). Constituency interests and delegation in EU and American trade policy. *Comparative Political Studies, 38*(10), 1271–1296.

Debusscher, P., & True, J. (2008). Lobbying the EU for gender equal development. In J. Orbie & L. Tortell (Eds.), *The European Union and the social dimension of globalisation* (pp. 186–206). New York: Routledge.

Decreux, Y., & Mitaritonna, C. (2007). *Economic impact of a potential free trade agreement between the European Union and India.* Paris: Report by CEPII CIREM for DG Trade.

De Gucht, K. (2010). Speech: Europe and Singapore: Partners in trade, partners for growth. Lee Kuan Yew School of Public Policy, Singapore, 3 March 2010. http://europa.eu/rapid/press-release_SPEECH-10-58_en.htm. Accessed 16 Jan 2014.

Derichs, C. (2013). Gender and transition in Southeast Asia: Conceptual travel? *Asia Europe Journal, 11,* 113–127.

DG Trade. (2013). European Commission trade with ASEAN Website. http://ec.europa.eu/trade/policy/countries-and-regions/regions/asean/. Accessed 16 Jan 2014.

Docksey, C. (1991). The principle of the equality between women and men as a fundamental right under community law. *Industrial Law Journal, 20*(4), 258–280.

Dür, A. (2008). Bringing economic interests back into the study of EU trade policy-making. *British Journal of Politics and International Relations, 10*(1), 27–45.

Eberhardt, P., & Kumar, D. (2010). *Trade invaders. How big business is driving the EU-India free trade negotiations*. Brussels: Corporate Europe Observatory.

ECORYS. (2009a). Trade sustainability impact assessment for the FTA between the EU and ASE-AN. Report for DG Trade, TRADE07/C1/C01 Lot 2.

ECORYS. (2009b). Trade sustainability impact assessment for the FTA between the EU and the Republic of India. Report for DG Trade in the European Commission, TRADE07/C1/C01—Lot 1.

Elsig, M. (2007). The EU's choice of regulatory venues for trade negotiations: A tale of agency power? *Journal of Common Market Studies, 45*(4), 927–948.

European Commission. (1994). Communication, towards a new Asia strategy, COM(94) 314 final, 13/7/1994

European Commission. (2001). Communication, Europe and Asia: Strategic framework for enhanced partnerships, COM (2001) 469 final, 4/9/2001.

European Commission. (2006a). Global Europe: Competing in the world, COM 567/2006.

European Commission. (2006b). Communication from the commission—A roadmap for equality between women and men (2006–2010), COM (2006) 92 Final, 1/3/2006.

European Commission. (2010). Growth, jobs and trade, COM (2010) 216.

European Commission. (2011). *Strategy for equality between women and men (2010–2015)*. Luxembourg: Publication Office of the European Union.

European Economic and Social Committee. (2011). Opinion of the European Economic and Social Committee on the role of civil society in the free trade agreement between the EU and India. REX/316, Brussels.

European Parliament. (2011). Resolution on the state of play in the EU-India free trade agreement negotiations, 11.05.2011, Strasbourg, N. P7_TA_PROV (2011) 0224.

European Union. (2010a). Framework agreement between the European Union and its Member States and the Republic of Korea. Official Journal of the European Union 23 January 2013 L 20/2. http://ec.europa.eu/world/agreements/downloadFile.do?fullText=yes&treatyTransId=14683. Accessed 16 Jan 2014.

European Union. (2010b). EU India relations background note. Press release 21.06.2010. http://europa.eu/rapid/pressReleasesAction.do?reference=MEMO/10/265&type=HTML. Accessed 16 Jan 2014.

Europe World. (2010). Big prospects for upcoming EU-Singapore FTA 5 Nov 2010. http://www.europesworld.org/NewEnglish/Home_old/CommunityPosts/tabid/809/PostID/1975/language/en-US/Default.aspx. Accessed 20 Jan 2012.

Garcia, M. (2012). The European Union and Latin America: 'Transformative power Europe' versus the realities of economic interests. Cambridge Review of International Affairs, OnlineFirst. http://www.tandfonline.com/doi/full/10.1080/09557571.2011.647762. Accessed 16 Jan 2014.

Garcia, M. (2013). From idealism to realism: EU preferential trade agreement policy. *Journal of Contemporary European Research, 9*(3), 521–542.

Gender Matters. (2013). UN/EU partnership on gender equality in development and peace website. http://www.gendermatters.eu/. Accessed 16 Jan 2014.

Horn, H., Mavroidis, P., & Sapir, A. (2010). Beyond the WTO? An anatomy of EU and US preferential trade agreements. *The World Economy, 33*(11), 1565–1588.

Hoskyns, C. (1996). *Integrating gender: Women, law and politics in the European Union*. London: Verso.

Hoskyns, C. (2004). Mainstreaming gender in the macroeconomic policies of the EU—Institutional and conceptual issues paper presented at the ECPR conference, Bologna June 2004. http://www.jhubc.it/ecpr-bologna/docs/179.pdf. Accessed 16 Jan 2014.

IBM Belgium. (2008). Trade sustainability impact assessment of EU-Korea FTA: Draft final report. Prepared for DG Trade.

Kaber, N. (2004). Globalisation, labour standards and women's rights: Dilemmas of collective (in) action in an interdependent world. *Feminist Economics, 10*(1), 3–35.

Khandekar, G. (2012). The EU-India summit: On the threshold of change. ESP Policy Brief No. 1, European Strategic Partnerships Observatory, FRIDE, Egmont.

Khorana, S., & Garcia, M. (2013). EU-India free trade agreement negotiations: One step forwards, one step back. *Journal of Common Market Studies, 51*(4), 684–700.

Khorana, S., & Perdikis, N. (2010). EU and India free trade agreement: Deal or no deal? *South Asia Economic Journal, 11*(2), 181–206.

Kolben, K. (2006). The new politics of linkage: India's opposition to the workers' rights clause. *Indiana Journal of Global Legal Studies, 13*, 225–258.

Koukoulis-Spiliotopoulos, S. (2008). The Lisbon Treaty and the Charter of Fundamental Rights: Maintaining and developing the *aquis* in gender equality. *European Gender Equality Law Review, 1*, 15–24.

Lightfoot, S., & Burchell, J. (2005). The European Union at the world summit on sustainable development: Normative power Europe in action. *Journal of Common Market Studies, 43*(1), 75–95.

Lisbonne de Vergeron, K. (2006). *Contemporary Indian views of Europe*. London: Chatham House.

MacRae, H. (2013). (Re-)gendering integration: Unintended and unanticipated gender outcomes of the European Union policy. *Women's Studies International Forum, 39*, 3–11.

Maes, M. (2009). Civil society perspectives on EU-Asia free trade agreements. *Asia Europe Journal, 7*, 97–107.

Manners, I. (2002). Normative power Europe: A contradiction in terms? *Journal of Common Market Studies, 40*(2), 235–258.

Manners, I. (2008). The normative ethics of the European Union. *International Affairs, 84*(1), 45–60.

Masselot, A. (2013). Does the European Union 'walk the walk' or Just 'talk the talk' of gender equality in water development projects in the Asian Region? *wH2O: The Journal on Gender and Water, 2*, 8–14.

McCormick, J. (2007). *The European superpower*. London: Palgrave.

McGuire, S., & Lindeque, J. (2010). Diminishing returns to trade policy in the European Union. *Journal of Common Market Studies, 45*(5), 1329–1349.

Meunier, S. (2000). What single voice? European Institutions and EU-US trade negotiations. *International Organization, 54*(1), 103–135.

Meunier, S. (2007). Managing globalisation: The EU in international trade negotiations. *Journal of Common Market Studies, 45*(5), 905–926.

Meunier, S., & Nicolaidis, K. (1999). Who speaks for Europe? The delegation of trade authority in the EU. *Journal of Common Market Studies, 37*(3), 477–510.

Meunier, S., & Nicolaidis, K. (2006). The EU as a conflicted trade power. *Journal of European Public Policy, 13*(6), 906–925.

Michell, T. (2003). The Middle East in the past and future of social sciences. In David L. Szanton (Ed.), *The politics of knowledge: Area studies and the disciplines* (University of California International and Area Studies Digital Collection, Edited Volume No. 3, pp. 74–118). Berkley: University of California Press.

Modwel, S., & Singh, S. (2012). The EU-India FTA negotiations: Leading to an agreement or disagreement? ORF Occasional Paper No. 32, Observer Research Foundation.

Paulus, L. (2009). The EU-India free trade agreement negotiations: Gender and social justice concerns. A memo for members of the European Parliament. Brussels: WIDE. http://www.wide-network.org. Accessed 1 July 2013.

Pollack, M., & Hafner-Burton, E. (2000). Mainstreaming gender in the European Union. *Journal of European Public Policy, 7*(3), 432–56.

Schimmelfennig, F. (2001). The community trap: Liberal norms, rhetorical actions, and the eastern enlargement of the European Union. *International Organization, 55*(1), 47–80.

Schimmelfennig, F., & Sedelmeier, U. (2004). Governance by conditionality: EU rule transfer to the candidate countries of Central and Eastern Europe. *Journal of European Public Policy, 11*(4), 669–687.

Sen, G. (2005). Neolibs, neocons and gender justice: Lessons from global negotiations, Occasional Paper No 9, United Nations Research Institute for Social Development.

Sen, N., & Nair, B. G. (2011). Human rights provisions in the forthcoming India-EU free trade agreement. *National University of Juridical Sciences Law Review, 4,* 417–437.

Sengupta, R., & Narendra, J. (2009). The current trade paradigm and women's health concerns in India: With special reference to the proposed EU-India free trade agreement. New Dehli: Centre for Trade and Development and Heinrich Böll Foundation. http://www.in.boell.org/downloads/Health_Report_mail.pdf. Accessed 16 Jan 2014.

Shivpuri, A. (2010). Towards a gender-sensitive trade regime. Trade policy analysis, issue paper, November 2010, South Asia Watch on Trade, Economics and Environment, SAWTEE. http://www.sawtee.org. Accessed on 16 Jan 2014.

Smith, M. (2006). The EU as an international actor. In J. Richardson (Ed.), *European Union: Power and policy-making* (pp. 289–310). Abingdon: Routledge.

Sprecht, B. (2009). A critical review of the trade sustainability impact assessment for the free trade agreement between the EU and the Republic of India from a gender perspective. Brussels: WIDE Network. http://www.wide-network.org. Accessed 16 Jan 2014.

Stratigaki, M. (2004). The cooptation of gender concepts in EU policies: The case of reconciliation of work and family. *Social Politics: International Studies in Gender, State and Society, 11*(1), 30–56.

Thompson, M. R. (2001). Whatever happened to 'Asian values'? *Journal of Democracy, 12*(4), 154–165.

True, J. (2009a). Trading-off gender equality for global Europe? The European Union and free trade agreements. *European Foreign Affairs Review, 14,* 723–742

True, J. (2009b). Trading-in gender equality: Gender meanings in EU trade policy. In E. Lombardo, P. Meier, & M. Verloo (Eds.), *The discursive politics of gender equality: Stretching, banding and policy-making* (pp. 121–137). Abingdon: Routledge.

United Nation. (2013). *UN ESCAP annual report 2013.* Bangkok: United Nation Publication. http://issuu.com/escap-publications/docs/escap-annual-report-2013?mode=embed&viewMode=presentation & layout=http%3A//skin.issuu.com/v/light/layout.xml. Accessed 16 Jan 2014.

Vogler, J., & Stephen, H. (2007). The European Union in global environmental governance: Leadership in the making? *International Environment Agreements, 7,* 389–413.

Wichterich, C., & Menon-Sen, K. (2009). Trade liberalisation, gender equality, policy space: The case of the contested EU-India FTA. WIDE-Network. http://www.wide-network.org. Accessed 16 Jan 2014.

Woolcock, S. (2007). *European Union policy towards FTAs.* ECIPE Working Paper 3/2007.

Yean, T. S. (2012). Negotiating for a Malaysia-EU FTA. Contesting interests from a Malaysian perspective. IFRI Centre for Asian Studies, Asie-Visions 57.

Young, A., & Peterson, J. (2006). The EU and new trade politics. *Journal of European Public Policy, 13*(6), 795–814.

Youngs, R. (2004). Normative dynamics and strategic interests in the EU's external identity. *Journal of Common Market Studies, 43*(4), 787–806.

Maria Garcia is a senior lecturer at the School of Politics, Modern Languages and International Studies at the University of Bath, UK. Her research focuses on the international political economy of free trade agreements, integration and EU-Asia relations.

Annick Masselot is an Associate Professor in Law at the University of Canterbury (College of Business and Law), New Zealand. Her research interests focus upon European Union law, comparative law, gender equality and equal treatment, social and employment law, reconciliation between work and family life, pregnancy and maternity rights. She is the author of *Reconciling Work and Family Life in EU Law and Policy*, (2010) London: Palgrave Macmillan (with E. Caracciolo di Torella). She has published articles journals such as the *European Law Review, European Law Journal, Columbia Journal of European Law, Feminist Legal Studies.*

Chapter 13
Russia's Complex Engagement with European Union Norms: Sovereign Democracy versus Post-Westphalianism?

James Headley

13.1 Introduction

Russia is in a unique position in relation to the European Union (EU). It is part of the wider European space; it is not a prospective member; it is a global power with significant economic and military clout; it has interests and presence both in Europe and in Asia; and it shares a high level of interdependency with EU Member States. Furthermore, as a result of the break up of the Soviet Union and the eastern enlargement of the EU, there is interest on both sides in the 'shared neighbourhood': the states of the southern Caucasus (Armenia, Azerbaijan and Georgia) and of eastern Europe (Belarus, Moldova and Ukraine).

These unique circumstances make Russia a vital case study in examining the encounter between EU norms and local practices. In this chapter I assess Russia's response to EU norms and how it reflects dominant Russian foreign and domestic policy thinking. Overall, I argue that the Russian response can be characterised as varying between resistance and rejection. At the same time, Russian policy makers challenge the very idea that Russia is a passive receiver of European norms from the EU, in some circumstances promoting Russia as an equal partner in developing common European norms: in other words, as a norm-maker rather than a norm-taker (Haukkala 2008). However, in some areas, Russia is willing to adopt what it regards as technical norms to promote greater trade with the EU.

This chapter will examine the particularities of the Russian response in three sections. In the first, it explores how the Russian response to EU norms is couched in terms of understandings of Russian identity but also increasingly as a rejection of the notion of pan-European norms. The second section shows how Russian policy makers distinguish between EU technical norms (relating to commerce and trade) and socio-political norms (relating to political system and practices and human

J. Headley (✉)
Department of Politics, University of Otago, Dunedin, New Zealand
e-mail: james.headley@otago.ac.nz

© Springer International Publishing Switzerland 2015   211
A. Björkdahl et al. (eds.), *Importing EU Norms,* United Nations University Series on Regionalism 8, DOI 10.1007/978-3-319-13740-7_13

rights). They aim to build pragmatic relations with the EU on the basis of the former, while rejecting any linkage with the latter. Distinguishing between specific norms developed and promoted by the EU, and the norm of regional integration itself, the final section argues that Russia's promotion of regional integration in the former Soviet space drawing on the EU model does not necessarily contradict its resistance to specific EU socio-political norms. However, Russia's adoption of the rhetoric of regional integration in the post-Soviet space is perceived by EU actors as a threat and a challenge to EU norms.

This analysis will focus predominantly on relations with the EU as an entity, rather than with its Member States. For simplicity, this chapter will often refer to 'Russia' and the 'EU', while acknowledging that they are not unitary actors. This research draws on a range of secondary literature on EU norms, EU-Russia relations, Russian perceptions of Europe/the EU and Russian foreign policy. In analysing the Russian position, the chapter refers to primary documents: significant declarations by Russian foreign policy makers, in particular, the President's annual address to the Federal Assembly and the 2013 Foreign Policy Concept. These help us to contextualise Russian policy, to discern the main themes and rhetorical nuances, and to analyse how Russian policy makers wish Russia to be perceived abroad.

13.2   Russia's Evolving Relationship to EU Norms: From norm-taker to Sovereign Equal?

In the initial period after the break-up of the Soviet Union, Yeltsin's Russia accepted a role as 'norm-taker' in becoming a Western-style liberal democracy and returning to the family of European, democratic states. In broad terms, Russia was a passive adopter of Western European political and economic norms of democracy and the market economy, and welcomed and encouraged help in its transition, through, for example, the EU's Technical Assistance to the Commonwealth of Independent States (TACIS) scheme. According to Lukyanov (2008, p. 1109), the main aim of the 1994 Partnership and Cooperation Agreement (PCA) between the EU and Russia was the 'Europeanisation' of Russia: without membership, Russia would 'nevertheless gradually approach the "European model", adopting EU norms and rules. The subsequent shift to a more assertive position has been well-documented and a number of explanations have been offered (Headley 2008; Lynch 2001; Shearman 2001). There are three factors that are relevant for an analysis of Russia's response to its encounter with EU norms.

Firstly, there was the apparent failure of the economic reforms. The reforms—known as 'shock therapy'—constituted a rapid and untrammelled application of neo-liberal economic theories, and their catastrophic impact had the effect of undermining the normative power of the West as a whole, including the democratic model with which the economic reforms were associated. Secondly, the reforms met resistance from those who disagreed with the transition to a full market economy, particularly but not only in the form in which it was being conducted. Many opponents believed that it was an alien imposition of values that were out of line with traditional Russian practices—if not the state-managed communism of the Soviet period, then a longer-standing communal approach (Mäkinen 2011). Here, critics also questioned whether liberal democracy imported from the West suited the more communal and authoritarian Russian historical practices. Thirdly, these responses were also couched in terms of another normative prior: the notion that international affairs were primarily constituted by the pursuit of state interests. Western states were perceived to be pursuing their own national interests, which not only did not coincide with Russian interests, but might even be contrary to Russian interests.

The policy response was to differentiate Russian from Western interests and to assert Russia's great power status. These ideas have underpinned Russia's overall foreign policy approach since the mid-1990s, particularly in the Putin era since 1999. Russia's attitude towards the EU has been encapsulated within this overall framework, but has undergone some shifts of emphasis in relation to shifting policy priorities and developments in relations with the EU, accompanied by shifts in conceptions of Russian and European identity.

Throughout much of the 2000s, there was an emphasis on Russia's European identity and also on its status as a major power that should be treated as an equal by other major powers. Particularly around the time of the 60th anniversary of the end of the Second World War in Europe, President Putin made a number of speeches asserting Russia's 'European-ness'. These ideas formed the basis of an article published in *Le Figaro*:

> The Russian nation has always felt part of the large European family, and has shared common cultural, moral and spiritual values. On our historical path—sometimes falling behind our partners, other times overtaking them—we have been through the same stages of establishing democratic, legal and civil institutions. Therefore, the Russian nation's democratic and European choice is entirely logical. This is a sovereign choice of a European nation that defeated Nazism and knows the price of freedom. (Putin 2005a)

According to this formulation, Europeans share both a common geography, history and culture, but also a set of values—freedom and democracy. Indeed, there is an essential link between the two since European values derive from European culture/history or have evolved with it (Headley 2012a). Putin (2005b, online) made this explicit in his annual address to the Federal Assembly in April 2005:

> Above all else Russia was, is and will, of course, be a major European power. Achieved through much suffering by European culture, the ideals of freedom, human rights, justice and democracy have for many centuries been our society's determining values.
> For three centuries, we—together with the other European nations—passed hand in hand through reforms of Enlightenment, the difficulties of emerging parliamentarianism, municipal and judiciary branches, and the establishment of similar legal systems. Step by step, we moved together toward recognising and extending human rights, toward universal and equal suffrage, toward understanding the need to look after the weak and the impoverished, toward women's emancipation, and other social gains.
> I repeat we did this together, sometimes behind and sometimes ahead of European standards.

These extracts demonstrate that Putin believed that in the past Russia had not been merely a passive recipient of European values and norms as developed in the West, but had also contributed actively to the development of European values and norms. Putin thus staked a claim to Russia's historical role as a norm-maker, which was also an assertion that Russia should be an equal partner in developing pan-European norms in the present.

However, Putin also questioned the extent to which pan-European norms should be developed and how deep and standardised they should be. It is useful here to distinguish between values and norms: values can be understood to be the broad ethical principles underlying specific ways of behaving in a range of contexts and policy areas; these specific ways of behaving—norms—are manifestations of those values (Headley 2012a). Putin claimed to accept the idea of Russia sharing common European values, placing Russia in the wider European cultural space, but argued that there were different ways of manifesting those values in specific cultural contexts. He concluded his *Figaro* article with the assertion that 'both large and small nations have equal rights, including the right to choose an independent path of development' (Putin 2005a),[1] which can be considered to be in tension with the notion of common European norms.

During Putin's second presidential term (2004–2008), the notion of common European norms receded, and the conception of different paths of development for different states came to the fore. For example, in his 2007 annual speech to the Federal Assembly, Putin (2007, online) declared:

> Our foreign policy is aimed at joint, pragmatic, and non-ideological work to resolve the important problems we face. In broader terms, what I am speaking about is a culture of international relations based on international law—without attempts to impose development models or to force the natural pace of the historical process. This makes the democratisation of international life and a new ethic in relations between states and peoples particularly important.

The slogan that came to be attached to this viewpoint was 'sovereign democracy', developed by the administration's loyal ideologue, Vladislav Surkov, although never officially endorsed by Putin (Mäkinen 2011; Sakwa 2008). This is supposed to be democracy in the international sphere, meaning that efforts to shape another country's development in a particular direction modelled on one's own experience is undemocratic. It is also a rejection of the idea of Europe-wide norms, the notion that specific ways of operating should be uniform across the continent; hence, it signifies opposition to the standardisation inherent in 'Europeanisation'. Nevertheless, it is presented in terms of democratic values, and therefore 'European values'; and Western European countries are considered to be displaying 'double standards' if they fail to recognise the equal rights of other sovereign states.

This outlook chimes with the approach of some communitarian political theorists who reject the idea of detailed universal rights and norms. For example, Walzer (1994) defends a notion of rights that allows for minimal cross-cultural absolute

---

[1] There are strong echoes here of Mikhail Gorbachev's concept of the Common European Home/House which served a similar purpose, although Putin does not use this metaphor perhaps because it is too closely associated with Gorbachev. Gorbachev also defended the 'right of every different nation to choose its own path of development' (Gorbachev 1987; Haukkala 2008, p. 50–51).

human rights and universal norms, but these are quite limited or 'thin'; he sees 'thicker' rights and norms being generated in each nation or culture. He argues that there are basic, 'minimalist' features of terms such as 'truth' and 'justice' that are understood by everyone, but the actual content of them is usually 'maximalist', arising out a particular society's values and norms. He uses this point to assert that there are a number of different 'roads to democracy', and a variety of 'democracies' at the end of the road. For example, he writes that he supported the 1989 Tiananmen Square demonstrators in their broad aims, but it is up to the Chinese people to develop their own form of democracy, which would have significant differences from the form of democracy in the United States, for instance. He concludes:

> Since I know very little about their society, I cannot foist upon the Chinese this or that set of rights—certainly not my preferred set. So I defer to them as empirical and social individuals. They must make their own claims, their own codifications (a Chinese Bill of Rights?), and their own interpretative arguments.

One problem with Walzer's 'thick/thin' distinction is the question of how we determine the boundary of communities in which morality is maximalist, i.e. at what level a particular society is constituted. Walzer assumes that it is at the level of nation-states and, in their defence of state sovereignty, Russian policy makers have tended to endorse this view (although I will show in the final section that Russian rhetoric has begun to identify cultures at the 'civilisational level', without necessarily implying that shared socio-political norms should be developed at that level). EU leaders, on the other hand, assert that it should be at the European level, and regard the EU as the leader in developing norms to reflect European values. So, the dispute between Russia and the EU is about whether there should be pan-European norms and, if so, how 'thick' or 'thin' they should be (see Headley 2012a for elaboration). In an article assessing Putin's 'project' from International Relations (IR) theory perspectives, Browning (2008) effectively makes the same point, but in the language of the English School of IR theory. He points out that the English School distinguishes between 'pluralist' and 'solidarist' variants of international society, such that debates are 'based on competing claims about the "thickness" of the normative content of international society' (ibid., p. 7): solidarists focus on universal human rights of individuals, while pluralists argue that states are 'at the heart of international society and have moral priority', so that states can only agree on minimal norms. In this debate, 'Russia is typically understood as favouring and defending a pluralist model of international society premised on a Westphalian model of sovereign equality' (ibid., p. 7).

I believe that there are some problems in the implicit identification here of a 'modern', sovereign Russia facing up to a 'postmodern', post-Westphalian EU,[2] not least because it seems to answer the question of what kind of entity the EU is in a way that has not yet been settled. Furthermore, Medvedev (2008, p. 221) argues that '[f]or all its postmodern imagery and the "rejection of power"…, the European Union is a direct descendant of the Western missionary tradition'. He suggests that

---

[2] For more explicit examples of this contrast, see Krastev (2007); Mezhuev (2008); Secrieru (2010).

the EU's approach is actually as 'bureaucratic' as Russia's, transposing the process of enlargement to relations with its neighbours rather than developing a political strategy vis-à-vis fully independent states. It is also based on a modern, rather than post-modern, 'othering' which seeks to transform the 'other' through 'European-isation'—essentially, a retreat to a 'colonialist interpretation of Westernness as goodness' (Medvedev 2008, p. 231)—rather than accepting its differences. Klinke (2012) makes an analogous point, directly challenging the 'postmodern label'. He argues that the EU displays archetypically 'modern' thinking in its conception of itself as postmodern: it sees itself as embodying the next stage of the development of humankind, in a teleological idea of progress.

In other words, the EU's assumption that it is a norm setter and has the right answers for the development of other states is a continuation of the 'civilising mission', a feature of the modern era, backed by its ability to exert power over weaker states. Although Whitman (2013, p. 174) suggests that the notion of Normative Power Europe (NPE) rejects any 'affiliation with colonial or neo-colonial practice', some EU policy makers do seem explicitly to endorse it (former President of the Commission, Romano Prodi for example; see Björkdahl 2005, p. 259; see also Korosteleva 2011). In any case, it is generally perceived in this way in Russia (Secrieru 2010, p. 9). For example, Tsygankov and Fominykh (2010, p. 23) of Moscow State University refer to the 'geopolitics of perception', arguing that EU actors believe that the EU 'plays an irreplaceable role and lays claim to indisputable advantages over all other models of development'. As Medvedev (2008, p. 211) puts it, Russia's bureaucratic centralism inevitably resists this tendency. Hence, the clash between Russia and the EU can be understood within a longer-term perspective of responses to Western European assertions of normative superiority, without necessarily framing it in terms of 'modern' versus 'postmodern'.

13.3 Contemporary Russia-EU Relations: Partnership for Modernisation?

During Dmitrii Medvedev's presidency (2008–2012), there were attempts to renew relations between Russia and the EU under the label 'Partnership for Modernisation'. The Partnership was to be built on recognition of interdependency and of the mutual benefits of cooperation over security and economic issues. There are different interpretations of the degree to which it has succeeded. For example, Baranovsky and Utkin (2012, p. 70) argue that it has finally got off the ground after a slow start, and is offering real funding opportunities for joint ventures. However, a more typical assessment is provided by Moshes (2012, p. 20), who argues that it was clear by the end of 2011 that the Partnership 'had essentially failed to make a difference. It did not go beyond declarations, multilateral and bilateral.' The EU and Russia have been unable to overcome their differences over fundamental issues and specific areas of interaction have proven more capable of creating division than understanding. These problems reflect divergent views of the purpose of the

Partnership and the wider nature of relations between Russia and the EU, questions that relate directly to Russia's response to EU norms.

From the Russian perspective, the Partnership suits Russian priorities, and indeed, 'modernisation' has been the buzz-word of Russian rhetoric at least since President Medvedev's article *Rossiia, vpered!* ('Go Russia!' or 'Russia, forward!') appeared in September 2009. It refers to the belief that Russia needs to move away from its reliance on export of natural resources, especially energy resources, and to develop a high-technology economy. In order to do so, it should look to the West as a source of ideas, technology and investment. However, the Russian authorities believe that Russia can do this without changing its socio-political system or the fundamental nature of its economy. This is what Olga Kryshtanovskaya describes as the Andropov approach (Mäkinen 2011, p. 152), but it is also reminiscent of Gorbachev's belief in interdependency, opening up to the West, but maintaining different 'paths of development'. Not only is this seen as possible, but it is believed that the EU will respond in kind because of its interdependency with Russia: as equal partners, both can stand to benefit.

Russian policy makers believe that trade can develop between the EU and Russia without deeper political or economic convergence; this is what Nikitin (2006, p. 6) calls the 'pragmatic, conservative' interpretation of the EU-Russia partnership. In line with arguments laid out above, they reject EU conditionality and interference in Russia's internal affairs, and defend Russia's right to its own 'path of development'. Associated with this strategy is an attempt to separate technical norms from socio-political norms. Russia is prepared to adopt legislation harmonising aspects of Russia's trade and business environment often by incorporating parts of the *acquis communautaire* (Tumanov et al. 2011, p. 125). This is because the EU is seen a norm-maker or leader in this area, and there is no point Russia wasting time and resources in developing its own equivalents. Furthermore, it is irrelevant whether EU norms in this area are better than alternatives that might be developed—the market strength of the EU and its importance for Russian trade means that there are strong practical reasons to harmonise with it (this is what Börzel and Risse 2012 call 'compliance pull'). Adopting common, 'thick' technical norms lays the basis for creating a common economic space between Russia and the EU—or, as Putin (2012, online) put it, 'a common economic and human space from the Atlantic to the Pacific Ocean'—hence promoting trade, jobs and higher living standards.

Whatever the future of technical partnership, it is clear that the EU (though not necessarily its individual Member States) rejects the delinking of its technical and socio-political norms. It sees them as inherently interconnected, believing that Russia cannot modernise its economy and become part of a wider shared economic and human space with the EU without also conducting political reforms. This is a matter of ethics, ideology and practicality. Firstly, there is a belief in the totality of liberal democracy, its ethical importance. In this respect, the decline in partnership is partly due to the widely-perceived regression in Russian democracy over the last decade. Secondly, in contrast to its individual Member States and economic agents within them, the EU is an inherently normative project, a fact which Manners's (2002) concept of NPE encapsulates. Particularly in Europe, its normative credibility is at stake; for example, as Moshes (2012, p. 21) points out, the EU cannot apply conditionality to countries such as Belarus while engaging fully with Russia without conditions if it wishes to be perceived as genuine and consistent in its promotion of its values in Europe.

However, it is also a practical question about the possibility of separating technical from wider socio-political and economic norms. At a broad level, there is doubt over whether there can be real engagement if human rights and the rule of law are not respected in Russia. On a more pragmatic level, without some level of trust, it is difficult to engage in trade and investment—and Russia is often perceived as an unreliable partner. For example, its image as a reliable energy supplier to the EU was badly shaken by the stand-off with Ukraine in early 2009, despite Russian efforts to show that it was Ukraine that was the instigator (Feklyunina 2012). Similarly, the tensions surrounding the TNK-BP joint venture seemed to show the unreliability of joint investments for Western companies, although in finally selling its stake BP has made a vast profit (Neate 2013). The point is whether, in the long term, Russia can be trusted to abide by the technical norms and legal standards that it is willing to adopt, without wider political change (Lukyanov 2008). For example, Moshes (2012, p. 21) suggests that the Partnership for Modernisation has failed because EU decision-makers had to recognise that a purely pragmatic approach did not work: 'the lack of rules, of an independent judiciary and of transparent contract enforcement makes European companies vulnerable to possible abuses in Russia'.

Delays in Russia's accession to the World Trade Organisation (WTO) seemed to reinforce this view since they were partly due to Putin's unwillingness to allow the infringement on sovereignty and power that adherence to such standards entail (Åslund 2010; Moshes 2012). However, now that Russia has joined the WTO, it is possible that this wider international framework may provide the necessary legal guarantees. Although this might help Russia in its attempt to separate political from technical norms—in the way that China, for example, has been able to—Russian actions in response to the EU's Eastern Partnership, discussed further in the final section, do cast doubt on its adherence to standard ways of behaving in the global economy even as a member of the WTO.[3]

In the EU's opinion, the Russian authorities' use of the economy for political purposes, and the insecurity this creates for other countries, makes Russia untrustworthy. This is particularly an issue with regard to energy. The EU perceives Russia as using its resources for geopolitical purposes and also regards the prominent state role in the energy sector as illegitimate. Indeed, through the 1994 PCA it has sought 'more active cooperation [with Russia] in developing the Law of Competition and gradual transition to market principles in the field of natural monopolies and state support' (Bordachev and Romanova 2003). However, Russian state control of the energy sector has increased since the turn of the century. In this context, the EU's

---

[3] Interestingly, former UK ambassador to Moscow, Anthony Brenton suggests that the EU should launch proceedings against Russia through the WTO over its partial trade embargo on Lithuania, widely interpreted to be punishment for Lithuania hosting the Eastern Partnership summit in November 2013 (The Guardian 2013).

Energy Charter Treaty (ECT) is designed to secure energy supply and prevent the Russian government from interfering in this economic area for political purposes. However, the Russian leadership perceives the ECT as a means to gain benefits from Russia without Russia receiving any reciprocal benefits (Secrieru 2010). By demanding access to Russian resources but restricting Russian ownership of infrastructure outside Russia, as they see it the ECT is the kind of self-interested action conducted at Russian expense, with normative window-dressing, that characterised the West's action towards Russia in the early 1990s. This is why Russia declined to sign the ECT, regarding it as a way for EU countries to gain 'energy security' (security of supply) and access to Russian assets, while Russia would gain nothing tangible in return: no 'security of demand' (in recognition that Russia also depends on the European market for its energy exports) and restricted Russian access to European markets and assets.

The dominant Russian perception, then, is that the EU is pushing its interests in the name of values/norms (see, for example, Baranovsky and Utkin 2012; Tsygankov and Fominykh 2010), while Russia is reasonably standing up for its own national interests and in doing so, is no different from EU Member States. Yet, DeBardeleben (2012) suggests that, in fact and perhaps ironically, Russia is promoting norms in the name of interests. She writes that '[r]ather than engaging in an explicit dialogue on the normative preference in Russia for a state-led approach to ownership and energy policy, the dispute over the Energy Charter comes couched in accusations and counter-accusations about protectionism and double standards' such that the 'normative basis of the conflict is obfuscated and redefined as a simple conflict of interest' (ibid., 427). Certainly, in referring to principles in order to defend its position, and in raising the issue of security of demand, Russia is proposing a principle that suits its own interests but can also be generalised. Indeed, Secrieru (2010, p. 15) takes this as evidence that Russia is 'showing zeal to switch its post-Cold War status from a "norm-taker" to a "norm-maker" in the European context'. In defending national control of natural resources, Russian officials also appeal to the principle of different paths of development as discussed above, just as Gorbachev did before them, even if Russia is certainly no longer a socialist state.

Although the EU may deny that its actions 'stem from a geopolitical logic' (Lukyanov 2008, p. 1114), in reality, then, for both the EU and Russia, 'interests interact with norms to drive policy' (DeBardeleben 2012, p. 424). Russia challenges the idea that the EU is only driven by norms, but also challenges the EU's self-declared role as norm-maker in economic matters, as well as the very idea of pan-European norms in relation to the level of state control of the economy. Hence, it perceives certain economic norms promoted by the EU as being in the category of socio-political norms that should be determined primarily at the state level, and should not affect trade relations. In other words, the EU is seen as presenting 'thick' socio-political norms as 'thin' technical norms, which shows that the question of where the boundary between technical and socio-political norms lies is itself a contested political question which may vary between states, cultures and traditions.[4]

---

[4] This is of course an issue within the EU itself, for example over privatisation of state-owned industries and assets, or the elaboration of budgetary and debt rules.

It is relevant here to note that, from a critical political economy perspective, Parker and Rosamond (2013) identify what they call a blind-spot in the Normative Power Europe position: its neglect of economic norms. They refer to the 'constitutive importance of economic liberalism ("market cosmopolitanism") to the EU's post-Westphalian character' (ibid., p. 229). In other words, the EU promotes neo-liberal economic norms that have the effect of undermining state sovereignty. It is therefore challenged by states such as Russia that seek to defend their sovereignty and also their right to exercise a strong state role in the economy. Whether the Russian state really is that different from EU Member States or other European states such as Norway in regard to its role in the economy, particularly in the energy sector, is debatable. For example, the 2013 Russian Foreign Policy Concept (FPC) declares that the Russian Federation 'provides state support to Russian enterprises and companies in getting access to new markets and in development of traditional ones while countering discrimination against Russian investors and exporters' (Ministry of Foreign Affairs of the Russian Federation [MFA] 2013, para 34d), which would not look out of place in the description of any country's foreign policy approaches. However, it is more the way that it does this that is problematic along with the merging of political and economic elites.

Besides energy, the greatest source of tension between the EU and Russia is the Eastern Partnership and Russia's own programme of integration in the former Soviet space. Here, it seems that Russian policy makers are themselves susceptible to the accusation of double standards, since Russia's rhetoric of non-intervention in the politics and economics of sovereign states belies its own interference in the domestic affairs and foreign policy choices of the former Soviet republics. I will now turn finally to investigate Russia's programme of Eurasian integration which is apparently modelled on EU integration.

13.4   Civilisational Identity and Eurasian Integration

In his conceptualisation of NPE, Manners (2008) suggests that integration in the EU is inherently a normative project because, by moving beyond a state-centric notion of sovereignty, it challenges normal ways of state behaviour and the structure of international relations, presenting the possibility of a post-Westphalian world. This does not mean that regional integration on the EU model is a norm (Lenz 2013)—one of the on-going debates in EU studies is precisely whether the EU is *sui generis*—but in its own policies the EU promotes regional integration using ethical arguments that it brings peace and prosperity, which is part of its own self-narrative. At the same time, many states in the world are seeking to build regional integration projects, looking to the EU as a successful model. These states include Russia (Moulioukova 2011; Secrieru 2010).

Russia is aiming to deepen integration within the Commonwealth of Independent States (CIS). A Customs Union was created between Russia, Belarus and Kazakhstan in early 2012, and Russian policy makers aim to transform it into a

Eurasian Economic Union over the next few years, and hope to enlarge its membership. The FPC calls the establishing of the Eurasian Economic Union a 'priority task' and states that Russia is 'aiming not only to make the best use of mutually beneficial economic ties in the CIS space but also to become a model of association open to other states, a model that would determine the future of the Commonwealth states' (MFA 2013, para 44). Furthermore, the FPC declares that this new union is being formed 'on the basis of universal integration principles'. In an echo of the narrative of EU integration, the FPC argues that with current global developments, '[r]egional integration becomes an effective means to increase competitiveness of the participating states' (para 19). Russia seems also to be emulating the terminology of the EU, not just in the name, but in the institutions, such as the Eurasian Economic Commission which Russia wants strengthened as a 'common standing regulatory body of the Customs Union and the Common Economic Space' (para 48d). The ultimate aim is the 'completely new freedom of movement of goods, services, capital and labour' (Putin quoted in Secrieru 2010, p. 10).

To underpin their policy priority of developing regional integration in the post-Soviet space, the Russian authorities represent Russia as part of a wider Eurasian civilisation, a region of countries sharing a common history, culture and to a certain extent language. For example, the FPC states:

> Russia intends to actively contribute to the development of interaction among CIS Member States in the humanitarian sphere on the ground of preserving and increasing common cultural and civilisational heritage which is an essential resource for the CIS as a whole and for each of the Commonwealth's Member States in the context of globalisation. (MFA 2013, para 44)

This echoes the EU's own identity rhetoric. However, there appears to be some tension evident in the FPC between the idea of Eurasia as a separate civilisation and as part of a wider European cultural space. For example, paragraph 44 claims that the envisaged Eurasian Economic Union 'is designed to serve as an effective link between Europe and the Asia-Pacific region', while paragraph 56 asserts that '[i]n its relations with the European Union, the main task for Russia as an integral and inseparable part of European civilisation is to promote creating a common economic and humanitarian space from the Atlantic to the Pacific' (MFA 2013). However, the tension might be resolved by considering these as overlapping, or perhaps nested, identities. Presenting it in this way can help to prevent clashes between regional integration projects but also serve the Russian policy aim of greater practical integration with the EU, perhaps in the form of inter-regionalism between the envisaged Eurasian Economic Union and the EU. After all, as Tumanov et al. (2011, p. 125) observe, the 'ultimate goal of the CES is Russian integration with the EU markets'; and this is backed by public opinion which wants Russia to have a partnership with both the EU and the countries of the CIS equally (ibid., p. 136).

An additional contradiction lies in, on the one hand, the assertion of state sovereignty and respect for different paths of development of different nations and, on the other hand, the civilisational rhetoric. Indeed, the framework for the operation of such paths of development and the values they represent seems to have shifted to the civilisational level. For example, in the section contextualising Russian foreign policy, the FPC states:

> For the first time in modern history, global competition takes place on a civilisational level, whereby various values and models of development based on the universal principles of democracy and market economy start to clash and compete against each other. Cultural and civilisational diversity of the world becomes more and more manifest. (MFA 2013, para 13)

Similar arguments are presented for the acceptance of diversity as opposed to standardisation at the civilisational level as were presented at the state level:

> In these circumstances imposing one's own hierarchy of values can only provoke a rise in xenophobia, intolerance and tensions in international relations leading eventually to chaos in world affairs. Another factor which negatively affects global stability is the emerging trend towards international relations dominated, as in the past, by ideological factors. (ibid., para 14)[5]

Although the FPC suggests that forging a 'partnership of cultures, religions and civilisations' will prevent a clash of civilisations (ibid., para 14), this is also a warning to the EU not to impose its norms in the former Soviet space.

Such allusions to commonality of norms/values above the nation-state level in Eurasia are likely to be seen as threatening by other states in the region, especially given the history of Russian domination (see Headley 2012b; an example is Sushko 2004). In practice, however, there has been little talk of common socio-economic or political norms linked to this civilisational identity or emerging through integration in the CIS, although there is a prevalent perception among the elites in Belarus, Moldova, Ukraine and Russia that the 'legal and political culture of [West] Europeans' contrasts with the 'communal and authority-abiding living in Eastern Europe' (Korosteleva 2011, p. 15). Instead, such integration is advocated on the pragmatic grounds that it suits the common economic interests of states in the region and is therefore of instrumental rather than inherent value (Vinokurov 2013). Such an approach shows again the Russian view that technical norms can be separated from deeper socio-political norms, and hence it does not mean that EU socio-political norms should be used in building Eurasian integration. The Eurasian context therefore supports Börzel and Risse's (2012, p. 9) assessment that '[e]mulation of institutional models such as the EU in different regional contexts could well be completely independent from any effort by the EU to promote certain norms or regulations'. And, despite talk of alternative paths of development, Russia is not promoting itself as a model to be emulated, unlike in the Soviet period (and it is certainly not perceived as a model by other states).

For these reasons, Eurasian integration is likely to remain intergovernmental in essence. As Lenz (2013, p. 219) puts it, the 'most fundamental ideational structure limiting EU ideational diffusion in regionalism is policy-makers' attitudes towards sovereignty'. We can see that in the security sphere, Russia is a founding member of the Shanghai Cooperation Organisation, whose founding norms/aims include

---

[5] Since the early 1990s, Russian foreign policy makers have categorised Russian foreign policy as pragmatic and non-ideological. If we define an ideological foreign policy as one based on a worldview which relates to a belief in the ethical superiority of a state's internal socio-political and economic system, then we can see that both the US and Soviet foreign policies during the Cold War were ideological; if the NPE concept is right, then so too is EU foreign policy today.

sovereignty of states (non-intervention in internal affairs), and defence of territorial integrity against separatism. These norms can be expected also to underpin integration in Eurasia and are analogous to the 'ASEAN values' of non-intervention and sovereignty, and the 'Pacific Way', the purported norms of mutual respect and dialogue among Pacific Island countries (Börzel and Risse 2012; Huffer 2006). The forms that integration has taken in South-East Asia and the South Pacific reflect this difference from the EU. Whether in practice a common market can be established without supranational political integration is debatable;[6] but even if a future Eurasian Economic Union can be governed intergovernmentally, it is an open question whether Russian authorities will accept the equality inherent in intergovernmentalism, let alone submit to the authority of bodies that may not be supranational in the EU sense, but will still need to exert impartial authority over all the Member States.

Russian proposals for an EU-type integration process have been greeted with scepticism by the EU, in stark contrast to its promotion of regional integration elsewhere in the world. One reason is that, this is not somewhere else in the world—it is in the EU's 'neighbourhood'.[7] While Russia is seen as contradicting European norms, the EU aims to project its interpretation of them in the wider European space, reflecting its belief that the EU is a norm-maker, other countries are norm-takers, and Russia is governed by a disrespect for those norms and is a challenge to them.

Russia's pressure on CIS countries to join the Russian-led integration project is taken as an example of this. The FPC warns:

> While respecting its Commonwealth partners' right to build relations with other international actors, Russia stands for the full implementation by the CIS Member States of their commitments within regional integration structures with Russian participation, ensuring further development of integration processes and mutually beneficial cooperation in the CIS space. (Russian MFA 2013, para 50; see also the Russian MFA declaration in response to the launch of the Eastern Partnership, Secrieru 2010, p. 17)

But Russia has moved beyond declarations. There have been an increasing number of instances of Russia using crude economic levers to pressure countries into choosing integration within the CIS and declining free trade agreements with the EU. For example, Russian authorities have excluded Moldovan wines from the Russian market for precisely this political reason, while couching the decision in terms of spurious quality concerns; and it is well known that Russia has threatened to raise the cost of energy supplies to Ukraine if it signs a Deep and Comprehensive Free Trade Agreement (DCFTA) with the EU, or alternatively, offers to reduce prices if Ukraine signs up to the Eurasian Union (BBC News 2013; The Guardian 2013).

---

[6] ASEAN does seem to be shifting towards a more European Union model (Wunderlich 2012), which may be part of a trend among regional organisations towards supranational governance (Lenz 2013).

[7] Interestingly, Secrieru (2010, p. 17) points out that Russian policy makers reject the notion of a 'shared neighbourhood' because, in line with the civilisational rhetoric, they conceive of the former Soviet republics as part of a common space—i.e. not separate from Russia—and divide the wider Europe into 'Brussels Europe' and 'Russia's Europe'.

As Korosteleva (2011) points out, both the EU and Russia seem to believe that the countries 'in between' have to choose one integration project or the other. On the EU's part, this is for the normative reasons outlined above, but also for practical considerations. For example, according to a spokesperson for the EU High Representative Catherine Ashton, if Armenia were to join the Customs Union, it would not be compatible with a DCFTA with the EU because a 'customs union has a common external trade policy and an individual member country no longer has sovereign control over its external trade policies' (RFE/RL 2012; see also Füle 2013).[8] But the EU also has economic interests in promoting greater integration between itself and countries such as Ukraine and Moldova (Tumanov et al. 2011), a political incentive in preventing them integrating more closely with Russia, and a security incentive in dealing with perceived threats.

In pursuing these interests, it also uses trade instruments. For example, the European Commission's suggestion that it may increase the quota of Moldovan wine imports shows that its trade policies are not independent of political considerations in relation to the wider context of these countries' relations with Russia (Füle 2013). Furthermore, it is clear that this is not a partnership; as Korosteleva (2011, p. 6) argues, the EU offers a 'false choice to the outsiders, or, more precisely, no choice at all: it is either co-operation on EU terms or no co-operation at all', and the partnership is more about 'projecting the EU model' (ibid., p. 8) onto outsiders. In promoting its norms, the EU does not only deal in 'soft power' (the attractive pull of its ideas). As Björkdahl (2005, p. 269) puts it, conditionality is 'in a sense a coercive means of persuasion and a way of imposing rather than diffusing norms'. The EU is exercising such 'hard power' conditionality in the Neighbourhood (for example, in linking a DCFTA with Ukraine to political reforms and improvements in human rights).

On their part, Russian policy makers deny that the countries in the former Soviet space have to choose between Russia and the EU (Lukyanov 2013), and criticise the EU for viewing it as a zero-sum game. However, their warnings against these countries cooperating with the EU belie these claims, as do their actual policies. Russia's coercive policies are also instances of 'hard power'. The difference from EU conditionality, however, is that the EU does not use these means to pressure countries into joining the EU or even into developing FTAs—it uses the offer of close association as a reward for adoption of EU norms. Russia uses economic instruments to pressure countries into developing a close association with it, but without linking it to reform of socio-political practices; these instruments are predominantly threats to withdraw already-existing trade advantages, such as lower energy prices or access to Russia markets. This is a tactic which in the long term could well be counterproductive (Treisman 2013; Valdai Club 2013). Arguments in favour of a union in the former Soviet space may have some validity, but not if the project is backed by coercion; while rhetoric about the inevitability of reintegration in the former Soviet space can also undermine the normative position (Headley 2012b).

---

[8] In response, Armenian officials have said that they would try to make provisions for a free-trade zone with the EU compatible with membership in the Customs Union which is now envisaged (Jozwiak 2013).

In fact, nearly all political forces in Ukraine and Moldova, for example, recognise the necessity and benefits of close trade links with both the EU and Russia and do not want to have to choose between them. Being forced to choose will be politically divisive and potentially destabilising (Korosteleva 2011). Russian policy might be more effective if it put its rhetoric that this is not a zero-sum game into practice. Furthermore, the very fact that Russia is able to use these punitive instruments shows that there is already a high level of interconnectedness in the CIS because of the legacy of the Soviet Union (see Headley 2012b and 2012c for elaboration). These are quite different circumstances from those that gave birth to EU integration (Libman and Vinokurov 2012). Russian policy makers could make more of the fact that, in many respects, the CIS already has features that the EU took many years to develop and seems to regard as normatively valuable. For example, there is visa-free travel among most of the CIS countries, whereas Russia continues to opine the lack of visa-free travel arrangements with the EU (Baranovsky and Utkin 2012; MFA 2013, para 58). In response to recent debate in Russia about illegal immigration, Putin continues to warn against the introduction of visas for travel in the CIS (RU facts 2013). Nevertheless, according to one of his advisers, Sergei Glazyev, in the long term deeper integration in the Customs Union, including a unified passport and visa system, may ultimately lead to the need for stronger controls on its external borders: 'such is the logic of the integration process in the Customs Union' (RU facts 2013). Deeper integration among a group of members of the CIS may therefore restrict access to it by people from countries outside the group, creating barriers where there was once free movement, while the possibility of maintaining free movement would be an incentive for countries to join the Union. In this case, Russia would be following the EU's lead.

13.5   Conclusion

The complexity of Russia's response to EU norms is a reflection of Russia's unique position in relation to the EU as well as the on-going debate over its identity. Russia's power, its geographical position and the interdependency between itself and EU Member States set it apart from other non-EU European states, but also from other non-European states that interact with EU norms. In fundamental ways, Russia is a rejecter or resister of EU norms. Russia has diverged in its internal evolution from the EU Member State model and refuses any EU attempts to influence its 'path of development'. It frames this resistance in terms of universal norms of state sovereignty and non-intervention. On the other hand, Russian policy makers do engage with the EU over its normative programme and at times promote Russia as a norm-maker. However, they demand that it be considered an equal to the EU in developing European or global norms.

In broad terms, Russian policy has shifted from promoting the idea of Russia as an equal developer of 'thick' Europe-wide norms as part of an assertion of Russia's European identity, to the rejection of the notion of Europe-wide norms. Russian policy makers accept the idea of broad universal values and some 'thin' universal norms, but argue that it is up to each state to develop its own 'thicker' socio-political norms reflecting the culture of that country. This position may serve the interests of the current Russian political and economic elite, but it is also promoted as an ethical position framed in terms of sovereignty and 'democracy in international affairs', against an EU—and wider West—that is using its power to undermine the sovereignty of other states, often in pursuit of its own interests. At the same time, Russian policy makers are prepared to adopt 'thick' technical norms that ease international trade but are not built on particular socio-political tenets. However, they disagree with their EU counterparts over whether these can and should be separated from 'thick' socio-political norms, and also over whether particular norms presented as 'technical' by the EU are actually socio-political—such as the degree of state involvement in the economy, which Russian policy makers see as a sovereign choice reflecting different 'paths of development'.

In many ways, this Russian position is not unique but is shared by the elites of other 'rising powers', in the 'BRICS' group of Brazil, Russia, India, China, South Africa, for example. States such as China and India also challenge Western normative hegemony, in the name of the values of democracy (at the international level, i.e. between states) and equality. They do not always question the development of 'thin', universal norms—indeed, the idea of sovereign equality between states is just such a norm which they see Western states as challenging. However, they argue that these norms must be elaborated in an open debate between equals. Often they see the differences of opinion over such norms as evidence of cultural diversity, which makes any universal norms likely to be 'thin' in content. Unlike prospective EU members, they also have fewer material incentives to conform to EU norms.

Russia's resistance to EU norms and also to the idea of pan-European norms being imposed by the EU is partly reflective of the dominant Realist outlook on international relations in the Russian elite. They perceive the policies of all states or state-like entities to be governed by national interests. However, they believe that it can be in the interests of all states to recognise certain norms of behaviour in international affairs. But they reject the idea that the EU has unique normative power. This outlook blinds them to the fact that normative language is not always window-dressing for interests, either for the EU or for Russia itself. However, Russian policy makers are placed on the defensive by a sense that their own input into the development of norms is rejected out of hand by EU policy makers because Russia is perceived as only pursuing its own interests and its policies as having no normative essence. To use Risse's (2000) terms—drawing on March and Olsen (1998)—EU actors therefore challenge Russia in terms of the 'logic of appropriateness', laying claim to the right to declare what is appropriate behaviour for a European state, while perceiving Russian actions to be governed only by the 'logic of consequentialism', i.e. of rational pursuit of self-interest (ibid.); whereas in fact, Russian policy makers are also at times using the 'logic of argument'—that is, making ethical arguments in defence of their position within an arena of debate among what they consider to be equals.

This is not to say that both EU and Russian actions and rhetoric are not governed also by interests, and not just state interests but also the interests of certain domestic actors. I do not have space to examine the domestic environment of norm creation and norm reception in Russia and in the EU, but certainly Russia's rhetoric and action is shaped not only by the outlook of the elite, but also by the interests of both the economic and political elite. However, critical perspectives also warn that we should not take the EU's normative language purely at face value either.

References

Åslund, A. (2010). Why doesn't Russia join the WTO? *Wash Quart, 33*(2), 49–63.

Baranovsky, V., & Utkin, S. (2012). Europe as seen from Russia. *Perspectives, 20*(2), 63–82.

BBC News (2013). EU warns Russia over trade 'threats' to ex-Soviet bloc. http://www.bbc.co.uk/news/world-europe-24061556. Accessed 12 Sept 2013.

Björkdahl, A. (2005). Norm-maker and norm-taker: Exploring the normative influence of the EU in Macedonia. *European Foreign Affairs Review, 10*(2), 257–278.

Bordachev, T., & Romanova, T. (2003). Russia's choice should provide for liberty of action. *Russia in Global Affairs, 2*(2). http://eng.globalaffairs.ru/number/n_841. Accessed 9 June 2012.

Börzel, T. A., & Risse, T. (2012). From Europeanisation to diffusion: Introduction. *West European Politics, 35*(1), 1–19.

Browning, C. (2008). Reassessing Putin's project: Reflections on IR theory and the west. *Problems of Post-Communism, 55*(5), 3–13.

DeBardeleben, J. (2012). Applying constructivism to understanding EU-Russian relations. *International Politics, 49*(4), 418–433.

Feklyunina, V. (2012). Russia's international images and its energy policy: An unreliable supplier? *Europe-Asia Studies, 64*(3), 449–469.

Füle, S. (2013). Statement on the pressure exercised by Russia on countries of the Eastern Partnership. European Commission Speech/13/687. September 11. http://europa.eu/rapid/press-release_SPEECH-13-687_en.htm. Accessed 23 Sept 2013.

Gorbachev, M. (1987). *Perestroika: New thinking for our country and the world.* London: Collins.

Haukkala, H. (2008). A norm-maker or a norm-taker? The changing normative parameters of Russia's place in Europe. In T. Hopf (Ed.), *Russia's European choice* (pp. 35–56). New York: Palgrave Macmillan.

Headley, J. (2008). *Russia and the Balkans: Foreign policy from Yeltsin to Putin.* London: Hurst and Co./Columbia University Press.

Headley, J. (2012a). Is Russia out of step with European norms? Assessing Russia's relationship to European identity, values and norms though the issue of self-determination. *Europe-Asia Studies, 64*(3), 427–447.

Headley, J. (2012b). Near abroads and arcs of instability: Conceptualising the region in the South Pacific and Eurasia. *Canterbury Law Review, 18*, 15–40.

Headley, J. (2012c). National and transnational challenges in the former Soviet Union and former Yugoslavia. *Global Change, Peace and Security, 24*(2), 251–269.

Huffer, E. (2006). The Pacific plan. A political and cultural critique. In J. Bryant-Tokalau & I. Frazer (Eds.) *Redefining the Pacific? Regionalism past, present and future* (pp. 157–174). Aldershot: Ashgate.

Jozwiak, R. (2013). Brussels sees problems with Armenia on customs union. RFE/RL. http://www.rferl.org/content/eu-armenia-customs/25097827.html. Accessed 23 Oct 2013.

Klinke, I. (2012). Postmodern geopolitics? The European Union eyes Russia. *Europe-Asia Studies, 64*(5), 929–947.

Korosteleva, E. (2011). The Eastern Partnership initiative: A new opportunity for neighbours? *Journal of Communist Studies and Transition Politics, 27*(1), 1–21.

Krastev, I. (2007). Russia as the 'other Europe'. *Russia in Global Affairs, 5*(4). http://eng.globalaffairs.ru/number/n_9779. Accessed 23 March 2008.

Lenz, T. (2013). EU normative power and regionalism: Ideational diffusion and its limits. *Cooperation and Conflict, 48*(2), 211–228.

Libman, A., & Vinokurov, E. (2012). Regional integration and economic convergence in the post-Soviet space: Experience of the decade of growth. *Journal of Common Market Studies, 50*(1), 112–128.

Lukyanov, F. (2008). Russia-EU: The partnership that went astray. *Europe-Asia Studies, 60*(6), 1107–1119.

Lukyanov, F. (2013). Russia does not want another Soviet Union. *Russia in Global Affairs, 11*(3). http://eng.globalaffairs.ru/redcol/Russia-does-not-want-another-Soviet-Union-16097. Accessed 12 Sept 2013.

Lynch, A. (2001). The realism of Russia's foreign policy. *Europe-Asia Studies, 53*(1), 7–31.

Mäkinen, S. (2011). Surkovian narrative on the future of Russia: Making Russia a world leader. *Journal of Communist Studies and Transition Politics, 27*(2), 143–165.

Manners, I. (2002). Normative power Europe: A contradiction in terms? *Journal of Common Market Studies, 40*(2), 235–258.

Manners, I. (2008). The normative ethics of the European Union. *International Affairs, 84*(1), 45–60.

March, J.G., & Olsen, J.P. (1998). The institutional dynamics of international political orders. *International Organization, 52*(4), 943–969.

Medvedev, S. (2008). The stalemate in EU-Russia relations: Between 'sovereignty' and 'Europeanisation'. In T. Hopf (Ed.) *Russia's European choice* (pp. 215–232). New York: Palgrave Macmillan.

Medvedev, D. (2009). Rossiia, vpered! *Izvestiia*, September 10.

Mezhuev, B. (2008). Modern Russia and postmodern Europe. *Russia in Global Affairs, 6*(1). http://eng.globalaffairs.ru/number/n_10362. Accessed 12 May 2013.

Ministry of Foreign Affairs of the Russian Federation (2013). Concept of the Foreign Policy of the Russian Federation. http://www.mid.ru/brp_4.nsf/0/76389FEC168189ED44257B2E0039B16D. Accessed 13 May 2013.

Moshes, A. (2012). Russia's European policy under Medvedev: How sustainable is a new compromise? *International Affairs, 88*(1), 17–30.

Moulioukova, D. (2011). Europe as the idea, model and reality: Complex nature of Europe's significance for Russia. *Jean Monnet/Robert Schuman Paper Series, 8*(3).

Neate, R. (2013, March 21). Rosneft takes over TNK-BP in $55bn deal. *The Guardian*. http://www.theguardian.com/business/2013/mar/21/rosneft-takes-over-tnk-bp. Accessed 24 Oct 2013

Nikitin, A. (2006). Russian perceptions and approaches to cooperation in ESDP. *Institute for Security Studies*.

Parker, O. & Rosamond, B. (2013). 'Normative power Europe' meets economic liberalism: Complicating cosmopolitanism inside/outside the EU. *Cooperation and Conflict, 48*(2), 229–246.

Putin, V. (2005a, May 7). The lessons of victory over Nazism. *Le Figaro*, p. http://archive.kremlin.ru/eng/text/speeches/2005/05/07/0748_type82912type104017_87601.shtml. Accessed 28 Sept 2005.

Putin, V. (2005b). Address to the Federal Assembly. April 25. http://www.kremlin.ru/eng/speeches/2005/04/25/2031_type70029_87086.shtml. Accessed 19 May 2005.

Putin, V. (2007). Address to the Federal Assembly. April 26. http://archive.kremlin.ru/eng/text/speeches/2007/04/26/1209. Accessed 6 Oct 2010.

Putin, V. (2012). Vladimir Putin on foreign policy: Russia and the changing world. Valdai Club. February 27. http://valdaiclub.com/politics/39300.html. Accessed 20 Feb 2013.

RFE/RL (2012, December 21). EU warns Armenia about Russia Custom Union. http://asbarez.com/107280/eu-warns-armenia-about-russia-customs-union/. Accessed 2 Oct 2013.

Risse, T. (2000). 'Let's argue!' Communicative action in world politics. *The Review of International Organizations, 54*(1), 1–39.

RU facts (2013, October 10). Putin's adviser threatened Ukraine with introduction of a visa regime. http://ru-facts.com/news/view/27008.html. Accessed 24 Oct 2013.

Sakwa, R. (2008). Russian political culture through the eyes of Vladislav Surkov. *Russian Politics and Law, 46*(5), 3–7.

Secrieru, S. (2010). Russia's mainstream perceptions of the EU and its member states. *SPES Policy Papers*.

Shearman, P. (2001). The sources of Russian conduct: Understanding Russian foreign policy. *Review of International Studies, 27*(2), 249–263.

Sushko, O. (2004). The dark side of integration: Ambitions of domination in Russia's backyard. *Washington Quarterly, 27*(2), 119–131.

The Guardian. (2013, October 17). How do you solve a problem like Russia? http://www.theguardian.com/world/2013/oct/17/problem-russia-syria-greenpeace-kremlin-europe-eu. Accessed 18 Oct 2013.

Treisman, D. (2013). Russia as a global policy leader: Can Russia define a new role for itself? *Russia in Global Affairs, 11*(2). http://eng.globalaffairs.ru/number/Russia-as-a-Global-Policy-Leader–16052. Accessed 8 Sept 2013.

Tsygankov, P., & Fominykh, F. (2010). The anti-Russian discourse of the European Union. *Russian Politics and Law, 48*(6), 19–34.

Tumanov, S., Gasparishvili, A., & Romanova, E. (2011). Russia-EU relations, or how the Russians really view the EU. *Journal of Communist Studies and Transition Politics, 27*(1), 120–141.

Valdai Club (2013). Experts speak out against pressure to accede to the Eurasian Union. http://valdaiclub.com/near_abroad/62500.html. Accessed 12 Oct 2013.

Vinokurov, E. (2013). Pragmatic Eurasianism: Prospects for Eurasian integration. *Russia in Global Affairs, 11*(2). http://eng.globalaffairs.ru/number/Pragmatic-Eurasianism–16050. Accessed 8 Sept 2013.

Walzer, M. (1994). *Thick and thin: Moral argument at home and abroad*. Notre Dame: University of Notre Dame Press.

Whitman, R. G. (2013). The neo-normative turn in theorizing the EU's international presence. *Cooperation and Conflict, 48*(2), 171–193.

Wunderlich, J. U. (2012). The EU an actor *sui generis?* A comparison of EU and ASEAN actorness. *Journal of Common Market Studies, 50*(4), 653–669.

Dr. James Headley is a Senior Lecturer at the University of Otago, New Zealand. His research interests include Russian foreign policy, nationalism and ethnic conflict, IR theory, and European Union enlargement. He is the author of *Russia and the Balkans: Foreign Policy from Yeltsin to Putin* (Hurst and Co./Columbia University Press, 2008) and co-editor of *Public Participation in Foreign Policy* (Palgrave Macmillan, 2012). He has a PhD and an MA from the University of London, and a BA (Hons) from the University of Oxford.

Chapter 14
The Diffusion of EU Norms to China: The Case of Tibet

Wenwen Shen

14.1 Introduction

In the past two decades, the human rights situation in Tibet has gained widespread currency within the international community. Within this context, the European Union (EU) is seen either as a sympathetic outsider, who reflects popular moral sentiment in the West, or—in the eyes of many Chinese—as an imperialist intruder. A cursory glance at EU-China relations reveals that periods of tension correspond with the publicity of human rights abuses in Tibet and/or the 14th Dalai Lama's European tours.

So far, legal and historical scholarship has not come to consensus on the nature of the Tibet question and its relation to international norms. Nonetheless, it is an important case that can help us understand the differences between how Europeans and Chinese understand this issue and the frustrations that each side feels with the other.

This chapter considers the rejection of EU norms with regard to the issue of Tibet. It applies the theoretical claims of Normative Power Europe (NPE) to an empirical analysis of Tibet. The issue has become a sticking point that reflects: the uneasy relationship between the EU's human rights concerns on Tibet and its implementation of Common Foreign and Security Policy (CFSP) towards China; the tension between the EU's normative and materialistic concerns; and the mismatch between norms of international law and the political reality of Chinese power.

Section one highlights the historical and political complexity of this issue. Section two identifies five norm-diffusion mechanisms—persuasion, invoking norms, shaping discourse, living by example and shaming—in the NPE literature (Manners 2009a, b; Aggestam 2009; Forsberg 2009) and demonstrates how theorising about normative power can contribute to our understanding of the EU's promotion of

W. Shen (✉)
School of History, Philosophy, Political Science and International Relations, Victoria University of Wellington, Wellington, New Zealand
e-mail: wenwen.shen@vuw.ac.nz

© Springer International Publishing Switzerland 2015
A. Björkdahl et al. (eds.), *Importing EU Norms,* United Nations University Series on Regionalism 8, DOI 10.1007/978-3-319-13740-7_14

human rights in external relations. In section three, the chapter's centrepiece, the five norm diffusion mechanisms is applied to anlyze the Tibetan case, illustrating the ways in which EU normative power is diffused and adopted or rejected. The conclusion evaluates the impact of these diffusion mechanisms.

14.2   The Tibet Question: Issues and Controversies

In international politics, the Tibet question asks what should be Tibet's political status vis-à-vis China (Goldstein 2004, p. 186; Anand 2006, p. 287). For the Chinese government, the so-called 'Tibet question' is raised only by forces external to China and demonstrates Western countries' continuing support for Tibetan separatists. For the Dalai Lama, on the other hand, the Tibetan Question is about genuine autonomy for ethnic Tibetans within China, although Beijing has accused him of covertly seeking independence (Financial Times 2013).

At the official level, all European governments acknowledge that Tibet is part of China and none has formally recognised the Tibet Government in Exile (TGIE). Yet, Europeans sustain the exile cause in other non-official ways such as the rallying of thousands of 'Tibet supporters', including: individual parliamentarians, rights activists, celebrities, artists and ordinary converts to Tibetan Buddhism.

14.2.1   The Chinese 'Occupation' of Tibet

At the core of the dispute is the historical status of Tibet. The main controversy focuses on whether Tibet has been independent or a part of China in recent history (Sautman and Dreyer 2006; Goldstein 2004). China's political position in Tibet is based, first and foremost, on the claim that China has controlled the territory since the mid-thirteenth century (White Paper 1992a, b). Tibetan exiles, on the other hand, maintain that Tibet has been an independent political entity for the past 2000 years. The Dalai Lama, for his part, has advocated a 'middle way' as preconditions for talks with China. He accepts Tibet as part of the People's Republic of China (PRC), but insists that Greater Tibet should become a self-governing political entity founded on a constitution that would grant Tibet Western-style democratic rights (ICJ 1997, p. 98). The PRC dismissed this offer as seeking an indirect form of independence (Xinhua News Agency 2008a, b).

In the past two decades, the EU's position on the Tibet question has generally been ambiguous and accommodating towards China. At no point has Tibetan independence been a major concern. Despite British attempts to control the area in the late nineteenth and early twentieth centuries, neither Britain nor other European countries have played a prominent role in Tibet's contemporary history. This stands in contrast to India, which is the primary host of exiled Tibetans, and to the United States (US), which supported the Tibetan cause financially and militarily in the 1950s and 1960s. Thus, despite their efforts to help the Tibet cause gain international visibility, EU policy makers have not committed themselves to support more than autonomy for Tibet under China. They have insisted that Tibetans should focus on China's violations of human rights, rather than on the core political issues many Tibetans wanted to raise: Chinese invasion and occupation of their country.

14.2.2   'Violation of Human Rights' in Tibet

International concerns about human rights abuses in Tibet focus on cultural extermination, political imprisonment and torture, the illegitimacy of China's sovereignty in the region, and the Chinese government's reluctance to fully embrace universal human rights. Since 2009, self-immolations by Tibetans protesting Chinese rule inside Tibet have given these issues particular prominence (ICT 2012).

In general, the Chinese government ignores international criticisms of alleged rights violations in Tibet, insisting Tibet is an issue of Chinese territorial integrity and national unity (Xu and Yuan 2006). From a Chinese perspective, Tibetans have enjoyed an unprecedented level of prosperity in economy, health and infrastructure, thanks to the Chinese Communist Party's economic reforms. The Chinese also recall Western silence over Tibet in the 1970s, and believe the 'so-called "Tibetan human rights problem"' has been manipulated by those with 'ulterior motives' (Zhang 1994, p. 172).

For many Europeans, concerns over and support for the Tibetan cause are framed in the discourse of human rights. In the Joint Statement with the US in response to the unrest in Tibet in 2008, the EU reiterated its human rights perspective towards the issue of Tibet. The British government also changed its discourse regarding Tibet in 2008, focusing on Tibet's human rights situation instead of its political status (Miliband 2008).

For Barnett (2001, p. 291), the concept of human rights offers a language that can respond to Western audiences' demand for criticism of China, while permitting Chinese officials to consider such criticisms as mild enough not to threaten China's fundamental interests in Tibet.

14.2.3   The Historical Legacy of European Imperialism

The official line of the Chinese government maintains that all pro-independence campaigns are driven by 'Western imperialism' with an aim to destabilise China and eventually destroy its territorial integrity and sovereignty (White Paper 1992b). It further argues that the Tibet question emerged as a direct result of the British expansion into Asia and Tibet (White Paper 1992b). For Goldstein (1997, p. 37), the double standard of British policy in the early twentieth century revealed its ambiguous and hypocritical attitude towards Tibet. The British sought to control Tibet for its strategic location as a buffer state in Central Asia and for its position as an entry point for commercial interests into the Chinese empire. Some scholars also argue that the failure of the British to comprehend the complex relation between Tibet and China led to an anachronistic understanding of pre-modern Tibet's relationship with China according to modern political and legal standards (Wang 2006; Anand 2006).

In view of Europe's imperialistic legacy, how do we know that Europe's 'normative power' in the Tibetan case should not be perceived as a mere expression of Eurocentric imperialism? On the one hand, the normative legitimacy of European foreign policy is clouded by the imperialist legacy of Britain in the eyes of the Chinese. On the other hand, in the eyes of the externally based Tibet support groups, the EU has a significant role to play concerning human rights violations inside Tibet. However, the problem lies in the Chinese rejection of the universalism of European norms. From a post-colonial perspective, China cannot view the values the EU promotes as 'universal' simply because it has had disastrous experience with Western imperialism which justified itself according to the same value system (Golden 2006, p. 268).

The EU's self-justification as a normative power, instead of as an imperialistic power, relies on the extent to which international human rights serves as an 'external reference point' as a crucial source of its legitimacy (Manners 2006, p. 170).

14.3   A Normative Power Perspective

Manners (2002) locates the sources of EU foreign policy among the EU's ontological attributes, arguing that the principles that guided the development and enlargement of the European project (peace, reconciliation, democratisation, multilateralism, human rights, etc.) are also the 'constitutive' features that make the EU a distinctive and unique polity and a 'normative power' (NPE) in international relations (Manners 2002, p. 252). In the context of EU foreign policy towards China, however, value pluralism makes the interpretation of NPE problematic. The case of Tibet provides a classic example in which the EU's notion of itself as a normative power upholding universal human rights norms is rejected by China in the name of state sovereignty.

In this chapter, the notion of NPE is adopted as an alternative to rationalist explanations for understanding and judging EU influence on China. In particular it uses the NPE framework to understand mechanisms through which norms might be diffused. 'The Tibet question' is an unlikely successful story for NPE as the EU has little leverage to influence China's Tibet policy. It nonetheless merits close examination because it offers insight into when and why EU norms are rejected. It also demonstrates how a normative power framework provides a nuanced perspective on understanding and judging policy effectiveness. In other words, this chapter observes the EU's normative power at work in the case of Tibet by looking at normative actions taken by the EU to promote its principled beliefs. Such actions include persuasion, argumentation, or conferral of shame or prestige, rather than coercion or material motivations. This approach demonstrates NPE at work, emphasising on how norms are diffused, and how normative power mechanisms are translated into EU foreign policy instruments.

With regard to how norms are diffused, Foot (2001, p. 9) suggests that, in the absence of a direct enforcement mechanism, one has to rely on moral persuasion, argumentation and/or shaming to elicit voluntary compliance in circumstances where norms are well-established international standards. For Tocci (2008, p. 9), methods based on dialogue, cooperation and engagement are normative because they reduce the risks of 'imposing allegedly "universal" norms through sheer power and against the needs and desires of local populations in third countries'. The use of persuasion, through constructive engagement and conferral of shame or prestige, is thus important if the EU is to be seen to 'be reasonable' in human rights policy (Manners 2009b, p. 795). Drawing from Manners (2002, 2009a, b), and his critics (Forsberg 2009; Aggestam 2009), there are five norm diffusion mechanisms underlying the policy approaches adopted by the EU towards China between 1989 and 2009. These five mechanisms include persuasion, invoking norms, shaping the discourse, power of example and conferral of prestige or shame. This chapter intends to evaluate whether these mechanisms have led to norm adoption, adaptation, resistance or rejection as outlined in the introductory chapter of this book.

14.4   Norm Diffusion

The foreign policy instruments involved in this case-study include high-level contacts with the Chinese counterparts in international forums, the issuing of statements, parliamentary hearings, resolutions concerning individual cases and European Commission delegations of the Troika ambassadors to visit Tibet. With the EU's internal divisions in mind, one needs to ask: (1) how consistent is the EU in promoting human rights norms; (2) are persuasion, instead of coercion, and engagement, instead of confrontation, more effective ways of norm diffusion and (3) are persuasion and engagement simply the result of the EU's political weakness?

14.4.1   Persuasion and Argumentation

The way NPE promotes principles through persuasion and argumentation can be translated into policy actions such as constructive engagement, encouragement of dialogue between participants and the use of eloquent rhetoric (Manners 2009a, p. 12; Forsberg 2009, p. 16). EU officials' visits in Tibet, inter-parliamentary visits, and human rights dialogue sit well within this group.

EU Officials' Visits to Tibet

Responding to the military crackdown in Lhasa in March 1989, the first delegation of Troika ambassadors and European Commissioner Martin Bangemann expressed the Twelve's concern to the Chinese government over the situation in Tibet, but no further action was taken. When the human rights dialogue was first launched in 1995, Troika visits were part of the negotiation package. Subsequently, a Troika mission took place in 1996 (EEAS 2012, online). After self-immolation cases in Tibet brought intense international scrutiny, China allowed the EU Special Representative (EUSR) on Human Rights, Mr Stavros Lambrinidis to visit China's ethnic Tibetan areas in September 2013, just 2 weeks before the United Nations' Universal Periodic Review was due to take place.

Given its confidentiality and China's close supervision throughout the visit, the actual process of fact-finding in these missions can hardly have been independent. Nevertheless, the EUSR visit represented an effort by senior EU officials to engage with human rights issues in Tibet in a more in-depth manner than before (EEAS 2013).

Inter-institutional Visits

The European Parliament readily took up a leading role in discussing the Tibet question, condemning the deterioration of the human rights situation in Tibet. Tibet has also often been the topic of inter-parliamentary meetings (Xinhua 2002).

However, the results of such visits often led to no concrete policy actions being extended, and the reporting of these events has been carefully controlled by the Chinese authorities. Institutions with little political remit, such as the European Economic and Social Committee (EESC), are less likely to put the Chinese authorities on the defensive. In September 2009, the EESC became the first EU institution to send an EU delegation to visit Tibet since the March 2008 unrest. The focus of the EESC President Mario Sepi's visit was on the social and economic aspects in Tibet Autonomous Region (TAR) over which China was much more prepared to cooperate (EESC 2009).

The result of the EESC visits seems to indicate that it was possible for the EU to find a way to address its concerns over Tibet and be welcomed by China, non-governmental organisations and Tibetans-in-exile all at the same time (ICT 2009). Thus, sending a low-profile body to deal with the most politically sensitive area of China's policy-making in a time of crisis proved to be a sensible way of balancing conflicting interests in EU relations with China.

Human Rights Dialogue

The EU-China human rights dialogue remains a long-term and regular forum for the EU to raise its concerns regarding Tibet. Since 1998, Tibet had been mentioned in several contexts, such as: 'the situation in Tibet, including the "patriotic education campaign"', 'the rights of minorities, including in Tibet', 'treatment of refugees and minority rights, including in Tibet and Xinjiang', and 'respect for cultural rights and religious freedom' (EU Annual Human Rights Reports 1998/9, 2001, 2002, 2003, 2004).

While the EU voiced 'grave concern' regarding the situation in Tibet, in its response, China simply reiterated its customary position on the situation in Tibet, on the role of the Dalai Lama and on China's position on further talks. Considering the lack of progress, human rights groups such as Amnesty International, International Campaign for Tibet (ICT) and the Tibetan Government in Exile (TGIE) repeatedly called upon the EU to reclaim the initiative by sponsoring a resolution against China at the forthcoming United National Committee on Human Rights (UNCHR). They feared the effectiveness of the dialogue approach had been compromised when other forms of pressure were abandoned (Macklin 1999; Agence France Press 1998).

14.4.2   Invoking Norms

Invoking norms is about the EU activating commitments to which the target country itself subscribes (Forsberg 2009, p. 17). In the Tibetan case, when China failed to adhere to international agreements to which it is a party, the EU would invoke the contravention of commitments to Tibet under international law. Policy instruments at the EU's disposal in such cases were most readily associated with European Parliament (EP) resolutions, declarations or *démarches*.

Until China had signed the International Covenant of Civil and Political Rights (ICCPR) in 1998 and ratified the International Covenant of Economic, Social and Cultural Rights (ICESCR) in 2003, self-determination, as a fundamental principle enshrined in these two Covenants, was not a part of the EP's normative repertoire with regard to the situation in Tibet. Instead, the human rights problem of Tibet was framed most often in terms of religious freedom and the rights of ethnic minorities. As a result, the EU had to rely on invoking individual legal provisions—such as Article 18 of freedom of religion under the Universal Declaration of Human Rights —rather than several United Nations' Conventions that were relevant for the same issue (EP 2001). While a large number of legal instruments remained irrelevant to the EP's position on Tibet, the problems of political status and human rights in Tibet persisted.

Furthermore, there was a tendency to deploy *démarches* and declarations to prioritise individual cases that violated norms deemed fundamental to the EU moral order. This is certainly the case when it comes to the death penalty. The EP issued *démarches*, declarations or/and resolutions in almost all the individual cases that involved death sentences or execution of Tibetans had been (EP 2005).

Overall, whenever the EU tried to activate commitments, China referred to either international law or to its own domestic laws. As a result, China would not recognise or reciprocate EU messages when it came to Tibet, let alone make concessions or compromise. This response is arguably rooted in China's positions based on such norms as absolute sovereignty. The norms that underpin the EU's discourse on Tibet, however, hold no normative power over China, simply because China perceives no legitimacy in the Union's actions.

14.4.3   Shaping Discourse

For Manners (2002, p. 239), normative power shapes discourses through the mechanisms of learning, adaptation or rejection of norms as a result of international norms and political learning by third countries. In the case of Tibet, this type of norm diffusion did occur in the early twentieth century, as the Chinese learnt the modern European diplomatic language to assert their relationship with Tibet in terms of sovereignty (Anand 2002, p. 8). Since the late 1980s, the West learned quickly to adopt human rights discourse to publicise the Tibetan cause. China's response to the EU concerns has always been assertive and consistent over the years, as China both resolutely and customarily rejects anything that might suggest the Tibet issue is more than a domestic issue, thus leaving no space for any external attempt to shape China's response.

Considering EP resolutions from 1987 to 2009, at least two trends can be identified in its discourse on Tibet. First, the broad range of issues that were initially under the EP's scrutiny was reduced almost entirely to individual cases. In the early 1990s, the EP passed resolutions addressing both Tibet's situation in general and individual cases, including: self-determination, population transfer and birth control policy, culture and religion, language, history, ecology, economy and health and hygiene. Between 1998 and 2009, however, seven out of nine Parliament resolutions were devoted to individual cases, five of which addressed just one case regarding the death sentence of a Buddhist Lama, Tenzin Deleg Rinpoche (EP 2005). The second trend since the late 1990s is that the situation in Tibet no longer stood alone as the subject of EP resolutions. Instead, it was raised alongside Xinjiang, as an example of China's repression of ethnic minorities and restriction of religious freedom, or as an example of the use of the death penalty for ethnic Tibetans who had committed political crimes.

Reacting to EP resolutions, Chinese official media preferred to criticise 'some parliamentarians' rather than the EU or the EP more generally. The main criticisms addressed 'amnesia concerning Europe's history and their ignorance of the Chinese autonomous region's current situation' (Xinhua 2009).

The Commission, on the other hand, has adopted a much more cooperative approach to the issue of Tibet, which is manifested by raising the Tibet issue discreetly within the newly established bilateral dialogue on human rights. According to the Commission's first Communication in 1998 on 'Building a Comprehensive Partnership with China', the EU 'attaches great importance to the respect for the cultural, linguistic and religious identity of ethnic minorities' on issues relating to Tibet (COM 1998, p. 10). In its updated version in 2003, the question of Tibet was only mentioned once in the context of ensuring a genuine autonomy for this region through encouraging China and the Dalai Lama to engage in dialogue (COM 2003). Since then, Tibet has not been mentioned in the Commission's policy papers.

The abovementioned patterns of development in the EU's response to the Tibet question can be understood as an accommodation and adjustment in its relations with China, while trying to uphold international human rights standards. However, as China's economy grew, so did the mutual interests between China and the EU. An ambiguous human rights language might be easy for the EU to pay lip service to, as the European domestic audience would see EU criticisms on China in words. However, by reducing the scope of norms under consideration and focusing on individual cases, one can argue that the EU's human rights discourse on Tibet became more defined, but also weaker overall. Therefore, instead of shaping China's discourse, the EU's discourse on Tibet ended up being shaped by China's non-negotiable position, the need to encourage the process of engagement and dialogue with China, and the dilemma between the EU's sympathy towards the Tibetans and its economic interests with China as a strategic partner.

14.4.4   *Living by Example*

According to Manners (2002), the notion of NPE is essentially about what the EU is, rather than what it does. As such 'living by example' might be the most important element of the EU's normative power. For example, the EU's handling of the independence of Kosovo and the Baltic countries may have implications for Tibet and the peaceful resolution of conflicts over its political status.

Kosovo and Domino Effects

The military intervention in Kosovo by the North Atlantic Treaty Organisation (NATO) forces made China extremely uncomfortable in 1999, as it too has regions—Tibet and Xinjiang—where ethnic groups have been seeking independence from PRC rule (Economist 1999). Fearing Tibet could become an 'Asian Kosovo', China's international response has been that it 'opposed interference in other nations' internal affairs no matter what the excuse or by what means and particularly opposed any random action that circumvents the UN'(The Guardian 1999). Domestically, China kept its media from reporting on ethnic cleansing of Albanians, and painted Milosevic as a patriot and hero, while presenting 'the US-led NATO' as an imperialist hegemon (People's Daily 1999 in the Guardian 1999). In 2008, Tibet's political status was given renewed attention in the light of Kosovo's independence. From an international law perspective, the right of Tibetans to self-determination is strong, and arguably stronger than that of Kosovars (Financial Times 2008).

Chinese scholars, on the other hand, accused the Western powers of holding self-contradictory double standards on the issue of human rights, self-determination and sovereignty in international affairs. And they too, like Western scholars, pointed to the tensions between the competing rights of the territorial integrity of states and the self-determination of peoples, both of which are guaranteed under international law (Xu and Yuan 2006, p. 306).

The Baltic Analogy

In the early 1990s, the Dalai Lama frequently made optimistic statements about Tibet's future following the path to independence of the Baltic States. He appealed to the Western governments to treat Tibet as they had the Baltic States (Becker in the Guardian 1990, 3 May: p. 8). For Mr Boutros Boutros-Ghali, UN Secretary General at the time, the Tibet case was also stronger than that of the Baltic Republics. This was because Tibet had a more credible leadership able to effectively communicate the moral and political foundations of its claims for self-determination (Falk 1994, p. 94). In addition, since the Dalai Lama is the only leader of the Tibetan self-determination movement and a recipient of the Nobel Peace Prize, he had already garnered wide support from the international community. Chinese scholars, on the other hand, carefully studied the collapse of Soviet Union and the independence of the Baltic States and the potential impact of these developments on Tibet's independence movement (Zhang 1994). Unlike the Soviet Union, the reason why the Chinese Communist Party did not fall to the wave of democratisation orchestrated by the West, lies in the government's successful economic reform and China's ethnic minority problems being sufficiently mild. In case Tibet follows the footsteps of the Baltic States, the Chinese government was advised: (1) to consolidate the Chinese Communist Party's leadership; (2) to ensure equality and solidarity among all nationalities; (3) to stimulate faster economic growth in ethnic autonomous regions; (4) to facilitate patriotic education in ethnic autonomous regions; (5) to crackdown splitist movement; (6) to unveil the historical truth to the world; (7) to stay alert against the threat of external anti-China forces (ibid., pp. 224–254).

14.4.5 Shaming

States are capable of feeling ashamed if they are concerned about their reputations. Reputation, in this scenario, is as a non-material cost resulting from the disapproval of other members of the normative community (Foot 2001, p. 10). Manners (2009a, p. 12) broadly defines shaming as public condemnation in multilateral fora or the use of symbolic sanctioning. Regarding Tibet, by increasingly resorting to public criticisms in recent years, European governments have found a less costly way to address the human rights problem in Tibet, both politically and economically.

For Western supporters of the Tibetan cause, the 2008 Beijing Olympic Games was used as a platform to give more publicity to Tibet. The Beijing Olympics were described by Thomas Mann, Chairman of the EP's Tibet Inter-Group, as an opportunity to 'keep our eye on the ball' (EP 2006). On the other hand, the Chinese Communist Party hoped to use the Games to promote a story that focused on three decades of high economic growth, the success of pulling millions out of poverty and the expectation in future to be respected and integrated into the global community (Askew 2009, p. 111). With this desire to gain due recognition from the rest of the world, the Tibet protest in Lhasa in early March was embarrassing for the Chinese regime.

In early April 2008, European Parliamentarians urged EU leaders to boycott the Olympic Games Opening Ceremony in Beijing on August 8 unless China resumed talks with the Dalai Lama (Spiegel 2008, online).

Other EU institutions steered clear of any mention of the Beijing Olympics and EU officials did not signal a boycott, although some Member States were contemplated their own action. Eventually Germany and Poland decided to avoid any ministerial-level participation in the ceremony. The Netherlands, Sweden and other nations ruled out a boycott, whereas the French and UK heads-of-state remained undecided until the last minute (Fox 2008).

On the Chinese side, the crackdown of protestors in Tibet led to public protests that disrupted international legs of the 2008 Beijing Olympics torch relay, particularly in London, Paris and San Francisco. The backlash against China's policy in Tibet generated anti-Western demonstrations in China and a boycott the French retailer Carrefour (BBC 2008, online)

China's decision to postpone the EU-China summit in December 2008 was a reaction to French President Sarkozy's plan to meet the Dalai Lama, while France held the EU's rotating Presidency (MFA of PRC 2008). Cancellation of a high-level summit with the EU over Tibet was an unprecedented move by China, which carried multiple implications for the EU. For Barnett (2008, online), 'there are internal divisions among the EU powers, and this is a squeeze to try and see who will stick to their principles and who believes they mustn't upset China.' It also showed China's increasing willingness to flex its strengthening global muscle (The Economist 2009, p. 31). Whereas a Chinese political commentator suggested that 'China thinks the Tibet issue is more important than its relation with Europe' (Agence France Presse 2008).

Overall, China's concern over its international image does provide the EU leverage over China, as massive public protests in Europe during the Olympic torch relay had embarrassed China. However, the process of 'shaming' China on the international stage also provoked nationalist resentments against Western governments and media. Within China, the official view of Tibet is universally accepted as the Chinese population has been subjected to decades of official propaganda providing the only source of information on the issue. Shaming might be successful in pressuring China into sharpening its propaganda overseas or hiring more international public relations firms, but it does not challenge China's fundamental concerns over its territorial integrity.

14.4.6   Norm Rejection

Despite the EU's effort, China has not fundamentally changed its official discourse regarding Tibet's status. Nor has Chinese domestic policy towards Tibet given in to external pressure, which China has bitterly opposed as interference of its internal affairs (Xinhua 2008b). The Tibet question thus captures the strong and weak normative behaviour among different EU institutions and some Member States, despite a similar rhetoric being adopted among them to confirm their official position on China's sovereignty and the human rights situation in Tibet.

Until the EU embarked on a policy based on cooperation and persuasion in 1998, the majority of the EU's concerns on Tibet had been mostly channelled through the EP's resolutions. Often belligerent and strident, these resolutions were insufficiently considered by other EU bodies and Member States, and they resulted in few tangible results (ICT 2009). The benchmarks of the human rights dialogue, as agreed by China in 2001, set out the EU's policy objective for Tibet as 'respect for cultural rights and religious freedoms' (COM 2007). The last time Tibet was mentioned in the Commission's Communication in 2003, the EU aimed to prioritise Tibet in its bilateral political dialogue with China to 'encourage China and the Dalai Lama to further strengthen ongoing direct contacts with a view to finding a mutually acceptable solution to the question of Tibet in the context of ensuring a genuine autonomy for this region' (COM 2003). However, significant hurdles remain before meaningful talks can be held between the Dalai Lama and the Chinese authorities (Goldstein 2004, p. 212).

Responding to the EU's concerns over the situation in Tibet, Chinese officials have consistently denied any human rights violations in Tibet. The Chinese Foreign Ministry's responses are often standardised, reiterating and emphasising the Chinese principle of non-interference as Tibet remains China's internal affair. It reads as if the Chinese government is convinced that criticisms based on human rights arguments were too mild to be threatening to China's fundamental interests over sovereignty and domestic stability.

In the eyes of Chinese political commentators, the Tibet issue has put a formidable strain on EU-China relations within the last decade. Some argue that the EU is motivated by the long-term interests to be seen as a normative power, and it does so by maintaining its criticisms of human rights violations in Tibet even during the global economic crisis (Jian 2009). Other narratives associate the EU's concerns over Tibet with China's rise, thus refer to the West's support for the Tibetan cause as 'some European politicians have ulterior motives and the vicious intention of containing and checking the emergence of China as a global power.' (China Daily 2009, online)

14.5 Conclusion

This case study demonstrates how norms promoted by the EU relating to the Tibet question have been rejected by China. The notion of normative power captures how the EU has addressed human rights problems in Tibet. The EU's actions have been based on legitimating human rights principles which the EU promotes through non-coercive means, including persuasion, invoking norms, shaping discourse, living by example and shaming. In the Tibetan case, the right to self-determination, as laid down in UN Charter, UNDHR, International Convent of Civil and Political Rights (ICCPR) and International Convent of Economic, Social and Cultural Rights (IESCR) and concluded in UN Resolutions, constitutes the legal and normative justification for the EU to invoke this principle when it addresses the Tibet question. The same should apply to individual human rights, including rights of ethnic minorities and religious freedom. In this respect, the EU's normative power and efforts to promote norms relevant to the Tibet question, despite being ambiguous and accommodating over the years, have all been rejected by China's non-negotiable position. At the core of this position is the conviction that the Tibet question should not challenge China's territorial integrity and historical ownership of the territory.

Despite the EU's efforts to address the Tibetan cause, the EU has not had any significant impact on the situation in Tibet. Responding to the EU's concerns over the situation in Tibet, Chinese officials have always insisted that Tibetans' religious freedom and standard of living have been hugely improved under the PRC's rule. China's international responses have always been a standard reiteration of the principle of non-interference over others' domestic affairs. As a result, it was the EU's position that ended up being shaped by China in its policy rhetoric over Tibet.

This analysis of the EU's responses to the Tibet question reveals the limitation of human rights as a central organising principle when it comes to the EU's external relations with an important trade and strategic partners. The Tibetan case also suggests that the EU's norm promotion is often in conflict not just with the EU's economic interests, but also with the need for engagement—a form of norm diffusion mechanism itself. Nevertheless, had the EU demonstrated greater unity and consistency, it could, at least, have marshalled a strong defence against China's 'diplomatic bullying' (Metten 2009).

References

Agence France Presse. (1998, February 26). Tibet government in exile asks EU to review human rights decision. Agence France Press. www.radioradicale.it/exagora/tibet-government-in-ex-ile-asks-eu-to-review-human-rights-decision. Accessed 20 Jan 2014.

Agence France Presse. (2008, 27 November). Angry China flexing muscle with Europe over Tibet: analysts http://www.phayul.com/news/article.aspx?id=23291. Accessed 29 Jan 2014.

Aggestam, L. (2009). The world in our mind: Normative power in a multi-polar world. In A. Gerrits (Ed.), *Normative power Europe in a changing world: A discussion* (pp. 25–36). The Hague: Netherlands Institute of International Relations. (Clingendael European Papers, 5).

Anand, D. (2002). A story to be told: IR, postcolonialism, and the discourse of Tibetan (trans) national identity'. In G. Chowdhry & S. Nair (Eds.), *Power, postcolonialism and international relations*. London: Routledge.

Anand, D. (2006). The Tibet question and the West: Issues of sovereignty, identity and representation. In B. Sautman & J. T. Dreyer (Eds.), *Contemporary Tibet: Politics, development, and society in a disputed region* (pp. 285–304). New York: M.E. Sharpe.

Askew, D. (2009). Sport and politics: The 2008 Beijing Olympic Games. *European Studies, 27,* 103–120.

Barnett, R. (2001). Violated specialness: Western political representations of Tibet. In T. Dodin & H. Räther (Eds.), *Imagining Tibet: Perceptions, projections and fantasies* (pp. 269–316). Boston: Wisdom.

Barnett, R. (2008, 24 November). Did Britain just sell Tibet?, *New York Times*. http://www.nytimes.com/2008/11/25/opinion/25barnett.html. Accessed 29 Jan 2014.

BBC. (2008, 19 April). Anti-French rallies across China, www.news.bbc.uk/2/hi/7356107.stm. Accessed 30 Nov 2014.

Becker, J. (1990) Tibetans discover new sympathisers,in the The Guardian, 3 May 1990, p. 8.

China Daily. (2009, 19 June). Tibet issue is a thorn in China-Europe ties. www.chinadaily.com.cn/opinion/2009-06/19/content_8300642.htm. Accessed 20 Jan 2014.

Council of the European Union. (1999). EU annual human rights report (1998/9). Brussels.

Council of the European Union. (2001). EU annual human rights report (2001). Brussels.

Council of the European Union. (2002). EU annual human rights report (2002). Brussels.

Council of the European Union. (2003). EU annual human rights report (2003). Brussels.

Council of the European Union. (2004). EU annual human rights report (2004). Brussels.

European Commission. (1998). Building a comprehensive partnership with China, COM (1998) 181 final. Brussels.

European Commission. (2003). A mature partnership-shared interests and challenges in EU-China relations, COM (2003) 533final, Brussels.

European Commission. (2007). Evaluation of the European commission's co-operation and partnership with the People's Republic of China, Country Level Evaluation, final synthesis report, April 2007, Brussels, p. 85.

European Economic and Social Committee. (2009). President Sepi declaration on the EESC mission to Tibet, CES/09/117. Accessed 25 Sept 2009.

European Parliament. (2001). Human rights: Religious freedom in People's Republic of China, 21 February 2001, Strasbourg.

European Parliament. (2005). Resolution on 'Tibet, the case of Tenzin Delek Rinpoche, OJC 201E, 18 August, 2005.

European Parliament. (2006). Meeting report, the 52rd meeting of the Tibet intergroup, 16 May 2006, Strasbourg.

European Union External Action Service. (2012). EU-China Relations: Chronology, http:eeas.europa.eu/china/index_en.htm. Accessed 30 Nov 2014.

European Union External Action Service. (2013). EU special representative for Human Rights Lambrinidis visits China, EU13-435UN, 20 September 2013.

Falk, R. (1994). Locating the right of self-determination of peoples as a principle of international law: General consideration. In R. McCorquodale & N. Orosz (Eds.), *Tibet, the position in international law: Report of the conference of international law relation to self-determination and independence for Tibet* (pp. 81-91). Sreindia: Hans Jörg Mayer.

Foot, R. (2001). Rights beyond borders: The global community and the struggle over Human Rights in China. Oxford: Oxford University Press.

Forsberg, T. (2009). *Normative power Europe (Once More): A conceptual clarification and empirical analysis*. Paper presented to the Annual Convention of the International Studies Association, New York. February 2009.

Fox, J. (2008) The Threat of a Boycott, in EUOvserver, 28 May 2008, www.euobserver.com/opinion/25885. Accessed 30 Nov 2014.

Golden, S. (2006). Socio-cultural aspects of the relationship between the EU and East Asia, with particular reference to China. *Asia Europe Journal, 4*(2), 265–294.

Goldstein, M. (1997). *The snow lion and the dragon: China, Tibet, and the Dalai Lama*. California: University of California Press.

Goldstein, M. (2004). Tibet and China in the Twentieth Century. In R. Morris (Ed.), *Governing China's Multiethnic Frontiers* (pp. 186–229). Seattle: University of Washington Press.

International Campaign for Tibet (ICT). (2009). Assessments and recommendations on Tibet, subcommittee on human rights. international campaign for Tibet, 1 December 2009.

International Campaign for Tibet. (2012). Storm in the grasslands: Self-immolations in Tibet and Chinese policy, international campaign for Tibet, 10 December, 2012.

International Commission of Jurists. (1997, December). *Tibet-human rights and the rule of law*. Geneva: International Commission of Jurists.

Jian, J. (2009, 27 March). Sino-EU ties hijacked by Tibet issue. Asia Times. www.atimes.com/atimes/China/KC27Ad01.html. Accessed 21 Jan 2014.

Macklin, S. (1999, 10 February). EU under pressure to mount protest. South China Morning Post.

Manners, I. (2002). Normative power Europe: A contradiction in Terms? *Journal of Common Market Studies, 40*(2), 235–258.

Manners, I. (2006). Normative power Europe reconsidered: Beyond the crossroads. *Journal of European Public Policy, 13*(2), 182–199.

Manners, I. (2009a). The concept of normative power in world Politics. In A. Gerrits (Ed.), *Normative power Europe in a changing world: A discussion* (pp. 9–24). The Hague: Netherlands Institute of International Relations, Clingendael.

Manners, I. (2009b). The social dimension of EU trade policies: Reflections form a normative power perspective. *European Foreign Affairs Review, 14*(5), 785–802.

Metten, V. (2009, 19 May). Europe needs a united front on Tibet. *European Voice*.

Miliband, D. (2008). Written Ministerial Statement, the Secretary of State for Foreign and Commonwealth Affairs, 29 October 2008.

Ministry of Foreign Affairs of the People's of Republic of China. (2008). Foreign spokesperson Qing Gang's remarks on postponing the 11th China–Europe Summit Meeting, 27 November 2008.

Sautman, B., & Dreyer, J. T. (Eds.). (2006). Contemporary Tibet: Politics, development, and society in a disputed region. New York: M.E. Sharpe.

Spiegel Online International. (2008, 24 April). Balancing Tibet and Trade: EU delegation faces difficult tightrope in China, www.spiegel.de/international/world/balancing-tibet-and-trade-eu-delegation-faces-difficult-tightrope-in-China-a-549409.html. Accessed 30 Nov 2014.

The Economist. (1999, 13 May). Bombs in Belgrade, bricks in Beijing. www.economist.com/node/321647. Accessed 21 Jan 2014.

The Economist. (2009, 19 March). A time of muscle flexing: As western economies flounder, China sees a chance to assert itself carefully. www.economist.com/node/13326082. Accessed 21 Jan 2014.

The Financial Times. (2008, 8 May). Tibet has stronger self rule case than Kosovo. www.ft.com/intl/cms/s/0/2db5ed0c-1cff-11dd-82-ae-000077b07658.html#axzz2qtiUT3k1. Accessed 20 Jan 2014.

The Financial Times. (2013, 7 November). An exclusive interview with the Dalai Lama. www.ft.com/intl/cms/s/2/d49d13aa-4749-11e3-b4d3-00144feabdc0.html#slide0. Accessed 21 Jan 2014.

The Guardian. (May 1999). Trampling on China's fears.

Tocci, N. (Ed.). (2008). Who is a normative foreign policy actor? The European union and its global partner, CEPS Paperback series, Issue 3.

Wang, L. (2006). Indirect representation versus a democratic system: Relative advantages for resolving the Tibet question. In B. Sautman & J. T. Dreyer (Eds.), *Contemporary Tibet: Politics, development, and society in a disputed region* (pp. 101–121). New York: M.E. Sharpe.

White Paper. (1992a). *Its ownership and human rights situation*. Beijing: Information Office of the State Council of the PRC.

White Paper. (1992b). *Origins of so-called 'Tibetan Independence'*, Beijing: Information Office of the State Council of the PRC.

Xinhua. (2002, 8 July). China's top lawmaker stresses ties with European Parliament. http://english.peopledaily.com.cn/200207/09/eng20020709_99366.shtml. Accessed 21 Jan 2014.

Xinhua. (2008a, 26 April). Tell you a true Tibet-Origins of so-called "Tibetan Independence". http://news.xinhua.com/English/2008-04/content_7987719.htm. Accessed 21 Jan 2014.

Xinhua. (2008b, 30 March). The Chinese side express strong dissatisfaction at the EU Foreign Ministers Council's unofficial discussion and comments on the situation in Tibet.

Xinhua. (2009, 14 March). Commentary: Amnesia, ignorance of some European Parliamentarians, Xinhua News Agency, news.xinhua.com/English/2009=03/14/content_11011604.htm. Accessed 21 Jan 2014.

Xu, M., & Yuan, F. (2006). The Tibet question: A new cold War. In B. Sautman & J. T. Dreyer (Eds.), *Contemporary Tibet: Politics, development and society in a disputed region* (pp. 299–312). New York: M.E. Sharpe.

Zhang. Z. (1994). International Relations and the Tibet Question [Guoji Guanxi yu Xizang Wenti]. Beijing: Tourism and Education Publishing.

Wenwen Shen is a lecturer of political sciences and international relations at Victoria University of Wellington. She holds a PhD in international relations from the University of Bath, UK, and has worked at the Brussels Institute of Contemporary China Studies (BICCS) at Vjrie Universiteite of Brussel and as a consultant for the European Parliament in Brussels. She has been a visiting fellow at the National Centre for Research on Europe (NCRE), University of Canterbury (NZ), the Center for European Studies at Australian National University, and Maastricht University and Renmin University in China. Her research interests concern EU-China relations, including Member States' relations with China, the EU in the Asia Pacific, human rights and human security.

Chapter 15
Conclusion

Annika Björkdahl, Natalia Chaban, John Leslie and Annick Masselot

This collection sets out to explore the responses of norm-takers to EU norm export along a continuum from norm adoption to rejection. Reading norm diffusion processes through the lens of our conceptual framework demonstrates complex and frictional processes of norm-maker and norm-taker interaction. First, our analyses show that the EU influence on norm-takers range from *intentional* and *active* to *passive* and *incidental*. The empirical analyses clearly demonstrate that there is a distinction to be made between how the EU projects norms *internally* and *externally*. Second, the *internal* and *external* dimension of EU norm export brings to the fore the spatial aspect of norm diffusion and distinguishes between norm-takers in various locales that are inside and outside the EU as well as at various geographical and spatial distances from the EU. Third, a key theme that runs through the volume is the relational aspect of norm diffusion, i.e. the interplay between norm-maker and norm-taker that is defined by interdependence, asymmetry and power. Fourth, domestic circumstances within norm-takers condition the reception of norms. For example, how exported norms fit with the recipient's normative context, elites' predisposition for socialization, learning and cultural filters may shape how local actors translate (or do not) norms into local institutions and practices.

A. Björkdahl (✉)
Department of Political Science, Lund University Lund, Sweden
e-mail: annika.bjorkdahl@svet.lu.se

N. Chaban
National Centre for Research on Europe, University of Canterbury,
Christchurch, New Zealand
e-mail: natalia.chaban@canterbury.ac.nz

J. Leslie
Political Science and International Relations Programme,
Victoria University of Wellington, Wellington, New Zealand
e-mail: john.leslie@vuw.ac.nz

A. Masselot
College of Business and Law, University of Canterbury, Christchurch, New Zealand
e-mail: annick.masselot@canterbury.ac.nz

© Springer International Publishing Switzerland 2015   247
A. Björkdahl et al. (eds.), *Importing EU Norms,* United Nations University Series
on Regionalism 8, DOI 10.1007/978-3-319-13740-7_15

We do not ascribe a role to the norm-taker, or any value to their responses other than the degree to which the imported norms reflect norms originally projected by the EU. Rather we describe and analyse the responses, i.e. the behaviour of the norm-taker. Our empirical cases from around the world clearly demonstrate that the movement of norms often is best characterized as a complex, multi-layered and frictional process where the EU and various norm recipients are involved in a give-and-take relationship that transforms the norm, the norm-taker and the EU. The chapters analyse both coercive, intentional, top-down imposition of norms, and unintentional, incidental norm-export *as well as* norm-takers' responses in terms of adoption, adaptation, resistance and rejection. We are thus able to clearly demonstrate the agency of norm-takers as both compliant and obstinate. Norm-maker/norm-taker encounters may produce hybrid outcomes containing components of, the norm exporter's and the norm importer's self-perceptions, perceptions of the other, and perceptions of the norm, obscuring their boundaries. This demonstrates how norm-takers exercise agency despite structural constraints such as asymmetrical power relations.

Instead of simply assessing the fit between norm-takers' and norm-makers' norms, institutions and practices, and then explaining outcomes as either 'acceptance' or 'rejection', the contributors to this volume describe intricate and tangled processes and effects by which norm-takers build congruence between EU exported norms (including norms previously institutionalized in a region) and local beliefs and practices. Thus, adopting an approach similar to Acharya (2004), we find that studies of norm dynamics should account for a range of responses to exported norms, from constitutive compliance to outright rejection, and evolutionary and path-dependent forms of acceptance that fall in between. In doing so, we assess the behaviour of the norm-taker such as adoption, adaptation, resistance and rejection, rather than the actor (i.e. adoptor, adapter, resister and rejector).

If we examine outcomes along the spectrum from adoption to rejection, can we discern any patterns that emerge between outcomes, on the one hand, and mechanisms of norm-transfer and power relations between norm-maker and norm-taker (including the local conditions of the latter), on the other? The broad range of empirical cases in this volume provided some preliminary insights into complex multilayered processes by which EU norms have (or have not) moved between actors. The following links modes of EU norm export, in combination with conditions prevailing among importers of EU norms, to the behaviours of 'adoption', 'adaptation', 'resistance' and 'rejection'.

15.1   Adoption

We begin by examining EU-level actors' intentional efforts to export norms to actors inside the Union. Such circumstances are also explored in the voluminous literature focusing on EU actors' undertakings to transfer norms to candidate and neighbourhood countries. Relevant literature argues that these circumstances provide EU actors the greatest resources with which to influence the behaviour of norm-takers. Formal, institutional powers such as infringement proceedings, as well as extreme levels of economic, social and political interdependence, give EU actors considerable leverage over norm-takers. However, the empirical cases of this volume demonstrate that, from their perspective, norm-takers retained considerable capacity to contest application and even adapt EU-level normative exports. Furthermore, this was true not only within 'new' EU Member States, but also in established members of EU-15. Despite Treaty obligations to adopt the rules and regulations of European Monetary Union, Czech politicians found ways to resist and 'adapt' their obligations in this issue area, although not in others. Similarly, there is evidence of resistance to adoption of EU-level norms on people mobility, particularly for third-country nationals, within and between Member States where people movements have a long and institutionalized history. Cases in this volume illustrate the resources—sanctions 'from above' combined with EU-level support for interests favouring mobility 'from below'—that EU-level actors can marshall to overcome resistance within Member States to EU-level exports 'downward'. Viewed from the perspective of norm-takers, 'adoption'—even under favourable circumstances—is a complex and often contested process, in which the outcome cannot be taken for granted. Much depends on the coherence and agreement with which common norms are accepted at the EU level. The impact of 'coherence'—and its absence—on EU behaviour is also a recurrent theme in literature on EU foreign policy and will come up again in this analysis.

We observe how the shifting balance of power impacts EU norms transfer when we move our focus from the efforts of EU actors to export norms vertically, within the Union, to attempts to export them horizontally, to other actors in the international arena. Our interest was towards actors both inside and outside the EU's Neighbourhood. In the latter case, asymmetrical power relations and interdependencies are often argued to give EU-level actors considerable leverage in their negotiations—for example, the EU's dealings with the African, Carribean and Pacific (ACP) countries to construct Economic Partnership Agreements (EPAs). Despite such leverage, however, many ACP countries have resisted adoption of EU norms for over a decade. In 2014 however, they were compelled to make concessions to EU normative power and signed EPAs adopting many of the EU exported norms. In some cases, they avoided comformity in practice or there was outright rejection. The experience of ACP countries discussed in this volume demonstrates the effectiveness of EU power resources as a means to export its norms when importers are resistant.

The utility of EU power resources in spreading norms was found to decrease rapidly as asymmetries between the EU and its external partners levelled out. Control over access to the world's largest internal market, at first glance, seems to provide EU-level actors a powerful tool with which to induce adoption of EU norms. Yet, the EU's economy, as it turns out, is a two-edged sword. Actors inside the EU have important interests in maintaining and growing material exchanges with outside actors. These material interests sometimes come into conflict with EU attempts to link market access for outsiders with adoption of EU norms like human rights and gender equality. For example, EU negotiators, despite a legal obligation to do so, have failed to maintain strong linkages between adoption of EU norms on gender equality and access to Europe's internal market in trade negotiations in the Asia Pacific. Again, EU internal conflicts over its own values and norms have shaped profoundly the Union's behaviour towards external counterparts.

Indeed, internal value conflicts happen to shape the EU's unintentional capacity to influence the values of other actors in the international system. Where, for example, the EU has succeeded in creating common internal product standards—such as in pharmaceuticals—external actors often have strong reasons (market access, regulatory cost savings) for adopting them. However, where internal divisions prevent creation of common standards—in food safety—external actors may be inclined to look elsewhere.

This observation brings us to alternative mechanisms of EU norm export that have less to do with the intentionality of EU actors. More precisely, it changes the focus to mechanisms of *reception* of EU norms, where intentionality lies with the norm-taker. In general, the cases in this volume demonstrate that these mechanisms are more likely to be associated with the behaviours of 'adaptation', 'resistance' and 'rejection' than with 'adoption'. There are important reasons for this. Most obviously, where EU actors have no intention of exporting norms, they are unlikely to expend resources to influence how EU norms are received. Accordingly, conditions around norm recipients are more likely to shape how norm-takers receive EU norms. This volume demonstrates that these conditions include the recipients' position in the international system and economy, their cultural filters and perceptions of themselves and the EU, as well as local institutions and constellations of domestic interests. It should be noted that the previous discussion implied the importance of local conditions even when EU actors sought to influence reception of EU norms—there is no reason to contest EU norms, if they do not conflict with local interests, values and filters. Local conditions, however, become increasingly visible and important in shaping outcomes of norm transfer as EU intentionality and power recede.

A norm-taker's position in the international economy and system plays an important role in whether and how EU norms are received. In part, this is another way of saying that a norm-taker's power relations vis-à-vis the EU matter. Large actors, like Russia and China, have more options in the international system than do smaller—especially trade dependent—actors. Russian and Chinese responses to EU norms are addressed below. For smaller actors, international constraints, particularly constraints of international security and economic competition, are more limiting. Access to EU markets and its limitation, for example, may impact profoundly the reception of EU normative exports.

European economic integration—and economic integration elsewhere (e.g. NAFTA)—influenced the decisions of policymakers in Australia, New Zealand and ASEAN to undertake their own version of economic integration. In the 1970s, UK accession to the EEC forced Australian and New Zealand policymakers to adapt to a world in which access to their producers' most important markets was curtailed or eliminated. In the 1980s, the Single European Market, the spectre of 'Fortress Europe', and a closed NAFTA bloc confronted Australasian and South East Asian policymakers with a renewed threat of compartmentalisation of the international economy. These developments and perceived forces of competition pushed for a deeper economic integration within ASEAN and between Australia and New Zealand. They also motivated these Asia-Pacific actors to search for solutions to the policy problems raised by their own economic integration.

15.2 Adaptation

Several of the volume's contributions investigate how policymakers in third countries received European integration as a 'model' for their own policy challenges. These cases demonstrate the complexity of the processes by which EU norm exports may be received. First, policymakers must interpret their own policy challenges as analogous to those faced by European policymakers. In the case of both trans-Tasman and ASEAN economic integration policymakers drew an explicit parallel between Europe and their own situation where competing jurisdictions impeded economic growth. However, although both drew analogies between their own situations and European experience, local conditions caused Australasian and ASEAN policymakers to receive European experience in different ways.

Australasian reception of European experience as a 'model' of integration demonstrates how ambivalence and local institutions permitted 'adaptation' of European norms to local practice. Australia and New Zealand shared with Europe not only the problem of competing regulatory jurisdictions but also similar democratic political systems, levels of economic development and liberal societies. These similarities drew Australasian policymakers' attention to European integration as a 'model' for rejuvenating their own economies. However, this attention was also filtered through Australasian policymakers' self-perceptions as 'victims' of European integration, Common Agricultural Policy and the Common External Tariff. As a result of their ambivalence toward the EEC/EC/EU's diversionary policies and aspirations for political integration, Australian and New Zealand policymakers adopted and refined the (economically) liberal normative content of European integration into an 'open' and (economically) 'liberal' version of regional integration in Australasia. Trans-Tasman integration provides a clear demonstration of normative 'friction' generating 'hybrid' norms.

Reception of European regional integration experiences by policymakers in the ASEAN case provides a counterpoint to the respective developments in Australasia. Similar to trans-Tasman regional integration, ASEAN integration reflects policymakers' desire to stimulate economic growth and development through economic integration. Also, similar to their Australasian counterparts, many ASEAN policymakers were ambivalent about the diversionary impact and political ambitions of European integration. What distinguishes Australasian and ASEAN policymakers' reception of European experience as a 'model' for regional integration are their differing attitudes towards and understandings of the relationship between national sovereignty and supra-national authority. Australasian policymakers adopted both the general forms that supra-nationality takes in the EU (i.e. 'pooled sovereignty' (majoritarian voting)) and trans-national agencies. However, while adopting the normative substance of European supra-national authority, Australasian policymakers gave their arrangements a very different—decentralised—design, avoiding creation of the institutions similar to the EU's Council, Commission and Court of Justice. ASEAN policymakers have done the opposite. They have 'mimicked' EU institutional design in terms of the ASEAN Secretariat, Committee of Permanent Representatives, etc., while rejecting the normative substance of supra-nationality by denying these institutions actual authority. Respectively, this volume argues that trans-Tasman integration represents a case of an adaptation and hybridization of EU experience, while ASEAN remains caught in resistance and hollow imitation of EU form without normative supra-national substance.

15.3   Resistance

In contrast to adaptation, resistance is characterised by the fact that the core of the recipient normative practice remains distinct from European practice. The original normative content of the export must be used but cannot be recognised as an EU norm. Although, actors' behaviours engage with European norms, the norm-takers intentionally or unintentionally choose to retain a local practice or they decide to adopt an alternative to European norms or maintain the *status quo*. At their core, norm-takers' practices are guided by norms that are distinct from European norm exports.

For example, EU trademark norms have seeped through the World Trade Organisation's agreement on Trade Related Aspects on Intellectual Property Rights (WTO TRIPS) and have indirectly been transmitted to New Zealand. However, this indirect transmission of EU norms also demonstrates that New Zealand is able to pick and chose aspects of the norms that suit it and resist and reject normative aspects that are more controversial and are not seen as suitable. Norms which are perceived to be beneficial are legally transplanted. By contrast, contested norms, within the EU legal order are rejected. This demonstrates how New Zealand is able to assert its legal independence without conditionality. Here the cultural filter of the historical legal links between New Zealand and the UK have proven to be beneficial. Where the British courts have expressed dissatisfaction with EU law, New Zealand's legislative and interpretative approaches have allowed New Zealand to escape unsatisfactory outcomes by resisting to import problems of EU trademark law. By choosing EU norms which are suitable for its own legal system, New Zealand has managed to set out comprehensive trademark systems, cleared of the controversial art of the exported norms, and more efficient than the EU normative profile. Importantly, the EU norms are not easily recognisable in New Zealand and they can only be traced by their 'legal DNA'. The result is the creation and the adoption of hybrid norms, which fit the norm-taker.

15.4 Rejection

Rejection of norms here implies a contestation between norms promoted by the EU and pre-existing normative and social orders of various norm-takers. Unlike previous research, which has addressed the questions of adoption or rejection and agency of norm-takers, the contributions to this volume emphasise a dynamic and frictional process of norm diffusion. In this process, EU norms, which may not cohere with the norm-takers, are rejected and fails to become part of the norm-taker's normative context, institutions and practices. The success of norm diffusion processes thus depends on the extent to which they provide opportunities for adoption, adaptation or if they can be imposed through coercive means. In most cases of norm rejection, there is no demand for EU norms, there is a contestation of who is a global normative power, and the geographical, social, political and cultural distance through which norms are projected obstruct norm adoption. In other cases, the exported norms may be feared and resisted simply because of their alien quality. The outcome of rejecting EU norms is that local practices do not comply with EU norms, that local institutions remain intact, and that the EU norms have not been adjusted to fit the local normative context and thus that there is a mismatch between EU norms and the local norms and practices.

Rejection of the EU's norms is particularly prevalent in cases where competing and powerful actors challenge the normative power of the EU on the global arena. In, addition, rejection also seems to be the automatic response in cases where there is a mismatch between EU projected norms and the norm-taker's normative, political, cultural and social context resulting in norm clashes.

Russia often rejects or resists EU norms. The complex Russian response to the EU's normative power is a reflection of Russia's relation to the EU. Russia's power, its geographical position and the mutual interdependency between itself and EU Member States set it apart from other states that are confronted with the EU's norm export and normative power. Russia has developed along a different path from the EU Member State model and refuses any EU attempts to influence its 'path of development'. Thus, Russia's policy has shifted from promoting the idea of Russia as an equal norm-maker of 'thick', Europe-wide norms, to the rejection of the notion of Europe-wide norms. Thus, Russia is seen as contravening EU norms in the 'shared neighbourhood', and Russia's rejection of EU socio-political norms is regarded as a stumbling block in developing a sustainable partnership.

Russia's position is shared by other 'rising powers', such as the 'BRICs'. Unlike prospective EU members, these states have fewer material incentives to conform to and comply with EU norms. China, for example, also challenges the EU's claim to normative hegemony. Illustrative of this is the question of Tibet in EU-Chinese relations. The EU's human rights policy and policy on self-determination challenge well-established Chinese norms pertaining to sovereignty and non-interference in internal politics of states— norms China often defends on the global arena. Thus, many norms promoted by the EU through non-coercive means such as persuading, invoking norms, shaping discourse, living by example and shaming have been rejected by China. On the issue of Tibet, the EU's normative power, although being projected in an ambiguous and accommodating way over the years, has been explicitly rejected by China's non-negotiable position on human rights norms.

The rejection of EU norms is not limited to China. The economic relations negotiations between the EU and the Asian region highlight the significant difficulties in diffusing norms through the medium of trade policies. A striking example is the gender equality norm promoted by the EU in its external relations. Gender equality is clearly visible in both the EU's legal obligations and the rhetoric displayed in co-operation and development policy documents, but explicit references to gender equality are conspicuously absent from trade policy. Most Asian states reject the EU's legalistic approach in linking of norms pertaining to gender equality to trade agreements. However, it is not necessarily a rejection of the values *per se*, but of the EU's mechanism of imposing them via conditionality clauses when negotiating Free Trade Agreements. The EU's prioritization of economic relations with key rising markets in Asia together with the Asian's countries systematic rejection of the inclusion of norms in Free Trade Agreement create a double barrier for the diffusion of gender equality norms. The Asian countries' rejection of gender equality norms through trade negotiations is both a rejection of the norms as such and of the means of exporting them. Zooming in on diffusion of norms pertaining to gender equality brings both power and the notion of normative clash to the fore.

The cases where rejection has been a dominant response to EU projection of norms demonstrate a powerful norm-taker with ability to challenge the EU normative power. The relationship between the norm-maker and norm-taker is not one characterized by asymmetry. Although Russia has been seen as a declining giant since the end of the Cold War, its new status of an 'emerging' power may explain why Russia fails to recognize the EU as the only or even the most important norm-maker for shaping the European normative context. From a distance, China is another 'rising' power with increasing global ambitions. Both China and Russia have displayed explicit rejection strategies that resulted not only in open rejection of norms promoted by the EU but also posted challenges to the EU's normative power.

15.5 Final Thoughts

This volume contributes to the advancement of the research agenda on norm diffusion and normative power by providing a novel conceptual framework that brings to the fore the agency of norm-takers, which is also reflected in empirical analysis of a broad range of cases of norm diffusion. A continuum of norm-takers' behaviours—from adoption and adaptation to resistance and rejection—presents a nuanced theoretical model to understand instances of intentional and unintentional transfers of EU norms internally and externally. While novel, this framework opens new avenues in the exploration of the EU as a 'normative power'. Our empirical analyses demonstrate that the predominant responses to EU norms are adaptation and resistance, or hybrid forms of responses, while straightforward adoption and rejection are rare. Future research may advance the agenda presented in this volume and address one of our most intriguing discoveries—the hybrid forms of norm-takers' responses to EU normative messages. One crucial explanation to the range of responses identified in our cases, as well as to the hybridity of responses, is a unique combination of various cultural filters specific to each norm-taker. Future research may further elaborate the types of cultural filters (including self- and xeno-perceptions considered in this volume) and account for their influences in single-country and comparative settings. As such, expanding the geography of such inquiry to other locations inside the EU and globally is another promising direction for the follow-up studies. Future consideration of a larger and more geographically diverse set of norm-takers will, possibly, lead to the identification of the new types of responses and of new hybrid responses that could build on the conceptual framework outlined here and advance our theorization of the norm-taker. Moreover, subsequent investigations may attempt a longitudinal analysis into the dynamics of norm diffusion to study multilayered and complicated interactions between the EU as norm-maker and various norm-takers examined in this volume. Research over time may help to assess if responses to EU normative messages are flexible or rigid, and what conditions—EU- and location-specific—are the key to the evolution of such responses. Nevertheless, this volume is the first to argue that a conscious systematic consideration of the agency of norm-takers provides one informed answer to the question if the EU's 'normative power' is reciprocated in Europe and around the word.

Prof. Annika Björkdahl is Professor of Political Science at Lund University. She has published on ideas and norms in International Relations particularly focusing on the role of the EU as an exporter of norms as well as on conflict prevention, peacekeeping and peace-building. Among her recent publications are *War and Peace in Transition* (Nordic Academic Press 2009), *Rethinking Peacebuilding: The Quest for Just Peace in the Middle East and the Western Balkans* (Routledge 2013) (with K. Aggestam). She has also published in *European Foreign Affairs Review, Journal of European Public Policy* etc. She has also been a guest professor at National Centre for Research on Europe, Canterbury University. She is currently the editor in chief of *Cooperation and Conflict*.

Dr. Natalia Chaban is Associate Professor and Jean Monnet Chair at the National Centre for Research on Europe, University of Canterbury, New Zealand. She has significant experience in analysing EU identity outside the EU, widely publishing and advancing methodological expertise in this regard. Since 2002, she has co-led a comparative transnational project on EU external perceptions comprising a multicultural team from 20 Asia-Pacific locations, as well as a 'mirror' perceptions project "Asia in Eyes of Europe". Among her publications is *The European Union and the Asia-Pacific: Media, Public and Elite Perceptions of the EU* (2008) Routledge (N. Chaban and M. Holland, eds.) and *Communicating Europe in Times of Crisis: External Perceptions of the European Union* (2014) Palgrave (N. Chaban and M. Holland, eds.) She has also published articles in journals such as *European Foreign Affairs Review, Journal of Common Market Studies, Journal of European Integration, European Law Journal, Mobilities*.

Dr. John Leslie is a Lecturer in Political Science and International Relations at Victoria University of Wellington (VUW). His research comparing economic integration in the European Union, between Australia and New Zealand and in the Asia Pacific has appeared recently in, among other outlets, *Journal of Common Market Studies Government and Opposition and the Asia Europe Journal*. During 2014–2015 John Leslie is on leave from VUW, acting as the European Union's Trade Officer in New Zealand. Research for and writing of this volume was completed before he began working for the EU.

Annick Masselot is an Associate Professor in Law at the University of Canterbury (College of Business and Law) New Zealand. Her research interests focus upon European Union law, comparative law, gender equality and equal treatment, social and employment law, reconciliation between work and family life, pregnancy and maternity rights. She is the author of *Reconciling Work and Family Life in EU Law and Policy,* (2010) London: Palgrave Macmillan (with E. Caracciolo di Torella). She has published articles journals such as the *European Law Review, European Law Journal, Columbia Journal of European Law, Feminist Legal Studies.*

Index

© Springer International Publishing Switzerland 2015
A. Björkdahl et al. (eds.), *Importing EU Norms,* United Nations University Series
on Regionalism 8, DOI 10.1007/978-3-319-13740-7

Printed by Printforce, the Netherlands